T0361168

THE CO-OPERATIVE ALTERNATIVE IN EUROPE: THE CASE OF HOUSING

The Co-operative Alternative in Europe: The Case of Housing

GREGORY ANDRUSZ
Reader in Sociology, Middlesex University

with contributions by
Bo Bengtsson
Prue Chamberlayne
Lars Nord

Routledge
Taylor & Francis Group

LONDON AND NEW YORK

First published 1999 by Ashgate Publishing

Reissued 2018 by Routledge
2 Park Square, Milton Park, Abingdon, Oxon, OX14 4RN
711 Third Avenue, New York, NY 10017, USA

Routledge is an imprint of the Taylor & Francis Group, an informa business

Publisher's Note
The publisher has gone to great lengths to ensure the quality of this reprint but points out that some imperfections in the original copies may be apparent.

Disclaimer
The publisher has made every effort to trace copyright holders and welcomes correspondence from those they have been unable to contact.

A Library of Congress record exists under LC control number: 98074438

ISBN 13: 978-1-138-34133-3 (hbk)
ISBN 13: 978-0-429-44019-9 (ebk)

Contents

Preface   vii
Acknowledgements   ix

Introduction   1

PART I: FROM CORPORATIST STATE TO CO-OPERATIVE COMMONWEALTH?   7

   Introduction to Part I   9
1 Conflicts in Political Economy and Social Theory   10
2 A Co-operative Culture   34

PART II: RUSSIA AND THE CO-OPERATIVE ALTERNATIVE   63

   Introduction to Part II   65
3 The Rise and Decline of the Co-operative in Russia   67
4 The Co-operative Revival under Gorbachev   95

PART III: HOUSING CO-OPERATIVES IN EUROPE   143

   Introduction to Part III   145
5 Soviet Russia: The Struggle against Statism   150
6 Marxist GDR: Cyclical Fortunes
   Prue Chamberlayne   178
7 Socialist Yugoslavia: Embryo of a Co-operative Republic
   Lars Nord   215
8 Social Democratic Sweden: A Story of Success
   Bo·Bengtsson   249

Conclusion   275
Postscript   285

Preface

This book has its origins in Gävle in Sweden, which was the venue for the first International Housing Research Conference in 1986. I had been asked to present a paper on housing in the Soviet Union. As I ruminated on a new approach to the existing information on the subject, the new General Secretary of the Communist Party of the Soviet Union, Mikhail Gorbachev, unknowingly came to my aid. In one of his speeches he remarked that the 'co-operative movement has not exhausted itself' and had much to contribute to the implementation of his idea of 'perestroika'.[1] This comment encouraged me to return to one of the enigmas of Soviet housing policy: why had the co-operative tenure performed so poorly given that, since 1964, it had received so much support from the country's most senior political actors? It seemed to me that it would be interesting to review the history of Soviet housing co-operatives in the context of the emerging co-operative revival.

The next step was to suggest that perhaps our understanding of housing co-operatives in a particular country could be enhanced by examining them dynamically in terms of their development over time and their relationship to other types of housing tenure.

Co-operatives, and co-operative housing in particular, have achieved, for different reasons and in different ways, the same minority status in both the UK and the USSR. Housing co-operatives have made a valuable contribution to the housing stock in Sweden and the GDR, but not in Yugoslavia. Was there any correlation between this fact and the size and role of the co-operative movement in individual countries more generally? This book examines a form of ownership which is neither 'private' nor 'state' in four countries.

Since 1989, when I took part in a workshop on co-operatives with specialists from several European countries, Europe has experienced a sea change. The Union of Soviet Socialist Republics, the German Democratic Republic and Yugoslavia no longer exist! This in itself could be taken to illustrate the futility of trying to conduct serious analyses of the present. However, the central focus of this book remains valid. I hope that it will make a small contribution to the further study of a social form which should no longer be regarded as an alternative of minority concern. The co-operative movement in its widest sense is the form which collectivism as an alternative to capitalism will take in the twenty-first century.

Note

1   The term 'perestroika' literally means 'restructuring', the English word which Margaret Thatcher used to describe her design for British society. For both of these political titans of the twentieth century, restructuring meant the transformation not only of economic structures but also of entrenched mind-sets. On Gorbachev's vision of perestroika, see M. Gorbachev, *Perestroika. New Thinking for our Country and the World*, William Collins, London, 1987; Archie Brown, *The Gorbachev Factor*, OUP, Oxford, 1997. On Margaret Thatcher's view, see D. Kavanagh, *Thatcherism and British Politics: The End of Consensus*, 2nd ed., Oxford, OUP, 1990; P. Mitford, *The Supply Side Revolution in Britain*, Edward Elgar, Aldershot, 1991.

Acknowledgements

I would like to express my gratitude to the following organisations for providing small grants which financed the workshop on co-operatives held at the Co-operative College, Stanford Hall in July 1989: the Nuffield Foundation, the Ford Foundation through the Joint Research and Development Committee of BASEES and the British Academy's Elisabeth Barker Fund. I would like to thank Bo Bengtsson, Johnston Birchall, Prue Chamberlayne, Jozsef Hegedus, Lars Nord and Ivan Tosics for participating in the workshop and for adding their considerable knowledge to the discussion. The National Swedish Institute for Building Research generously provided me with a six-week travelling fellowship to visit their Institute in Gävle, which offered a stimulating working environment. Katie Lewis has been far more than a copy editor. Finally, a big word of thanks to Libby and Katya, who were there literally at the dawn of this project, coaxing and cajoling me to finish and an Amstrad to behave. They have each in their own inimitable ways contributed to the project coming to fruition.

Introduction

This book offers a tentative exploration of the trend in European societies towards more decentralised, local forms of social and economic organisation. In doing so it mirrors an intellectual trend in sociology which is trying to establish a new balance between structure and action in which actors play a greater part in the construction of the social orders which they inhabit. Individuals and groups in different situations, through their interactions and their negotiations, re-create familiar and create novel structures and new ways of achieving their own self-defined goals.

The founders of sociology were aware that the market mechanism, despite its importance, could not in itself ensure the maintenance and reproduction of the social order. Nineteenth century utilitarianism was largely dismissive of solidarity and trust as integrating factors in society. The common legacy of the titans of social thought (Durkheim, Marx and Weber) was that the outcome of the evolutionary process, wanted or unwanted, was socialism and with it the growth of the state and bureaucracy. Their heirs in the twentieth century regarded modernisation as synonymous with urbanisation, industrialisation and bureaucratisation, which meant the concentration of people in large cities, huge factories and burgeoning bureaucracies. The 'end-state' would see a convergence between modernised societies which, in the period after 1945, were typologised as communist and capitalist systems. In the main the so-called convergence theorists, and Fukuyama is no exception, predicted that convergence would be unidirectional: the 'superior' capitalist system would absorb through its survival the less evolutionary successful communistic form of social and economic organisation. They assumed that social systems which permitted the co-existence of different property forms and competing political parties were functionally more efficient. Those predicting that the outcome of history is a market-oriented economy within the cast of Western liberal democracy believe either that this is inevitable or that it would be the end result wherever individuals are allowed to choose the type of economic and political system within which they wish to live. Neither transcendent Reason nor ordinary human common sense could, in their view, countenance the idea of an alternative.

1

Yet each society records in its modern history how certain segments of the population have reacted to the inequities of their societies and put forward alternatives to the emerging individualist ideal. In Britain in Cromwellian times, the Ranters and Levellers were, in Christopher Hill's words, among those who sought to 'turn the world upside down'.[1] For E. P. Thompson, in the tumultuous years of the early nineteenth century individuals in their small groups censured nascent capitalism and planted the seeds of the liberty tree.[2] Dennis Hardy has surveyed these small group challenges in the nineteenth and twentieth centuries in England and their attempts to form their own 'alternative communities'.[3]

These authors have in their different ways found themselves, like Max Weber, in 'debate with the ghost of Marx'. They felt themselves at odds both intuitively and theoretically with the structured rigidity of Marxism's Hegelian reductionist teleology, especially as espoused in its Althusserian form.[4] The categories of the Marxist dialectic, labour and capital, while crucial determinants of social development, failed to encompass the myriad individual challenges. Many individuals, enjoined to sacrifice themselves to a creed of selfishness, egoistic individualism and competition, chose to counter it with a view of harmony and co-operation. Their actions were theorised by others such as Proudhon, Fourier, Owen and Kropotkin (for whom, more even than the others, the dominant factor in evolution was voluntary co-operation, not competition). But it was Mill and Marx, not Morris, who came to dominate European economic and political thought.

Following the Second World War, European societies were faced with a series of inter-related problems. Some of these were the direct outcome of the wartime destruction of industry and the social and technical infrastructure. Others were rooted in the very social and economic structures of European states, inherited from the nineteenth century, which had given rise to fascism in its various guises. The peoples of Europe demonstrated at parliamentary elections that the policies which governments had conventionally employed before 1939 were no longer acceptable. The outcome was a massive penetration by governments in social and economic affairs. The philosophy of *dirigisme* to varying degrees characterised the majority of European states by the mid-1950s. In the Soviet Union and Eastern Europe the state had nationalised and centralised control over most sectors of the economy, although in some countries agriculture did not succumb to this model. In market-oriented societies state ownership was more restricted and the levers of control more indirect and sophisticated.

Perhaps nowhere was the new role assigned to the state as visible as in house building. The toppling of this policy issue from the apex of the political agenda of many countries in the early 1980s coincided with the anti-statist, pro-market counter-revolution. The political debate, which had for four decades centred on attempting a theoretical determination of the boundary between the private and public (or state) sectors, had shifted rightwards.

At the heart of the debate on the location of the private–public boundary lies the notion of property. For more than a century a passionate debate has taken place on the origins of Roman landed property: some people claim the priority of common property, whilst others assert that immovables were subject to private ownership from the beginning. The conclusion reached by one school on the origins of private property is that, since the first references to property linked it to movables (persons – *familia* – and cattle – *pecunia*) and failed to refer to the land, this 'justifies the view that movables were the very first objects of private property'. This is taken as support for the argument that 'in Rome, as with many other peoples, the common landed property of the clan [*gentes*] preceded the system of private property in land'.[5] According to this school of thought, collective ownership prevailed in Greece and Rome where, until Justinian's time, the *ager publicus* was a public estate and only its use could be granted. Marx and Engels and subsequent Marxist scholars and political systems have made this the fundamental premise for organising society.

Needless to say, not everyone accepts this version of historical 'fact': Hayek, to name but one of the most significant opponents of this view, contended otherwise.[6] (See Chapter 1 below.) Proponents of private ownership rest their case ultimately on the teachings of Thomas Aquinas, according to whom temporal goods received by human beings from Divine Providence belonged to them as to ownership but not as to use, thereby laying the ideological basis for a system of private ownership and controlled use.

The European political traditions of the twentieth century, which have followed the parallel historical paths of Mill and Marx, derive from this long theoretical – at times metaphysical – controversy positing collective against private ownership. There are two main explanations for the fervour of the debate. Firstly, since there are no direct sources detailing the origins of landed property in Rome, evidence cited by the contenders to truth is sharply disputed. Secondly, the outcome of this adversarial, academic argument becomes a weapon placed at the disposal of the field marshals of the ideological battle. For this reason, the related issues of 'property' and 'ownership' form a primary leitmotiv of the book.

Research interests in the social sciences, which closely correspond to actual changes in policies and popular sentiments (however generated), have in recent decades oscillated between 'the local' and 'the national' focus, with occasional attempts at synthesis. Since the 1970s the pendulum has consistently swung towards the 'local', the micro or small-scale which are now, more than just rhetorically, the driving motor of governance and public activity. This is readily visible in the shift from macro- to micro-economics and from sociology to psychology: that is, a shift in focus from large-scale forces shaping social processes to individual (household, enterprise) responses to actual events. Within sociology too there have been adaptations to this changing ideational climate, reflected in the attention paid to local councils,[7] neighbourhoods, community structures and, perhaps above all, the voluntary sector. The latter is also referred to as the 'non-profit' or 'NGO' (non-governmental organisation) sector, depending on context.

A number of factors can be adduced to help explain this change in orientation. Firstly, technological change – especially the revolution in communications and information technology – means that the concentration of people in large enterprises and companies located in large cities is no longer a technical imperative. Completely new settlement patterns are emerging, in particular the so-called 'Edge Cities', which are in effect the opposite of dormitory towns: suburbs with more jobs than commuters. Already up to one-third of all Americans live in the country's 200 'Edge Cities', which contain two-thirds of *all* office space in the United States of America.[8] Moreover, the 'crystallisation' of human knowledge and capacities in microcomputers enables a few people to complete tasks which formerly required the efforts of many.[9]

Small, privately owned companies, not requiring large capital investment, are regenerating themselves, if not as co-operatives in a legal sense, then as co-operatives in terms of the work ethos.[10] In addition, technological change is necessitating a redefinition of the boundaries between the formal and informal economies, the relationship between paid and unpaid work, and the role of the voluntary and co-operative sectors. It is now generally accepted that a considerable amount of work in modern industrial societies takes place outside the formal accounting system, sometimes through what is referred to as the 'reciprocal exchange of labour'.[11]

Secondly, the current interest in local initiative and participation is reflected in the prominence which these ideas, in particular the notion of subsidiarity, have assumed in political debate. Thirdly, the shift in orientation partly reflects changes in the social structure, the general level of education and the higher level of political awareness. This is giving rise to demands for greater openness in the dissemination and accessibility of information ('transparency') and greater democratisation of decision making ('accountability').

Social decay and deterioration in the physical fabric of particular loci in society produce social instability, feelings of insecurity and high mobility rates. While some people deal with this situation by escaping it, others remain and seek to defend and enhance their space by employing tenants' advisors, and campaigning for neighbourhood offices, larger or better equipped local health centres and polyclinics and the encouragement of new hybrid professions such as nurse-practitioners. These individuals, groups and institutions serve as supportive networks for people facing economic hardship, domestic difficulties and alienation from both the local and larger society. Some of these functions can be financed by a combination of contributions made by residents (user payments) and by grants provided by various tiers of government. Initiatives such as self-management schemes are likely to involve the better-off and better educated and more dynamic, since such people are more aware of the tangible benefits to be gained from their activities.

The companion ideas of 'active citizenship' and the 'stakeholder society' encourage individuals in informal groups and formal associations to publicise their increasingly diverse needs and demands, then to campaign and organise to have them met. These already include the provision of recreation, education, health and child care, accommodation and employment. Individuals who are unable or unwilling to satisfy their needs for housing directly through the marketplace (because the privately rented sector is too small and/or inappropriate, or because the cost of purchase is beyond their reach) have periodically, depending on circumstances, rediscovered the benefits of collective or co-operative action.

The new socialism, which develops dialectically in opposition to the new free marketeers, supersedes bureaucratic statism. The state has demonstrated its inability, partly because of its vastness and remoteness, to respond to people's needs. It has acted as a fetter on human creativity and inhibited individuals from using their capacity to shape and control their local (residential) and immediate (work) environments. Since systems of total state ownership and of private property tend to generate negative social behaviour, a lack of responsibility, insecurity and feelings of powerlessness, it is worth examining whether the propensity 'to do good' and to realise oneself as a human being can best be achieved through a co-operative property form.

Notes

1   C. Hill, *The World Turned Upside Down: Radical Ideas During the English Revolution*, Penguin, Harmondsworth, 1975.
2   E. P. Thompson, *The Making of the English Working Class*, Penguin, Harmondsworth,

     1968.
3   D. Hardy, *Alternative Communities in Nineteenth-Century England*, Longman, London, 1979.
4   E. P. Thompson, *The Poverty of Theory & Other Essays*, Merlin Press, London, 1978.
5   G. Diosdi, *Ownership in Ancient and Preclassical Roman Law*, Akademiai Kiado, Budapest, 1970, pp. 26–33.
6   F. von Hayek, *The Fatal Conceit. The Errors of Socialism. The Collected Works of Friedrich August von Hayek*, ed. W. W. Bartlett III, Routledge, London, 1988.
7   In the sociological and political discourses of the 1960s and 1970s local councils and municipal government were referred to as the 'local state'. (For instance, C. Cockburn, *The Local State: Management of Cities and People*, Pluto, London, 1977.)
8   One example of an Edge City is the settlement forty miles west of Manhattan, one of a dozen amorphous suburb cities in New Jersey containing over thirty separate municipalities. The population, in excess of 1 million people, is policed by a score of different forces. The area is known to real estate agents as '287-78' because it lies near the intersection of these two interstate freeways. J. Garreau, *Edge City: Life on the New Frontier*, Anchor, New York, 1991.
9   M. Castells, *The Rise of the Network Society: The Information Age*, Vol. I, Blackwell, Oxford, 1996.
10   In one small British engineering company the staff decide their own salaries and hours of work, set their own budgets and double as salesmen, cost accountants and quality control inspectors. Central to the company's success is its ethos of trust, teamwork and self-reliance (M. Streeter, 'Message from the workers' paradise: we're doing fine', *Independent*, 25 July 1997, p. 10).
11   P. Pahl (ed.), *On Work*, Blackwell, Oxford, 1988; E. Sik, 'Small is Useful or the Reciprocal Exchange of Labour in Hungary', in P. Galasi (ed.), *Labour Market and Second Economy in Hungary*, New York, 1985.

PART I
FROM CORPORATIST STATE
TO CO-OPERATIVE
COMMONWEALTH?

Introduction to Part I

The end of the Second World War marked more than the defeat of fascism. It also marked the rejection of the conventional economic wisdom that had dominated the inter-war period, where 'normalcy' meant a return to the Gold Standard and a belief in the efficacy of free markets and in the dictum '*laissez-faire* should be the general practice: every departure from it, unless required by some great good, is a certain evil'.[1] The Allies who had defeated fascism in war were intent on ensuring that national and international measures should be taken to ensure that as far as possible the economic causes of that war should not be allowed to recur. The outcome was state intervention and the formation of the corporatist state.

Keynes and Marx walked in step for the first thirty years after the war. Then, in the mid-1970s the West broke step and rejected Keynes. A little over a decade later, Marx suffered the same fate. Normalcy once more became economic regulation not by governments but by markets. The issue now is the search for a new collectivist approach to social organisation.

Note

1   J. S. Mill, *Principles of Political Economy*, (1848), Longman, London, 1909, p. 950.

1 Conflicts in Political Economy and Social Theory

> So when I consider . . . the state of all flourishing commonwealths today . . .
> I can see nothing but a conspiracy of the rich who are aiming at their own
> advantage under the name of the commonwealth. They invent and devise all
> ways and means, by which they may keep without fear of losing all that they
> have amassed by evil practices, and next to that may purchase as cheaply as
> possible and misuse the labour and toil of the poor.
>
> Thomas More, *Utopia*

In September 1990, after a year of truly cataclysmic changes in the political
geography of the world which accompanied the collapse of the 'actually
existing socialism'[1] in East and Central Europe and the Soviet Union, a
military crisis in the Middle East involved the United States and the USSR in
a joint, agreed policy towards a belligerent Iraq. This provided some grounds
for optimism that the advanced industrial nations had reached the point of
formulating a new world order. Underlying the new political alignments are
the global structural environmental and economic crises. The two are
intricately linked, for increases in GDP are positively correlated with
increasing energy consumption, and the latter, since the Club of Rome Report
(*The Limits to Growth*) in 1972, has been seen as a keystone in the
environmental crisis.

Much is owed to the perspicacity and boldness of Mr Gorbachev. But the
reason he acted as he did and his overtures were heard and accepted both
within his empire and without was that the economic cost of the arms race
could no longer be sustained by the superpowers. For some, though, this was
a triumph of the marchers' reason – part of the long march of Reason. History
has yet to judge whether the efforts of the tens of thousands who took part in
the peace movement made a significant contribution to the termination of the
Cold War and the abandonment of the MAD process.[2]

There are cycles in human thought which move between polar opposites,
for instance, authoritarianism and libertarianism. The eighteenth century was
intoxicated by the newly discovered omnipotence of 'reason', which was
expected to explain passions, politics and deities. With the publication of

Spinosa's *Ethics*, the world became reduced to an arithmetic problem. There could be no place for instinct and tradition in the new logic.

The antithesis to this *Weltanschauung* peaked at the end of the nineteenth century and early decades of the twentieth. The irrational, the 'intuitive', the 'unconscious' and the volatility of the crowd were captured and reflected in T. S. Eliot's *The Waste Land*, and in the works of Freud and Sorel.[3] At its zenith this way of thinking foreshadowed the nemesis of the free market philosophy and its supplantation by the institutional and intellectual bearers of the seed of rationality – the welfare state and scientific Marxism. Under Marxism-Leninism the laws of politics and society were as inexorable as the laws of thermodynamics. One of the slogans of the October 1917 revolution was: Communism = Soviet Power + Electrification. There was a profound belief in science: the social world was controllable and could be planned once the laws of social development were understood.

By the end of the 1980s, reaction had once again set in against the absolute knowability of the social world and its economic functioning. Today, not only in Russia, there is no longer a grand faith in science; governments are seen as being no more able to control the trade cycle than they can the weather. 'Science' itself has become debased and scientists are chided for polluting the world from their detergent laboratories. There has been a questioning and even partial rejection of the idea that *Homo sapiens* can control the environment. For this reason, among others, the ground has been well prepared for the almost joyous embrace of Adam Smith. The general acceptance of his hidden hand is revealing; it returns us to mysticism, superstition and the *deus ex machina*.

Macro-economic demand management by government, the Keynesian prescription, has been denounced and derided. Its place has been taken by micro-economics, in which each individual and household is sovereign in the market in the sky. The substitution of the 'macro' by the 'micro' in economics was accompanied by the shift from sociology to psychology: social ills and problems were the product, not of structures (and if so, then not amenable to 'engineering'), but of individual failings. Hayek, while drawing on the work of sociologists, refused to acknowledge their contribution to his own thought. He deliberately denied the existence of sociology as a discipline: he discussed 'social Darwinism', but omitted to mention Herbert Spencer, its originator. The reasons for this neglect are to be found in his highly disparaging discussion of the subject:

> The socialist bias of constructivism (i.e. rationalism) . . . displays its inability to comprehend economic phenomena most crudely in sociology.

. . . Sociology itself might also be called a *socialist* science, having been openly presented as capable of creating a new order of socialism. . . . Sociology proceeds in sovereign disregard of knowledge gained by established disciplines that have long studied such grown structures as law, language and the market.[4]

Corporatism and Beyond

Karl Mannheim, also a sociologist, was aware of the direction of change brought about by technology and the way in which society was increasingly organising its members in terms of the most efficient orchestration of means and ends. He concluded that there was a decline in the 'capacity to act intelligently in a given situation on the basis of one's own insight into the interrelations of events'. However, he did not suggest that everything should be left to the market.[5] In the post-war decades the 'means' chosen came to be conceptualised as corporatism.

This concept is itself difficult to define, partly because of the range of topics addressed under this heading and the disagreements over what constitutes the essential elements of the theory.[6] Its virtue inhered in its offering a credible and distinctive alternative to pluralism as a way of interpreting organised interests and the manner in which they were integrated into the work of governments and their bureaucracies.

An important attempt to offer a concise statement on corporatism in the context of liberal democracies was made by Schmitter in 1974.[7] According to him, corporatism consists of a system of functionally differentiated interest groups which are recognised or licensed by the state and granted a monopoly in exchange for observing certain controls on their selection of leaders and for filtering the demands they put forward. This last point is very important. These 'interest organisations' did not necessarily fully represent their members' interests and could instead act as regulators of those interests by, for example, restraining even the legitimate wage demands of their membership, by tacitly or overtly accepting an incomes policy. This suggested that demands placed on the agenda by interest group mediators emanated from the organisation rather than from the individual members, or that the demands of the latter are shaped by their representatives, within their own conclave.

In contrast to pluralism, which views the political arena as consisting of pressure groups competing in the marketplace, corporatism was a system of state-licensed monopolies. Such a system emerged because 'bourgeois dominated' polities need stability in an environment characterised by the concentration of ownership, increasing competition between national economies, and a growth in the public domain.

Other authors saw corporatism as a distinctive form of political economic organisation differing from both capitalism and socialism. In fact one writer described it as 'an economic system in which the state directs and controls predominantly privately owned business according to four principles: unity, order, nationalism and success'.[8] It was a social formation that had developed as a consequence of structural changes in the economy, such as the increased concentration of investment resources in a smaller number of large industrial conglomerates, declining profitability, higher expenditures on research and technological development, and intensified international competition. These all had the effect of drawing the state more and more into the economic arena. This interpretation was in a sense a generalised sketch – an academic cartoon – of the trend in the UK and other industrialised societies. It represented another sort of 'third way' – neither capitalism nor socialism, but a hybrid in which the dominant power groups in society were 'incorporated' into the state machinery to maintain social, economic and political stability. Corporatism was adapted to explain the compromise reached during the Brezhnev era between the political leadership and various interests.[9]

The major European states had to find ways of dealing with the turmoil of 1968 and the impact of the oil crisis of 1973, which brought with it the threat of higher inflation and economic dislocation. The trade unions were strong (their membership figures were buoyant) and yet there was mounting evidence that full employment might not be sustainable. Moreover, despite burgeoning public expenditure it seemed that the post-war commitment to the other pillars of the welfare state might also be difficult to maintain. The post-Keynesian era had dawned, although Friedman's dome still lay beneath the horizon.

Although political parties still appealed to the public to participate in the parliamentary decision-making process, in fact deals were being done behind closed doors with leaders of powerful interest groups – 'the beer and sandwiches at No. 10 syndrome' (until Margaret Thatcher became mistress of the house). Corporatism was an expression of the high point of consensus politics. However, in retrospect these manoeuvres were attempts by national governments to employ domestic institutional measures to tackle essentially international problems. This type of politics represented a rational way of resolving conflicts over the distribution of goods and services in both private and public sectors. The theory appeared to apply to, and adequately describe, the political ordering of affairs in the UK and USSR in the late 1970s under the unimaginative, docile and compromising leaderships of James Callaghan and Leonid Brezhnev.

At the 'meso' level, corporatism was evident in certain economic sectors where public policy functions were being devolved to private groups. Whole sectors, properly comprising part of the public domain, could be seen to be operated and regulated by private interest associations who performed 'public' roles. The activities of water boards, for example, were regulated neither by market forces nor by state bureaucracies answerable to Parliament.[10] Studies carried out on 'quasi-autonomous government organisations' (quangos), especially in the public sector, uncovered a disturbing aspect of the functioning of liberal democracies, namely that they contained sectors which were quasi-public associations, responsible neither to shareholders nor to the electorate. From the standpoint of the 1990s the boards and associations falling into this category were an 'unstable' political-economic form and already in transition to becoming private.

It is now being suggested that a supranational corporatism is emerging which has to meet the needs of an integrated Europe. The future European political economy will be held together by a combination of technocratic professionalism shared by all the major players regardless of divergent specific interests and by a dense and durable web of bi-, tri- and multilateral bargaining relationships involving both public and private bodies. Ideally, this system should maintain order in the supranational organism by ensuring that all parties practise self-restraint and consent to compromise. However, there are serious limitations to extending the concepts and institutions of the national corporatist state to the supranational level.

The international organisations set up after 1945 – OECD, GATT, UNCTAD, the World Bank and IMF – have far from outlived their usefulness. But during the 1970s it became clear that there were no technically viable institutional mechanisms to provide mutually acceptable political solutions to the economic and ecological problems faced by national governments functioning in the international arena. In their absence, national corporatist strategies were deployed. The medicine prescribed was no more than a placebo. Rather than use the breathing space to find new institutional mechanisms, as in the 1920s politicians looked back to the 'golden age' of free trade: capital markets were deregulated, the powers of trade unions eroded through the legislative process, and the promise of full employment abandoned. Neo-corporatism expired and the mythological saviour, market forces, was ushered in.

Corporatism had been called into existence to overcome the vestiges of the bi-polar conflict between the two classes, 'labour' and 'capital' (which by now was an oversimplification of a much more complex social structure created by massive and irreversible changes to the economic structure). The period witnessed the growth of a non-manufacturing sector and of a large, better educated and articulate middle class whose concerns became increasingly focused on 'green issues' – the quality of life and the environment, consumer protection and gender. Placing these issues on the political agenda marked the emergence of social movements which cut across class boundaries and in doing so rupture the old class-based politics. The new social movements in advanced Western societies are not primarily concerned with a redistribution of wealth but with a redefinition of national and international issues, such as justice (for instance, the use of nuclear power or the location of nuclear power plants), education and censorship, human rights and both the built and the natural environment. The very nature of these concerns excludes, as a solution to them, the use of a distributive mechanism premised on the mechanism of the exchange economy.[11]

The emergence of the Green movement in Germany epitomised an aspect of a trend in European societies. In the late 1960s there had been extra-parliamentary opposition to inner-city decline and the effects of the urban renewal policies that were introduced to arrest it. In the 1970s the Greens built on this earlier opposition and championed 'first-person politics' in place of its sibling 'politics in service of the proletariat'. The *Wende,* or turning point, in German politics coincided with that occurring elsewhere. Local authorities began to look for new and alternative ways of meeting their obligations and the expectations of their electorates (soon to be renamed 'clients' and 'customers') about the level of services (and their delivery) to which they considered themselves entitled. This applied especially to welfare and other 'cultural' services, whose costs were rising. The central government, which was also demanding economic restructuring, applied a range of fiscal restrictions that reinforced existing pressures causing unemployment. Under these circumstances, political parties saw, contemplated and then adopted ideas and policies developed in the 'alternative camp'. Most notable among these have been: (1) the attempt to incorporate the 'informal' labour market into the main economy through a variety of state agencies which were established to offer advice and assistance to small enterprises; (2) the adoption of the self-help ethos, generically referred to as 'community care', which is hailed as a rescue vehicle for social services; and (3) ideas on recycling and energy conservation and generation.

As far as this book is concerned, a crucial element in the demise of corporatism has been the technological revolution associated with information technology and micro-electronics generally. Apart from anything else, these changes have opened up the possibility for the formation of smaller production and organisational units. Post-Fordist in scale, postmodern in style, these units are flexible, adaptable and easily dismantled and require flexibility of their employees. A corollary of this development has been the whittling away at one of the central features of the *raison d'être* of unions and employers' associations, namely the national agreement. Local-level bargaining and greater involvement of employees in decisions affecting their livelihood and quality of life become more important than decisions taken at the centre. Technological change coincides with social change and the maturation of populations who wish to be better informed about global issues – the erosion of the ozone layer – and about matters of more direct and immediate concern. The overall outcome of these changes is a movement towards greater decentralisation which strikes a death blow to national corporatism. Even at the local level and in individual sectors, the corporatist principle has been eroded. This is true even of Sweden.[12]

Central to the present global restructuring process, especially in the revolutionary transformations taking place in Russia and East and Central Europe, has been the deregulation of capital markets that began in the early 1980s. In the *Communist Manifesto*, published in 1848, Marx wrote:

> The bourgeoisie, by the rapid improvement of all instruments of production, by the immensely facilitated means of communication, draws all, even the most barbarian, nations into civilisation. The cheap prices of its commodities are the heavy artillery with which it batters down all Chinese walls. . . . It compels all nations, on pain of extinction, to adopt the bourgeois mode of production, it compels them to introduce what it calls civilisation into their midst i.e. become bourgeois themselves.[13]

The torrent of commodities produced by the more efficient capitalist countries of Western Europe might have breached the Berlin Wall. But history will probably reveal that the Trojan horse was the capital market. Under its pressure, the rigidities of the West European 'mixed' economies gave way first. It was only a matter of time before the accumulated rigidities of countries to the East would succumb.

Some theorists regard the events of 1989–90 as the triumph of 'people power', and posit that the revolt of the masses was provoked by a universal craving for 'liberty', 'democracy' and more obvious material benefits. Some will be more inclined to stress the failure of a type of system riven with faults and beyond reform. Others would argue with Maynard Keynes that:

> . . . the ideas of economists and political philosophers, both when they are right and when they are wrong, are more powerful than is commonly

understood. Indeed the world is ruled by little else. Practical men, who believe themselves to be quite exempt from any intellectual influences, are usually the slaves of some defunct economist. . . . I am sure that the power of vested interests is vastly exaggerated compared with the gradual encroachment of ideas. Not, indeed, immediately, but after a certain interval . . . soon or late, it is ideas, not vested interests, which are dangerous for good or evil.[14]

Innovative ideas have a gestation period before they are advanced in a coherent and understandable way. When first presented in the marketplace they may appear radical and challenging and be for that reason ignored, neglected or refuted. The gestation period continues but it reaches another stage during which the insidious process of their co-optation begins. The recent history of the Green movement (and the British Liberal Democratic party) testifies to this process, with the legitimate cry 'you stole my issue' often rending the air in the political arenas.[15]

Since a strong organised labour movement has always been a condition for corporatism, the advent of the single European market in 1992 has all but removed any possibility for its restoration. In future, labour – all working people – will be protected by the implementation and further consolidation of the Social Contract, embedded in the Maastricht Treaty, and in supranational legislation. Human rights, including freedom of movement and non-discrimination, will be protected by law, ultimately through the European Court of Justice. Collective bargaining between employers' associations and trade unions will not disappear altogether, but will gradually become outdated.

Just as NATO has had to adapt itself to the new geopolitical environment, so will the ILO and other Europe-wide organisations representing all-embracing socio-economic classes. According to some observers, 'In the absence of supranational employer associations and facilitating state intervention, all that the unions can hope to accomplish in building what the Commission has euphemistically called a "European industrial relations system" are consultations and perhaps negotiations with the headquarters of large multinational firms'.[16] Moreover, it is imperative that they do adapt. The political rights of the 'European citizen' are ill protected by the European Parliament, which is too weak, in the short term, to defend and enhance the social rights of its citizens, or the rights of employees in the workplace. This systemic development might serve as a stimulus to the growth in co-operatives within an overarching legal framework in the new regionalised Europe.

Strong, regional industrial districts already exist. They have well-developed social and technical infrastructures which enable firms working within them to compete in the international marketplace. Local and regional governments work closely with different interest groups to provide facilities for small, innovative firms with low capital needs to start up. If it is possible to identify a form of corporatism, then it is akin to that envisaged by Durkheim as a solution to anomie in industrial societies, which he saw as being modelled on medieval guilds.

In fact, towns and regions are themselves behaving like their medieval forebears, such as the Hanseatic league, in that they act as solidary units in promoting the interests of their own citizens. They advertise the merits of their towns (Milton Keynes, Peterborough) and regions (Baden-Württemburg) and send emissaries to the political decision-making centres at the national (London) and supranational (Brussels) level. But these emissaries travel with a brief negotiated at the local level between various actors whose interests, agendas and numbers (in the sense that new actors enter the arena and others exit) cannot be conceived as constant. The generation of (local) society and its economic profile is an outcome of praxis, a dynamic exchange of material and non-material needs between individuals in time and space.[17]

As has been pointed out, if unions move their centre of gravity to the regions, then they will inevitably lose any chance of influencing decisions in the 'political management of interregional externalities'.[18] Since such regionalised unions would be co-operating with local employers in order to further the interests of 'their' firms and region in the inter-regional free market competition, they might find it extremely difficult to argue for more assistance to go to less developed regions. Because the ideological environment in which they operate compels them to act in this way, national and supranational governments are obliged to intervene to bring about a distribution of resources which otherwise would not occur.

A Challenge to Friedrich August von Hayek

In one recent volume of his collected works, Friedrich Hayek began by quoting Ludwig von Mises to the effect that: 'If we wish to save the world from barbarism we have to refute Socialism, but we cannot thrust it carelessly aside'.[19] One must similarly say of Hayek's writings, which are powerful, polemical, didactic and dogmatic, that they too must be subjected to serious challenge and not rejected out of hand.

In his book, *The Fatal Conceit: The Errors of Socialism*, Hayek argued that 'our civilisation depends . . . on what can be described as the extended order of human cooperation, an order more commonly, if somewhat misleadingly, known as capitalism'.[20] This extended order 'resulted not from human design or intention but spontaneously'. His whole work was dedicated to 'proving' this (unprovable) assertion which, incidentally, he described as a 'scientific study'.[21] Yet, his declarations were doctrinaire in their formulation: 'Socialist aims and programmes are factually impossible to achieve or execute, and they also happen . . . to be logically impossible'.[22] And, just as the Church once reasoned that erroneous ideas can only lead mankind into the pit of eternal damnation, Hayek considered that: 'The dispute between the market order and socialism is no less than a matter of survival. To follow socialist morality would destroy much of present humankind and impoverish much of the rest'.[23] In this fashion he raised the defence of capitalism to the virtue of a crusade, following in the footsteps of his namesake, St Augustine, who set the precedent for the ecclesiastical war over ideology in the Middle Ages. However, one fairly constant theme in history is that missions undertaken in the name of ideals have not relied solely on peaceful persuasion and have been content to employ aggression clothed as a holy war.

For Hayek, the superiority of capitalism (the market order) resides in its having 'evolved' and survived whilst societies lacking the traditions, habits and structures of this order failed in the competition between human groups. He quoted with approval the statement by Carr-Saunders that '. . . man and groups are naturally selected on account of the customs they practise just as they are selected on account of their mental and physical characters. . . . Those groups practising the most advantageous customs will have an advantage in the constant struggle between adjacent groups over those that practise less advantageous customs'.[24] He gave this view an intellectual update by citing Karl Popper to the effect that 'cultural evolution continues genetic evolution by other means'.[25] All cultural development rests on the inheritance of acquired characteristics 'in the form of rules guiding the mutual relations among individuals which are not innate but learnt'.[26] The comparison of social evolution with genetic change in biological organisms has occupied a dominant niche in sociological theory since the mid nineteenth century. Hayek appropriated the idea by stating that cultural evolution is a process of continuous adaptation to unforeseen events which could not have been forecast. This is another reason why 'evolutionary theory can never put us in the position of rationally predicting and controlling future evolution'.[27] Furthermore, biological and cultural evolution both rely on the same principle of selection, namely reproductive advantage. They also depend on competition as a means of 'preserving existing achievements'.[28]

Positing an alternative to this Darwinian view, Kropotkin, at the beginning of the twentieth century, argued that voluntary co-operation, not competition, was the dominant force in evolution. He too drew upon the anthropological studies and the history of ancient Greece to demonstrate his point.[29] But then, Hayek did not like Aristotle's views. Like any other dogmatist, he was not content merely to draw upon other names in the directory of scholarly prophets, but had to demonstrate the superiority of their intellectual antecedents. Thus, Hayek claimed that the 'idea of evolution is older in the humanities and social sciences than in the natural sciences', for Darwin had derived his ideas on evolution from reading Adam Smith. The new dogma has also to challenge the founding fathers of philosophy. Aristotle's 'utter incomprehension of the advanced market order in which he lived' had the unfortunate effect of leading to the proclamation of Aristotelian ethics as virtually the official teaching of the Roman Catholic Church. This had a 'damning effect', in the eyes of Hayek, for it caused the early modern Church to condemn interest as usury, to preach the notion of a 'just price' and show contempt for gain.

Luckily, David Hume had the sense to see that the market made it possible 'to do a service to another without bearing him any real kindness'. Yet not everyone is aware of this insight, with the result that 'a naive and childlike animistic view of the world', one permeated with Aristotelian thought, has come to 'dominate social theory and is the foundation of socialist thought'.[30] The writing of Descartes contributed to this invidious thinking: Cartesian rationalism discards tradition and claims the paramountcy of pure reason, which itself can build a new world and a new morality and draw up new laws. Hayek fundamentally disagreed with this view. For him, as for Edmund Burke, 'morals, including our institutions of property, freedom and justice, are not a creation of man's reason, but a distinct second endowment conferred on him by cultural evolution'.[31] Tradition is itself 'the product of a process of selection from among irrational, or, rather, "unjustified belief" which, without anyone's knowing or intending it, assisted the proliferation of those who followed them'.[32] The sifting process which creates customs and morality takes into account, he argued, many more facts about existence than could an individual. From this point of view, tradition is 'in some respects' wiser than human reason.

Hayek gradually came to display a suspicion, if not an antipathy, towards intellectuals, for 'rationalists tend to be intelligent and intellectual; and intelligent intellectuals tend to be socialist'. This phenomenon was explained by the fact that 'intelligent people will tend to overvalue intelligence, and to suppose that we must owe all the advantages and opportunities that our civilisation offers to deliberate design rather than to following traditional rules'.[33]

But, contrary to Hayek's assumption, simply removing state planners – who are but a creation of 'intelligent people' – does not mean that individuals in modern society are suddenly free to maximise their choices. One of the doyens of organisational theory, who considers that 'organisations (are) the key phenomenon of our time, and thus politics, social class, economics, technology, religion, the family . . . take on the character of dependent variables',[34] has been led to ask 'what kind of a society is being created within the large employing organisations'?[35]

Perrow's question arises because the bureaucracy of large organisations has become for its employees more than a source of wages that can be freely spent on consuming the goods and services of other organisations. Today up to 45 per cent of a large organisation's labour costs are paid in fringe benefits. From one point of view, employers who provide or make available a whole range of services are applauded for being progressive. But Perrow wonders whether there is cause for concern when the 'generosity' of organisations removes from employees a little more choice, which was previously 'subject to family and kin, neighbours, peer groups, and religious or ethnic ties'.[36]

The intrusion of the welfare state into our lives and its intervention in the economy may be deplored by market theorists, but the state provides services to individuals, not on condition that they are employed, but on account of their being citizens. The state can find other ways of delivering services to its masters – its citizens, through decentralised agencies and more or less autonomous groups. Therefore, statisation is not the only road to serfdom: the 'organisational society' also creates its own form of dependency, one which bears a price, ultimately that of insecurity – the equivalent of the price demanded by Mephistopheles of Faust.

Hayek suggested that his argument was akin to that employed by Freud in his *Civilisation and its Discontents*, involving as it does the conflict between the instinctive desires of human beings and the learnt rules of conduct, except that the two men reach different conclusions, with Hayek believing that 'an atavistic longing after the life of the noble savage is the main source of the collectivist tradition'.[37] Yet, in his rejection of the paternalistic state, for which he wishes to substitute a mythically free individual in the marketplace, Hayek has more in common with Freudian thought than he would like to accept.

Of course, Hayek was writing within a tradition which includes more recent thinkers than Hume and Smith. The Cambridge economist, Colin Clark, writing in 1941, claimed that: 'long-period world economic equilibria develop themselves in their own peculiar manner, entirely independently of political and social change'.[38] Schumacher, referring to this 'metaphysical heresy', retorted that in the long term world economic equilibria can be known because they are dependent on political and social changes. In his view, since the future is always in the making out of the past, about which a great deal can be known, 'the future is *largely* predictable, if we have solid knowledge and extensive knowledge of the past'.[39] (The condition that it cannot be wholly predicted is owing to the 'mysterious and irrepressible factor called human freedom'.) Evidently, it is not just doctrinaire Marxists who face the opprobrious charge of 'the poverty of historicism'. Nor is a language of scorn the sole prerogative of Hayek; Schumacher dismissed Clark's analysis as employing 'sophisticated and ingenious methods . . . to produce a work of spurious verisimilitude'.[40]

There is something misanthropic in Hayek's work, for despite his belief in the virtue and beneficence of evolutionary processes, he contends that 'evolution cannot be just' and that 'to insist that all future change be just would be to demand that evolution come to a halt'. The apparent reason for this is the teleological purpose of evolution, which 'leads us ahead precisely in bringing about much that we could not intend or foresee'.[41] Any single individual or organisation (or government) can have only partial knowledge of all the events to which the market order is constantly adapting through price signals. This 'adaptation to the unknown' is most effectively achieved by decentralising decision making, thus enabling more information to be taken into account. Other economists point out in a similar vein that history has repeatedly demonstrated that market responses are much quicker than legal responses to changing economic conditions. But it is not a matter of ´whose response is the more rapid', the market or the computer prediction. It is a question of whether governments (or groups of individuals) should engage in modelling and calculating probabilities on the grounds that although the 'future cannot be forecast . . . it can be explored'.[42]

One of John Locke's applauded insights was that, if a political authority wants to maintain and encourage peaceful co-operation among individuals – on which prosperity rests – then it has to enforce a particular form of justice – one which cannot exist without the acceptance of private property. But, in order to prevent the abuse of property, competition has to be ensured. Private property (which Hayek preferred to designate 'several property') was regarded as 'generally beneficial in that it transfers the guidance of production from the hands of a few individuals who . . . have limited knowledge to a process, the extended order . . . thereby benefiting those who do not own property *nearly* as much as those who do'.[43] This might have some validity as far as a certain range of demands and needs are concerned, but the so-called 'extended order' seems at a loss to transfer resources 'for socially necessary purposes'.

There is no explanation why 'The morals of the market do lead us to benefit others, not by our intending to do so, but by making us act in a manner which will have just that effect'.[44] The implied motivation for our actions is altruism, which is demonstrated through voluntary gifts made to charities. As far as the question of determining the relative rewards to individuals is concerned, the inadequate answer given is that: 'Nobody can ascertain, save through the market, the size of an individual's contribution to the overall product, nor can it otherwise be determined how much remuneration must be rendered to enable him to choose the activity which will add most to the flow of goods and services'.[45] The Thomist notion of a 'just price' and the idea of distributive justice, which are determined by people in their everyday lives, are shunted aside by the *deus ex machina* of the market: 'Mankind could neither have reached nor could now maintain its present numbers without an inequality that is neither determined by, nor reconcilable with, any deliberate moral judgements'.[46]

Adam Smith and his Adherents

The notion of a 'just price' is too easily ridiculed and rejected by the paradigm in which everyone (as well as everything) in the economic marketplace has his or her price. Indeed, central to the market philosophy are prices and the functions which they perform. Milton Friedman identifies three basic functions. The first is the transmission of information about, for instance, demands, tastes and resource availability. Secondly, prices offer an incentive to minimise costs and to allocate resources to their most highly valued uses. Thirdly, they distribute income. As far as the second (apparently reasonable) function is concerned, it has to be remarked that few decision-makers act on the basis of price information alone, especially when making major investment decisions.[47] As to the third, the governments of many industrialised countries, especially since 1945, but in some states since the 1930s, have been trying to separate the distribution of income from market determination.

The vitriol poured on Keynesian economics and especially the former state socialist societies of Eastern Europe can be traced in part to the fact that one of the most important experimental economic decisions in modern history, the decision to move to a more fully planned economy, meant a reversal in the relationship between prices and planners. Prices were no longer to determine planners' decisions, planners would determine prices. That particular experiment has come to an end. The fact that it was tried at all explains the inquisitorial malevolence with which it has been attacked: heretics must be condemned, damned and punished. The debate initiated by Oscar Lange in 1936 on how to inject market elements into centrally planned economies (and thus on various versions of 'market socialism') has now been all but totally removed from government economic agendas set and discussed by the World Bank, IMF and the members of G7. A moratorium has also been placed on its opposite: how far aspects of a command economy can be introduced into a market system to create a 'mixed economy'. Until recently most professional economists were not unsympathetic to some element of planning in a mixed economy. The economic collapse of the Soviet empire has seen the (temporary) triumph of market capitalism and the ridicule of anyone calling themselves an economist and advocating any form of central planning.

The often quoted Yugoslavian experiment seemed to many to offer a compromise between the two systems. Its biggest failing, according to Friedman, lay in the linkage of property rights to employment status. That is to say, workers had no transferable rights to the productive enterprise, so that they were owners of the enterprise only while working in it. Therefore, Yugoslavia could have no capital market – a serious problem for all those who sought to reform the administrative-command economies from the late 1960s onwards in Poland and Hungary and in the first years of perestroika in the Soviet Union. Friedman accepted that the path adopted by Yugoslavia was an advance on the fully-fledged command economies, in that power and responsibility were more dispersed, but the indivisibility of property rights and their lack of transferability not only hampered the formation of a capital market, but impeded risk-taking and innovation.

Friedman, an economist of impeccable market credentials, concedes that while there is not really a satisfactory substitute for a full-scale free market, some departure from the ideal may be desirable. Not only are people willing to sacrifice efficiency for other goals, but 'the market is simply not capable of doing some things' and there are also troublesome 'externalities'.[48] But this is the extent of the concession: it appears that only national defence is the exception, for Friedman even opposed the existence of the United States Food and Drug Administration, on the grounds that this, like education, health and the prison service, can be provided by the private sector.

Paradoxically, Adam Smith, the patron saint of market capitalism, did not hold the capitalist or bourgeoisie in high esteem. In so far as he regarded businessmen, politicians and legislators as being interested solely in their own self-interest, he may be seen as a forerunner of public choice theory.[49]

Moreover, he reserved a very definite role for government as the provider of social services, including such public works as bridges, canals, highways and 'institutions for promoting instruction of the people'. In other words, Smith was not a consistent advocate of markets and opponent of government intervention. Much in his analysis and prescriptions remains unpalatable to modern advocates of *laissez-faire*.

Adam Smith's basic objection to the society of his time was to the injustice of privilege, reflected in the monopoly powers exercised by government and business, and to the inefficiency which came from the unfair advantages enjoyed by monopolies and the high prices which they charged. The relevance of these first criticisms of late eighteenth-century Britain to the former administrative-planned economies of East and Central Europe and Russia is sufficiently evident to make further comment unnecessary. Equally pertinent to the condition of these (and other industrial) societies is Smith's view on the psychological cost of economic growth:

> In the progress of the division of labour, the employment of . . . the great body of the people comes to be confined to a few very simple operations. . . . But the understandings of the greater part of men are necessarily formed by their ordinary employments. The man whose whole life is spent in performing a few simple operations, of which the effects are always the same or very nearly the same has no occasion to exert his understanding, or to exercise his invention in finding out expedients for removing difficulties which never occur. He naturally loses, therefore, the habit of such exertion, and generally becomes as stupid as it is possible for a human being to become.[50]

Smith's aim was to emphasise the mental mutilation which extreme forms of the divisions of labour could create. The torpor arising from specialisation could make the individual 'incapable of bearing a part in any rational conversation' or of formulating 'any just judgement concerning many even of the ordinary duties of private life'.[51] In order to counter the deleterious psychological effects brought about by improvements in economic welfare, he advocated a programme of compulsory education and the cultivation of the arts. His censure of the mode of production, too often ignored by those who quote him so readily in support of capitalism, did not contain advice on a solution. However, the validity of his depiction (and its moral gravitas) was to act as a spur to those who did want to tackle the problem, including Robert Owen and the early co-operators.

His championing of *laissez-faire* and, *ipso facto*, the commercial and manufacturing class was far from unqualified. He was not, as he is often portrayed, an advocate of granting total freedom of action to entrepreneurs; indeed, he was highly critical of entrepreneurs as a group. He complained of 'the mean rapacity, the monopolising spirit of merchants and manufacturers', declaring that unwise policies pursued by governments can readily be blamed upon merchants and manufacturers whose 'interested sophistry' has 'confounded the common sense of mankind'.[52] He cautioned that legislative proposals emanating from the business class 'ought always to be listened to with great precaution' and only adopted after a close scrutiny for 'it comes from an order of men, whose interest is never exactly the same with that of the public, who have generally an interest to deceive and even to oppress the public'.[53]

Smith attributed four main good qualities to individuals: a propensity to 'truck and barter'; an urge to better their condition; a propensity to save, since they are essentially frugal; and prudence. On the other side of the balance book, firstly they are lazy, with everyone wanting to improve their position but with the least exercise of effort; secondly, they are hypocritical and will seek to disguise their private interest as being the public interest; and thirdly, because of a tendency to 'monopolise', 'people of the same trade seldom meet together' without their conversation ending 'in a conspiracy against the public, or in some contrivance to raise prices'.[54]

It is this combination of human qualities that made Smith so opposed to mercantilism, a system in which the government issued extensive regulations governing the use of labour and capital. Mercantilism represented the successful assault of the business community on a helpless public, allowing avaricious and monopolising merchants to exploit the machinery of government for their own purposes, without really contributing to the nation's welfare. For these reasons, mercantilism as a system failed to combine the individual's drive for self-betterment with increasing the general welfare. On the other hand the corporatist system (described earlier), established two hundred years after the publication of *The Wealth of Nations*, did, as was intended, promote the general welfare. Its failing, perhaps, was that it encouraged the 'bad' qualities in the human psyche that Smith had listed. He proposed to substitute for mercantilism, just as modern exponents of his views propose to substitute for corporatism, an alternative based on competition. They believe this will encourage, if not compel, people to behave in ways that simultaneously benefit both the private and the public interest.

The institutional order advocated by Smith pivoted on the notion of competition, which he saw as the means of ensuring that entrepreneurs, in pursuing their own self-interest, would 'naturally' promote the general public's welfare. His attitudes and opinions were highly coloured by the political context within which he lived. Government was oligarchical – and could hardly be described otherwise since only 3–4 per cent of the adult male population was enfranchised. (Neither Adam Smith nor David Hume was entitled to vote.) Parliament was the bastion of the privileged and thus hardly given to respond to public needs. He considered it axiomatic that, to the extent that governments – composed of politicians and bureaucrats – have power, they will take full advantage of the opportunities available to them to enrich themselves. Moreover, they will do as little as possible in order to enjoy the benefits of privilege: 'Landlords, like all other men, love to reap where they never sowed – that is, as soon as the land of any country has all become private property'.[55]

Smith's descriptions, analyses and prescriptions derive from his understanding of human psychology and the structure and *modus operandi* of the society in which he lived. The need for human co-operation was central to his notion of psychology. However, co-operation and reciprocity occurred, he thought, not through individual benevolence but through the perception each individual has of the personal benefit to be gained from 'helping' someone. Hence his famous statement:

> It is not from benevolence of the butcher, the brewer or the baker that we expect our dinner, but from their regard to their own interest. We address ourselves, not to their humanity but to their self-love, and never talk to them of our own necessities but of their advantage.[56]

This astutely formulated dictum should be seen within the context of his overall project on moral issues, which was highly critical of mercantilism and corrupting monopolies. The motive force behind co-operation between human beings might be consciously or unconsciously selfish or it might even be a selfish gene. On the other hand, the opposite might be true; the driving force might be selflessness. These are metaphysical questions. While the co-operative movement is imbued with moral meanings which are critical of unbridled individualism, which it challenges, its success depends on being a practical alternative in the organisation of human affairs.

One of the key problems of the Friedman argument is that it tends to suggest that externalities, like oligopolies, are marginal and rare occurrences. Smith, from what has been said above, would have been far more sceptical about their 'marginality'. Perhaps he would have responded as did Alec Nove, who pointed out:

> If unemployment was due only to labour market imperfections, if

economies of scale did not lead to the emergence of large and economically powerful corporations with powers over prices, if the distribution of property bore any recognisable relationship to present or even past economic merit, then [Friedman's] case would be cast-iron. . . . The institution of bankruptcy is indeed a method for dealing with misallocation and inefficiency. . . . But to invest massively in capacity which is consigned to the scrapyard soon after it becomes operational is not quite what we mean by efficient use of resources.[57]

In a text written in 1983 Nove proposed an economic system consisting of five types of property ownership. The majority of goods and services would be provided by enterprises operating in market competitive conditions, with material incentives linked to the satisfaction of demand at least cost. The long-term interest of the employees could be linked to the long-term future of the 'self-managed' enterprise by a lump-sum payment related to length of service and the appreciation of the enterprise's assets, similar to the 'with profits' policies offered by insurance companies.[58] Nove concluded his 'Comment' by challenging Friedman's complacency and pointing out that a market economy may be a necessary condition for human freedom, but it is certainly not a sufficient condition for, as we know, in many countries today its maintenance requires a military dictatorship.

Nove's moderate and considered 'Comment' must have been unknown to Francis Fukuyama (or it went unheeded) for, according to the latter, the past generation has witnessed two developments of world historical significance. 'The first is the emergence of liberal democracy as the only global ideology and the second is the victory of market principles. These two revolutions are closely connected and represent a larger, secular pattern of evolution'.[59] For Fukuyama, liberal democracy and advanced industrialisation are closely connected; the former 'inexorably' following the latter. He uses the economic development of countries in East Asia as the model for his 'theory', pointing out that their 'growth demonstrates that latecomers to the process of economic development are in no way disadvantaged and can achieve the highest levels of technology and consumption provided that they remain connected to world markets and permit free competition at home'.

Russian Co-operatives and the Socialist State

Exactly a century ago, the Russian Populists (*narodniki*) had also argued that the latecomers to history could benefit from the 'privilege of backwardness'. But they differed fundamentally with Fukuyama: they totally rejected *laissez-*

faire capitalism as the vehicle which would enable them to reap that privilege. Some would argue that that was their great mistake. However, in their view, the privilege of backwardness meant that, having witnessed the horrors and inhumanity of early capitalism in Western Europe, they could take steps to prevent Russian society from travelling along the same path. The alternative which they posited was ultimately a conservative one, in that they wished to preserve their country's unique communitarian institutions and traditions. They differed from modern European conservative parties, which some see as having achieved a balance between a *laissez-faire* system (which they allege brings freedom and prosperity), on the one hand, and communities, which preserve values, on the other.[60]

Russian capitalism, it is said, 'was born in the Crimean War and died in World War I'[61] and by the end of the nineteenth century was heavily dependent on foreign capital investment, which had grown from 13.4 per cent of GNP in 1861 to 30 per cent in 1914.[62] In 1899 Count Witte, the then Minister of Finance, wrote to the Tsar informing him that the influx of foreign capital was the sole means for Russia's industrialisation.[63] Small firms did not play a part in his policy for the country's economic growth. The tsarist state provided a legislative framework for industrial growth and much of the direct investment. Instead of encouraging and relying upon indigenous managers and entrepreneurs, it preferred to 'import' them from Europe. Only after 1900 did the state relax its grip and allow a middle class – albeit nurtured by the state – to play a more active part in the country's industrialisation. Thus, from its earliest origins down to the present day, Russian industrialisation has based itself firstly on large productive enterprises. Secondly, the country depended heavily on foreign investment. Thirdly, the state played an enormous role directly and indirectly in the industrialisation process. Fourthly, partly as a cause and partly as an effect of these features, an autonomous sphere of market-oriented economic activity was never central to the everyday lives of the majority of the population.

Only in 1990 did the former Prime Minister of Russia concede that Peter the Great's state and Stalin's party had at last to surrender their entrepreneurial function to 'individual and family-labour activity, co-operatives, joint stock and leasehold enterprises for we must view the entrepreneurship of citizens and their freedom of economic initiative as a powerful lever'.[64]

Keynes, in the passage already cited, indicated the importance of ideas over vested interests. There is evidence for this maxim in the pre-eminence of Keynesianism after 1945 in Western Europe and in the predominance of Marxism in Eastern Europe. Over time ideas which had once been innovative and revolutionary became a doctrine among the groups who grew up with them and who came to constitute new, consolidated 'vested interests'. Alternative ideas – some of them wholly novel and others resurrections from an earlier period – presented themselves for adoption. Over the past 150 years one set of ideas in particular has suffered rejection at the hands of 'vested interests'.

At a meeting of the First International, Marx joined battle with Bakunin and Proudhon, whose ideas were moulded to form an 'anarcho-syndicalist' approach to the transformation of capitalism.[65] The revolution in Russia in February 1917 had syndicalist overtones, and for a while Lenin supported slogans and discussion of workers' control. But in 1921 the Workers' Opposition emerged as a protest movement against the bureaucratisation of industry, the introduction of Taylorism and Trotsky's anti-labour policies. When it published its manifesto on the restoration of workers' control in industry,[66] it was denounced as 'anarcho-syndicalist' and proscribed.[67]

Until the 1970s, the centrist and statist view of Marxism held sway amongst the social democratic political parties and trade unions in continental Europe, although the voice of decentralised anarcho-syndicalists remained strong in France, Italy and Spain (after the death of Franco).

Socialism meant modernism and modern meant monumental and mechanical: large factories, large cities and huge bureaucracies, whose virtues of speed, predictability and impersonality were acclaimed by Weber and that generation of capitalists and socialists alike. The bureaucratic form was the most efficient means of achieving specified goals. Economic growth has been one of the 'successes' marked to the credit of those who championed the path that had historically been taken. Rejected alternatives have periodically been called up and reinvestigated and reinterpreted.

Periods of actual or anticipated military conflict have led to extreme forms of centralisation and the imposition of strict constraints on private economic activity, archetypally in the societies of East and Central Europe and the former Soviet Union. The transition from small, private ownership to state ownership occurred in these countries at the end of the 1940s. The existence of group interests, including those of co-operatives, was regarded as a hindrance to the growth of political centralisation. Yet, during the transitional period from old (capitalist) forms of management to new ones, the co-operative would have ensured both a greater self-interest amongst producers in the final results and a greater direct connection between individual and collective interests. The general rejection of the co-operative form of labour organisation and property ownership – on the grounds that it preserved 'petty bourgeois' tendencies – had dire economic and undesirable ideological consequences.

Ironically, Russia and other formerly state socialist countries, in order to shorten the transitional period from the old (state socialist) forms to 'the market' (regarded as the path to prosperity), have rejected the co-operative mode, on the ideological ground that it preserves socialist elements. Culturally acquired habits that are absolutist or purist die hard: the demand by Marxism that *all* property should be publicly owned has been replaced by the desire for *all* property to be privately owned. At present the spectre stalking Europe is not pragmatism; the issue of ownership is not being decided on the basis of the merits of each case, but by the dogma of privatisation. It is equally ironic that Russian society, with its highly centralised state, should have been the birthplace of Michael Bakunin and Peter Kropotkin, the two principal progenitors of modern ideas on the minimalist or wholly absent state and a totally decentralised form of 'government'.

Notes

1   R. Bahro, *The Alternative: A Contribution to the Critique of Actually Existing Socialism*, Verso, London, 1977.
2   There is no sole 'agent' or 'agency' to explain major historical changes. Conflicts and contradictions within structures (such as the pride and price of Star Wars and Soviet paranoia and economic failure) are the prime movers. But pressures from below, in the form of social movements, do exert an influence, especially when they embody an immanent reason. At particular conjunctures a charismatic Alexander can cut the Gordian knot which dangerously entangles human affairs.
3   On Sorel's doctrine of spontaneous, non-rationalised activity, see G. Sorel, *Reflections on Violence*, (Paris, 1908) trans. T. E. Hulme, New York, 1914. Sorel's name has been linked with those of Freud and Nietzsche as 'the great prophets of the modern age' (H. Stuart Hughes, *Consciousness and Society: The Representation of European Social Thought 1890–1930*, Alfred A. Knopf, 1958, New York, Chapters 4 and 5).
4   F. von Hayek, *The Fatal Conceit: The Errors of Socialism. The Collected Works of Friedrich August von Hayek*, ed. W. W. Bartlett III, Routledge, London, 1988.
5   K. Mannheim, *Man and Society: In an Age of Reconstruction*, (1940) Routledge and Kegan Paul, 1960, London, p. 59.
6   P. Williamson, *Corporatism in Perspective*, Sage, London, 1989.
7   P. Schmitter, 'Still the Century of Corporatism?', *Review of Politics*, 36, 1974, pp. 85–131.
8   J. Winkler, 'Corporatism', *Archives Européennes de Sociologie*, no. 17, 1976, p. 103.
9   See V. Bunce and J. Echols, 'Soviet Politics in the Brezhnev Era: "Pluralism" or "Corporatism"?', in D. Kelley (ed.) *Soviet Politics in the Brezhnev Era*, Praeger, New York, 1980; V. Bunce, 'The Political Economy of the Brezhnev Era', *British Journal of Political Science*, 13, April 1963.
10 P. Saunders, 'Corporatism and Urban Service Provision', in W. Grant (ed.), *The Political Economy of Corporatism*, Macmillan, London, 1985.
11 R. Grundmann and C. Mantziaris, *Habermas, Rawls and the Paradox of Impartiality*, EUI Working Paper SPA no. 90/1, European University Institute, Florence, p. 8.
12 L. Lindqvist, 'Corporatist Implementation: The Case of Privatisation in Swedish Public

Housing', *Housing Studies*, vol. 3, no. 3, 1988, pp. 172–82.

13   K. Marx and F. Engels, 'Manifesto of the Communist Party', (1848) in K. Marx and F. Engels, *Selected Works in Two Volumes*, vol. 1, FLPH, Moscow, 1962, p. 38.

14   J. M. Keynes, *The General Theory of Employment, Interest and Money*, (1936), Macmillan, London, 1961, p. 383.

15   R. Roth, 'Local Green Politics in West German Cities', *International Journal of Urban and Regional Research*, vol. 15, no. 1, March 1991, pp. 75–89.

16   W. Streeck and P. Schmitter, 'From National Corporatism to Transnational Pluralism: Organised Interests in the Single European Market', *Politics & Society*, vol. 19, no. 2, June 1991, p. 158.

17   These ideas are explored in a theoretical way by sociologists and geographers. See, for example, A. Giddens, *Central Problems in Social Theory: Action, Structure and Contradiction in Social Analysis*, Macmillan, London, 1979.

18   W. Streeck and P. Schmitter, op. cit., p. 155.

19   L. von Mises, *Socialism*, (1922) Liberty, Indianapolis, 1981, cited in Hayek, op. cit., p. 4.

20   Hayek, op. cit., p. 6.

21   Ibid., p. 7.

22   Ibid., p. 7.

23   Ibid., p. 7.

24   A. M. Carr-Saunders, *The Population Problem: A Study in Human Evolution*, Clarendon Press, Oxford, 1922, pp. 223, 302.

25   K. Popper and J. Eccles, *The Self and its Brain*, Routledge and Kegan Paul, 1977, p. 48.

26   Hayek, op. cit., p. 25.

27   Ibid., p. 25.

28   Ibid., p. 26.

29   P. Kropotkin, *Mutual Aid: A Factor of Evolution*, Heinemann, London, 1902.

30   Hayek, op. cit., p. 47.

31   Ibid., p. 52.

32   Ibid., p. 75.

33   Ibid., p. 54.

34   C. Perrow, 'A Society of Organisations', *Theory and Society*, vol. 20/6, December 1991, p. 725.

35   Ibid., p. 754.

36   In the United States, the range of services which an increasing number of organisations place on offer to their employees is extensive: marital and retirement counselling, educational opportunities, training programmes, sex therapy, tax advice, sports and recreational facilities, medical care, travel services and child care facilities.

37   Hayek, op. cit., p. 19.

38   C. Clark, *The Economics of 1960*, Macmillan, London, 1941, cited in E. Schumacher, *Small is Beautiful: A Study of Economics as if People Mattered*, Abacus, London, 1974.

39   Schumacher, op. cit., p. 190.

40   Ibid., p. 78.

41   Hayek, op. cit., p. 74.

42   Schumacher, op. cit., p. 200.

43   Hayek, op. cit., p. 78.

44   Ibid., p. 81.

45   Ibid., p. 119.

46   Ibid., p. 118.

47   J. Kornai, *Socialist System, Political Economy of Socialism*, OUP, Oxford, 1992.

48 M. Friedman, *Market or Plan*, Centre for Research into Communist Economies, 1984, p. 20.
49 See, for example: P. Abell, *Rational Choice Theory*, Edward Elgar, Aldershot, 1991. For a criticism of this approach, see B. Hindness, *Choice, Rationality and Social Theory*, Unwin Hyman, London, 1988.
50 A. Smith, *The Wealth of Nations*, ed. J. R. McCulloch, Book V, Chapter 1, Part 3, Article II, 1901, Ward, Lock & Bowden, London, p. 616.
51 Ibid.
52 A. Smith, *The Wealth of Nations*, ed. R. Cambell, A. S. Skinner and W. B. Todd, OUP, Oxford, 1976, p. 494.
53 Smith, *Wealth of Nations*, 1901 ed., p. 215.
54 Smith, *Wealth of Nations*, 1976 ed., p. 145.
55 Smith, *Wealth of Nations*, 1901 ed., p. 53.
56 Ibid., p. 27.
57 A. Nove, 'Friedman, Markets and Planning: A Comment', in M. Friedman, op. cit., p. 32.
58 A. Nove, *Economics of Feasible Socialism*, Unwin, London, 1983.
59 F. Fukuyama, *The End of History and the Last Man*, Free Press, New York, 1992; 'Two sets of rules for a split world', *The Independent*, 7 September 1990. Fukuyama's provocative essay, 'The End of History?' was first published in *The National Interest*, no. 16, 1989. It is interesting that this author, too, 'borrows' heavily from the storehouse of sociological thinking. In this case, Fukuyama owes a debt to another sociologist, Talcott Parsons, and his theory of pattern variables, which included many of the societal attributes which are preconditions for liberal democracies.
60 D. Willetts, *Modern Conservatism*, Penguin, Harmondsworth, 1992.
61 W. Blackwell, *The Beginnings of Russian Industrialisation, 1800–1860*, Princeton University Press, Princeton NJ, 1968.
62 O. Crisp, *Studies in the Russian Economy before 1914*, Macmillan, London, 1976.
63 G. Guroff and F. Carstensen (eds), *Entrepreneurship in Imperial Russia and the Soviet Union*, Princeton University Press, Princeton NJ, 1983.
64 N. Ryzhkov, *BBC Summary of World Broadcasts: Soviet Union*, 26 May 1990, p c1/c12. Of course, the concession had in fact been made in 1988 with the Law on Co-operatives and the discussion surrounding its introduction and implementation.
65 From Proudhon the syndicalists took their belief in the self-governing workshop which would be the basic unit of a free and decentralised society. They presented a trenchant ethical critique of industrial society, the state and the increasing tendency within socialism to come to terms with the existing political system. Hence their view that central authority and the power of elected and appointed officials in the trade unions should be kept to a minimum. See G. D. H. Cole, *The World of Labour: A Discussion of the Present and Future of Trade Unionism*, (1913), 4th edn, Bell, London 1919.
66 See M. Beissinger, *Scientific Management, Socialist Discipline, and Soviet Power*, I. B. Tauris, London, 1988, Chapter 1.
67 On 1 May 1989 Moscow was the forum for the founding conference of neo-anarcho-syndicalists. They held a minute's silence for all anarchists 'who fell in the struggle with the repressive machinery of the state' (*Volya*, no. 1, 1 July 1989.) In September 1989 they reported that they had 300 members in 26 Soviet cities. 'The reason we are not very numerous is because we are very selective in our choice of members' (personal communication).

2 A Co-operative Culture

> It is not private ownership, but private ownership divorced from work,
> which is corrupting to the principle of industry; and the idea of some
> socialists that private property in land or capital is necessarily mischievous
> is a piece of scholastic pedantry as absurd as that of those conservatives
> who would invest all property with some kind of mysterious sanctity.
>
> R. H. Tawney, *The Acquisitive Society*

A co-operative culture is not an atavistic and irrational reaction to existing
cultural structures. It is a mode of organisation which grows out of the 'old'
structures to reveal the latent possibilities that lie within them and presents a
rational opportunity to remedy the maladies constantly being reproduced in
them.[1]

Background and History

Two main types of organisation are collectively owned and run by their
members in accordance with principles first laid down in Rochdale in 1844
and subsequently adopted in modified form by the International Co-operative
Alliance (ICA) in 1966: producer co-operatives and consumer co-operatives.
Producer co-operatives are defined as being formed by those who wish to sell
the product of their labour. Such associations include house-building and
agricultural co-operatives. Housing co-operatives fall within the second
category. Co-operative activities may be classified more comprehensively as
belonging to five principal categories: agricultural, industrial (producer or
'worker'), consumer (retail), credit and housing co-operatives.

The laws governing co-operatives are complex and differ from country
to country. The nature of the political regime determines the range of
activities in which co-operatives may engage or be encouraged to engage.
Prior to the revolutions in Europe beginning in 1987 and culminating with the
unification of Germany in 1991, organisations designated co-operatives in
some countries were not accepted by the ICA as being eligible for such
designation. Since the status of co-operatives as non-profit-making
associations might enable them to claim tax allowances and other privileges

accruing to non-profit and charitable institutions, some organisations might fraudulently claim to be co-operatives when they are not.

Whether co-operatives flourish or are completely marginal types of organisation depends very much on cultural factors. These comprise a subjective environment, as distinct from another set of influential factors with which this environment interacts, such as the legal and financial framework, taxation and national insurance. The latter constitute an objective environment.

Social Trends

The aim of democrats in the eighteenth and nineteenth centuries was to achieve a political equality which had already been largely conceded in the courts, where all were (supposedly) equal before the law. For those writing in the Age of Reason and for their descendants alike, traditions and social mores were the trappings of aristocratic corruption and privilege which needed to be stripped away to liberate the individual in body and mind. The restructuring of attitudes which accompanied the Protestant Reformation was integral to the 'spirit of capitalism' and the new social relationships representing that spirit. As social thinkers have long recognised, the benefits of the Reformation and then the progressive aspects of the Benthamite utilitarian calculus and later still its existentialist derivative all carried a price: autonomy was accompanied by alienation.

This systemic problem only fully matured with the firm establishment of industrialism in the twentieth century. Until then the majority of everyday problems that human beings had had to solve collectively had been at the community or neighbourhood level. In terms of the span of human history and social development it is only very recently that ordinary people have become involved in matters and decisions about which they have scant knowledge but which affect the lives of millions of people.

As industrialisation progressed, capital investment became concentrated in fewer hands, in larger firms and workplaces and in huge urban agglomerations. People reacted to the insecurity, uncertainty and hardship which affected the first generations exposed to industrial capitalism by creating new solidarities such as Mutual Benefit and Friendly Societies, trade unions and co-operatives. In time these, too, grew in size, as part of the universal trend towards the bureaucratisation of society. As cities increased in size and density, legislation granted more power and authority to municipal authorities. At first, the decentralisation of decision making to local government away from the centre helped to give people control over their lives again. Gradually, however, local government in large cities also became remote from individual affairs. Now the advanced industrialised societies are experiencing a decline in the size of urban settlements, as people move to suburbs and smaller towns.

As far as the workplace is concerned, the growth in scale of the manufacturing unit, and the greater power of employers, came to be matched by organisations representing the workforce, most notably trade unions, whose size and resources conferred considerable power on their full-time officials. The bureaucratisation and crystallisation of power in social democratic political parties and trade unions, representing the political and economic wings of labour respectively, was dissected and criticised at the beginning of the century by Robert Michels in his theory of the 'iron law of oligarchy'.[2]

Today, more people are again employed in smaller workplace units. In the United States the proliferation of small manufacturing firms is such that officials concerned with economic development are having to readjust their concepts and policies to take into account the changing size and organisation of manufacturing units. A government agency has a different, much easier task when negotiating the opening (or closure) and location of a branch manufacturing plant employing several thousand workers, than when it is trying to meet the requirements of thousands of smaller enterprises covering many different and distinctive industries.

The worlds that individuals inhabit are again growing smaller and, in some ways, more knowable. The terrain on which the struggle for control takes place has also changed. This shift in scale is reflected in the emphasis attached by the World Bank, the EU (through its TACIS programme), the Organisation for Security and Cooperation in Europe (OSCE) and the Know How Fund (financed by the British Foreign Office) to providing support to the development of small and medium-sized enterprises in the former Soviet Union and Central and East European countries (CEECs).

During the course of the twentieth century, whenever problems have become too huge and remote from the experience of very large sections of the population, so that people feel unable to understand the causes of the problems and can see no way of solving them rationally, electorates have been prompted to choose governments and leaders who have attended to and cultivated their more 'instinctual' emotions. As Simmel observed in his essay, 'The Metropolis and Mental Life', the metropolitan person, constantly bombarded with external stimuli, is prompted to protect the self by 'reacting with the head instead of the heart' and to cultivate a blasé attitude towards the world. The modern money economy and the calculative exactness of practical life which it brings have transformed the world into an arithmetical problem. Money is concerned solely with what 'is common to all: it asks for the exchange value, it reduces all quality and individuality to the question, how much?' In thus creating a society in which life is 'composed more and more of impersonal contents', the individual summons the utmost in uniqueness and particularisation in order to preserve his or her most personal core. 'He has to exaggerate the personal element in order to remain audible even to himself.' As a result the carrier of human values is no longer the 'general human being' in every individual but the person's qualitative uniqueness and irreplaceability. The function of the metropolis, according to Simmel, is to provide the arena for the struggle between (and reconciliation of) these two different ways of defining the individual's place in society.[3]

When the immensity and complexity of the task seem to defy solution through rational deliberation, fascism and other authoritarian forms of corporatism have been modes offering a salve to both substantive economic problems and more diffuse emotional ones; they have presented ways of overcoming the *Gemeinschaft–Gesellschaft* dichotomy by appropriating and politicising affective terms and notions such as *Heimat* and *Volk*. In the 1930s a largely instinctual motivation to survival and self-interest (achieved through scapegoating, stigmatising and ultimately war) led human beings to make a compromise with what they mistakenly saw as their rational joint interest.

Thus, paradoxically, the process of centralising power and authority in political and economic institutions, while imposing a rational order on a world run and controlled by administrators, has frequently been based on the less well-understood feelings widespread among the population concerning their lack of control. The right-wing authoritarian regimes of the 1920s and 1930s and then the Stalinist economic and political authoritarian edifices which were erected in the decades after 1945, as well as corporatist structures in the social democratic regimes of Western Europe, contributed to the gradual recognition among élites in the 1970s that, while decentralisation might mean a loss of control, the gain in 'freedom' could lead to a release of initiative and creativity in the population and ultimately preserve the unity of the state and society, which politicians were beginning to fear was threatened by centrifugal forces.

But the motivation to foster an environment conducive to individual creativity has little to do with 'personal growth', and is only partly concerned with cultivating a nation of entrepreneurs. The stimulus to change has its origins in the state's decision to effect a fundamental change in its obligations to provide for its citizens. Actuaries and accountants, among other specialists within the state apparatus, have concluded that, since the state is financially unable to provide for the needs of its citizens and meet their expectations, it must withdraw from the political compact with the voters and compel them to enter the marketplace to purchase medical services, education and retirement care. In this way states are seeking to resolve their fiscal crises.

The Co-operative Principle

In 1844 the Rochdale pioneers formalised the principles of co-operation which were later to be adopted by the International Co-operative Alliance. From Rochdale the co-operative movement began its passage across Europe. In Britain the consumer sector grew steadily and never relinquished its position as the largest in Europe, growing from 1.75 million members in 1901 to 6.5 million in 1931 and peaking at almost 13 million in 1961 before the decline set in. By 1986 it had 8.1 million members and a market share of 4.9 per cent.

In 1882 the Co-operative Producers' Federation (CPF) was established in Britain with the aim of offering financial and marketing assistance to manufacturing co-operatives. Within ten years of its foundation, it was representing 119 societies with 21,000 members, but by 1910 the number had already fallen to 86 societies, declining to 41 in 1944 and to 9 in 1981. There was a brief period in the 1920s when, under the influence of 'guild socialism', the idea of workers' co-operation regained a certain fashionable currency. Then in 1958 a Society for Democratic Integration in Industry (SDII) was founded, changing its name to the Industrial Common Ownership Movement (ICOM) in 1971.[4]

The co-operative form of property ownership emerged as a reaction to the individualism of industrial capitalism and, as an ideology, represented a fusion of Utopian socialism, Christian ethics and democratic socialism. Described as 'hybrid' or 'illegitimate', 'aberrant' or 'transitional', it has always inhabited the no man's land between the 'private' (individual, capitalist ownership) and 'public' (state ownership). In the case of Britain the very word used to describe the phenomenon is lodged in the structured vocabulary of the nineteenth century and has tended, with some notable exceptions, to be associated with obscurantists, mystics, idealists and philanthropists – people who are earnest but ploddingly slow, unfashionable, and concerned with a healthy life (spiritually as well as gastronomically) and organically grown food. They have been regarded as being as marginal to society as the organisational forms they have proposed.

So, while co-operatives may be described (though not easily defined), the description will not displace popularly inherited images. They do nonetheless have one central defining feature: whereas, just like other forms of business organisation, the co-operative must survive in a market economy, unlike most other enterprises it is motivated to succeed primarily by providing satisfaction to its members. In the case of the UK this is made even more concrete by the Industrial and Provident Societies Acts, which recognise as co-operatives those businesses which are conducted for the mutual benefit of their members. In such organisations control has to be on the basis of 'one person, one vote' for all voters, and not according to the individual member's financial investment in the co-operative. The rate of interest payable on share and loan capital must not exceed that needed to attract and keep the necessary capital. The amount distributed as profit should be credited to the individual member in direct proportion to his or her participation in the enterprise's activities.[5]

The financial affairs of co-operatives are the source of some of the trauma tormenting co-operative practitioners and their theorists alike. Until recently the Industrial Common Ownership Movement (ICOM) in Britain insisted that producer co-operatives should not draw upon external equity finance and that no one should hold more than a nominal £1 share. The remaining assets were held collectively. The (moral) strength of this 'purist' co-operative form was outweighed by the financial vulnerability that this strict requirement caused. On the other hand, the regulations governing the Co-operative Producers Federation (CPF) stipulate that, whilst each member must hold one share, there is no maximum limit.

The statutes of a particular co-operative can be drawn up to meet the specific needs and demands of its membership. For instance, in some cases equity holdings can be acquired and shares allowed to appreciate with the growth in the co-operative's net asset value. Although the Charter or Statutes chosen by a co-operative can vary, they are all bound by the key principle, already mentioned, that members have only one vote each regardless of the size of their shareholding. This leaves two issues outstanding: can the co-operative employ hired labour, and can people not working in the co-operative take part in decision making by virtue of holding shares in the co-operative? At stake here is more than just a principle, since the use of hired labour, especially in profitable co-operatives, can lead to their dilution and eventual conversion into private firms.[6]

The section on the financial organisation of co-operatives in a publication by the International Labour Office stated that:

> [the] capital of a co-operative society is essentially variable. It increases automatically with the admission of new members or the purchase of additional shares. . . . A share in a co-operative does not stand to earn and

cannot earn a dividend; all it can earn is a fixed and limited rate of interest.
. . . It cannot receive a premium over its nominal value, and when it is refunded only the amount actually paid up on the share is returned after deduction of a due proportion of any losses incurred by the capital of the society.[7]

The detailed practical issues of the distribution of surpluses (profits) and reserves, the collective and individual ownership of reserves, and the manner in which capital is (or may be) raised need not detain us. They are technical and resolvable. Nevertheless, the long-term survival of producer co-operatives is highly dependent on the regulations governing individual equity shareholding and accumulation and the use of hired labour.

Hired labour is not an issue in consumer co-operatives, which are owned by their customers, who become members and employ people to work for them; producer co-operatives, on the other hand, manufacture goods and provide services and are owned and controlled by those working in them. Co-operatives are also classified by size, which is an important variable. Small-scale co-operatives are usually set up initially to meet local needs. Their small size enables them to respond more quickly to changing local and more distant demands and to be more innovative in a dynamic environment. In a sense they approximate closely to the liberal model of the perfectly competitive market. Although they do not have to restrict the scale and range of their activities to serving local demand, once co-operatives exceed a certain size, they begin to develop bureaucratic and professional management structures and become susceptible to the 'iron law of oligarchy'; in the process they tend to sacrifice the loyalty of their members and workers.

In the eyes of co-operative theorists and practitioners:

> as the membership and area of operations increase, the social bond and the moral solidarity which distinguish a co-operative from a profit-making concern are weakened and the personal relations between members and administrators begin to disintegrate. . . . The virtues of efficiency and also of education are in danger of being weakened. . . . This danger can be avoided . . . (but) the optimum size for a co-operative society cannot be settled on the basis of dogmatic assertion: each individual case must be dealt with separately.[8]

This touches on two of the guiding principles of the co-operative movement. One is that it has a federative structure. That is to say, the basic units at each level determine, on their own initiative, the dividing line between those functions which they reserve to themselves and those which they delegate to the federal body.[9] A second underlying tenet of the co-operative movement has always been the paramount importance attached to education. In 1946 a representative of the Swedish co-operative movement, which was already financially prosperous, declared that, if their movement were to begin afresh and were offered a choice between two options, on the one hand an educated membership but no capital, or 'a large amount of capital and ill-informed members, our experience would incline us to choose the former'.[10]

The View of Co-operatives

Co-operatives are attractive to political parties and ordinary citizens for a variety of reasons. They appeal to political and economic liberals on three main counts. Firstly, they promote self-help and, because they also believe in consumer choice, accept competition. Secondly, for social democratic, if not Marxist, socialists, they are attractive because of their collectivistic and non-profit orientation. Thirdly, they are attractive both to individuals who prefer a working environment which they can control and plan themselves and to people who reject the profit-maximising capitalist employer as much as the inefficient, bureaucratic state employer. However, those who reject the private enterprise system because it 'employs the human urges of greed and envy as its motive power . . . (which) demand continuous and limitless economic growth of a materialist kind, without proper regard for conservation',[11] have in the past overwhelmingly tended to opt not for co-operation but for a statist form of ownership, where the state is the employer. Conversely, those who repudiate state ownership rush to embrace its antithesis, the private enterprise system.

For this behaviour to change, people must come to believe that a co-operative can actually deliver material benefits: a job, an income and livelihood from a producer co-operative, or a dividend from a retail co-operative or shelter from a housing co-operative. People do not form and join co-operatives for the principle alone. They do so because it represents an effective way of organising production or delivering a service and because, in insisting on an individual's rights and responsibilities, it is more democratic. Arguably, the most important feature of co-operation to individuals and society is the fact that the ultimate authority in an enterprise is inseparable from ownership and accountability; those who possess the rights of ownership also assume responsibility and thus become accountable. The democratic element which confers power on all members of a co-operative necessarily carries enormous obligations.

Disparagers of the co-operative movement frequently point out that the vast majority of members (or employees) have no interest in participating in decision making. Generally speaking this is true. But then roughly one-quarter of the British electorate do not exercise their democratic right at general elections. The turnout at local government elections is in the range of 25–45 per cent and is frequently less than 25 per cent. At national elections for the European Parliament just 34 per cent of those registered as eligible to vote in fact do so. It is rarely said, however, that people should be disenfranchised because they do not cast their vote. The gaining, through universal suffrage, of the right to participate in politics marked a real advance in human affairs. Despite flaws in the working of democratic institutions, the principle is rarely challenged. The further society moves away from that condition where life is 'nasty, brutish and short', the greater the opportunities for human beings to control their destinies, exercise their freedom and judgement and realise their individual potentialities.

European nations profess to be political democracies because they uphold the right of citizens to participate in the political process on the basis of 'one person, one vote'. They maintain that this equality ensures mutual respect for individuals and the system's legitimacy. Parity of esteem will in time also have to be conceded in the workplace; but it will not be respect if what is conferred is merely the right 'to be consulted and to advise'. Ownership, not control, grants equality; and in turn it imposes the obligation of responsibility. The industrial co-operative represents a secular trend in advanced industrial societies towards a greater diffusion of power, authority and responsibility in the workplace and elsewhere in social life.

'Co-operation' is as old as, but no older than, 'competition' and there seems little purpose in trying to determine from Pliny's tablets or anywhere else which of the twins emerged first, although the writings of Pliny the Younger point to the problems which decentralised government bring. Discovering whether 'in the beginning', as Marx declared, human beings lived communally or, as Hayek equally strongly insisted, human association was based on private property, is of historical interest. Of greater significance is knowing where an author stands on this matter *today*, for all theoretical systems and economic doctrines rest on (shallow and visible or deeply buried) metaphysical foundations.

According to philosophers and historians (both amateur and professional), at different points in human (or a particular society's) history people have lived more co-operatively than competitively or the converse. (Or they have predicted that they should or would do so.) Marx and Engels chided Thomas More and Robert Owen for being 'utopian'. Why? Because they imagined that a co-operative (or other collectivist) mode of organising society could be 'willed' into being once this or that great person had pronounced the wisdom of doing so, and once property-owners could be persuaded to surrender their holdings voluntarily. Engels's 'scientific' socialism, on the other hand, had discovered in the theory of surplus value (when fused with the Hegelian dialectic) that a collectivist (communalist, communist) mode of social organisation would succeed or supersede competitive capitalism and possessive individualism.[12]

From Marx's point of view, co-operatives were not only condemned by capitalism but, worse, they condemned themselves. All of them were (and are) obliged to function in a capitalist system. Some of them even accepted the notion of freedom of enterprise, which would permit them to 'gain a surplus' (that is, make a profit), and oblige them to face competition and risk and to be dedicated to meeting consumer demand.

Trade Unions and Co-operatives

The goal of reformers in the nineteenth century was to advance political democracy by extending the franchise, thus removing the abuses of power and institutional corruption. During the early stage of capital accumulation industrial democracy was not on the horizon. Instead, workers formed trade unions in order to protect themselves, and Friendly Societies and Mutual Aid Associations in order to provide for themselves against adversity. Unfortunately for the co-operative movement, while trade unions and consumer co-operatives could live in harmony with one another, neither could co-exist amicably with the notion of producer co-operatives: trade unions chose to use their growing power to promote municipal and state socialism, while the consumer was protected through a network of retail co-operatives.

After a century of developing and negotiating, trade unions could pride themselves on having gained representation on the boards of directors of industrial enterprises. The policy of *Mitbestimmung* was introduced in Germany in 1952 and was followed twenty years later by an EEC directive proposing employee representation on the boards of all large companies operating in the EC. In the UK the Bullock Report on Industrial Democracy, which reviewed the same subject, was published in 1977.[13] Governments and political parties regarded these moves as marking the extension of industrial democracy.

Robert Michels, on the basis of his analysis of Social Democratic parties and trade unions,[14] concluded that this approach to democracy had an inherent weakness. Trade unions have their own corporate short- and long-term agendas, which require their representatives on boards of directors to be guided by their primary loyalty (as defined by the union), which is to the union, and not to the workforce in the firm on whose board they are sitting. Thus, even today, whereas the managers on the board derive their authority from the firm's shareholders, the heads of trade unions derive their authority, not from the firm's employees, but from the union itself.

The final quarter of the twentieth century has witnessed a considerable weakening in the power of the unions in Britain and elsewhere in Europe – a process that is unlikely to be reversed. A variety of factors have contributed to the slow emasculation of the unions. High unemployment has played its part; so have legislation and the formation of cells of 'conservative' trade unionists. Above all, massive structural changes have occurred in the economy: the demise of the old staple industries, which began in the 1920s, is virtually complete.[15] Computers and robots have revolutionised the manufacturing firms which remain, while the growth in information technology has transformed the way in which the balance of payments is recorded.[16] A damaging wind is also blowing from another direction. In the UK one-quarter of private-sector firms have introduced share-ownership schemes. This development also contributes to the conceptual and institutional erosion of trade union functions. Admittedly, the shareholding of employees is invariably so small that they are able to exercise very little influence over a board's decision making. In addition, since the shares are tradable on the market, employees are tempted to sell their interest. Nevertheless, the effect of these changes in the participatory relationship of employees to the firm is to introduce a wider public to the notion of share ownership.

In contrast to Sweden and Germany, where trade unions were heavily committed to providing co-operative or non-profit housing themselves, in Britain the trade unions have not even adopted a position of neutrality. In 1978 the National Union of Public Employees (NUPE) published a booklet which argued in a way very reminiscent of that used against the co-operative movement in Russia and in some of the other centrally planned economies (CPEs). The substance of NUPE's position may be summarised as follows: the capitalist classes have created a 'ladder to home ownership' which is financially beneficial to them and which is attractive to the public since it offers them 'control' over their housing situation. The co-operative is a rung on this ladder to ownership. The 'problem' arises when, because more and more people have stepped onto this rung, increasing sums of public money are channelled into helping them onto the ladder. This happens to the detriment of council house building. The union's solution to the housing shortage and the need for democratically controlled housing is a socialist housing policy, based on public housing.[17] This view was already obsolete in 1978. Most of the left-led debate on the promotion of home ownership and the privatisation of council housing focused on criticising it as an attempt to reinforce the hegemonic notion of the property-owning democracy. In hindsight, it failed to identify in this policy the foundations of the 'actuarial society' – one in which the burden of welfare benefits would be too large for the state to sustain, so that the housing asset would be required at the point of retirement to be converted into an annuity to make a small contribution towards the financing of the home-owner's pension and care. Since this policy option was widely unpopular amongst a broad swathe of the active electorate and could, in any case, only fund some of the long-term costs of the elderly, it has been shunted off the main line, while the new policy train of private pensions (with its first-, second- and third-class carriages) rushes towards the final stations of life.

The attitudes of shareholders, managers, trade unions and the public at large to the role of unions in the bargaining and decision-making process vary from country to country. In the final analysis the task of unions is to negotiate the highest wages and obtain the best conditions possible for their members. Trade unions behave as they do because that is their *raison d'être*. Their role in society was redefined in the USSR and in the other CPEs where wage bargaining and wage determination were not trade union functions. Instead, unions were just another agency available to help the state (Communist Party) to achieve its goals, which, since it was a workers' state, could not be contrary to the interests of employees in state enterprises and organisations. Logic determined that in societies where the means of production were owned by the state, which was a 'state of all the people', there could be no conflict between labour and capital. This theoretical issue lay at the root of the banishment of Yugoslavia as a heretic from the socialist fold. It explains why the debate over establishing co-operatives in the USSR in the late 1980s was so acrimonious.

But it is not just in Russia and the other 'states in transformation'[18] that the relationship between labour and capital has to be rethought. All European societies have to confront an old challenge in a new way. Instead of capital employing labour (which then has to create agents to represent its interests), labour must become the owner of the capital which it employs. There is probably no better educator to democracy than knowing that the responsibility for success or failure rests with oneself. Industrial democracy will enhance political democracy, for the experience of power, authority and responsibility in the workplace will lead individuals to be more attentive to what is happening in the wider political domain. The reconceptualisation of the profane relationship between labour and capital may be of a magnitude akin to Luther's reconceptualisation of the sacred relationship between man and god, in that it questions the need for a mediating agent (trade union, priest).

Strong government, it is argued, is only possible where one party has a majority that enables it to govern by implementing a clear set of policies with a mandate from the electorate. In liberal democracies, strong is taken to mean two main parties. A plurality of parties is regarded as leading to weak government.[19] Of course, the 'strongest' form of government is where there is just one (vanguard) party. Similarly, very large manufacturing companies, conglomerates with monopolistic or oligopolistic positions in the economic (as opposed to political) marketplace, have been regarded as the surest way for national economies to survive and prosper in the international competitive arena. Questions of the size, representativeness, efficiency and legitimacy of these large, concentrated and centralised organisations have come under increasing scrutiny since the mid-1970s.

Frontal assaults on trade unions, alternating with peaceful periods of a steady whittling away at these labour organisations, have accompanied the demise of the 'corporatist compromise' arranged by governments between organised labour and capital. The diminution in the power of unions could benefit the producer co-operative, which has historically been bound by and subordinated to trade unionism. Yet, as the next millennium approaches, there are few discernible signs of much genetic mutation in the organs of collectivism or socialism, which continue to reflect the double helix of labour's struggle to protect itself during the rise of industrial capitalism. Trade unions sit uneasily with workers' co-operatives. They feel the best way of advancing industrial democracy is for them to gain seats in the boardroom, so that they can participate in the management of industry and commerce on behalf of labour. In a word, they adhere to a pre-Reformation belief in the indispensability of their role as intermediary between sacred labour and Mammon.

Yet only a co-operative economy can break the macro-economic deadlock in which the trade unions force up the price of labour, bringing about inflation, which is then countered by the government forcing massive unemployment in order to maintain the value of the currency. The 'discipline of the (international) marketplace' has now been used, to different degrees, in virtually all European governments since the mid-1980s, with the result that 20 million people in the European Union are without full-time employment. But, in attacking inflation through the employment exchange, the state becomes overburdened by its welfare debt. In order to curb expenditures on welfare benefits, governments are transferring the burden of social costs from the government to the employer and the employee as, for instance, in the reduction in the British Government's support for sick pay.[20]

Co-operatives as Solution

Co-operation does not always presuppose that ownership has to mean 'held in common', where 'everyone owns everything, and no one owns anything'. In this respect the British Labour Party (including the authors of the Party's 1918 Constitution) assumed a similar ideological stance to that of the former Communist Parties in Eastern Europe in their common belief that co-operation is a lower form of socialism. Dissension around the question of ownership flourishes within the co-operative movement itself. Although essentially agnostic on the issue of collective or individual ownership in co-operatives, the British Co-operative Development Agency, which was set up in 1978 with the primary task of promoting, in theory and practice, the idea of industrial co-operatives, did not agree with those who chose to define co-operation as being exclusively collective ownership.[21] The lack of success of producer co-operatives in Britain has been matched by their success elsewhere in Europe. They are to be found in Italy[22] and in the much discussed and dissected Mondragon group in Spain. In 1980 the latter, which consists of industrial co-operatives and supports financial, social and advisory services, employed over 20,000 people.[23] The experience of the Mondragon co-operative inspired the creation of an agency in the UK, Job Ownership Limited (JOL), to promote the creation of co-operatives along Mondragon lines. As far as Italy is concerned, the output of co-operatives under one of the principal umbrella organisations of producer co-operatives, the communist- and socialist-controlled LEGA, makes it the fourth largest grouping in Italy. Moreover, it is noteworthy that Italy, which has the largest co-operative sector in the Western world, also had until recently one of the most rapidly growing economies in Europe, with a per capita income which is now higher than that of the UK. Its economic achievement has been partly attributed to the size of its small-business sector, which includes many co-operatives. It may be far from pure coincidence that it was the Italian Communist Party, the largest in Europe, which coined the term the 'historical compromise' to describe its political philosophy of Eurocommunism and the term *la terza via* to describe a concrete aspect of the compromise between socialism and capitalism: for one large segment of Italian opinion the industrial co-operative constitutes 'the third way'. One of the central tenets of *la terza via*, self-management, is governed by another, the discipline of the marketplace.

The 'third way' has little or nothing in common with the function prescribed in Britain for producer co-operatives in the 1970s, namely that they should be formed as 'rescue operations' when private enterprise failed and large numbers of employees faced unemployment.[24] The political climate of the 1970s was conducive to factory occupations by workers ('sit-ins'). These last-ditch defensive actions against closure and loss of employment resulted from the fact that the trade unions had been rendered quite powerless, since there were no owners with whom to bargain. The grievance had to be transferred to the political realm and the deliberating chambers of local councils and the central government.

Even accepting that co-operatives had a benign role to play as 'salvationists', the goals ascribed to them could be quite contradictory. On the one hand, newly formed co-operative undertakings were expected to restore to robust health (that is, profitability) what appeared to be, if not terminally ill, at least very sick, patients. On the other hand the company's workforce, the local community and political interests all hoped that the co-operative would save jobs. These goals were frequently incompatible, for to make the enterprise economically viable required a reduction in the workforce. Interestingly, if ironically, studies of co-operatives which had been formed out of bankrupted private enterprises found that they were successful in instituting wage cuts and large reductions in the workforce, and in loosening trade union demarcation lines.[25] Although the vast majority of co-operatives have not been created with the aim of staving off liquidation and redundancy, there was speculation that the genesis of co-operatives lies in a notion of 'pragmatic acceptance'.

This concept, which emerged during the 1960s, suggested that the absence of radicalism and class consciousness among the working class, large sections of whom voted for conservative parties, was a consequence of the workforce's pragmatic approach to the social system: the system was actively or passively accepted because it met people's material interests. This view was criticised on the grounds that, since acceptance of the status quo was based on material interests, the social system was inherently fragile: it was held together largely by a cash nexus which, once broken, perhaps through redundancy, would allow the underlying feelings of lack of control and meaninglessness to come to the surface.[26] The formation of three worker co-operatives out of bankrupt firms in 1974 allowed the validity of the cash nexus thesis to be tested.

In contrast to the predictable positions adopted by the Conservative Party – that factory occupations were illegal acts and were in any case wasteful projects to which government resources should not be committed – and the Labour Party – that the establishment of these co-operatives played an educative function in the political radicalisation process, the investigation concluded that co-operative organisations can be pragmatic accommodative responses designed to restore the cash nexus within the present system. The trade union chairman of one co-operative observed that 'the bulk of our workforce was more concerned about a weekly wage than they were about a co-operative'.[27] Thus the experience of worker co-operatives, especially in the UK, like the radical alternative communities set up in different places over the last two hundred years,[28] has never seriously challenged the structures, values and *modus operandi* of established society.

Where producer or housing co-operatives are formed by the expropriated or weak in the marketplace, their members know that they are engaged in a trade-off with government and authority more generally.[29] In the main, they represent strategies on how to survive within the existing structure of society. Although some of those involved in the endeavour consider their actions to be motivated by higher concerns, in objective historical terms their behaviour is a collective form of self-help.

In Britain, the number of producer co-operatives has been growing, although not dramatically. They rose in number from 19 in 1975 to 305 in 1980 and to 1,476 in 1986, when they had over 28,000 members.[30] These figures have to be seen in the perspective of a national workforce of over 20 million people. The turnover of the worker co-operative sector at £200 million per annum remains low, with the eleven largest enterprises accounting for 43 per cent of the total turnover.[31] If the activities of the six co-operative sectors in the UK were combined, they would represent about nine million members in approximately 2,500 co-operatives, employing 150,000 people and with an annual turnover of £7,400 million.[32] As regards size, over 70 per cent of producer co-operatives have fewer than ten workers, and only 3 per cent (ten in all) have over 100 workers. The principal reason for this size profile is that many of the newly created co-operatives are in low-paid service trades requiring low-qualified workers operating in poor working conditions. This is likely to change in the future, as producer co-operatives expand in sectors at the interface of services and manufacturing, such as information technology.[33]

As already mentioned, a society's culture and whether or not a co-operative tradition exists constitute important variables encouraging or restraining co-operative development in a particular country. Together they construct a subjective environment which creates and perpetuates images, nurtures prejudices and moulds opinion in ways which dispose the public and institutions favourably or unfavourably towards co-operatives. For instance, accountants, solicitors and bankers 'know' how small, private firms are formed, the body of law and regulations governing their activities and how they function; they are far less well informed and sure about 'co-operatives'. In the contrary case, where a country has a long tradition of co-operation, where the co-operative form is taken for granted and known to be a 'normal' and effective organisational form, the institutional complex that comprises the co-operatives' objective environment is well adapted to their needs.

Co-operatives in Eastern Europe

Whereas in Britain co-operatives developed 'within the womb of capitalism' and worked within it, elsewhere, especially in Central Europe, they grew out of essentially feudalistic structures. According to one account they were adopted in the region for three main reasons.[34] Firstly, its ideology corresponded to the needs of nationalists, who found in the co-operative movement a 'powerful weapon in their struggle for economic, cultural and political self-determination'. Secondly, they did not threaten the dominant institutional structures. Thirdly, they offered an agency for mobilising capital and labour during a period of rapid economic development. Co-operatives were regarded by nationalists as an important tool for achieving the goal of self-determination, and Pluta argues that this explains why they emerged amongst the oppressed nationalities, such as Slovaks, Poles and Czechs, before they did among the dominant nationalities – Germans, Russians and Magyars.[35] But if nationalists wooed them and the church supported them (not least because they seemed to counter the growth of anti-clericalism), then socialists and liberals shunned them.

Pluta's evidence does not seem to justify his conclusion that co-operatives 'played a significant role in central and east Europe in the late nineteenth and early twentieth centuries'.[36] But it is possible that they assisted the struggle for cultural survival among minorities and the development of a national consciousness. In economic terms they provided a path out of financial indebtedness by marshalling and mobilising resources for use in those sectors such as agriculture, services and small-scale manufacturing which were unattractive to capital and finance. In 1989 at the point of transformation of the countries in the region, co-operatives and other mutual aid associations could have mobilised resources.

In 1976 the organ of the co-operative movement in Czechoslovakia – where the first co-operative society in continental Europe was established by a group of artisans and farmers in 1845[37] – declared that 'today the co-operative movement is an inseparable part of the socialist economy and has a firm place in satisfying the immediate needs of citizens'.[38] Such rhetoric did not reflect their true status, which remained that of minor actors in the country's economic development. Their future, as seen from the late 1970s, looked brighter: any post-reform government would have to rely on co-operatives in the agricultural and service sectors since 'reprivatisation would be extremely difficult, if not impossible, since virtually none of the present means of production existed when the communists took over'.[39] In this context, and bearing in mind that capitalism requires particular skills and aptitudes, some commentators thought even then that the co-operatives would have an important role to play when reform eventually came, though this role would vary depending on each country's past co-operative traditions, level of economic development and political culture.[40]

Although the optimism expressed in some circles in the decade prior to the (counter-)revolution in 1989 has not yet been justified by reality, the success of various communist(ic) parties in Bulgaria, Poland, Slovakia, Romania and Lithuania since 1993 indicates the continuing belief in collectivist modes of organising production and distribution.

Co-operatives in Poland, even during the 'old' regime, played an important part in retailing, services and agriculture. Workers' co-operatives played a far greater role here than in the other socialist countries. Industrial co-operatives were found in textiles, clothing and footwear and in the timber, chemical and electrochemical industries.[41] By the 1970s the Polish government was trying to direct workers' co-operatives away from manufacturing in order to meet the vast unsatisfied demand in the service sector. Expansion did take place, and by the end of the decade co-operatives were providing a wide range of services ranging from tailoring and home and car maintenance to foreign language teaching and medical and dental treatment.[42]

This interpretation of the wide-scale presence of co-operatives is open to the criticism that, although official statistics classified a number of activities as being part of the socialised sector of the economy, many organisations were co-operative in name only; in reality they were nothing other than privately owned enterprises.[43] The validity of this charge is not easily tested; when the subject of analysis is co-operatives, where one observer finds harmony, another finds rampant exploitative capitalism.[44]

Co-operatives in a Changing Climate

In 1984, the author of the so-called Novosibirsk Report commented that the administrative-command economy, which had been useful for the industrialisation of a backward, poorly educated peasant country like the Soviet Union, had become outmoded. In classical Marxist terms, the 'social relations of production were no longer compatible with the forces of production, in fact they were a fetter on them'. Above all, the rigidly hierarchical, bureaucratic system was, she said, alienating for a population that was now highly educated and politically more sophisticated.[45] This observation also has relevance for other European countries where the pedagogic philosophy and teaching methods are based on individual project work, which is thought to encourage independent thought.

The fettering effect of social relations applies to all European societies, especially where a central pedagogic value and objective of education is that the citizens of tomorrow should accept the existence of different interpretations of the social and natural worlds. They are also made aware that a variety of policies can be pursued in trying to solve problems. This approach can be, firstly, disturbing for individuals, because it extends the range of their existential choices; secondly, threatening for élites, since ultimately it empowers large sections of the population; and, thirdly, potentially destabilising for society, for it abandons (and denies the legitimacy of) a single integrating set of norms, values and common historical heritage. It is also disturbing on the grounds that, as Durkheim recognised, one cause of anomie is that people are increasingly educated beyond the requirements of their jobs, or, at least, the multimedia technology is available for this to happen. The inherently positive and negative aspects of these structurally determined developments are part of the preparation of individuals to become 'active citizens' in the future.

In other words, intrasystemic pressures are building up to find new ways of organising decision making, including the involvement of more people in co-ownership schemes as a way of developing industrial democracy. This could be a way of harnessing the creativity and initiative of new recruits to the labour market who otherwise may become alienated from hierarchies and bureaucracies. It is no accident that the co-operative movement is well developed in those countries where there is strong support for democracy, since education lies at the heart of the movement and democracy:

> The educational task that must be carried on among the members is, first and foremost, to keep alive in them the feeling that the co-operative society is not an organisation set up independently of them to serve their needs, but rather a business that belongs to them and depends on them for its efficiency and prosperity. They must have instilled into them the knowledge, motives and ability that will make them into real co-operators imbued with the will to assist in the joint enterprise because they are

conscious not only of their collective interests but also of the moral ties and freely accepted collective responsibilities which unite them to their fellow members. Lastly, education must make them feel they are members not only of the co-operative society but also of the movement, the movement that does not represent a mere commercial system, but is also a movement of ideas, a new conception and a new organisation of human relations.[46]

The new parliamentary states of East and Central Europe and Russia are inspecting and trying on for size the clothes of multi-party democracy. At the same time, the movement towards political federalism in the European Union is compelling the longer-established liberal democracies in Western Europe to review their political attire. The hugeness of the political superstate with its supranational agencies is too remote to grasp. The new technologies require, or at least present the opportunities for, the introduction of novel organisational and more democratic forms. The pace of technological change demands flexibility, which itself necessitates that employees are better informed and more involved in an enterprise's activities. This may best be achieved through extending industrial democracy through ownership.

This leaves one crucial question unasked and unanswered: who is to provide social welfare services? Do co-operatives have a role to play here too? As Europeans enter the twenty-first century, in this sphere at least the case for a concerned, centralised state remains a strong one. Hitherto the nation state has sought to try to equalise the life chances of its citizens by the use of grants and incentives to induce industry to move to different localities in order to provide jobs and raise income levels. Now the supranational state seeks through its regional policy to accomplish a similar redistributional objective. To the extent that the nation and supranational (European) state will continue to use taxation revenue to provide social services, these might be distributed through local networks of co-operatives and other voluntary associations. Where state funds are reduced or totally withdrawn, citizen-consumers might set up co-operatives and other forms of mutual aid associations, as they have for nursery provision in Sweden where, perhaps signalling a long-term trend, hundreds of 'nursery co-operatives' were formed in the early 1990s.

As part of this process, the aim is to separate the commissioning of services from their actual provision. The path away from the universal social service, staffed by professionals and delivered by a bureaucracy that has expanded as its competencies have been extended incrementally by a central government responding to lacunae in its earlier legislation and changes in social policy, is through a devolved structure of private or trust agencies.

Although the main funding of the social services will, for the time being, be financed from taxes, the actual assessment of need, the service provision and its monitoring will be undertaken by charities, trusts and qualified individuals.

The Move to Smaller Units

Beginning in the late 1960s and early 1970s, most West European countries experienced a new wave of co-operatives. In the majority of countries (with notable exceptions, especially Italy), even when aggregated they have been small in number and marginal as a consequence. Some of the thematic issues which they addressed were later incorporated within the much broader social movements which grew out of them. This growth and metamorphosis is epitomised in the formation of 'Greens' and ecology movements which, having formalised their organisational networks, accomplished the leap in status from pressure group to political party. The recent setbacks in their electoral support may be explained by the fact that key clauses in their manifestos are now proudly proclaimed from the platforms of the major political parties. Ecology parties have suffered from an appropriation of their agenda, in a manner akin to that experienced by co-operatives whose customers for organically grown products now have their needs met by the large retail food chains.

A second discernible trend over the past two decades has been for capitalism to call a halt to the trajectory of certain economic sectors and return, as it were, to its roots. A new role has been found for the small enterprise. It is the growth of the small and medium-sized firm which may augur ill for the industrial co-operative. The timing of the resurgence in smaller manufacturing and servicing units has varied from country to country, but it is widely regarded as a successful means for generating employment and economic growth.

The small firm in Italy was integral to the country's economic miracle, most visibly perhaps in the textile industry in Prato. And in the USA, the wealthiest economy in the world and the home of some of the largest corporations, small firms employ 'nearly two-thirds of the blue-collar labour force and supply the bulk of the parts and components used in the production' of finished goods for both domestic and export markets'.[47] Significantly, in economically retarded Britain, where small firms have for a long time made a smaller contribution to the gross national product, compared with Germany and Italy for example, legislators have been late to offer assistance to smaller enterprises. Since discovering in the late 1970s that the latter were essential to the country's economic recovery, the British

Government has passed legislation to help small firms.

This rediscovery of the small firm was premised on a variety of observations and ideological predilections. In the first instance, there had been a belated awakening in the UK to the fact that small firms are making a large contribution to the success of the German and other economies, including that of the United States. The 'white hot technological revolution' of an earlier Labour government in the 1960s, which had fostered amalgamations between large manufacturing units, has been placed in cold storage: thirty years later, huge industrial and commercial conglomerates began to 'downsize' into smaller units. Secondly, the small firm fitted well with the Conservative Government's desire to revive a decaying 'enterprise culture'. Another perceived prerequisite for the revitalisation of this culture (grounded in 'Victorian values') is a reduction in the size of the public sector through the privatisation of activities provided by the state.[48] Finally, intervention in the form of enterprise agencies became necessary in order to overcome the traditional difficulties faced by the small firm: restricted access to capital, lack of management skills (including the ability to market, and a lack of capacity to undertake research and development).[49]

Although Business in the Community emphasises the effectiveness of the agencies in generating and maintaining jobs and on the survival rate of enterprises they assist, little firm evidence exists to uphold this claim. The Co-operative Development Agency similarly points out that rising unemployment has been a stimulus to the setting up of co-operatives and advisory agencies to support them. It also stresses the impressive survival rate of co-operatives. Like privately owned small businesses, co-operatives need training in management and other business skills. To a greater extent than 'traditional' small businesses, they also lack access to finance for investment and growth. Thus, a strong case can be made for the creation of a co-operative credit and finance agency, along the lines of the local enterprise agencies, but catering specifically to the needs of co-operatives. In general, however, the climate in many societies is more favourable to privately owned small businesses than co-operative enterprises, because the private firms conform to the hierarchical structure dominant in liberal democracies.

The initiatives undertaken in the UK so far are a long way from the sort of national network programme introduced by the Danish Government in 1989 and by schemes adopted in Germany and Italy. All three countries have found a way, through different types of networks, of combating the many problems faced by small businesses.[50] For instance, groups of firms co-operate to share overhead costs, particularly those which need to gain access to expensive technologies. This allows them to compete in rapidly changing markets. They can also combine into networks in order to undertake market research and forecasting, to purchase materials and to hire financial consultants or managers – tasks generally beyond the limited resources of a single small firm. Combining for these purposes can lead to the joint exploitation of niche markets through production networks. Moreover, the combination of highly specialised and segmented markets and computerised production systems works to the advantage of small networking firms. Unlike the large enterprise they are unburdened by traditional management structures and procedures, which are a constraint on rapid response.

In a number of industries this development has been a direct result of institutions and individuals having to adapt to a changing environment. Changes have resulted from both endogenous institutional factors and exogenous (international) factors. In the case of the former, change has been propelled by the consequences of the acrimonious disputes between labour and management in the late 1960s which led to production losses, low gains in labour productivity, a fall in market price competitiveness and to a failure to respond to demand and fashion. Exogenous factors include the increase in the oil prices in the 1970s and uncontrolled rises in the Third World debt and the impact that this eventually had on the sale of, in the case of Italy, farm machinery produced by large manufacturers. The need to survive under these conditions gave rise to an explosive growth in small enterprises and the evolution of manufacturing networks, assisted by city and regional governments in collaboration with labour and employer associations.

The dirigiste, planning-from-above, approach is in transition. A distinctly different partnership between the state and the producers in the economy is emerging; it is more co-operative. Alterations to traditional vertical links between the state and civil society are accompanied by changes in the horizontal links and modes of contact within civil society. Firms located within a region (such as Saarland–Alsace-Lorraine), whose population may be larger than some European states,[51] are now being encouraged to think co-operatively instead of competitively about ways in which they can maximise their mutual interests. These evolutionary trends point in the direction of industrial democracy and co-operation. Even in the heartland of free enterprise capitalism, clothing manufacturers in one district of Massachusetts 'have, through their co-operative efforts in market development, skill training, and day care, improved the quality of work life as well as firm productivity'.[52]

The workplace is of central importance to people; it can be a loose or dense network of relationships and attachments, many of which people experience but never articulate. The geographical space in which the workplace and residence are located constitutes an environment directly affecting the quality of life of individuals who work and live in them. Organisations with no party affiliation (such as Development Trusts in Britain) have been established to bring together the public, private and voluntary sectors with the express aim of renewing an area physically and and socially.[53]

Social and Economic Planning

There is no necessary conflict within European geographical space between decentralisation of government and the surrender by nation states of their already attenuated 'sovereignty' to a larger political entity. Universal entitlements within a political space, such as civil liberties and the maintenance of standards in the provision of elementary services such as education, health, pensions and social security are probably best defended and enhanced by the existence of a greater wealth-generating political-economic unit. The normative role of this political organisation could be as great as its tax-levying powers. In fact, the social purposes for which revenue is raised through taxation would be directly associated with broader and longer-term normative objectives. It would be utopian to dismiss the concern that national governments have with economics; however, the current preoccupation with the subject is almost fetishistic in that 'efficiency' and 'competitiveness' have become objectives in their own right and at the expense of a concern for the 'social'.

In 1989, during the early days of reform in the former Soviet Union, the Supreme Soviet for the first time gave precedence to social planning over economic planning in its socio-economic plan for the next decade. Since then, the navigators of a hegemonic capitalist spirit have done their best to reset those priorities. Yet, no matter how diligently the Soviet Union and then its successor states have applied themselves as pupils – in the belief that the higher standard of living found in Western countries is sufficient proof of the superiority of the latter's economic system – the yield of their economies has in most cases continued to decline. Nevertheless, late capitalism persists in peddling the same items from the same tray – more competition and more consumption. It does so by invoking macro-economic modellers whose ever more sophisticated mathematical equations singularly fail to predict major global economic events accurately.[54]

The counter-revolution against Keynesianism is all but complete and another orthodoxy is being installed in its place – one which is distanced from much of the world around it and unable to describe or subscribe to anything like the *Theory of Moral Sentiments* in which Adam Smith found it necessary to embed his interpretation of society. The extent to which a new orthodoxy might be said to be established is captured in the fact that in 1986 John Smith, prior to becoming leader of the Labour Party, confirmed that three initial thrusts of a future Labour government's economic policy would be renationalisation (beginning with British Telecom), the establishment of a National Enterprise Board, and added impetus to fund co-operatives.[55] But then John Smith personified what is now described as 'Old Labour'.

Conclusion

Some questions concerning co-operatives are open to empirical analysis and verification, while others are much broader and more theoretical. The latter ask, for instance, whether or not co-operatives offer an opportunity for the creation of an alternative, collectivistic economic system. Do human associations conforming to conventionally accepted definitions of 'co-operative' comprise a viable property form? More specifically, can housing co-operatives offer their members an alternative way of living, or are they a mechanism meeting the need for shelter of those whom neither the state nor private sector can satisfy?

Although it will probably never be a dominant form and replace capitalist or state-owned enterprises, the co-operative does exist as an alternative. G. D. H. Cole once remarked, 'Social institutions have two, and only two, legitimate purposes – to ensure to men the supply of the material means of good living and to give men the fullest possible scope for creative activity'.[56] Capitalist and statist forms of organisation and ownership might be the best means of securing the first purpose, but probably not the second.

By the beginning of the twentieth century, the labour movement in England had more or less completely turned its back on co-operation and workers' participation and decided to make its long-term objective the transfer of the means of production from private into public ownership. This goal remained enshrined in the famous Clause 4 of the Labour Party's Constitution until its repeal in 1995. At the end of the twentieth century, the status of the Clause is akin to a holy relic. In weaning itself from its legendary mother the Party has not sought a 'third way', but has anchored itself in the safe intellectual haven constructed by the neo-liberals. One reason for the crisis that overtook the Party in the late 1970s and led to the foundation of the SDP was its unwillingness to heed Tawney's observation:

The objection to public ownership, in so far as it is intelligent, is in reality largely an objection to over-centralisation. But the remedy for over-centralisation is not the maintenance of functionless property in private hands, but in the decentralised ownership of public property.

'New' Labour has looked closely at Tawney and the critique presented by the faction which became the SDP.

As Marx pointed out in *The Communist Manifesto* and Durkheim in *The Division of Labour*, capitalism was an advance on the collective and community-related system of production and provision available to primitive societies. The case for co-operation (or communism) cannot be made purely in the name of the superior value of 'collectivism'; it has to demonstrate that it is at least as good at generating wealth as are other modes of organisation, and better at distributing it. There are prima-facie reasons for believing that co-operatives can meet these criteria, not least because in industrial co-operatives there is no conflict of interest between labour and capital: the owners of capital in a producer's co-operative cannot strike against themselves. However, in 1986 there were only an estimated 10,000 people working in co-operatives – not enough for even blind optimists to see Britain turn into a nation of co-operators.

Notes

1   For a clear exegesis of the meaning of co-operation, see W. Watkins, 'The Nature of Co-operative Principles', in *Co-operative Principles in the Modern World*, Education Department, Co-operative Union, Stanford Hall, Loughborough, 1987.
2   R. Michels, *Political Parties*, (first published in German 1911) Free Press, New York, 1967. See also: I. Zeitlin, *Ideology and the Development of Sociological Theory*, Prentice-Hall, Englewood Cliffs NJ, 1968, Chapter 14.
3   G. Simmel, 'The Metropolis and Mental Life' (1906), in P. Hatt and A. Reiss (eds), *Cities and Society*, Collier-Macmillan, London, 1957, p. 645.
4   J. Thornley, *Workers' Co-operatives*, London, Heinemann, 1981.
5   *Guide to the Law relating to Industrial and Provident Societies*, HMSO, London, 1978, Chapter 5.
6   H. Miyazaki, 'On Success and Dissolution of the Labour-Managed Firm in the Capitalist Economy', *Journal of Political Economy*, vol. 92, no. 5, October 1984.
7   International Labour Office, *Co-operation: A Workers' Educational Manual*, Geneva, 1956, p. 47.
8   Ibid., p. 60.
9   Ibid., p. 73.
10   H. Elldin, 'The Importance of Education and the Co-operative Movement', paper submitted to the International Conference on Co-operative Education (16th Congress of the ICA), Zurich, 1946.

11   E. Schumacher, *Small is Beautiful*, Abacus, London, 1974, p. 220.

12   K. Marx and F. Engels, *The Manifesto of the Communist Party* (1848); F. Engels, *Socialism: Utopian and Scientific* (1877). Both works are included in Karl Marx and Friedrich Engels, *Selected Works in Two Volumes*, FLPH, Moscow, 1962.

13   *Report of the Committee of Inquiry on Industrial Democracy*, HMSO, London, 1977. Its recommendations that, in companies employing more than a certain number of workers, the board of directors should contain equal numbers of directors (representing shareholders), trade unionists (representing the workforce), and independents who could break deadlocks should they arise, were never implemented.

14   R. Michels, op. cit.

15   However, a major public opinion survey undertaken at the end of 1992 showed an increase in support for trade unions in the UK. This was a response to the widespread insecurity caused by the undifferentiating contagion of unemployment. It testifies to a conviction in the value of local, work-based solidarity, rather than to a resignation to the workings of the blind forces of the market.

16   A symptom of the times is the growing importance of 'intellectual property rights' and legislation governing this issue. Laws on patents, though still critical, refer back to a previous, manufacturing era.

17   NUPE, *Up Against a Brick Wall – The Dead End in Housing Policy*, NUPE, 1978.

18   The term 'transformation' is preferred to 'transition', since the latter implies 'movement towards' some identifiable and known end state. Moreover, this end state is presumed by the World Bank, the IMF and the United States Government to be that envisaged by Fukuyama, namely capitalism and liberal democracy.

19   The UK and Italy are representative of polities at opposed ends of the multi-party spectrum.

20   In 1991 the British Government reduced its contribution to sick pay from 100 per cent to 80 per cent. In 1993 it reduced it by a further 20 per cent. This will compel more workers to take out private insurance. The Department of Social Security informed the Public Accounts Committee that the sick-pay system, which relies on self-certification for the first seven days, would be better policed if companies had to share a greater proportion of the costs.

21   This organisation was given the pitifully small sum of £200,000 in order to provide an advisory service on co-operative formation, marketing and alternative sources of finance for co-operative associations. The paltriness of the grant accounts for, firstly, the organisation's gaining all-party support in Parliament and, secondly, its failure.

22   A. Zevi, 'The Performance of Italian Producer Co-operatives' in D. C. Jones and J. Svenjnar (eds), *Participatory and Self-Managed Firms*, Lexington Books, Lexington, 1982.

23   See, for example: A. Cambell, *Mondragon 1980*, ICOM, Pamphlet no. 9; K. Bradley and A. Gelb, 'Motivation and Control in the Mondragon Experiment', *British Journal of Industrial Relations*, vol. XIX, no. 2, July 1981; K. Thomas and C. Logan, *Mondragon: An Economic Analysis*, Allen & Unwin, London, 1982; R. Oakshott, *The Case for Workers' Co-operatives*, Routledge, London, 1978.

24   For instance, the collapse of industry in Liverpool's Vauxhall district threatened the community of people living there. In 1986 the local residents responded to the threat by raising £8 million for the largest self-build project in Europe. They had two principal goals: firstly, to prevent the creation of yet another wasteland in the city following the closure of a large sugar refinery and the demolition of the buildings; and, secondly, to provide accommodation (145 housing units) for local people.

25 The *Scottish Daily News* saw its workforce fall from 1,942 to 500 and the Meriden motorcycle factory from 1,750 to 626 workers. See K. Bradley and A. Gelb, 'The radical potential of cash nexus breaks', *British Journal of Sociology*, vol. 31, no. 2, June 1980.

26 J. Westergaard, 'The Rediscovery of the Cash Nexus', in R. Miliband and J. Saville (eds), *The Socialist Register*, London, Merlin Press, 1970.

27 Cited in: K. Bradley and A. Gelb, op. cit.

28 D. Hardy, *Alternative Communities in Nineteenth Century England*, Longman, London, 1979.

29 C. Grace and M. Kingham, 'Can Tenants Run Housing?', *Fabian Research Series 334*, Civic Press, 1980.

30 Co-operative Development Agency, *Directory of New Co-operatives and Community Businesses*, London, 1986.

31 K. Jefferis, *Co-operative Union 1985*, London, 1986.

32 P. Clarke, *Co-operation between Co-operatives – Today, Tomorrow, Forever?*, Co-operative Development Agency, London, n. d., circa 1987.

33 About two-fifths of all producer co-operatives in Britain are printers – one of the oldest craft unions dating back to the guild system.

34 L. Pluta, 'Introduction' in A. Balawyder (ed.), *Co-operative Movements in Eastern Europe*, Macmillan, London, 1980, p.16.

35 Ibid., p.17.

36 Ibid., p.19.

37 J. M. Kirschbaum, 'The Co-operative Movement in Slovakia, 1845–1948', in Balawyder, op. cit., pp. 30–33.

38 L. Kovalcik, 'Approaching the Congress of the Central Co-operative Council', *The Czechoslovak Co-operator*, no. 1, 1976, p. 2, cited by S. Kirschbaum, 'The Co-operative Movement in Socialist Slovakia', in Balawyder, op. cit., p. 70.

39 Ibid.

40 E. Loebl, 'Comment on S . Kirschbaum', in Balawyder, op. cit., p. 79.

41 J. Gajd, 'Workers' Co-operatives in Polish Industry. Their Role and Development', in Balawyder, op. cit., pp. 157, 162.

42 Ibid.

43 A. Korbonski, 'The Private Sector in Poland: Problems and Prospects', in Balawyder, op. cit., p. 170.

44 I am reminded of Robert Redfield's reply to Oscar Lewis's research findings which contradicted his own, which had been carried out in 1926. Redfield had found in the 'folk society' of Yucatan a Rousseauesque paradise (which enabled him to elaborate his theory of a rural–urban continuum); Lewis, his former student, found murder, robbery and domestic violence. Redfield's reply to the outcome of the restudy undertaken 25 years later was that the two researchers had been looking for different things. See R. Redfield, *The Little Community* and *Peasant Society and Culture*, University of Chicago Press, London, 1956.

45 'The Novosibirsk Report', published in *Survey: A Journal of East & West Studies*, vol. 28, no. 1, 1984. The report was later attributed to T. Zaslavskaya. See Chapter 4 below.

46 International Labour Organisation, *Co-operation: A Workers' Educational Manual*, Geneva, 1956, pp. 110–11. The core values expressed in this quotation are as central to Mr Blair's vision of a stakeholding society under the Labour Party as they were to Mr Major's notion of the active citizen under the Conservative Party.

47 C. R. Hatch, 'The Power of Manufacturing Networks', *Transatlantic Perspectives*, no. 22, Winter, 1991, p. 3.

48   Department of Trade and Industry, *DTI – the Department of Enterprise*, Cmnd. 278, HMSO, 1988.

49   The grant aid provided by central government since 1986 came to an end in 1991, at least as a means of core funding enterprise agencies. Since then, state finance has been channelled through various government departments for specific projects and under contract for training and counselling. See Business in the Community, *Review of Local Enterprise Agency Network*, BIC, 1989.

50   Whereas the British Government focused its attention on establishing an agency to help individual firms by offering advice and counselling, the Danes were training officials to become network brokers with the task of looking for mutual commercial opportunities for firms who are competitors.

51   Denmark has a population of only 5.1 million.

52   Hatch, op. cit., p. 6.

53   In 1986 the Prince of Wales described the Development Trusts as 'the third force', which could mobilise the public, private and voluntary sectors.

54   P. Ormerod, *The Death of Economics*, Faber & Faber, London, 1994.

55   J. Cunningham, 'The workers' co-op movement wins new political friends', *Guardian*, 6 November 1986.

56   G. D. H. Cole, *Essays in Social Theory*, Oldbourne Science Library, London, 1962, p. 97.

PART II
RUSSIA AND THE
CO-OPERATIVE
ALTERNATIVE

Introduction to Part II

The study of the history and fortunes of co-operatives in Imperial and then Soviet Russia and now in the Russian Republic is of interest in a number of respects. Although the theoretical idea of the co-operative as a form of social and economic organisation posited against capitalism is not generally thought to have originated in Russia, it was well suited to Russian civil society. Declared illegitimate by the tsarist autocracy, co-operatives found favour amongst representatives of all other sections of the population. They enjoyed a short-lived boom in the aftermath of the 1905 Revolution and played an important role during the First World War.

In the period after the 1917 revolution, Lenin and dominant Bolshevik factions pronounced the co-operative movement heretical and illegitimate, but it regained legitimacy during NEP (the New Economic Policy which Lenin introduced in 1920). After struggling to maintain its identity, status and acceptability as a socialist form, it succumbed to the command economy introduced by Stalin. Even the 'thaw' under Khrushchev saw no improvement in the position of co-operatives.

As a social phenomenon, co-operatives survived the vicissitudes of the following seventy years and with the introduction of perestroika entered a new springtime. In the 1980s they finally came to take their place as an authentic socialist form in a renascent civil society. During the heady days of 1986–90 their early development prior to, and after, October 1917 was subjected to new interpretations and their historical and contemporary value and meaning were re-assessed. The urges in Lenin in 1917 and in Stalin a decade later to aim for and then impose a 'higher' form of socialism were matched by Yeltsin's palace coup in the dying embers of 1991 to impose a 'higher' (purer) form of capitalism.

Probably nowhere else in the world have co-operatives been so affected by government caprice. Rarely have they been so elevated in people's minds as a vehicle for class advancement. Both the Tsar and his advisors on the one hand, and Lenin and his subsequent commissars on the other, thought that they were attacking the organisations of a threatening class enemy. The autocracy feared any challenge to its hegemony, so it mattered little that the co-operatives were drawing into their ranks individuals from different sections of the middle class, the more prosperous peasants and skilled craftsmen, as well as poorer and weaker sections of the urban and rural working class and peasantry. Lenin, too, was antipathetic to co-operatives: firstly, in his eyes they were dominated by 'bourgeois and petit bourgeois elements', and, secondly, Stolypin's agrarian reforms were having partial success and members of the working class and the 'middle peasants' were discovering practical advantages to be gained from co-operative membership, which made them less disaffected with the tsarist regime.

Co-operatives in Russia have flourished during periods of regime crisis, when the state has made concessions to the demands of economic liberals, who were also political radicals, as the bourgeois have generally tended to be in their society's transition to capitalism. These have been times of uncertainty and transition; they have coincided with the rise of an articulate 'middle class' demanding a voice against, first, an autocracy grounded in a belief in a mystical divine right and, later, a dictatorship resting on its conviction that it had a scientifically determined right to decide and govern. On the whole co-operatives were not, in the case of Russia (or the Soviet Union), a predominantly working-class movement.

One of the most striking features about the continuing revolution in the economic, social and political life of Russia is the immensity of the task, which in some ways is more complex and difficult than the overthrow of tsarism in 1917 and the 'second revolution' inaugurated by Stalin in 1929, not least because the latter was determined not to be thwarted by open debate (*glasnost*). In complete and striking contrast to the first General Secretary of the Party, the last General Secretary, Mikhail Gorbachev, set out to revitalise the local soviets and restore power to them, to legislate for self-management at the enterprise level and to promote co-operatives through a series of promulgations and decrees. In 1987, co-operatives could be seen as representing the revival of the political and socialist revolution of 1917 that had been asphyxiated in the 1930s.

3 The Rise and Decline of the Co-operative in Russia

The History of Co-operatives in Russia up to 1917

Fertile ground?

The Russian intelligentsia of the nineteenth century was acquainted with Western reformist ideas. This is evident from discussions held amongst the Decembrists[1] and the acknowledged influence of St Simon on Herzen and his circle. At the end of the 1840s a group grew up around M. V. Petrashevskii to discuss Fourier's *The New Industrial World*.[2] Others discussed the meaning of Owen's *New Lanark*, Cabet's *Icaria*, and the notion of progressive taxation advanced by Proudhon.[3] The strictness of the censor prevented dissemination of these works other than by word of mouth.

Robert Owen's concern with 'all those systems which create the unending desire to buy cheap and sell dear' was well received by reform-oriented co-operators, who, later in the nineteenth century, cited with approval Holyoake's axiom that capital should not be the source of profit but the necessary and powerful instrument for the satisfaction of people's needs.[4] Their espousal of co-operative associations as unions founded on the twin pillars of equal rights for all members and self-government – which gives rise to the principle 'one person, one vote' – was a code for broader political objectives. Equal rights and self-government entailed the responsibility of the participants for the affairs and obligations of the association and, through universal suffrage, of all citizens for the local and central state.

The first open Russian propagandist and theoretician of associations of workers was N. G. Chernyshevskii.[5] It was through articles in his journal, *Sovremennik*, that Russians in 1859 learned of the work of Owen. Instructing as the works of West European reform-oriented writers were, Chernyshevskii was interested in devising a plan of development which would take into account Russia's norms and mores. The distinguishing cultural feature of Russia was its common ownership of land with individual working of it, which could easily be transferred to a higher stage of communal working of the land. Such was the popularity and influence of Chernyshevskii among democrats of his time that later writers considered that the foundations of the co-operative movement in Russia owed an important debt to him.[6]

Throughout the nineteenth century most Russian peasants held land in social ownership (*obshchestvennoe vladenie*). According to this form of ownership all male members of rural society (*sel'skoe obshchestvo*) were entitled to an equal allocation of the periodically redistributed land. All land was regarded as belonging to the rural society and not to individual peasants who, though permitted to lease their allotment on a temporary basis, were prohibited from selling or mortgaging it. On those occasions when a peasant chose not to use his entitlement, it reverted to the community, which reallocated it until such time as he required it.[7]

The periodic redistribution of the land by the *mir*[8] was regarded as an instrument for resisting both the concentration of land ownership and the subsequent formation of a landless proletariat which would be driven to work in capitalist industry. At the same time some populists were keen to point out that a Russian form of 'labour association' (*trudovaya artel'*) had been in existence long before co-operatives evolved in Western Europe.[9] This institutional structure was regarded as the foundation stone for a co-operative mode of industrial development. Russian advocates of consumer and credit co-operatives drew a distinction between their germination and potential in Russia and in West European countries, where the land was cultivated by individual farmers: 'Our poor people have carried with them through their sorrowful history one great source which must be preserved and developed at all costs; all friends of the people must offer advice and personally assist the development of our commune into an agricultural association'.[10]

For all these reasons, in his debates with the Russian Populists in the last decade of his life Marx commented that: 'the special research into this subject [the rural community] which I have conducted ... has convinced me that this community (*mir*) is the mainspring of Russia's social regeneration'.[11] In his view Russia stood at the crossroads and could, if it chose, avoid the path of capitalist development. However, the Social Democrats, which included the Bolsheviks, considered that, though the path to socialism was painful, no other existed: capitalism was a necessary and inevitable stage through which all countries had to pass. For the Socialist Revolutionary Party, on the other hand, an alternative lay in the formation of 'unions' (*soyuzy*) and 'associations' (*tovarishchestva*), that is, co-operatives,[12] whose advantages were already visible in a few examples of collective action.

Although the standard of living and the working conditions of the members of these loose co-operatives improved, they still received less than the cost of their labour because, firstly, the *artel* had to pay interest on money borrowed and, secondly, such producer co-operatives did not in themselves 'eliminate "parasitic" intermediaries. Only when socialism was achieved and all the means of production were in social ownership would this evil be removed'.[13] In other words, the Socialist Revolutionaries rejected the Bolshevik position, that co-operatives did not offer a viable path for the advance towards socialism, but neither did they regard a society of co-operatives as synonymous with socialism. In this sense, they were precursors of the Bolshevik leadership's acceptance of the co-operative road during the 1920s: co-operatives constituted a viable and preferable form of social relations once socialism had been established. Tangible material interests apart, co-operative ownership, as the Bolsheviks were to come to accept, could help to 'educate people to a new way of life, to accustom them to think together, manage their own affairs and prepare them for a future socialist economy'.[14]

The Socialist Revolutionaries were in certain respects heirs to the Populists (*narodniki*). Like them, they believed that, because three-quarters of Russian peasants owned the land communally, the transition from commune ownership to co-operative ways of working the land would be easy. However, Lenin thought otherwise. In his view, since capitalist relations had already been established in the countryside and the country at large had embarked upon the capitalist path, the die had already been cast.[15]

The cultural context would seem to have been propitious for the germination of the co-operative idea and the co-operative movement. German and French peasants, who held land as private property, found it much more difficult to combine in associations. Yet, ironically, agricultural associations were far more common outside Russia. The explanation for this paradox – and the fact that 'in this huge country there are no more than 4,000 different types of co-operatives and only a handful of *artels* like those found in Pavlovo' – lay with the bureaucratic machinery of the Ministry of Internal Affairs, which took a year or more to ratify a co-operatives' charter and was obstructive to those that were successful.[16] If the position of the old regime was a barrier to development, the polemical stance taken by Lenin and the Bolsheviks *vis-à-vis* both the Populists (for their defence of the inherent virtues of the *mir*) and the Socialist Revolutionaries (for their support of co-operatives) hardly promised any more fertile a political-ideological environment for their growth than that found under tsarism.

Early Difficulties

The first co-operative societies in Russia were established in the Baltic region, where news of the success of consumer societies in Germany and England was initially received. Given the strong cultural links between the Baltic states and Germany, some regarded 'Schultze-Delitzsch as the spiritual father of the Russian co-operative movement'.[17] Following the foundation of a consumer co-operative in Riga and then Revel in 1865, others were set up in St Petersburg, Pskov, Kharkov, Odessa and elsewhere.[18] However, even before the ratification of the first consumer association charter in Riga, the idea of consumer co-operatives had been put into operation 'in the back of beyond in the Urals' (*v Ural'skom glushi*). This has led to the assertion that 'the idea of consumer co-operatives in Russia developed wholly or to a significant degree independently of elsewhere', appearing first of all in 1864 in the Urals. Because of their indigenous origins, the forms which co-operatives took 'were far from the same as those found in Western Europe'.[19] Nevertheless, doubts were raised about the capacity of a peasantry which had only been fully emancipated in 1861 to formulate by themselves the notion of consumer co-operatives. For this reason, Ballin, one of the pioneers of the co-operative movement, regarded the intelligentsia (under the influence as much of Chernyshevskii's *What is to be Done?* as of Holyoake's history of the Rochdale Pioneers) as the instigator of co-operatives.[20]

Schultze-Delitzsch saw credit associations as a way of strengthening the small independent producer, but in Russia, as a result of their cultural origins, these institutions were interpreted as an instrument for developing producers' *artels* and co-operatives. Moreover, in contrast to the insistence of Schultze-Delitzsch that the initial creation of a co-operative had to be based on the resources of its membership and that any person wishing to join a co-operative had to be able to afford a share, Russian co-operators recognised that such conditions were pointless in a society just emerging from serfdom and suffering from poverty. Capital to finance the formation of rural banks would have to come from the *zemstva*,[21] which were institutions of local government established in 1864.

In fact the *zemstva* did try to provide financial assistance and other resources for co-operatives, but their attempts often failed. In one, not untypical, instance, peasants formed themselves into a *kustar artel* to manufacture nails. But, instead of using the money lent to the artel by the Tver *zemstvo* for nail production, the peasants saw the donation as a generous act of charity on the part of this official organisation, and immediately distributed it among themselves for their individual personal use. The efforts of the Tver local government to help various co-operative ventures over a fourteen-year period after 1869 were all, to one degree or another, unsuccessful. Financial mismanagement and lack of the necessary expertise to operate any machinery that was introduced frequently contributed to failure. The fact that the recipients considered the money a gift or act of charity meant that they tended not to have a 'responsible' attitude towards its use.[22]

Another consequence was that the *zemstva* found it difficult to recover loans; either there was nothing to recover or the obligation to return what had been received was not acknowledged. The impersonal rules of a Weberian 'rational-legal society' were far from being the norm in nineteenth-century Russia: the traditional Russian merchant offered his word to repay his debt at the next annual trade fair rather than offer a bill of exchange.[23] Cultural traditions prevalent in serf and merchant families – most of whose heads could neither read nor write – reinforced the tendency toward short-run profit maximisation. However, traditional norms and practices, which emphasised personal contacts and bribery, were in part a functional adaptation to a society dominated by a pervasive and arbitrary bureaucracy.[24]

This bureaucracy observed with suspicion any coalition of individuals under whatever guise. Unlike their English counterparts, who could discuss issues selected by the membership, Russian co-operators were allowed to debate only those matters specified on the agenda, which had previously been vetted by the local chief of police, who usually supervised the meetings.

Bureaucrats from the lowliest clerk in a village to the provincial governor used a multiplicity of administrative strategies to obstruct the development of co-operatives. These could take the form of a fiat, as when in 1869 the Ministry of Internal Affairs, responding to a request from the Khar'kov co-operative society to convoke a conference of representatives of all consumer co-operatives, ruled that 'the activities of consumer societies are only permitted within the boundaries of a city; general links between co-operatives are not allowed and must not be allowed'.[25]

The Government rigorously obstructed the formation of unions of societies as part of its antipathy to any independent coalition, on the grounds that it could develop into an organised political pressure group.[26] Or it employed the time-honoured device of taking a long time to process the applications of would-be co-operatives. The Government's fear of autonomous collectivities was demonstrated in the powers given to provincial governors and local mayors, who required no pretext or provocation to close a co-operative society.

As a result of such legal and administrative harassment, the first congress of Russian consumer co-operatives was not held until 1896, following which the St Petersburg section established a 'Permanent Commission for the Affairs of Consumer Associations'. Two years later a union of consumer co-operatives covering the Moscow province was established. This gradually became the leading consumers' union in the country and in 1903 began publishing its own journal.

Artels *and Credit Co-operatives*

A negative attitude to co-operatives from above was supplemented by ignorance, illiteracy and lack of initiative from below. Land shortage added yet another obstacle to the formation of agricultural co-operatives. A limited antidote to this situation was the encouragement given to the establishment in villages of *artels* of *kustars*, that is, of individuals involved in a whole range of handicrafts: carpentry, tailoring, metal- and leather-working, wood- and stone-carving, and the production of cutlery, toys, locks, harnesses, samovars, buttons and barrels.[27]

One representative Russian view of the *artel* was that it had nothing in common with the producer co-operatives found in England. In contrast to the latter with their permanent organisation, written charters and elected officers, the Russian *artel* was fluid and temporary, with no fixed statutes. In those sectors, such as tanning and dairying, where more advanced technology was employed and peasants formed larger *artels*, joint ownership of machinery 'was based not on the co-operative spirit but on a purely capitalist basis, where the minority [of *kulaks*[28] and wealthier *kustars*] exploited the product of the labour of the majority'.[29]

At the turn of the century, two opposing views on the future of co-operatives prevailed. One regarded co-operation between peasants and among *kustars* combined into *artels* as a viable (if not the only) path for the Russian masses to take in order to escape poverty and their torpid condition. The other considered the high-minded ideals promoted by the *narodniki* and the *zemstva* doomed to failure: increasing poverty, alleviated by what the peasantry regarded as acts of charity, created despondency and reinforced traditional patterns of behaviour, all of which militated against self- betterment through personal initiative. On the other hand, in reality, especially after 1905, some of the (better-off) *kustars* became small capitalists while others utilised the *artel* – which had been the only form of legally organised labour – to agitate for reform, including the right to join trade unions. In 1906 the first so-called independent workers' co-operatives were established in St Petersburg, and gradually became an arena for the struggle between the Mensheviks, who predominated, and Bolsheviks. The former urged workers to join consumer co-operatives as a means of combating the high cost of living; the latter declared that high living costs could only be fought by the direct action of the organised proletariat.[30]

Producers' co-operatives developed primarily in Siberia. The region had been relatively untouched by the 1905 revolution, and its rich grazing land was suitable for cattle breeding and thus butter production. Migrants from the over-populated regions of European Russia were themselves 'achievers', while the willingness to work in teams – the first step towards co-operation – was a concomitant of migration. By 1914, 70 per cent of Siberia's butter production came from co-operative *artels*, and it was distributed on the market by four Siberian unions of co-operatives.[31]

Credit co-operative associations also came into prominence, especially in the countryside. Their importance has to be seen in terms of the role of agriculture in the national economy: in the period 1910–13 annual exports amounted to 1,200 million roubles ($650 million), of which grain accounted for 42.9 per cent and agriculture generally 69.2 per cent. Credit societies and their unions, which contributed much to increased productivity on the land, gradually assumed a major role in the development of the national economy.[32]

The presence of a Central Bank was a necessary condition for the existence of credit institutions, for there was no other institutional mechanism to channel money from unions with surplus funds to co-operatives lacking finance to expand their business activities.[33] Following the fairly rapid expansion of co-operatives in Russia after 1907, a thorough study of co-operative banks in Western Europe was commissioned. Its report and draft proposals for a National Bank were discussed at the first All-Russian Co-operative Congress held in Moscow in 1908. The bank's Charter was finally ratified by the Council of Ministers in 1911. When it opened for business in 1912, the Moscow Narodny Bank – which the State Bank refused to recognise – was in the hands of co-operators; only 15 per cent of the bank's shares were held by private individuals.[34]

The Shape of the Movement

Between 1875 and 1891 the state registered 186 consumers' co-operatives. By the turn of the century their number had reached 800. Although, initially, membership was predominantly middle-class (teachers, officers), by the end of the nineteenth century they contained representatives of all classes. Even so, Russian co-operatives seem to have had proportionately more middle-class members than did English co-operatives. However, this fact needs to be corroborated by detailed studies on the class composition of co-operatives. According to one contemporary source, in 1905 up to 300,000 people (of which one-half were drawn from the working class) were affiliated to consumer societies.[35] At this date Russia had 996 consumer co-operatives, the largest of which had 12,000 members.

The first All-Russian Co-operative Conference was convened in 1908. According to one eyewitness, it was composed of 'a sprinkling of military uniforms mingled with the cassocks of priests, but peasants and working men predominated'.[36] The Government tolerated the assembly for a week but then intervened and dissolved it. This and the unstable legal position of co-operative bodies impeded their establishment and evolution. The hostility of the nation's political organs and industrial magnates notwithstanding, 1908 saw the formation of the first Siberian Union of Co-operative Creameries. This was followed in 1912 by the creation of Consumers' Unions in Warsaw and Perm and the Association of Consumers' Societies of Southern Russia and in 1913 of the Transbaikal Trading Association.[37] One leading co-operator attributed the comparatively weak development of co-operatives in Russia not just to political conservatism and caprice and capitalist self-interest, but also to the country's low level of capitalist development.[38]

Despite the slow growth of co-operatives, by 1914 Russia had, according to conservative estimates, over four million households – with at least 20 million individuals – who were part of the co-operative movement.[39] On the eve of the Russian revolution in 1917, over 50 per cent of all peasant households in Siberia were members of some form of dairy, credit or consumer co-operative.[40] The All-Russian Union of Consumer Co-operatives commanded enormous capital and credit resources, owned large numbers of factories, and had its own river fleet on the Volga and its own fishing industry on the Caspian Sea.[41] But even the most enthusiastic supporters were forced to concede that, whilst there were tens of thousands of co-operative associations, individuals with experience and skill working in this sector were numbered in their hundreds. This shortage was compensated by 'fervent and unending arguments about the "essence" of co-operation which degenerated into mysticism and medieval metaphysics, arguing over principles which had long been clear and generally accepted'.[42]

Contemporary Russian commentators on the co-operative movement, writing as observers or as 'activists', were often members of the liberal intelligentsia – radical, but not revolutionary, socialists. Loyal to the co-operative tradition, they were seeking an alternative path to capitalism. In some cases the founders of co-operatives 'were drawn from the intelligentsia favourably disposed to the people'.[43] This involvement enabled the intelligentsia to assuage its thirst to engage in some form of public activity.[44] On the other hand, delegates to the first congress of Consumer Associations in 1896 had all the appearance of quite high-ranking civilian and military officials. As far as the old Bolsheviks or even recent Soviet authors were concerned, these co-operators were defined as Utopian socialists or, less generously, as those who pursued 'the same petit-bourgeois and bourgeois anti-socialist path as the co-operative movement in the West (with the exception of those co-operatives led by the Bolsheviks)'.[45]

No doubt a comparatively high proportion of consumer, rural, credit and other co-operatives were dominated by 'bourgeois elements', both in the countryside and in the town.[46] In fact, in some instances the term 'co-operative' seemed to contemporaries to be a complete misnomer. For example, the luxurious and ornate building in St Petersburg belonging to the Guards' Officers High School Society was referred to as a 'co-operative enterprise'. Yet, like the majority of consumer societies, its membership was strictly limited to a select circle of individuals. Such social exclusiveness furnished the Bolsheviks with a *casus belli* against co-operatives. This bias was referred to in a small pamphlet entitled 'What does the consumer society give to working women?',[47] which observed that it was 'unfortunately true that workers' co-operative associations are developing slowly'[48] while in the countryside co-operative membership was 'mainly confined to the prosperous *kulak* and "top-of" the middle peasant stratum'.[49]

Tugan-Baranovskii categorised co-operatives as peasant, working-class and *petit bourgeois*.[50] The third group consisted of minor officials, representatives of the liberal professions and a section of small-scale entrepreneurs drawing an income from both their own labour and capital. To the extent that the latter relied on their own labour they were genuine co-operators, otherwise they were capitalists and exploiters of labour. This class essentially drew its inspiration from Schultze-Delitzsch, combining consumer societies, banking and credit associations and unions of craftsmen. In his view they did not gravitate towards collectivism nor to any other new economic form and could easily revert to purely capitalist associations with nothing at all in common with co-operatives (as happened to many Schultze-Delitzsch credit–savings societies in Germany).

For Tugan-Baranovskii nothing could be more blatantly false than the assertion by many advocates of co-operatives that they had a non-class character.[51] Each of its three trends – proletarian, peasant and *petit bourgeois* – had its own character and direction of development. However, whilst this meant that it was impossible to combine all co-operatives in one organisation, it did not mean that there was an inevitable antagonism between them. Of some importance for the whole of Soviet history was his observation that, unlike with West European societies, no evidence existed of any antagonism between working-class and peasant co-operatives. Moreover, he did not think that this situation would change in the future; relations between the two classes could remain amicable. Tugan-Baranovskii and others did not agree that only co-operatives falling under the ideological tutelage of the Bolsheviks could be socialist.

One study on the subject stated that it was expressly concerned with the co-operative movement from a 'sociological standpoint, as a new social force, creating new social relations and presenting the masses with new attitudes'.[52] In fact, pre-Revolutionary writers often saw co-operatives in two-dimensional terms. On the one hand, co-operation had a 'technical' aspect, describing the collaboration of two or more people; on the other, it had a 'social' aspect, meaning a 'form of combining human effort on the basis of voluntary collaboration'.[53] According to Nikolaev, writing in 1908, the co-operative was a powerful force, not for assisting the transformation of society within a capitalist framework, but as a much more powerful force for bringing about a future socialist society. The essence of a co-operative was that it should be free and voluntary, independent and democratic and – 'if the co-operative movement is really seeking to challenge and supersede the capitalist organisation of society' – have a 'labour base'.[54] This last requirement depicts the class dimension of the co-operative movement and the view of some that action had to be taken to make co-operatives more attractive and accessible to larger sections of the working class and less prosperous peasants.

Nonetheless, it was specious to argue, as the Bolsheviks did before and after 1917, that, since the better-off benefited disproportionately from consumer societies, the Russian intelligentsia, which strongly advocated co-operation, was consciously or unconsciously 'misguided'.[55] Moreover, according to Antsyferov, the psyche of the peasant masses was evolving at an astonishing speed from an extreme form of individualism towards co-operative association. In his view, a special co-operative 'environment' was beginning to be created even in the remotest villages.[56] By contrast, Lenin chose to see rural life as being increasingly characterised by socio-economic differentiation and disharmony.

Since virtually all Russians acknowledged that their country would remain a peasant country for a long time to come, considerable emphasis was placed on the multidimensional development of agriculture and agriculture-related industry. The link between small-scale industry and agriculture – unlike in the West – had not been wholly severed but was maintained in the primitive form of *kustar* industry. More than this, all social classes, with the exception of small traders, and the state and local government had a mutual interest in the widespread and unrestricted development of co-operatives.

From a narrow fiscal point of view, their development was absolutely necessary: the massive state debt could only be discharged by exporting large quantities of agricultural produce. It would become ever more difficult to sustain the export of millions of tons of wheat unless the harvest was increased. Both the state and local government budgets were constantly growing, with the *zemstva* budgets doubling in the period 1906–14. Some people thought that the *zemstva* would not be able to meet the ever increasing demands placed upon them unless they could rely more on co-operative organisations.[57]

Modern Parallels

These nineteenth-century views on the imperative of developing co-operatives for the economic salvation of Russia were to be unmistakably parallelled in the period before Gorbachev was ousted by Yeltsin. Small-scale industry and craft production (*kustar*) strongly emphasised the need for credit co-operatives to enable them to survive. A cogent case existed for introducing policies aimed at sustaining *kustar* industry; it was integral to satisfying domestic demand and to providing goods for export in order to improve the balance of payments. Newly opened foreign markets were being lost: the Poltava *zemstvo*, for instance, was compelled to turn down large orders placed in New York because it could not deliver the quantities required.[58] The whole situation, it was argued at the time, would be radically improved by passing a wide, general, enabling law on co-operatives which would stimulate the development of the whole national economy.[59]

Even a cursory examination of the co-operative movement in the period before 1917 sheds light on the cultural context which, at the end of the 1980s, was to kindle agents both inimical and friendly towards the development of co-operatives. In both periods the autocratic yet fearful state and its labyrinthine bureaucracy, which acted so negatively towards the early strivings of co-operators, formed the first line of opposition. The second line of opposition came from entrenched economic interests which viewed with annoyance the emergence of an institutional form intent on eroding their source of power and profit. Thirdly, despite the passage of time and regime change, there were those who shared a millenial belief in equality: 'the main law of life should be that anyone born into the world/commune (*mir*) should receive as much land as he can work with his own hands (*svoimi silami*)'.

That belief bears a close resemblance to condemnations of wide earnings differentials heard in the 1980s, but with one important difference. Then, it was believed, the abolition of private ownership in land and its conversion into 'the wealth of the whole working population' would precede (and make easier) the social ownership of factories, railways and the means of production generally.[60] As the 1980s turned into the 1990s, the privatisation of enterprises and other means of production preceded the privatisation of land.

Communists and Co-operatives, 1917–29

From Revolution to New Economic Policy

No organisation rendered more assistance to the country during the First World War than the co-operative movement. The Moscow Narodny Bank financed commercial developments in Siberia, whose co-operatives supplied the military with food, financed military hospitals, purchased war bonds and provided temporary relief to soldiers' families. Towards the end of the war, the co-operatives emerged as the biggest movement in the country and, in the eyes of some, as popular as the revolutionary ideas sweeping the country.[61]

The government which succeeded the autocracy in February 1917 adopted a new, much friendlier stance towards co-operatives. Not only did the Mensheviks continue to support them, but the fresh stimulus given by the Provisional Government culminated in their becoming the world's leading co-operative movement; the most important group was the consumers' associations, headed by the Moscow Union of Consumer Societies. In 1917 the latter was reorganised and merged into a national union, the Central Union of Co-operative Societies (*Tsentrosoyuz*). This organisation ran its enterprises on a purely capitalist basis, but as a model employer paying wages according to special rates agreed with the trade unions. It also provided its workforce with hygienic working conditions, social insurance, pensions and medical care; this did not, however, prevent strikes occurring.

In the course of 1918 the Central Union began to acquire real estate throughout the country, including slaughterhouses, tea-packing plants and cheese factories, office buildings, warehouses, publishing houses and libraries.[62] By the end of 1918 it was running 95 offices: 50 in Russia, 20 in Siberia, 7 in Turkestan and 18 abroad, including London, Stockholm, and New York.

By 1919 co-operative organisations represented 100 million people in

80,000 local organisations and 500 unions with the potential, by virtue of the movement's size, to act as a political force. The Provisional Government courted them in the hope that they would take on the burden of organising the country's food supply. Although some delegates to the third All-Russian Congress of Co-operatives held in Moscow in April 1917 had argued that the co-operatives should distance themselves from politics, the majority voted to pledge the support of the co-operatives to the new government.

The majority of co-operators condemned Kornilov's attempted *putsch* in July 1917, but were none the less unwilling to sever connections with the middle classes. Instead, they insisted on the need to strive for a coalition of all classes. This position led to a rupture in the ranks of the membership; representatives of labour co-operatives rejected this policy and advocated a more radical socialist platform. They were in a strong position to do so, for in 1918 the membership of the consumer associations consisted of 47 per cent peasants, 45 per cent workers and 8 per cent middle class.[63] On the other hand, the peasant and working-class delegates and members were not unanimous in their outlook, with some taking the middle class and more prosperous peasant as their reference groups. The question is whether the co-operatives, having rendered invaluable support to the embattled soviets against capitalism during the first year of the revolution, had now themselves become capitalist, thereby making a clash with the Bolsheviks inevitable. Given the enormous diversity of co-operatives, it is no surprise that there was no unanimity or consistency in their political allegiances, which tended to vary from region to region. But this was not the only reason: the categories 'capitalist' and 'socialist' were so vague that individuals were inclined to redefine the category to which they belonged depending on the changing circumstances.

With the approach of elections to the Constituent Assembly in 1918, a special All-Russian Co-operative Conference was convoked. Some of those who had earlier counselled against co-operators becoming involved in politics were now among the most vociferous advocates of entering candidates at the election. The platform adopted by the Conference included: concluding an honourable peace treaty, handing over the land to those who worked it, and establishing a democratic constitutional government.

War, revolution and blockade isolated Russia from Western Europe and impelled local manufacturers to play a larger role in the domestic economy. By 1920 over twelve million peasants were working in the *kustar* sector, particularly in the provision of leather and felt boots and bast (hemp) shoes, so that 'practically the whole country was shod by the *kustars*'.[64] In August 1918 the Russian *kustars* founded a national union under the title of The All-

Russian Co-operative Association for the Manufacturing and Marketing of Kustar Products (*Kustarbyt*).

The attitude of the Bolsheviks towards co-operatives in 1918 was as misguided as the decision taken in that year to collectivise agriculture – although Stalin's imprint on the collectivisation policy added callousness to dogma. The assault on the 'old ways' as a means of encouraging an acceptance of the new order led the Soviet Government to move, as had its tsarist predecessor, against the Moscow Narodny Bank, which controlled the entire co-operative credit network, the very backbone of the agricultural areas. To that end, in December 1918 the Moscow Narodny was nationalised.[65] In so far as the Bank was converted by the decree into the co-operative section of the State Bank, it retained its independence over many of its operations. Elsewhere, the declaration of a state monopoly in a number of products forced co-operatives to recognise that they were now mere agents of the Government and minor players in the Soviet system. In a number of respects these actions repeated and reinforced a cultural pattern in which those in authority exercised power arbitrarily by fiat and hastily promulgated decree. The feeling of insecurity thus created was reminiscent of the outside interference experienced by the embryonic co-operative movement under tsarism. The wilful and doctrinaire action taken by the tsarist authorities against co-operatives supplied the Soviet regime with a negative role model for use against all subsequent attempts to form co-operatives.

A decree of April 1918 clarified the Bolsheviks' view on consumer co-operatives and their 'new' concept of co-operatives, namely that the movement should cease to be a private social one and instead involve the whole of society.[66] At this time Lenin was very much opposed to voluntary forms of co-operation. Freedom of action for co-operatives based on the principles of voluntariness and independence was abolished in March 1919. Members of co-operative boards, including that of *Tsentrosoyuz*, were appointed by the Government. In reality, although they became economic agencies of the state, co-operatives occupied a much more important role than originally assigned to them by the Government. For a short period they were in form and function precursors of the modern quango.

The attempt at a revolutionary *shturm* to collectivise agriculture in 1918–19 was shortlived and an experience which led the VIII Congress of the RKP(b) in December 1919 to stipulate that collectivisation had to be premised on 'voluntariness, conversion on the basis of practical experience, the creation of the necessary material conditions and the most important co-operative principle, that of self-government'.[67] The voluntary aspect of co-operation was paramount, especially, it was thought, since 80 per cent of the population were peasants cultivating their own land.[68] The same Congress passed a resolution stating that consumer societies should be developed within a framework of the existing co-operatives 'which are the most important consumer organisations representing in the sphere of distribution the best legacy of capitalism'. It acknowledged that, rather than abolish co-operatives, it was better to develop them 'along communist lines'. This would encourage initiative and discipline among the working population and eventually lead to the fusing of all co-operatives into a single society covering the whole country.[69] Such statements, like Lenin's 'It is not the co-operatives that have to adjust to NEP but NEP to the co-operatives',[70] were saturated with broad theory and dogma. The attention paid to political considerations was sometimes deft, but more often crass and clumsy.

NEP and the Co-operative Restoration

Until the attempted coup in 1991, much was made of Lenin's statement in his pamphlet *On Co-operation* that, where the proletariat has defeated the bourgeoisie, socialism is 'a system of civilised co-operators with socialised ownership of the means of production'.[71] This was interpreted to mean that the promotion of co-operatives was not a way of developing NEP; rather, NEP had as its goal the maximum development of co-operation and its general conversion into a nationwide form of social organisation.[72] The evolutionary path towards socialism, advocated by pre-revolutionary co-operators functioning in a capitalist society, was now finding support amongst some Bolshevik factions as the correct path forward under socialism.[73] Those citing with approval Lenin's views on co-operatives tend to ignore his view that: 'Co-operation is one aspect of state capitalism [and] co-operative capitalism resembles state capitalism in the sense that it facilitates agreements between the state (i.e. Soviet government) and capitalists'.[74] The New Economic Policy – which was certainly a form of state capitalism – in promoting the maximum development of co-operatives would, in Lenin's view, 'reconcile the interests of private trade with government control and so make private traders work for the general good'.[75]

The aim of Lenin's principal work on co-operatives was twofold: firstly, to point out to officials in government and economic organisations the mistakes they were making in their interpretation of the role of co-operatives; and, secondly, to try to enrol the mass of the population in the co-operative system. By 1924, when politicians were expressing their concern at the success of private traders they turned to the co-operatives as a means of curbing the former's activities and capturing their markets. On the other hand, the attitude of trade unions was less favourable to co-operatives. In their view co-operatives only supplied one-quarter of workers' needs, were inefficient and had high overheads. In addition, they failed to pay sufficient heed to their customers' demands and were corrupt.[76] In this regard the position espoused by Soviet trade unions was similar to that of their counterparts in western Europe, especially in the UK.

The attitude of the Communist Party to the co-operatives in 1920 was accurately reflected in a statement by the appointed chairman of *Tsentrosoyuz* that 'after three years' struggle against the old co-operative movement, there is nothing left of it'. In the eyes of one of the supporters of the pre-Soviet co-operative, the emasculation of co-operatives was not the result of a free struggle of ideas, human abilities and talents. Because of this, old-style co-operators remained optimistic about their future, with the Board of the Central Co-operative Society of Flax Growers declaring at the time of its compulsory closure that 'the present calamities, which have had such an effect on Russian co-operatives, are only temporary. They will continue to exist and flourish'.[77]

In this the co-operators were to be proved correct. The introduction of the New Economic Policy at the X Party Congress in 1921 was immediately accompanied by a decree on 7 April allowing consumer societies to resume their activities of exchanging commodities on the market and restoring the right to hold shares and to raise funds. This was followed by a decree on 17 May 1921 which reinstated the right of individuals to form producer *artels* which could hire workers as long as their number did not exceed 20 per cent of the shareholders. By the end of the year the Government prescribed ways of returning nationalised enterprises to their former co-operative owners. Factories employing over 200 workers were entitled to form themselves into co-operatives.

Because of the extremely adverse trade balance, special privileges were granted to forest *artels*, which combined, in September 1921, to form the All-Russian Union of Forestry (*Vsekoles*). Its level of profits, however, compared unfavourably with those of foreign competitors, such as Canada, Sweden, Norway and Finland. Whereas Russian co-operatives exported goods in the form of raw or semi-manufactured products, their competitors exported finished products such as doors and window frames. The story has a familiar and tragic resonance: Russia was, and remains in the 1990s, an exporter of mainly primary goods with little added value.

These concessions to co-operatives in the face of food shortages and low industrial output (themselves due to shortages of machinery and management skills) recalled the grudging concessions the tsarist authorities made when faced with economic and political crises. However, for the co-operatives to play their full role in reviving the economy would require reforming the system of banking, finance and taxation. The Bolshevik leadership's political insecurity and doctrine-bound approach prohibited contemplation of such a policy. The Commissar for Finance, Krestinsky, rejected suggestions to re-establish a co-operative bank: 'If a co-operative bank is formed, foreign loans would be used in the interests of the co-operatives, so that while the economic life of Russia might be improved, the ruling system would be weakened'.[78] This transparently narrow political self-interest was only partly justified by his additional observation that: 'With such a bank existing in our country, bourgeois Europe, which admits the necessity of granting relief, would grant this relief through these co-operatives, and thus take away the ground from under our feet'.[79] Similar sentiments were again to be expressed in Russia in 1987–88 in the course of a Conservative backlash against perestroika.[80]

Nevertheless, following persistent demands by the co-operatives themselves and the evident inability of the State Bank to meet the needs of the whole co-operative movement, the Government sanctioned the establishment of a co-operative bank, the All-Russian Consumers' Bank. Although organised along the lines of the Moscow Narodny, it differed from it in that the new bank dealt solely with consumer co-operatives. In January 1922 a very large demand for loans led to a decree sanctioning the creation of co-operative credit associations.

Of course, the frequent bellicose and paranoic statements of Soviet officials and politicians could well be construed as justified responses to a hostile international environment. The Allies' decision to re-open trade with Soviet Russia was not an altogether altruistic and benign gesture. Economic recession in Western Europe was threatening political and economic stability and Russia's demand for manufactured goods offered a safety valve. At the same time, the Allies declared their intention to deal only with co-operative societies. This gave rise to media articles entitled 'Neither Lenin nor Kolchak, but Russian Co-operatives' and to the argument that using co-operatives as the channel for international trade would weaken the Soviet Government's control over the economy, which would eventually culminate in the demise of the communists. Grounds for optimism that this would occur and that communists would give way to co-operators were strengthened by a decree issued in May 1924 which embodied a return to the principles on which the Russian co-operative movement had developed prior to the revolution. However, the brief period between 1918 and 1924 was long enough to bequeath to the co-operatives an overgrown, costly, bureaucratic administrative machine.[81]

Ever since the time of Peter the Great, the Russian state had intervened to support priority manufacturing sectors. But, although both tsarist and Soviet governments neglected to commit resources to consumer goods (apart from vodka), they only grudgingly allowed capitalist enterprises and co-operatives to meet unsatisfied consumer demand. Nevertheless, in spite of the numerous obstacles which they faced, it was the co-operatives, not the state or 'large' capital, which took the initiative to introduce, for example, insurance schemes. *Tsentrosoyuz*, building upon its earlier health insurance[82] programmes, began offering fire and transport insurance and property insurance for Consumers' Unions in 1918. These collective self-help schemes, like the earliest insurance schemes in nineteenth-century industrialising Britain, were mutual benefit societies pre-dating health provision by statutory authorities, which are now being revived in Russia , the UK and elsewhere in Europe.

Co-operative Growth – Political Conflict

Thus, in the early years of NEP co-operatives were regarded as a 'powerful economic factor' and accorded a new lease of life. Integral to the Government's policy towards them, as towards virtually all other groups which it did not regard as totally heretical and threatening, was the obligation to set up communist cells within co-operatives 'in order to lead the movement in the most efficient way toward the universal adoption of communism'.[83] However, despite exhortations to increase the number of communist instructors within the co-operative movement, of the 869 instructors in the All-Ukrainian Union of Consumers only 6 per cent were members of the Communist Party.[84] Not only did the Communist Party fail to preponderate in the key area of instruction and to control all positions on the boards of co-operative associations, but it was compelled to abandon rigid doctrinal positions in favour of economic policies designed to achieve prosperity. However, by the end of the decade, the political apparatus was again coming to prevail over economic and purely commercial interests. In the changing climate the proto-Stalinist faction in the Party became increasingly annoyed and piqued over the Party's lack of control and semi-subordinate status in relation to the co-operatives. Still, even though the autonomy of co-operatives was being whittled away as they became more and more the agents of government policy,[85] as late as 1927, as during War Communism, peasants preferred to deliver their grain to agricultural and consumer co-operatives rather than the state. The result was that during the 1920s Moscow's consumer co-operatives (*gorpo*) controlled a third of the capital's trade turnover. Siberian dairy co-operatives, which now controlled 72 per cent of peasant households engaged in dairy farming, maintained their pre-revolutionary success.[86] Prosperous dairy co-operatives, unlike less remunerative potato co-operatives, were largely controlled by *kulaks*.[87] By the mid-1920s, up to 70 per cent of basic consumer goods manufactured by state industry were being sold through consumer co-operatives.[88]

Just as with the decree of April 1918, which had attacked the bourgeois domination of the co-operatives, voices were raised attacking the predominance of *kulaks* in the agricultural co-operatives.[89] The fact that *kulaks* were also probably in a controlling position in village communes justified scepticism that the traditional communes provided the basis for a gradual transition to collectivism. Nonetheless, as late as December 1928 land redistribution was tolerated and the existence of the *mir* and land community defended as 'a step on the road to more collective forms'.[90] According to Carr and Davies, the 'admittedly inadequate statistics' revealed that '30 per cent of peasant households belonging to agricultural co-operatives were poor peasants, 60 per cent middle peasants and 10 per cent *kulak*' – although 50–60 per cent of *kulaks* were members.[91] Co-operatives became even more suspect following the fall from favour of Bukharin, who had been one of their principal protagonists.[92] Following a decree of September 1935, virtually the whole of the urban co-operative trading network was absorbed within the state retailing system, leaving only a small number of co-operative shops.[93]

Credit co-operatives, so vital for a flourishing co-operative sector, suffered, as they had in the nineteenth century, from not being able to use alternative sources of finance to maintain their operations. Since deposits by members were negligible and membership fees extremely low, the co-operatives were heavily dependent on state credit. By 1928, 27 per cent of all peasant households were members of credit co-operatives.[94] Contrary to declared policy intentions, the more prosperous peasant households benefited disproportionately from the system. They received larger advances, repayable at lower interest rates over a longer period.[95] Legislation specifically favouring poorer peasants essentially failed to achieve the desired objective: apart from the fact that individuals without any resources of their own might not have been able to put credit to good use, they were regarded by credit co-operatives as unreliable business risks.

In 1925–26 co-operative industry – which included manufacturing plant belonging to consumer, agricultural and industrial co-operatives – was responsible for 6.4 per cent of the production of large-scale industry (that is, of so-called census industry, which included units with over 16 employees or over 30, depending on whether or not mechanical motive power was used), rising to 9 per cent in 1928–29.[96] Co-operative industry was principally concerned with food products and controlled 17 per cent of gross production of all 'census' food industry. As in the pre-revolutionary period, it also included 'sawmills, printing works, tanneries, and small workshops producing metal goods, cotton textiles and soap'.[97] In the same year small-scale industry accounted for 25 per cent of manufactured products, principally consumer goods. Three-quarters of its workforce of 3.6 million worked in the countryside, and of those 89 per cent retained a connection with industry (compared with 15 per cent of urban workers).[98] The workforce in this sector preserved many of the features of the 'worker-peasant' characteristic of the pre-revolutionary period. [99]

Enterprises falling into the category of 'small-scale' consisted almost entirely of artisans who worked long hours for low levels of renumeration and were frequently dependent on middlemen. In 1926, almost 10 per cent of all artisans belonged to 5,800 primary co-operatives, the majority of which were producer *artels*. A further estimated 364,000 artisans belonged to 'unofficial' or 'independent' co-operatives. Like agricultural co-operatives these were charged with being 'bogus'. That is to say, they were really private capitalists using the co-operative form to evade controls on the number of hired workers and to benefit from privileges enjoyed by co-operatives, such as no control on wages, hours worked and working conditions.[100] As will be seen, these issues and complaints came to prominence again in the 1980s as a source of controversy over the nature of co-operatives, not least the criticism made in 1927 that the 'overwhelming majority of "labour *artels*", including those belonging to official co-operative unions, were of a capitalist nature'.[101]

The debates surrounding co-operatives in the 1980s mirrored in a number of respects those that came to a dramatic peak in the last years of NEP. On the one hand, artisan industry received official support. The XV Party Congress in 1927 reaffirmed the first five-year plan's provision for an expansion of artisan and handicraft industry in order to help alleviate the shortage of goods.[102] Local authorities and other state bureaucracies were urged to cease their contemptuous treatment of artisan industries. On the other hand, those opposed to small-scale industry argued that it was incompatible with the new technology and that private capitalists were exploiting artisans.[103] Fear of artisans being influenced by capitalists, coupled with a deteriorating supply situation, meant that independent artisans suffered in terms of the quantity and quality of the metal allocated to them.

Recognising the importance of small-scale industry and artisan crafts, the state compromised and decided to support 'official' co-operatives. It was hoped that channelling sales and supplies through these co-operatives would attract both artisans and 'independent' co-operatives to become members.

However, although by 1929 industrial co-operatives accounted for 'about one-third of the gross turnover of small-scale industry',[104] the majority of artisans remained outside the system. By 1939 artisans who were 'members of *artels* of industrial co-operatives', together with the non-working members of their families, comprised 2.3 per cent of the total population.[105]

In the mid-1950s small producer co-operatives, whose operations included over 114,000 workshops employing 1.6 million workers, were responsible for the manufacture of 40 per cent of all furniture, 70 per cent of metal plates and dishes and 43 per cent of outer knitted garments. This sector contained 100 design offices, 22 research laboratories and two scientific research institutes.[106] The argument used for their abolition was to prevent duplication of work already being done by state enterprises. During perestroika this policy was described as having 'robbed society of one of its most powerful driving forces of economic progress, namely, competition' and having created a framework for the growth of monopolies.[107]

Membership and trade turnover of consumer co-operatives increased after their revival in 1925, as they gradually became integrated into the system of marketing industrial goods through syndicates. Mistrust by sections of the Party notwithstanding, consumer co-operatives proved better at competing with private traders than did state trading organisations. They came to hold a key position in economic policy and were thus too valuable to be discarded.[108] Membership of consumer co-operatives grew rapidly from 12.3 million in 1926 to 32.7 in 1929, by which date 58 per cent of all peasant households belonged to consumer co-operatives.[109] It was anticipated that, during the first Five-Year Plan, the proportion of retail trade handled by the co-operatives would rise to 88 per cent of industrial goods, and 56 per cent of agricultural products.[110]

Granting such a major role to consumer co-operatives allowed the state to exert pressure on them to reduce prices. In so far as this affected their profit margins, finance for investment had to come from other sources. They could have raised the fee charged to members, but since this would have run counter to the Government's policy of encouraging more poor peasants to enrol in co-operatives, they had instead to rely on state credit: the Government's social policy to make co-operative membership accessible to all conflicted with the goal of making the co-operatives more self-financing from internally generated resources. Furthermore, in seeking to make consumer co-operatives the principal channel for the distribution of consumer goods to the whole population, the Ministry of Trade (*Narkomtorg*) came into conflict with *Tsentrosoyuz,* which reasoned that, unless co-operative shops were reserved for members only, no one would have an incentive to join.

The egalitarian policy was only superficially laudable, for at the same time as it was imposing upon the co-operatives the need to discriminate against the rich and assist the poor, the Government was creating a privileged bureaucratic stratum. Additionally, the more the state intervened in price setting by co-operatives and affected their economic decision making in other ways, the less co-operatives were able to expand and remain strong self-financing agencies. Yet, to the very end of NEP those institutions dealing with money and credit remained quite orthodox in their lending practices, showing greater concern for creditworthiness than for the social destination of their loans. Sound finance and a developed banking infrastructure were recognised by tsarist and Soviet Finance Ministers alike to be the cornerstone of a successful co-operative sector and economy generally. However, the decision had been taken to move towards a more fully planned economy, one of the most important experimental economic decisions in modern history.

Conclusion

The population in the Soviet Union during the 1920s was socially differentiated and conflicts were coalescing around class interests. But a dogmatic preoccupation with social class drew co-operatives into the vortex of entrepreneurial extinction. The essential conflict was couched in class terms. And, according to Marxist theory, class was defined in terms of property. In this one relationship is found the justification for Bolshevik policy, strategy and dogmatic assertion. The original first Five-Year Plan for the development of the economy (1928/29–1932/33), which had been approved by both the Party and Congress of Soviets in April/May 1929, was essentially defined by the principles of NEP and co-operative development. With the decision in the autumn of 1929 to sharply accelerate the speed of collectivisation, other forms of co-operation in agriculture ceased to exist until 1988.[111] By the latter part of the 1930s, consumer co-operatives had disappeared from the cities.[112]

The 'curtailment of co-operatives' in the late 1920s came to be explained by their new protagonists in the late 1980s as being 'due to numerous objective and subjective reasons'. These included the fact that the 'profundity of Lenin's understanding of the socialist system as a "system of civilised co-operators" was not grasped by very many political party leaders, to say nothing of the rank and file of the party members, still less the mass of non-party people'.[113] The tragedy of the 1930s was to be repeated fifty years later with the 'reformers' in command of the good ship *Rossiya* behaving as perversely as did the commissars in the 1930s.

The decision in 1986 to restructure the economy and radically review the existing political and economic system has led historians to re-examine the factors responsible for the policies adopted fifty years ago. In the Gorbachev period, revisiting the past was accompanied by a revision of ideas on the practicality of alternatives which were rejected.[114] The starting point for the review was the issue of co-operation in the 1920s and the collectivisation of agriculture in the 1930s.[115] A re-examination of the Leninist co-operative plan and its role in a socialist society was central to the argument of those who considered 'one of the most important tasks of *perestroika* to be the democratisation of the economy on the basis of co-operation'.[116] The re-study required 'a re-conceptualisation of the essence and significance of collectivisation, in so far as the latter substituted the multifarious forms of co-operation in agriculture into one form of productive co-operative. It posed the question of whether collectivisation was a great social revolution representing a step forward toward socialism by a peasant country, or a tragedy'.[117]

There is one footnote to this general conclusion. The demise of the co-operative was not synonymous with the elimination of all non-state economic activity. This continued to exist in two main fields – agriculture and small-scale building work. In the case of the former, despite being ideologically frowned upon and restricted in the scale of its operations, the private household plot was a major contributor to local and national food consumption, with Uzbeks and Georgians travelling thousands of miles to markets in Russia. Building workers, often itinerant, the so-called *shabashniki*, who undertook contract work, also faced considerable harassment. Although employed mainly as repairers rather than as constructors of new buildings, they filled a recognised niche in society for the provision of a vital service: for example, constructing farm outbuildings, single-storey houses in smaller towns and car garages in cities.[118] The legal reforms initiated by Gorbachev's perestroika sought to harness the skills and initiative of such individuals.

Notes

1   The name 'Decembrists' was given to the Russian revolutionary group who led an unsuccessful revolt against Nicholas I in December 1825. Most of its members were army officers from aristocratic families and élite regiments, and had acquired a first-hand knowledge of the West in the Napoleonic campaigns. Their aims were to establish basic freedoms and a constitutional government in Russia and to abolish serfdom..

2   K. A. Pazhitnov, *Istoriya kooperativnoi mysli*, 2-oe izd., Petrograd, 1918, p. 237.

3   See *Sbornik: Na slavnom postu*, St Petersburg, 1900 g.

4   Pazhitnov, op. cit.

5   Chernyshevskii never actually used the term 'co-operation', a word which first appeared in Russian texts in 1866.

6   Pazhitnov, op. cit., p. 257. This decade saw the publication of a series of monographs on the subject. See, for example, N. Kachalov, *Arteli v drevnei i nyneshnei Rossii*, St Petersburg, 1864; N. Ziber, *Potrebitel'nyya obshchestva*, St Petersburg, 1869; A. Yakovlev, *Ocherki narodnago kredita v Zapadnoi Evrope i v Rossii*, St Petersburg, 1869; N. Kolyupanov, *Prakticheskoe rukovodstvo k ustroistvu sel'skikh i remeslennykh bankov*, St Petersburg, 1870.

7   I. V. Maiorov, *Trudovoe tovarishchestvo. (Kooperatsiya)*, St Petersburg, 1907, p. 16.

8   The Russian *mir*, or village commune, had existed at least since the sixteenth century and was a form of peasant self-government. It had considerable powers over individual peasant households, including tax collection and land redistribution. It was regarded by Slavophiles and Populists (*narodniki*) as a uniquely Russian institution which snould be preserved. The word *mir* translates into English as 'world', 'community', 'peace'.

9   A. Malakhov, *Russkaya kooperatsiya i kommunisty*, London, 1921, p. 12. An industrial *artel* essentially consisted of a team of peasants working together and sharing their collective earnings equally.

10   V. F. Luginin and A. V. Yakovlev, *Sel'skiya ssudnyya tovarishchestv*, St Petersburg, 1870.

11   K. Marx and F. Engels, *Selected Correspondence*, Moscow, 1956, p. 412; A. Walicki, *The Controversy over Capitalism*, Clarendon Press, Oxford, 1969, especially Part III, Chapters 3 and 4.

12   Maiorov, op. cit., p. 4.

13   Ibid., p. 20.

14   Ibid.

15   V. I. Lenin, *The Development of Capitalism in Russia*, St Petersburg, 1899.

16   Maiorov, op. cit., p. 25.

17   Pazhitnov, op. cit., p. 260. There is evidence that Schultze-Delitzsch wanted to visit Russia in order to set up the first society.

18   K. Ballin, *Pervaya pamyatnaya knizhka russkikh potrebitel'nykh obshchestv*, St Petersburg, 1870, pp. 46–7.

19   Pazhitnov, op. cit., p. 260.

20   *Vestnik kooperatsii*, no. 2, 1910.

21   *Zemstva* were institutions of self-government created by a law of January 1864 aimed at modernising and democratising local government and at stimulating local initiative to meet the urgent needs of the countryside.

22   Lenin, Khrushchev and Gorbachev in particular, among successive Soviet leaders, frequently chided Russian (and Soviet) citizens for their 'lack of responsibility'.

23   T. C. Owen, 'Entrepreneurship in the Structure of Enterprise in Russia, 1800–1880', in G. Guroff and F. Carstensen (eds), *Entrepreneurship in Imperial Russia and the Soviet Union*, Princeton University Press, Princeton NJ, 1983, p. 61.

24   Ibid., p. 83. Even in St Petersburg, the 'window on the West', where joint stock companies were more common, the latter 'actually perpetuated the old patrimonial pattern of state domination, while the smaller, less technologically advanced share partnerships struggled for an economic livelihood outside the state's control. . . . By 1880 neither had been able to break free of the state's awesome power' (ibid., p. 74).

25   'Pervoi vserossiiskoi kooperativnoi s"yezd v Nizhne-Novgorod' in *Sputnik kooperatora*,

Petrograd, 1916, p. 93.

26   Because of the popularity of the *zemstva* and their proximity to their electorates, the central government punished them by reducing their income.

27   *Kustars* were small rural producers whose activities were normally confined to winter. They usually used only hand tools, though mechanical devices appeared after 1906. For a full discussion of this group, see O. Crisp, *Studies in the Russian Economy before 1914*, Macmillan, London, 1976, pp. 48–54.

28   The term came to be applied to those peasants who were, comparatively speaking, better off than others.

29   A. Volgin, *Osnova narodnichestva*, St Petersburg, 1896, p. 57. Thus prosperous *kustars* were small capitalists who took advantage of their workers (poorer *kustars*), paying them less than factory employees. As in cottage manufacturing in England, self-employed *kustars* laboured longer than the 16 hours a day customary for factory workers. (See P. Maslov, *Usloviya razvitiya sel'skikh obshchin v Rossii*, St Petersburg, 1903, p. 406.

In the Pechora region in the far north, fishing co-operatives were established, based on the *artel* system in operation for centuries in the north of the country. The members of a fishing *artel* usually entered into an oral contract before the commencement of the season and decided on the quantity of nets, string and food to be supplied by each of the 5–15 members. They exchanged (rather than sold) their catch for goods brought by a merchant, who frequently held a monopolistic position. Bartering was frequently accompanied by money-lending, which virtually enserfed the entire population of the area, including small shopkeepers. They were rescued from this situation by the creation in 1909 (by the local authorities, not the fishermen themselves) of a co-operative credit society. By 1918 a large number of co-operative associations had formed themselves into the Pechora Union of Co-operative Societies. Among the tangible benefits offered by the co-operatives were the educational campaigns instituted by the societies, the introduction of modern methods of fish preservation, and the elimination of the middleman.

Members of these *artels* resemble groups of workers (*shabashniki*) working in the building trade in Soviet Russia in the 1970s. (See G. Andrusz, 'Soviet Housing Policy in Transition', in J. Sillince (ed.) *Housing Policy in the USSR and Eastern Europe*, Routledge/Croom Helm, London, 1990).

30   E. T. Blanc, *Co-operative Movement in Russia*, Macmillan, New York, 1924, pp. 54–5.

31   D. Ilinskii, *Siberskie kreditnye kooperativnye obshchestva i Moskovskii Narodny Bank*, Moscow, 1917, p. 10; N. Makarov, *Krestyanskoe kooperativnoe dvizhenie v Zapadnoi Sibiri*, Moscow, 1910.

32   See Blanc, op. cit., p. 79.

33   A co-operative society's capital had three components: an entrance fee of 2–10 roubles, the sale of shares (10–20 roubles) and loans. The general assembly decided how many shares a new member was entitled to purchase. In English consumer co-operatives, profits were distributed solely in proportion to purchases, thus removing any inducement to hold more than one share. By contrast, in Russia dividends were paid on the number of shares held. A century later, in the late 1980s, the issue of the right to possess multiple shares was central to the polemical debate on the future of co-operatives in the USSR.

34   A. Antsyferov, *Moskovskii Narodny Bank*, Moscow, 1917.

35   V. F. Totomiants, *Svod svedenii o deyatel'nosti potrebitel'skikh obshchestv v Rossii voobshch i za 1903 god v chastnosti*, St Petersburg, 1905, pp. 19–21. See the same author's other works: *Potrebitel'nyya obshchestva: Istoriya, teoriya i praktika*, St Petersburg, 1908; *Kooperatsiya v russkoi derevne*, St Petersburg, 1908.

A burgeoning literature on different aspects of the co-operative movement appeared particularly after the 1905 Revolution. See, for instance: I. Kh. Ozerov, *Obshchestva potrebitelei*, St Petersburg, 1897; V. Vorontsov, *Artelnyya nachinaniya russkogo obshchestva*, St Petersburg, 1895; A. I. Chuprov, *Melkii kredit i kooperatsiya*, St Petersburg, 1909; A. N. Antsyferov, *Ocherki po kooperatsii*, St Petersburg, 1911; N. P. Giber, *Sistema kooperatisya*, St Petersburg, 1911; S. N. Prokopovich, *Kooperativnoe dvizhenie v Rossii: Ego teoriya i praktika*, St Petersburg, 1913; N. V. Chaikovskii, *Soyuz Sibirskikh maslodel'nnykh artelei*, Moscow, 1914; A. V. Merkulov, *Istoricheskii ocherk potrebitel'skikh kooperatsii v Rossii*, St Petersburg, 1915; N. G. Bryanskii, *Moskovskiya proizvoditel'no-trudovyya artel*, St Petersburg, 1915; M. L. Kheisin, *50 let potrebitel'skoi kooperatsii v Rossii*, St Petersburg, 1915.

36   A. A. Nikolaev, *Teoriya i praktika kooperativnogo dvizheniya*, Moscow, 1908, p. 19.

37   J. V. Bubnoff, *The Co-operative Movement in Russia. Its History, Significance and Character*, Manchester, 1917.

38   Totomiants, op. cit., p. 7 and passim.

39   In January 1911 Russia had 4,767 'consumer' co-operatives (rising to 7,665 a year later) with half a million members and a turnover of 90 million roubles – equivalent to roughly 13 per cent that of co-operatives in England at that time. The Moscow Union of Consumer Co-operatives contributed about 7 per cent of total turnover. Credit, banking and financial co-operative associations comprised another important group. In 1911 Russia had 3,411 loan–savings and 5,063 credit associations with an estimated 1.5 million and 2.3 million members respectively. This may be compared with Germany (where this type of co-operative was the most developed in Europe), which had 17,493 credit associations. Expansion before 1914 was rapid: credit associations increased to 10,401 with 6.9 million members and the loan–savings co-operatives to 3,728 with 2.2 million members. In other words, the number of co-operatives rose by two-thirds while the membership witnessed a 2.3-fold increase. See A. N. Antsyferov, *Ocherki po kooperatsii: Sbornik lektsii i statei, 1908–1914*, Moscow, 1915. In contrast, *producers* co-operatives were very poorly developed. See Antsyferov, *Moskovskii Narodny Bank*, pp. 169–170.

40   B. V. Ivanov, *Osushchestvlenie Leninskogo kooperativnogo plana v Sibiri (1920–1927 gg.)*, Tomsk, 1977, p. 7.

41   Malakhov, op. cit., p. 14.

42   Antsyferov, *Ocherki po kooperatsii*, p. 313.

43   Malakhov, op. cit., p. 12.

44   Antsyferov, *Ocherki po kooperatsii*, p. 296.

45   A. P. Klimov, *Potrebitel'skaya kooperatsiya v sisteme razvitogo sotsializma*, Moscow, 1980, p. 16.

46   Their leaders were 'local marshals of the nobility, *zemstva* officials etc.' J. V. Bubnoff, op. cit., p. 47.

47   G. David, *Chto daet potrebitel'skoe obshchestvo zhene rabochego*, Moscow, 1918. This booklet was first published in Russia in 1905 and reprinted in 1918.

48   Ibid., pp. 12–13. Her final paragraph (pp. 18–19) perhaps sheds light on her politics:

> The co-operative movement is the soil in which women can help to improve the lives of all workers and assist them in their striving for a better, just and human existence. This work does not present an obstacle to your family interests and responsibilities; it does not draw you away from that work which is closest to your heart. On the contrary, here there is a merging of personal and public interests.

49   B. V. Ivanov, op. cit., p. 7.

50   M. I. Tugan-Baranovskii, *Sotsial'nyya osnovy kooperatsii*, Petrograd, 1915.

51   Ibid.
52   A. A. Nikolaev, *Teoriya i praktika kooperativnogo dvizheniya*, Moscow, 1908, p. 5.
53   Antsyferov, *Ocherki po kooperatsii*, p. 162.
54   Nikolaev, op. cit., pp. 10–14.
55   Bubnoff, op. cit., p. 47.
56   Antsyferov, *Ocherki po kooperatsii*, p. 162.
57   Bubnoff, op. cit., pp. 298–305.
58   Ibid., p. 304.
59   Ibid., p. 306.
60   Maiorov, op. cit., pp. 29–30.
61   Blanc, op. cit., p. 131; E. M. Kayden and A. N. Antsyferov, *The Co-operative Movement in Russia during the War*, Yale University Press, New Haven, 1929.
62   Blanc, op. cit., p. 138.
63   Ibid., p. 147.
64   Ibid., p. 148.
65   J. V. Bubnoff, 'The Nationalisation of the Moscow Narodny Bank', *The Russian Co-operator*, February 1919, vol. 3, no. 2.
66   V. I. Lenin, 'The Immediate Tasks of the Soviet Government', *Collected Works*, vol. XV, 1922, pp. 207–8.
67   V. P. Danilov, 'Problemy istorii kooperatsii i kollektivizatsii sel'skogo khozyaistva v SSSR', paper presented at the Anglo-Soviet Conference on Recent Developments in Soviet and British Historical Thinking on the Period since 1917, London, 22–24 March 1988.
68   Z. Stencel-Lensky, *Co-operation in Soviet Russia*, London, 1920, p. 20.
69   *Programma i ustav RKP (b)*, Moscow, 1919, p. 139 and passim.
70   V. I. Lenin, *Polnoe sobranie sochenenii*, 5th ed., Politizdat, Moscow, 1958–65, vol. 64, p. 195.
71   Ibid., vol. 45, pp. 372–3.
72   Danilov, op. cit., p. 4.
73   G. Stepanov, *Poltrebitel'skie obshchestva i rabochii klass*, Moscow, 1920, p. 16.
74   V. I. Lenin, *Collected Works*, vol. XVIII, part 2, 1922, p. 219.
75   See International Labour Organisation, *The Co-operative Movement in the Soviet Union*, Geneva, 1925, p. 270.
76   Ibid., pp. 218–21, 307.
77   Stencel-Lensky, op. cit.
78   N. Krestinsky, 'Russia's New Financial Policy', *Soviet Russia*, vol. V, no. 6, pp. 234–5.
79   Ibid.
80   L. March, *Egor Ligachev: A Conservative Reformer in the Gorbachev Period*, Research Papers in Russian and East European Studies No. REES97/2, Centre for Russian and East European Studies, University of Birmingham, 1997.
81   International Labour Office, op. cit. p. 342.
82   Although the *zemstva* had pioneered the formation of health services and were acknowledged as best placed to fulfil this function, they frequently failed to do so.
83   This tactic was not to be confined within the boundaries of the Soviet Union, for an 'active struggle for the emancipation of the co-operatives from the leadership and influence of the bourgeois compromiser' had to be continued worldwide through a co-operative department organised within the Third Communist International (Blanc, op. cit., p. 266.)
84   A. G. Orloff, 'The Revival of the Co-operative Movement in Russia', *The Russian*

Economist, London, 23 March 1922.

85   E. H. Carr and R. W. Davies, *Foundations of a Planned Economy, 1926–1929*, vol. I, Macmillan, London, 1969, p. 16.
86   A. A. Nikolaev, *Promyslovaya kooperatsiya v Sibiri 1920–1937*, Novosibirsk, 1988.
87   Carr and Davies, op. cit., p. 150.
88   P. Fedirko, *We're Working with the Prosperity of the Peasant in Mind*, Novosti, Moscow, 1989, p. 4.
89   Carr and Davies, op. cit., pp. 34, 149–53.
90   Ibid., p. 126.
91   Ibid., p. 150.
92   I. Bukharin, 'O Kooperatsii', *Sovetskoe potrebitel'skoe obshchestvo*, 2, 1989, pp. 44–9.
93   Postanovlenie Sovnarkoma i TsK VKP(b), 'O rabote potrebitel'skikh kooperatsii v derevne', 29 September 1935.
94   Carr and Davies, op. cit., p. 155.
95   Ibid., p. 206.
96   Ibid., pp. 385, 934.
97   Ibid., p. 385.
98   Ibid., p. 390.
99   E. M. Dement'ev, *Fabrika: Chto ona delaet naseleniya i chto ona u nego beret'*, Moscow, 1897; M. Tugan-Baranovskii, *Russkaya fabrika*, izd., 2-oe, 1900.
100 Carr and Davies, op. cit., pp. 390–93.
101 Ibid., p. 393.
102 *KPSS v rezolyutsiyakh, s"ezdov, konferentsii i plenum TsK*, Moscow, 1954, vol. 2, p. 49 (cited in Carr and Davies, op. cit., p. 394).
103 Both points of view could be heard in the debates surrounding the 1988 Law on Co-operatives. (See Chapter 4.)
104 Carr and Davies, op. cit., p. 399.
105 Goskomstat, *Narodnoe khozyaistvo SSSR za 70 let*, Finansy i Statistika, Moscow, 1987, p. 11.
106 L. I. Abalkin, 'Vozrozhdenie kooperatsii', *Sovetskoe potrebitel'skoe obshchestvo*, 2, 1989, p. 5.
107 Ibid.
108 Carr and Davies, op. cit., pp. 653–4.
109 Ibid.
110 Ibid., p. 655.
111 Danilov, op. cit., p. 18.
112 Fedirko, op. cit., p. 4.
113 *The System of Civilised Co-operatives in the System of Socialism*, Novosti, Moscow, 1989, p. 23.
114 R. W. Davies, *Soviet History in the Gorbachev Revolution*, Macmillan, London, 1989.
115 See for instance, of the many texts on this subject, R. W. Davies, *The Industrialisation of Soviet Russia. The Socialist Offensive: the Collectivisation of Soviet Agriculture, 1929–30*, Macmillan, London, 1980.
116 Danilov, op. cit., p. 1. See also *Kommunist*, no. 18, 1987, pp. 28–38.
117 Danilov, op. cit.
118 A. Simurov, 'Ustupili mesto shabashnikam', *Pravda*, 20 November 1983; A. Sukontsev, 'Zhigulevskie stradaniya', *Pravda*, 19 December 1984.

4 The Co-operative Revival under Gorbachev

Introduction

The resurrection of co-operatives, which for fifty years had lain dormant as a property and organisational form, can be charted from the Plenary Session of the Central Committee of the CPSU in April 1985, the XXVII Congress of the CPSU in February 1986, and the XIX Party Conference in June 1988 to the allocation of 40 seats to co-operative representatives in the new Parliament of people's deputies.[1]

In its main contours the Soviet economic system that was in existence in the mid-1980s was the same as the one that had come into being in the 1930s. This model had three forms of property (or 'economic subjects'): state enterprises (which were state property), state co-operatives, and family household economies (essentially the private household plot of land). In the late 1980s this was described by some people as representing an Asiatic mode of production (or a 'system of administrative terror'), where people were motivated to act not by market signals but by a pattern of privileges and punishments. The aim of perestroika from the start was to expand the second and third forms of property at the expense of the first.

The statements legitimising the existence of co-operative property found in chapter two of the 1977 Soviet Constitution (Articles 10–18), entitled *The Economic System*, were intentionally vague. The articles were not wholly reassuring about the future of co-operatives, for they conveyed the impression that over time they would disappear. Just nine years later, at the XXVII Party Congress in 1986, Mr Gorbachev came out as a champion of co-operatives, stating that they had 'far from exhausted their potential'.[2] He went on to say that 'wherever the need exists, utmost support should be given to the establishment and growth of co-operative enterprises and organisations'.[3] This announcement was in fact a policy statement, for it was followed by a series of Party and Government decrees on the setting up of co-operatives in different spheres of economic activity.[4]

In August 1986 the Council of Ministers published a decree allowing co-operatives to be established in one sphere of activity, namely the processing or recycling of raw materials and waste products. Within six months over 13,000 co-operatives had been registered. This was the first stage in the Government's programme of creating new areas in which co-operatives could function. Fears were now being voiced by important political actors at the Plenary Session of the Central Committee held in June 1987 that co-operatives and 'individual labour activity' were tantamount to the restoration of private economic practices.[5]

These developments were paralleled by a barrage of decrees affecting the institutional edifice that had been erected over the past six decades. It began with the Law on State Enterprises, enacted in June 1987.[6] This was accompanied by a whole range of decrees enumerating the new functions of the major State Committees (Gosplan, Gossnab), changes in the method of determining prices and enhancements to the role played by banks in the process of reorienting the whole economic system.[7] Alongside the legislation affecting the organisation of the economy, the Central Committee of the CPSU and the Council of Ministers issued a decree which laid the foundation stone of the country's political transformation: 'On improving the activities of the republican organs of administration'.[8]

Of greater significance than the 1987 Law on State Enterprises, which failed to achieve its objectives, was the decree on 'Individual Labour Activity',[9] which permitted individuals or families to obtain permits to run small businesses in such areas as private medicine, tuition and house repairs. This was shortly followed by a decree encouraging the use of existing legal provisions to expand co-operatives in the manufacturing and service sectors.[10] Then came the Law on Co-operation,[11] which was accompanied by a range of 'lower level' governmental acts on, for instance, joint ventures, leasing arrangements and share ownership. Despite cries that the changes were being introduced too slowly, the actual pace of legal transformation was really quite rapid. Following the Law on Leasing came the Law on Property, the Law on Land and the Law on Local Self-government. This corpus of legislation signalled that the country was travelling in a radically new direction.

On 26 March Gorbachev delivered a strong speech in defence of co-operatives to the Fourth All-Union Congress of Collective Farmers: he spoke of the advantages of co-operatives, saying that they were flexible, could meet demands unsatisfied by the state, especially for services, allow disadvantaged groups to be integrated into the economy, and provide employment. This so-called 'situational approach' (*situatsionnyi podkhod*) or 'incrementalism' continued until the publication of the draft Law on Co-operatives [12] in March 1988, which after a nationwide debate quickly passed onto the statute book in May and came into force on 1 July 1988. Opposition to the Law emerged immediately, compelling the first major amendments and restrictions on co-operatives to be made in December 1988. Co-operatives thus became the issue around which supporters and opponents of fundamental reform could crystallise.

The overall outcome of this burst of legislative activity was the creation of a wholly new economic structure consisting of state enterprises, individual family firms, co-operatives, joint ventures, joint stock companies, leasing concerns and *de facto* (if not *de jure*) private enterprise. Co-operatives occupied an important place in this evolving system. They represented neither an 'intermediate' nor a 'transitory' property form. Nor were they the culmination of the Government's decision to shift away from the publicly owned, centralised, administrative-command economy. They were indicative of a society in transition towards an expansion in the size and realm of non-state property; towards, that is, a society described by Hayek as 'several property'. The old Stalinist single-property form was replaced; and even the anticipated 30 per cent of the economy which was to be retained under state control would henceforth run quite differently from in the past, not least because it would also have to operate in an environment open to market forces.

The emergence of different types of property ownership adds another dimension to the country's social stratification. It inevitably gave rise to property-group interests. The interplay between the property-groups led to the formation of political factions (some within the Communist Party itself), which by 1991 were beginning to mature into formal parties.[13]

The Ideological Debate

In a number of respects the situation which faced Gorbachev when he became General Secretary of the Communist Party of the Soviet Union (CPSU) in 1985 was similar to that faced by Lenin when he introduced the New Economic Policy in 1920 after a period of extreme centralisation when money had all but disappeared as a medium of exchange. Co-operatives were to form an integral part of Lenin's policy. Similarly, in 1986 the radical changes in economic and social policy heralded by perestroika were necessitated by the need to reverse declining growth rates in production and productivity and to counter bureaucratic rigidities throughout the system. In his speech to the XXVII Party Congress, the last ever General Secretary of the Communist Party of the Soviet Union pointed to the necessity of 'taking a fresh look at some theoretical ideas and concepts. This applies to such major problems as the interaction of the productive forces and the production relations, *socialist ownership* and its economic forms, the co-ordination of centralism with the autonomy of economic organisations and so forth'.[14]

A report submitted to the Central Committee of the Communist Party in 1984 described the existing economic system 'that had taken shape during a period of extensive economic development' as being out of date and a brake on development.[15] In order to rectify the situation, 'long established ideas, let alone prejudices' had to be removed. The Party Leader continued this line of argument, pointing out rather poignantly that 'unfortunately, there is a widespread view that any change in the economic mechanism is practically a retreat from the principles of socialism'.[16] Co-operatives were identified as one of the means for reviving the fortunes of the economy. Industrial co-operatives, which survived purges, industrialisation and the Second World War, were closed down by a series of legislative decrees in the 1950s. Looking back on them in 1988, Aganbegyan, the leading pre-perestroika economic reformer, judged them to have been 'quite widespread in industry, especially in the production of consumer goods'.[17] Gorbachev took up the point:

> We also stand for full clarity on the question of co-operative property. It has far from exhausted its possibilities in socialist production, in providing better satisfaction of people's needs. Whenever the need exists, utmost support should be given to the establishment and growth of co-operative enterprises and organisations. These should become widespread in the manufacture and processing of products, in housing construction . . . and in the sphere of services and trade.[18]

He wanted to see an expansion in services to ease the burden of domestic work, make it easier to have a car serviced and a flat repaired.[19] References were made elsewhere in the report to the need to give every form of encouragement to the building of co-operative and owner-occupied housing.[20] But the renewed emphasis on co-operatives meant more than just improving the way in which the economy operated; it was indicative of a return to 'experimental' socialist forms associated with Lenin and the New Economic Policy.

The references to socialist democracy and the greater involvement of the population in the management of the country were also a return to Lenin's socialist vision as expressed in *State and Revolution*. Gorbachev pointed out that society's development was 'inconceivable and impossible without a further development of all aspects of socialist democracy'. Government should not be the privilege of a narrow circle of professionals for 'we know that the socialist system can develop successfully only when the people really run their own affairs, when millions of people are involved in political life'.[21] The Party Programme explicitly referred to the role of co-operatives in this context: 'The Party helps to improve the work of co-operatives and other co-operative organisations and associations, regarding them as an important form of socialist self-government and an effective means of developing the national economy'.[22]

These views uttered on the world stage in 1986 were among the first lines of a drama whose first act ended in December 1991 when Gorbachev was unceremoniously and crassly expelled from the Kremlin. Some of the scenes were almost dominated by the polemic over the future of co-operatives. In 1998, as Act 2 continues to unfold, there is scarcely sight or sound of co-operatives.

As late as 1986, for the vast majority of Soviet philosophers and economists co-operatives constituted the single most important obstacle to the country's technical and social progress. In 1985 even the Institute of Economics of the USSR Academy of Sciences was still contending that by 1990 there would be a merging of collective farm (co-operative) property with state property, for by then the important transition to a classless society would have been basically completed.[23] Conventional wisdom still held that social progress could be measured by each further increment of statisation.[24] A year later, this stance was being denounced as formal, abstract reasoning which favoured state over co-operative ownership on the basis that nationalised property ensured that all individuals were completely equal in their relationship to the means of production. Those hostile to co-operatives were castigated for identifying all progress in socialist society with, firstly, the institution of a legally equal relationship between workers and the socialised means of production and, secondly, the ever increasing dominance of the state in regulating the economy.[25]

According to the 'reformist' faction, there was sufficient historical evidence to show that, when the limits to further statisation were transgressed so that literally all aspects of economic life were 'supposed' to operate according to a single blueprint drawn up by the planning authorities, both the economy and people's consciousness were subjected to 'undesirable and objectionable deformations'.[26] The critique came from within the paradigm and bore its hallmark in its ponderous language. Nevertheless it pointed to an important linkage in Soviet Marxism between the long march of socialism and the 'permanent statisation of property'. When glasnost allowed closeted critics of the system to examine the ideology, they found that the system was flawed because it neglected the human factor; the society contained a defective gene which cultivated passivity and a culture of dependency amongst very broad sections of the population.

Gorbachev's introduction of the notion of the 'human factor' into political discourse justifies drawing a parallel between him and Martin Luther. In the first instance, this was the first time in Russian history that 'the individual' was elevated to a position of prominence over the collective. In this sense, perestroika was the Russian equivalent of the Reformation. The second parallel lies in the fact that Mikhail Gorbachev, like Martin Luther, began by attacking corruption (associated with indulgences [privileges]) within the established church (the Communist Party and the Catholic Church respectively). Neither man envisaged leaving the church or creating a new religion; they sought to reform the doctrine and practices of their systems by working within them.[27]

The paternalistic system of government combined with the statisation of property had created an 'irresponsible attitude towards resources'. This criticism was applied to explain the degradation of the environment, the criminal waste of energy, the Chernobyl disaster and the poor upkeep of residential accommodation. Because resources which in theory belong to everyone in fact belong to no one, little incentive existed among the population to use them economically. By the same token, low productivity and poor motivation resulted directly from the fact that workers did not own the fruits of their labour.

In less than three years the orthodoxy which had grown up over the previous sixty years had not just been subjected to verbal abuse. It had become the *heresy*. Its former supremacy had been supplanted by its opposite, the privatisation of property. Henceforth, each increment of privatisation was deemed a measure of social progress. The radical quality of the new orthodoxy is reflected in the view expressed by one economist:

> Today's economic proposals all point in one direction – privatisation. Our economy simply cannot survive without private ownership. . . . We cannot afford to wait decades or even centuries for private ownership to evolve naturally as it did in other countries. We need a fully-fledged market economy now. . . . Privatisation must involve giving away state property to the public or selling it for just symbolic sums.[28]

This sense of demanding and uncompromising (I want it now!) urgency for the immediate and rapid transformation of the economy and society is nothing novel in Russian history. Peter the Great in the eighteenth century set himself the task of introducing modern industrial technology into the country and Europeanising Russian society. His new city and window on Europe, St Petersburg, was built at horrendous human cost. Apart from westernising courtly habits, many of his other achievements did not survive his lifetime. Then, in the latter part of the nineteenth century Count Witte set about industrialising and liberalising the economy. But the *political* progress brought by the liberal democratic revolution in February 1917, the subsequent abdication of the Tsar and the decision to convoke a Constituent Assembly proved too slow for Lenin, and his decision to force the pace of change inaugurated civil war, further destruction of the backward economy and further misery. At the end of the 1920s the *economic* progress being made by the country was too slow for Stalin: the result was the massive suffering, starving and privation caused by collectivisation and the five-year plans. As the country entered the final decade of this century, radicals were once again forcing the pace. Gorbachev, rather than being perceived as having learnt the lessons of his country's history, was pilloried for lack of daring and vision and for acting as a bureaucrat hindering change.

Neither Engels in *Anti-Duhring* nor Marx in *A Critique of the Gotha Programme* had made any mention of the possibility that co-operative forms could be used as a way of organising labour in a communist society or in the earlier transitional (socialist) stage. However, Engels had at times expressed some guarded support for co-operatives – to the effect that he and Marx had never doubted the utility of employing co-operative forms of production in the transition to a fully communistic economy.[29] It is difficult to escape the feeling that their generally non-committal and dismissive attitudes towards the co-operative property form had at least something to do with their hostility towards the anti-statism of Bakunin and the co-operative decentralism of Proudhon.

Marx expressed his views on co-operatives in the Charter of the First International, written in 1864.[30] The experience of establishing co-operatives was, he thought, one of the main achievements of the proletariat in the preceding fifteen years. Co-operatives had shown themselves to be formative in introducing workers to the ideas of collectivism and mutual aid, thereby preparing them for socialism. They were, therefore, the first breach in the system of capitalist relations, but still no more than an intermediate stage between capitalism and socialism. As a 'lower' form of socialism, they could not arrest the development of capitalism or adequately alleviate poverty, since co-operative membership was confined to the more privileged sections of the working class. Co-operatives were relegated, in Marx and Engels's schema, to the function of 'preparing' the material and ideological ground for the growth of socialism within the womb of capitalism. They had their origins under capitalism and were destined to die with it since, under socialism, the co-operative was superfluous.[31]

The change in attitude that Marx and Engels held towards co-operatives took place over decades. Lenin, always in a hurry (perhaps because of his knowledge of his genetic endowment of arterial sclerosis and therefore of the need to act quickly), reduced his change of mind to seven years. Socialism was perceived as being based on direct state control over all production and distribution, which was managed through a highly centralised system.[32] In his 'socialism as book-keeping phase', Lenin, along with many other leading Bolsheviks during the period of War Communism, considered that the whole of the national economy right down to the smallest detail should be subordinated to the state. That is, the state was to determine in the case of each individual enterprise what to produce, how to produce it and how to distribute what was produced. The planning of socialist production was rigidly and simply linked to administrative methods of managing the economy. (It was left to Stalin to actually oversee the construction of this system, which Brezhnev's men tried to perfect and which Gorbachev was left to dismantle.) Lenin's ideas on the management of the economy, formulated in the abnormal but no doubt thrilling conditions of revolution and civil war, formed part of the legacy that he left to his successors.

In 1919 he was still adhering to the position that co-operative enterprises were an integral part of the capitalist economic structure. As late as March 1921, in his tract *The Tax in Kind* he continued to declare that 'the small commodity producers' co-operatives . . . inevitably give rise to petty-bourgeois, capitalist relations, facilitate their development, push the small capitalists into the foreground and benefit them most'.[33] In so far as co-operatives always aimed at making a profit, they were market-oriented. In this sense, the co-operative did carry within it the germ of capitalism. Within two years this observation was transformed from an indictment (associated with 'counter-revolutionary socialist revolutionaries and Mensheviks') to an encomium.

By 1923 enterprises had been re-established on a commercial, cost-accounting basis and money circulation had replaced barter. When Lenin recognised that a socialist economy like any other would probably be built on 'personal interest', the theoretical obstacles to including the co-operative enterprises within the structure of the economy evaporated.

During perestroika, Soviet authors came to maintain that, for Lenin, the virtue of the co-operative movement resided in its offering each individual the opportunity to demonstrate initiative. Moreover, it allowed a fusion of personal economic interest with group interest and, through a series of mediating units, with the national interest. The principal problem for Lenin, as for all socialists, was how to establish the boundaries between the private and public, the point at which the private interest should be subordinated to the general interest and the way in which they could best be combined. The ultimate theoretical reason adduced by Lenin to justify this ideological shift was that by 1923 'political power is in the hands of the working class [and] this political power owns all the means of production'. Suddenly, under Soviet power, 'much that was fantastic, even romantic, even banal in the dreams of the old co-operators (Owen, Fourier), . . . is becoming an unvarnished reality'.[34]

The volte-face and discovery of the virtues of co-operation were premised on the real problems facing the state and society. These problems were partly the creation of the immediate circumstances of revolution and civil war, partly the outcome of Bolshevik ideology and partly a consequence of the cultural legacy of tsarism.[35] These factors reinforced one another to produce a centralised and overbureaucratic economy and polity. While reflecting upon the problems of economic management Lenin discovered the benefits of the co-operative system: it was anti-bureaucratic and encouraged individual effort and initiative.

The bureaucratic mind was a singularly important obstacle to development, for it impelled each lower-level agency to transfer responsibility for decision making whenever possible to a higher authority. As a result minor problems which should have been resolved by people on the spot accumulated at the apex of the Party and state structures.

At the XI Party Congress, one of the graphic examples chosen by Lenin to illustrate the weakness of a system which required that decisions had to be agreed with the Centre may be paraphrased as follows: One month proved to be insufficient time for 4,700 senior officials within the Soviet administrative system to reach a decision to purchase, on exceptionally favourable terms from a French merchant, tinned meat for Moscow's starving population. Eventually, the organisation responsible for food arrived at an agreement with the Ministry of Foreign Trade. But they then had to wait until the matter had been discussed in the Politburo. During this period the tinned meat rotted in the ship's hold.[36]

Such practices as this, both past and present, led Lenin (and writers today) to refer to the revival of Russian Manilovism, after the character in Gogol's *Dead Souls* known for his smug complacency, inactivity and daydreaming. The situation repeated itself in January 1992 when, during a severe meat shortage in the capital, a container-load of meat from Britain was held up in Moscow by health inspectors. There was *some* justification on the part of the Russian officials, but without the intervention of international television cameras it is likely that the delay spoken of by Lenin would have been replicated.[37]

Communist bureaucrats, Lenin complained, set up committees, held meetings and compiled plans to spend millions or trillions of roubles, yet were totally unconcerned about saving the kopek which they had been given and even less about attempting to turn it into two kopeks. This criticism has more than a faintly familiar ring: both Gogol and Gorbachev would immediately and intuitively understand the criticism. Small wonder that a number of senior Russian politicians, economists and commentators in present-day Russia warn against large sums of money being granted or loaned to their government or to other petitioners for fear of it disappearing into a big black hole.[38]

It was in order to overcome this particular and generalised problem and to avoid being 'dragged down by the foul bureaucratic marsh of writing papers, talking about issuing decrees and generally drowning in the sea of paper'[39] that Lenin emphasised the need to be more selective in the recruitment of officials. However, he soon came to realise that the basic cause of the inertia found in the Soviet administrative apparatus and of the problems of managing the economy were systemic. In other words, recruitment policy was a relatively minor problem: the changes which were necessary could not be implemented by streamlining the state's personnel department. Had he lived he might also have realised that the plurality of property forms which he was recommending was fundamentally incompatible with a political system called the 'dictatorship of the proletariat' – a polity which, under his aegis, in 1921, having already proscribed other political parties, now banned political factions within the single party. The fatal flaw of co-operatives, as seen by Lenin prior to the revolution, was that, in so far as they functioned as commercial bodies, under the pressure of competition they had a tendency to be converted into joint stock companies. It was not this 'flaw' that was 'fatal', but Lenin's political dictatorship.

Schoolman-like squabbling over the sacred texts concealed an important question on the usefulness of Marxism as a method for analysing both the social forces involved in the co-operative movement and the polemical debate to which it had given rise. The period from 1986 to 1991 saw a war being waged at both levels. Completely in keeping with the new rationality – which condemned 'cant, sophistry and scholasticism' in favour of applying a utilitarian calculus to institutions and structures – defenders of 'nationalised' property were being required to corroborate their arguments with factual, empirically based evidence. At the heart of the debate sat the key words in the

Marxist lexicon: class relations and class power.

Fear of the class implications of co-operatives had made Marx and Engels (and many Bolsheviks) circumspect in their approach towards them. Many in the Party and most of the élite were, with good cause, afraid that if the co-operatives grew richer through gaining control over economic resources, their growth would be at the existing élite's expense. The case levelled against co-operatives by the *nomenklatura* in Gorbachev's time was never really about equality. After all, although Marx and Lenin declared that socialism meant the abolition of private ownership of the means of production and the abolition of classes, they did not reduce social progress in socialist society to ensuring that everyone stood in equal relation to the socialised means of production. And even if such equal relations were somehow established, Marx could be cited on the necessity of guarding against 'communism of the barrack room' based as it is on the 'envy of the lumpen'.[40]

In the course of this intense debate between 1986 and 1991, interpretations of income distribution and equality became more sophisticated. Once again attention was drawn to Lenin's critical review of the damaging effects that the policies pursued under War Communism (1918–21) had had on the economy. When these policies were rescinded in 1921, he acknowledged and stressed that the movement towards full equality simply by confiscating and nationalising property would be to no one's benefit, especially if there were no workers or peasants available and willing to work. In his view, 'attracting people to work is the most important and most difficult problem of socialism'. The case for giving people incentives and for income differentials had therefore been acknowledged. Thus, the struggle which Gorbachev was waging with his opponents was no longer about ensuring equality of income between citizens; it was about the right of existing groups of resource controllers and allocators to determine who got what. The co-operatives were seen, and rightly so, as Trojan Horses.[41]

The theorising of equality and co-operation within Soviet Marxism is fundamentally linked to the question of class and, *ipso facto*, to property relations. For this reason the tone of the ideological debate attained a particularly high pitch of antagonism. From as early as 1987 this was manifested in the maturation of factions within the Communist Party to form groupings akin to separate political parties. The *real* differences of opinion – which parties represent – were obscured by the iconic culture's construction of a conflict between Gorbachev and Yeltsin. Already by 1988 Gorbachev was draped in Kerensky's mantle, appearing as the statesman of moderation and compromise. Yeltsin had visibly and willingly become the populist and 'maximalist', and thus in an ironic way, a Bolshevik, at least in strategy.

Soviet sociologists had even before perestroika ceased to analyse the social structure in terms of classes, as defined by the most restricted Marxist paradigm. Glasnost now allowed a public discussion to take place on how people have different interests and needs and different access to goods and services, which depend on their occupation, their role in society and in the management of the economy, their place of residence and nationality. Some groups were recognised as being better able than others to articulate their needs and have them met. A consequence of such empirico-theoretical revelations was to condemn and then reject the myth that everyone stood in an equal relationship to the means of production. It also led to a repudiation of the mandarin proposition that the merging of property forms was inevitable.

From the beginning of restructuring (personified in Gorbachev), which was also the formalisation of the 'new' social system, the leadership realised that its Soviet Marxist theorisation of social class was no longer 'appropriate' for analysing social stratification. However, there was a double-edged bite to this newly discovered realism: it was now both realistic and a necessary feature of the new social system to recognise that the complexity of Russian society means that there is a plurality of social groups – not simply the working class, peasantry, 'white collar' workers and the intelligentsia. Indeed, the old Soviet analysis was oversimplified. Ironically, the social system that has emerged since the demise of the USSR is very amenable to Marxist analysis; this, of course, is one of the reasons for the 'reformers' to abandon and demonise Marxism. Inevitably, the interplay between the conflicting interests of these groups logically led to the formation of political factions (some within the then Communist Party itself).

The Law on Co-operatives insisted that state organisations must give all the help they could to foster co-operatives and increase the efficiency of their operations. Equally important, they had to refrain from putting obstacles in the way of individuals wanting to set them up. The contribution of the mass media was seen as vital, for it was their task to cultivate a moral and psychological atmosphere which would reassure people that being a co-operative member was a socially worthwhile activity. The Law – which allowed any group with a minimum of three members over the age of 16 to form a co-operative – had a number of principal objectives: to boost the economy, encourage its democratisation, and provide employment for workers made redundant in the state sector; to make co-operative membership attractive to very large sections of the population; and to meet the growing unmet demand for consumer goods and services, including food and a range of manufacturing products, thereby reducing queues and shortages.

It was hoped that the size of the black (second) economy would decline as more entrepreneurs operating illegally became incorporated into the formal economy. This would in turn increase local and central government revenue through taxes on members' and workers' incomes and the profits of co-operatives. The higher levels of remuneration received by co-operative workers, because of their higher productivity, would, it was believed, act as an incentive to the development of economic competition between co-operatives themselves and between co-operatives and state enterprises. The co-operatives were at the heart of Russia's grand mass apostasy. Co-operatives, in their various guises and domains, represented one specific kind of response to the newly and candidly acknowledged diversity in Soviet society. The state quickly realised that it had tapped into and released two opposite elemental forces in the society: a desire by some to 'truck, barter and trade' and thereby become richer; and an equally strong desire by others to enforce the communism of the barrack room. As the parlous condition of the economy became known and it tottered towards the brink of collapse, moods of inertia and resignation came to dominate, rather than demands by workers for self-management and workers' control.

Positive features of the co-operative movement which had been highlighted by Lenin and other protagonists in the 1920s were once again pointed out. They were held, for example, to promote an 'organic synthesis between the general and the specific, collective and individual' and, in providing a school for learning the traditions and norms of democracy and self-government, had an educative function helping to foster a psychological disposition antithetical to the culture of dependency.[42] Furthermore, in participating, a 'genuine economic relationship is forged between the individual and the means of production, between labour and its fruits, and an attitude of thrift is inculcated'.[43] But the historical origins and legitimation for co-operatives were no longer seen as deriving from Lenin's tablets alone, for 'these new co-operatives draw upon deep traditions in Russia's distant past. It is frequently forgotten that a form of co-operative economy was widely developed before the October Revolution'.[44]

In September 1989 the Soviet Sociological Association hosted the four-yearly conference of the International Sociological Association. The co-operative movement dominated discussion on the first day, when events were likened to 1917. Speakers reiterated that, although initially perestroika had only affected the upper echelons of society, over the previous twelve months the process of restructuring had begun to resonate amongst large sections of the population. The latter were themselves agents of change through national movements, strikes, the formation of independent trade unions and a proliferation of informal groups. The active involvement of the mass of the population in the redistribution of power and property – which was revolutionary in its essence – was crucial in order to prevent the existing economic and political monopolies from stabilising and then containing the restructuring process at its present level. Amidst the euphoria, where the dominant discourse involved denunciations of the state and monopolies and calls for (a never clearly defined) devolved self-government, it was left to a representative of the co-operative movement in his speech to challenge the anarcho-syndicalists for their Luddism.

These innovations required, almost as a *sine qua non*, legislation on the leasing of capital and land. Existing provisions allowed too much scope for arbitrary interference by local authorities and state enterprise officials.[45] New legislation enacted in November 1989 established, among other things, that the produce from the leased property (land or capital) belonged to the leaseholders, and that state agencies could no longer veto the transfer of state-owned property to leaseholders.[46]

The process of reform had its own logic, so that the issue of leasehold was followed by legislation on actual property ownership. One of the underlying intentions of the initiators of the reform was, firstly, to make a statutory declaration that the state no longer had a monopoly of ownership and, as a corollary, that other property forms, such as co-operatives, leaseholding and joint stock companies should be of equal legal standing.

Just as inexorably, in so far as it granted legal recognition to the private ownership of the means of production, the legislation raised two questions: firstly, would the reinstatement of private ownership lead to the restoration of capitalism; and, secondly, if that were to be the consequence, would it be accompanied by the re-emergence of all the exorcised manifestations of exploitation, unemployment and vast disparities of income and wealth? The wording of the law finally adopted in May 1990 represented a tactical, short-term compromise on the right to full, unrestricted private ownership, especially in the most sensitive area, that of land.[47] There were to be another three years and another confrontation at the White House before the advocates of private property could claim a major victory. But even seven years on, individuals cannot own the freehold to land.[48]

The outcome of the ideological battle fought in favour of co-operatives is open to different interpretations. For some the battle has been lost; co-operative ownership has been pushed aside in favour of private ownership. The whole debate in the Supreme Soviet and in the country over the Law on Co-operation was a testing ground for the assault on statist socialism. The next stage was for international capital to wage war on any form of socialistic or collectivist mode of ownership, of which the co-operative was the most easily identifiable and assailable.

Activities

There were few spheres of economic activity in which co-operatives could not engage. The law allowed them to be established in industry, construction, transport, trading, public catering and services. Producer co-operatives could be set up for: the production, procurement, processing and sale of agricultural produce; the processing of by-products and recycled material and the extraction of minerals; the repair and servicing of equipment; and road and housing construction. They also operated in the fields of recreation and health and in the provision of legal, scientific research, planning, technical design, engineering and other consultancy services, advertising and promotional work, and they engaged in the training of specialists and the setting up of technical training enterprises. In 1989 a group of sociologists and psychologists advertised the services of their co-operative, 'Confidence', which operated a data bank of information on people's 'personal interests'.[49] Another co-operative, 'Mars', was set up by artists, sculptors and art critics to establish a museum of modern art in Moscow.[50]

Then, as if capitulating to the anti-co-operative lobby, in December 1988 the Government issued a decree which it referred to as 'regulating certain types of co-operative activity'.[51] The areas proscribed were: weapons, explosives, fireworks; narcotics; poisons; medical services in the following fields: treatment of cancer; treatment of people suffering from infectious diseases including venereal and contagious skin complaints; treatment of drug addicts and the mentally ill in need of urgent hospitalisation; observation and treatment of pregnant women; surgical operations including abortion. Also prohibited were: the preparation and distribution of medicines; manufacture of alcoholic spirit and wine; operating gambling and card games; the manufacture, buying and selling of articles made from precious metals; providing private general education; publishing works of science, literature and art; producing cinema and video films and organising the exchange, sale and lending and public viewing of films; carrying out any form of foreign currency transaction or taking on a commission basis goods belonging to foreign nationals; manufacturing and restoring icons, church plate and religious symbols. A second supplement specified the types of activities in which co-operatives had the right to engage but only on the basis of contracts concluded with enterprises and institutions specialising in a particular line of activity – for instance, the manufacture, alteration and repair of articles of semi-precious stones and amber; the manufacture of cosmetics and perfumes; helping with foreign tourists.

Typically, in the 'Age of Reform', radicals denounced these restrictions as a triumph for conservative forces. In fact, most of the items and subjects included on this list of restrictions would have been controlled by statutory regulations in most West European countries. The inclusion of videos within the prohibition was directed as much at the making and circulation of pornographic films as at seditious anti-socialist propaganda, while the restrictions on those practising medicine mark the establishment of the sort of more sophisticated controls that already existed in West European countries.[52] However, in too many cases there were no legitimate grounds for excluding co-operatives from providing much needed goods and services; the reality was that the co-operative movement had been forced into retreat by the Soviet bureaucratic behemoth. Nevertheless, despite these new regulations, co-operatives continued to operate within or on the boundary of these forbidden zones.[53] The co-operative movement, acting as a politically astute pressure group, criticised the new regulations, challenged their legality and denounced them as a discouragement to co-operative development.[54] Then, in October 1989, after a sustained anti-co-operative campaign, the Supreme Soviet introduced certain amendments to the Law on Co-operatives.[55]

Consumer co-operatives, which essentially remained part of the state system for distributing goods and food products to the population, began to complain that they were unfairly discriminated against in comparison with 'non-state' co-operatives.[56] The latter, benefiting from the new Law on Co-operatives, were not constrained, as were the statist consumer co-operatives, by the imposition of normatives in the form of commands, instructions and recommendations. Nonetheless, they felt the heavy hand of the state to be omnipresent, and argued that only two 'plans' should come from above: one specifying the level of profits and the other the relationship between the rate of growth of the wage bill and growth in the amount of work performed.

This perception of advantage affected attitudes towards work and the earnings potential in state and non-state co-operatives. In the 'new wave' co-operatives individuals could earn 'by the sweat of their brows' salaries three times the size of those paid to employees in consumer co-operatives. The apparent difference in earnings failed to take into account, however, that the state enterprises were in a better position to obtain goods in short supply, since they were still part of the state's resource-allocating system.[57] This meant that the higher wages in the co-operative sector were highly contingent, being dependent on their ability to obtain materials.[58] Moreover, the low salaries paid to those in state enterprises were compensated for by the sometimes considerable illegal supplementary earnings made by employees by virtue of their access to products in demand. On the other hand, privileges available to members of consumer co-operatives (primarily access to goods) were regarded by some commentators as largely illusory, since they scarcely ever existed, especially for the 100,000 remote villages with over 7 million inhabitants lacking any fixed retail network and condemned as being without a future.

In 1989 Moscow's consumer co-operative chain (*gorpo*) had 2,000 member-shareholders. It was a voluntary organisation whose representatives' meetings decided on the admission of new members, who were charged a (nominal) entrance fee of 50 kopeks and a share deposit of 10 roubles.[59] The benefits were alleged to be quite considerable: members could be elected and elect others to managerial posts; they had preferential rights over non-members in the purchase of goods and benefited from discounts on the sale price; they also received a dividend from the co-operative's profits. In addition they were given preference in the acquisition of shares (*aktsii*) and other securities which the Moscow society had planned to issue.[60] Moscow's status as the capital city also enabled it to attract foreign capital for consumer co-operative ventures. However, because of the numerically small size of the membership and equally small membership fees, necessitated by the need to ensure 'equal access' to the co-operative, this part of the consumer sector lacked capital for investment. The issuing of shares, bonds and other securities was a precondition for co-operatives to be able to expand and fulfil the role that Soviet reformers expected of them.

It was a reflection of the time that a leading advocate of co-operatives, P. Bunich, in 1988 prophesied that in the long run goods requiring a high technical input and large-scale 'capital' would be specialised state enterprises, since they could cut costs and prices because of mass production. Co-operatives would, he stated, concentrate on the manufacture of goods requiring significant inputs of labour, producing in small batches and non-repeatable runs.[61] The question which this posed at the time was whether Bunich actually believed that his forecast was true for the short run and that in the longer term state enterprises would become joint stock companies. Or whether he believed that the co-operative sector (because of its private quality) would always occupy a relatively small niche in the economy. Of course, his allocation of fields of activities to the state and co-operative sectors respectively has to be interpreted in terms of its conformity to the rules in the Soviet game of 'ideology chess'.

Because of the huge amount of waste in the manufacturing process, the

Government placed stress on the use of waste- and by-products. Instead of throwing their waste onto scrap heaps, ministries and enterprises were asked to sell these products to co-operatives. Whether or not the incentives provided for in the decree would have been sufficient to encourage enterprises to take on this extra work will never be known.

There were cases of co-operatives fulfilling functions hitherto not undertaken by the state, such as 'strengthening outside doors of flats to prevent thieves breaking in', and of supplementing the activities of state organisations in 'doing battle against insects and teaching children how to draw and paint'.[62] On the other hand, state officials attacked co-operatives precisely because they not so much supplemented as replaced the state sector. Even worse, this substitution 'does not contribute to a growth in commodities, but instead reduces services'.[63] While it was anticipated that they would serve as the motor force of change in areas of manufacturing, their long-term future always lay in the much neglected service sector.

While co-operatives could be expected to continue to meet consumer demand for goods and better shopping facilities, one sphere in which it seemed likely that they would thrive was in providing social services, thereby assuming roles played by the voluntary sector in the UK. This posed the question of whether in some social fields co-operatives, as voluntary associations, would in the future require local authority subventions. This social aspect of the co-operative movement had a second dimension. Profit-making co-operatives stood at the interface of the state and the charitable, voluntary sector. For instance, one Moscow co-operative restaurant, which contributed to ecological projects organised by a large-circulation magazine, made donations for victims of a major railway disaster which occurred in 1989 near Ufa, and on Sundays provided free dinners for the poor, elderly and invalid. However, the local soviet interpreted the 'serving of old ladies as no more than window dressing to cover for drunken orgies and extortion which take place in the evening'.[64] The link between the growth of co-operatives and the transfer of the obligation for the provision of social services from the state to the private sector and non-governmental organisations prefigured projects to support such a shift financed by the EU a few years later.

At the founding conference of a new umbrella organisation designed to co-ordinate, among other things, the diverse charitable and 'peace keeping activities' of co-operatives and to focus on ecology, health protection and co-operative tourism, many participants stressed the importance of working with national charities, 'not only because they would help solve social and ecological problems, but because they would also improve people's attitudes towards co-operatives'.[65] The provision in the law (art. 21.2) that contributions from profits to charities were exempt from tax marked another vital turning point in the structure, functioning and theory of the Soviet welfare state. Any future analysis of social policy in Russia should take into account the fact that the Government of Mikhail Gorbachev may be credited with introducing legislation on charities.[66]

The growing number of single-parent families and the explicit preferences expressed by women for part-time work meant that co-operatives offered those bringing up small children an opportunity to use their aptitudes and capacities outside the home.[67] Other groups targeted as potential co-operative members were pensioners, invalids and students. Preference in joining co-operatives was also to be shown to workers made redundant from state undertakings (art. 40.2). This could have led to a symbiotic relationship between state enterprises and co-operatives.

In a period of increasing hardship, retrenchment and falling state revenues, vulnerable social groups are especially at risk. The potential for co-operatives, in the sense of mutual associations, to assist this sector was considerable. The void created by the state's withdrawal was not being filled by private enterprise. In any case the latter would be able to see profitable advantage in some of these fields of activity only after the society had reached a higher level of economic and social development. Even then it would only cater for the needs of a prosperous minority of the population. Where their activities concern helping members of vulnerable social groups, co-operatives, as voluntary associations, might decide to dispense with the name 'co-operative'. Ideologically, Western governments and international aid agencies have found the appellation 'charity' or 'voluntary organisation' more appealing than 'co-operative' since the latter is associated with socialist collectivism, while 'charity' connotes ethical business and the philanthropic impulse of the prosperous, and 'voluntary organisation' suggests bottom-up, self-help activity .

In general, those wishing to form co-operatives tended to be the more enterprising and most skilled workers and thus less likely to be made redundant. In an interview involving the Minister of Finance and a foundry supervisor in a car assembly plant, the latter pointed out that 113 of the people in his charge had left to join co-operatives over the past twelve months and 'they were the most qualified workers. Now they are earning 900–1,000 roubles a month [in contrast to the average industrial wage of 220 roubles] and they are worth the money'.[68] These high incomes, which state enterprises were unable to pay, had two consequences: firstly, many enterprise directors tried to convert from being state to co-operative undertakings; and, secondly, there was an outflow of highly qualified workers in industry and construction into co-operatives.[69] Therefore, co-operatives held a special appeal to workers in high-productivity, profitable enterprises. This was particularly true where co-operatives were formed by employees leasing equipment, premises or transport from the enterprise which they served as a co-operative.

It was foreseen that the development of long-term contracts, self-financing, self-management and the gradual displacement of a centralised distributional system by a market, would require more highly trained employees in fields and professions virtually unknown in Russian society. Sales and marketing executives would have to be well acquainted with the regional economy and its potential as a source of inputs and market for outputs. They would also have to carry out market research, conduct advertising and promotional campaigns and produce catalogues and prospectuses.[70] Many of these services would have had to be bought in from other co-operatives specialising in consultancy and training.

Since individuals who were not co-operative members can 'participate in the activities of co-operatives on a contractual basis in their spare time' (art. 4.2), the law provided for the local soviet to regulate 'the ratio of the number of people employed in the co-operative under labour contracts to the number of co-operative members'. This was intended to prevent 'the use of co-operatives for private enterprise employing hired labour under the guise of the creation of a co-operative' (art. 40.2). These controls were designed to prevent a situation arising where, say, a co-operative producing a technical product or something for mass consumption was based on the labour of its few members – chairman, deputy chairman and administrative staff, and the remainder of the workforce were on contract. In view of the diversity of activities in which co-operatives were engaging, it would have been impossible to stipulate a statutory ratio.[71] On the other hand, this reasonable statutory flexibility could have been used as a legal weapon by local soviets who had a grudging attitude towards co-operatives. The unseemly and naive rush to the market and privatisation which occurred immediately after Gorbachev had been forced to vacate the Kremlin in December 1991 does not invalidate the social importance of this legislation which, in general, conformed to labour-protection legislation in Western Europe.

Fears and criticisms expressed about the formation of 'bogus co-operatives' by entrepreneurs, who might and did use the organisation as a legal way of exploiting labour, paralleled those criticisms that had been voiced before the demise of co-operatives in the 1930s. The crucial difference between the 1930s and the 1980s was the strengthening of the judiciary and the rule of law under Gorbachev. So, although the Government might still act hastily and 'unreconstructed' officials might behave capriciously in their relationship to co-operatives, nonetheless, individuals and institutions were increasingly (though very slowly) coming to rely on the law courts as a way of challenging the arbitrary use of power.

This said, evidence existed of officials cynically usurping the notion of the 'rule of law'. One of the pioneers of the Moscow co-operative movement, the restaurant 'Farkhad', was threatened with closure by the district catering trust, with whom the lease was signed, and by the local soviet. The co-operative's appeal against the termination of the lease was upheld by the district procurator's office. In another incident, a trading co-operative was requested to vacate its premises even though the co-operative was profitable and exporting to Austria. The argument employed by a senior local soviet official had a disingenuous quality: the state organisation should not have leased the premises in the first place. Yet it had done so because the previous state enterprise had moved elsewhere. Nonetheless, 'co-operatives must not oust state trade and must find premises for themselves or come to us and ask to be allocated space. The fact that we have none is another matter altogether. Difficulties must never overshadow the law'. The official added for the journalist's benefit: 'Please note that we acted strictly in conformity with the law'. Yet, in at least one case, co-operatives had been closed on the grounds that the decision to do so was 'not a matter of what the law says [about the rights of co-operatives] but a matter of people's interests'.[72] Such a view was, of course, a flagrant contradiction of the very notion of the rule of law.

Journalists reporting these cases interpreted the various government decrees, resolutions and circulars issued during 1989 to mean that local soviets and state economic organisations, believing co-operatives to be no longer in favour, felt safe to move against them. Besides deploying their well-practised delaying tactics, they were punctilious in their observance of the law.[73] In the latter half of 1989 co-operators and commentators were using the platform offered by *Moscow News* to point out that a major shift in policy had taken place. It was common knowledge that co-operatives met their real opposition at the local level, where politicians and local government officials could deploy a number of obstructive devices. However, when it was a matter of the price of materials trebling and co-operatives having difficulty in gaining access to their own bank accounts and being overburdened by heavy taxes, it was the central state which was acting in a hostile fashion.[74]

Control over the allocation of premises and taxation were the two levers operated by the local and central states respectively to make life difficult for co-operatives. The artists' co-operative 'Mars' negotiated for a number of Soviet artists to exhibit in Greece. A Greek millionaire sponsor concluded a contract with the co-operative to allow artists supported by the co-operative to spend time working in Greece. 'But the officials resent our being a co-operative and we have difficulty finding premises.'[75] In view of a general shortage of both residential and non-residential accommodation, officials had a convenient excuse for refusing to allocate space to co-operatives. There was also almost certainly a strong element of anti-intellectual sentiment and envy amongst bureaucrats whose chagrin was heightened by the sort of free foreign travel agreement negotiated by this co-operative.

Local soviets also had to devise strategies 'to counter tendencies towards the formation of monopolies' (art. 41.4), attendant cutbacks in production and the charging of artificially high prices. However, proscribing certain activities could (and did) inadvertently bring co-operatives enormous financial benefits by creating more of the same old grey and black economies.[76] On the other hand, in the eyes of large sections of the population, the more co-operatives there were, the more acute became the shortage of certain products.[77] Undoubtedly, not all those martyred by these attacks on co-operatives merited beatification, for there were often justifiable complaints that the higher prices charged by co-operatives for their goods and services were not matched by higher quality. There were also instances of articles purchased in state shops being resold by co-operatives at higher prices without any added value.[78] One rejoinder offered to placate the faint at heart and sceptical was that, according to the 'laws of supply and demand', an abundance of goods and services would lead to a lowering of prices to a level where co-operatives would no longer be able to make a fortune from buying up goods from the state.

The style and message of some Soviet writing on co-operatives, competition and monopolies suggested that the Soviet citizen was already being offered a breakfast of classical economics by Harriet Martineau. The prescription of 'more competition' presented by economists was countered by the politician's penchant for greater local government intervention. Unlike the economist, the politician regretted that the local soviets had been deprived of any economic means for influencing the development of co-operatives.

Growth in Co-operative Activity

Consumer co-operatives in the Soviet Union traditionally differed little (if at all) from state shops and were largely concentrated in the countryside, where they sold food and consumer goods. In the 1980s, with 60 million members and 35 million employees working in 6,450 consumer co-operative 'cells', they too were ripe for revitalisation within the framework of reforms introduced under perestroika. By 1989 their retail trade turnover had reached

98.6 billion roubles from 390,000 retail outlets and 108,000 public eating places. They were accounting for about 27 per cent of total retail sales and operating 21,000 industrial enterprises.[79] It became commonplace to point out how, until very recently, 'consumer co-operatives were literally converted into a state department and managed just like any other ministry or committee. Instructions and orders setting plans, limits, the wage bill and wage rates are all received from above'.[80]

But these hierarchical arrangements were not solely to blame for the inertia and absence of imagination found in consumer co-operatives; every shareholder and worker in the co-operative had to 'undergo a change of heart and break with the custom of always waiting for someone to issue an instruction before taking action'.[81] The charge of Manilovism, mentioned earlier, still stands and remains a serious impediment to the implementation of changes. Gorbachev was compelled to repeat that co-operatives could not be 'planted' from above, but could only come from creative initiative from below. Yet, academic protagonists of co-operatives retorted that consumer co-operatives continued to be dominated by a huge statised, highly centralised management system cut off from the rank and file and simply unable to provide co-operative workers and member-shareholders with genuine forms of self-government.[82] The restructuring of the way in which goods and services were produced and distributed had to take place simultaneously with a psychological restructuring of the population. Co-operatives were regarded by reformers as a key and critical instrument in effecting that change of mind.

Unfortunately, the changes that were necessary if co-operatives were to develop could have negative effects. For instance, in 1988 retail turnover for both state and co-operative trade was included in the state's 'order' (*zakaz*). In other words, a co-operative's material inputs and outputs were part of the state's plan. But then, when, beginning in 1989, the 'state order for turnover' was made to apply to state trading bodies, real dangers were immediately created for those sections of the population whose consumer needs were being met through co-operative outlets.[83] Past precedent demonstrated that where shortages existed – and these were ubiquitous – state enterprises were, not surprisingly, given preferential treatment in supplies. Thus, the political and legal gains made by co-operatives when they gained independence of the state order system was likely to be countered by the economic cost of freedom from state tutelage. This contradiction could only be overcome by a far more radical transformation of the economic system, which continued to be highly regulated.

Official statistics on the number of co-operatives, their activities, average size of membership, the number of individuals employed and the value of output were acknowledged to be inaccurate. The State Committee on Statistics (Goskomstat), which should be reasonably reliable, put the number of registered co-operatives at 32,561 at the end of June 1988. This represented an eightfold increase over a twelve-month period. The total number of people employed by co-operatives stood at 459,000, while gross output was valued at 1.04 billion roubles, having increased from 29.2 million a year earlier. Thirty-nine per cent of the registered co-operatives were involved in providing consumer services, 16 per cent were engaged in public catering and 27 per cent in some form of material production. Some of them had now become large undertakings: in 1988 the 'Shtamp' engineering co-operative in Moscow, for instance, had 1,000 employees. Between January and December 1988, over 14,000 producer co-operatives were set up, with a membership of over 150,000.[84] Goskomstat disclosed that in April 1989 the number of co-operatives had risen to 99,300, employing 1.9 million people. By January 1990, the respective figures were 210,000 and 5.5 million.[85] The production of consumer goods represented around 26 per cent of turnover. Construction and medical care – both of which were showing signs of success – accounted for about 15 per cent and 2 per cent of total turnover respectively.

By the end of 1988 Moscow had 3,000 co-operatives; the output of the sector had increased 25-fold over the twelve-month period.[86] In value terms about 29 per cent of the gross output of the nation's co-operatives was being produced in co-operatives located in the capital.

As a result of the grievous shortage of cafés and restaurants, popular discontent with the situation and the low level of capitalisation required to set them up, catering proved a fairly easy point of entry into the *terra incognita* of co-operative activity. These eating places became an immediate source of complaint from customers and would-be diners because of the extortionate prices charged. This complaint was in most cases justified; prices were much higher in co-operatives than in state restaurants. On the other hand, the very low prices charged in the latter reflected the high state subsidy on food products. The second phase of development, of equal if not greater importance in the long term, was the increase in business and professional services, including management consultancy. In some cases co-operative ventures in this sphere required larger investments.

These figures testify to the growth which occurred in the number of co-operatives, their membership, turnover and range of activities. At the same time, co-operative members and their supporters were perpetually bemoaning their fate and speaking apocalyptically about the impending collapse of the movement. The language used reflected something of a siege mentality, as for instance when the President of the National Union of Consumer Societies referred to the paradox that 'as co-operatives grow in number and economic power, their very existence is in question'[87] – an unfortunate phraseology reminiscent of that employed by Stalin (for instance, in his *The Right Deviation in the CPSU(b)*).[88]

The growth of co-operatives in the face of quite considerable institutional opposition (maintained by conservative popular support) owed something to the fortitude and organisational ability of the co-operators themselves. They had not been slow to seize the legal guarantees available to them and set up support networks offering training, accountancy and managerial and legal advice to one another or to prospective newcomers and to the population at large. In 1988 *FAKT* was established in Moscow as a co-ordinating centre for the co-operative movement (and the 'alternative economy' more generally). It also housed the offices of the already highly successful business newspaper, *Kommersant*. The willingness of people to commit their savings, borrow and work long hours to build up the enterprise served as a barometer of attitudes towards the stability of the political climate and confidence in the rule of law.

The infrastructure necessary for the efficient functioning of a modern, sophisticated industrial society extends beyond the conventionally defined 'commanding heights'. Today, that infrastructure implies the widespread use of information technology, including facsimile machines, reprographic equipment, electronic bank transfer facilities, detailed (and reliable) statistics on the economy and the production and processing of income tax return forms. The means and degree to which the state is, can or should be directly involved in funding and controlling this 'infrastructure' is not easily determinable. However, the rapidity of change and nature of the technology in some of these fields is such that small-scale enterprises have clear advantages over larger ones. The co-operative, which is based on a particular set of social relations and organisational structure, as a small-scale enterprise, has additional advantages.

An important aspect of the development of co-operatives was their relationship to the informal ('second' or 'black') economy. As in any country, estimates of the aggregated size of this sector are open to serious dispute. According to the estimate, in 1989 the capital assets deployed in the second economy amounted to 500 billion roubles, while turnover in this sector was calculated as having risen from 5 billion roubles in the early 1960s to 90 billion at the end of the 1980s.[89] The history of this informal economy has been well documented, as have its functions and significance to the Soviet economy at large. The networks of individuals who managed to obtain raw materials and equipment necessary for an enterprise to meet the targets laid down in its plan were the lubricators of the system. Inevitably over time these quasi-legal arrangements dealing with the flow of commodities between state enterprises crystallised into illegal forms of individual and group ownership of property. At this point white-collar crimes, tolerated because they were intrinsic to intra-systemic economic circuits, crossed an important threshold. Those involved were no longer merely enjoying a few perquisites associated with assisting the operation of the public economy; they were members of an amorphous social group concerned with the aggrandisement of personal wealth.

This development was an inevitable concomitant of perestroika, one of whose premises was the legalisation of individual and family economic activity and co-operatives in order to encourage extra-state economic sectors and to draw the illegal 'shadow economy' into the 'light'. An unintended consequence was to increase the crime rate.[90]

In a number of respects, the behaviour of co-operatives, which became the subject of investigation by journalists and state officials, had its origins in features endemic to the Soviet economic culture – embezzlement, false declarations of financial and output plans and their outcomes. The latter were supplemented by additional illegal (but traditional capitalist) habits, at that time specific to the co-operatives, such as providing false income tax returns.

Co-operative Property and Finance

The work of Ludwig von Mises and Joseph Schumpeter on the relationship between ownership, socialism and the functioning of the economy took on an immediate contemporary interest during the co-operative phase. Von Mises – who had argued that only if there were markets in capital and land could they be valued to reflect their productivity and different uses – suggested that socialist ownership was inherently inefficient.[91] At the same time Schumpeter was explaining why socialist economies lacked the technological dynamism which capitalist entrepreneurship necessarily ensured. The underlying logic of their analyses was already propelling the Soviet Union (and other East European countries) towards changing the laws governing property rights.[92]

One of the central aims of the reformers was to create an economic system in which consumer satisfaction would be a primary motivating force for producers. This was to be achieved by the development of markets for commodities. Such a shift in orientation from a command-administrative economy would tackle the systematic and chronic problems of the inefficient and wasteful use of resources, hidden reserves, shortages and poor quality.[93] Reform cannot, however, be restricted to the creation of markets for commodities, but has to extend to permitting markets in capital and land. In his book, *Perestroika: New Thinking for Our Country and the World*, published in 1987, Gorbachev reiterated that 'Public property was gradually fenced off from its true owner – the working man'.[94] The challenge to an almost exclusive form of state ownership made its appearance in proposals to create legitimate individual, family and co-operative forms of ownership.[95] Those opposing change in ownership regarded leasing and renting from the state as preferable alternatives.[96] This position was one of many face-saving compromises and ideological evasions designed to preserve the status quo.

Co-operative ownership was regarded by the Law on Co-operatives as a form of socialist ownership and on a par with state ownership. This status ensured that its property could neither be confiscated nor be transferred to state enterprises or any other group without the consent of a general meeting of its members. Only the latter had the right to sell, lease or transfer its buildings, equipment, stocks and other material assets. Co-operatives were legally permitted to own buildings, machinery, transportation, finished products and other property consistent with their activity. Their property derived from members' contributions, the income generated by sales, bank credit, and the 'revenue from the sale of shares or other securities issued by the co-operative' (art. 22.1). If a co-operative wanted to expand production or convert its operations into providing new commodities or services for which a demand had increased or emerged, it could, after gaining authorisation, issue shares for sale equal to the gross annual income secured by its total property (art. 22. 4). With Soviet economists beginning to discuss primary and secondary markets for shares, co-operatives provided a sort of test-tube for experimenting with a functional equivalent to a stock market. In the eyes of economists, the restriction of selling securities to co-operative members and their employees prevented the development of a secondary market in shares and therefore a market valuation of the performance and assets of not just co-operatives but all organisations.

The Law gave co-operatives access to bank credit. Loans, however, had to be repaid within two years, with interest charged at from 0.75 per cent to 1 per cent depending on whether the loan was long-term (a maximum of two years) or short-term; a higher rate of 3 per cent was levied on overdue loans.[97] These rates may be compared with those asked of state enterprises, which were required to pay 0.5–8 per cent on short-term and 10 per cent on overdue loans. Thus, in 1988 co-operatives were being offered some favourable advantages *vis-à-vis* state ventures. At the same time, co-operatives, unlike state enterprises, could fail: if a co-operative consistently failed to meet its settlement obligations, then the bank could declare it insolvent and raise the question of the co-operative's liquidation with the local soviet.

Prior to 1917 and again during the 1920s considerable attention was paid to the setting up of co-operative banks. The idea emerged again in 1988 when it was believed that, apart from financing co-operatives and providing competition for the state banks, they could borrow hard currency from Western financial institutions whose governments might consider that support in the form of credits to an independent co-operative sector could yield long-term political benefits.[98] Within the financial sector there were also plans to set up co-operative insurance agencies, some offering new profit-bearing types of insurance and others providing a normal range of services for state enterprises (for instance, against commercial risk, unstable rates of exchange, and fire and theft).

Prices, Rewards and Taxation

The Law required prices to reconcile two competing desiderata: on the one hand, 'prices and tariffs for a co-operative's goods and services must reflect the socially necessary cost involved in producing and selling goods' (art. 19. 1). In other words, prices should not be 'speculative' and should somehow conform to Marxist precepts on price formation. On the other hand, however, prices should 'take into account customer appeal and quality', thus reflecting market demand. In a very real way, this policy towards price formation by co-operatives was preparing the population for the freeing of prices which eventually came about, in Russia, in January 1992. Consumer demand rather than cost was to be the principal determinant of price. The whole notion of watchdog bodies monitoring the prices charged by co-operatives was, in a sense, unrealistic.

In the tertiary sector, market-clearing pricing was the norm, while in other spheres of co-operative activity, pettifoggery, prejudice and unwarranted zealousness on the part of officials in regulating prices prevailed. Officialdom's zest for control was frequently demonstrated by the termination of a co-operative's activities. Where goods were produced to meet a state order or manufactured from raw materials supplied to the co-operative by the state, they had to be sold at centrally set prices – although even these could vary if the co-operative contracted with the client to make an additional charge (or allow a discount) in order to meet certain quality specifications and delivery deadlines. Price setting presented a clear area of conflict: the prices charged were the major, if not the sole, determinant of co-operative incomes which, as already indicated, substantially exceeded, sometimes by 100 per cent, the incomes of workers in state enterprises engaged in comparable work.

These differences in earnings were attributed by some to productivity levels which were double or treble those achieved in state enterprises. These higher levels were themselves a result of the imposition of greater discipline on the workforce – whether a self-discipline of members or an employer-dictated discipline on hired labour. This is not to imply that co-operatives operated sweatshop regimes; productivity was higher largely because the state sector suffered severely from absenteeism, drunkenness and time-wasting.[99] The traditional means of trying to instil discipline – moral appeals by peers, work collectives and comrades' courts and the withdrawal of rights to holiday passes – were now being replaced by the discipline of the marketplace. Although the movement was very gradual and only affected a small number of people, it did signal the changes to come. The higher earnings compensated those working in co-operatives for the absence or loss of important fringe benefits associated with employment in state organisations and enterprises.

A person's legal position in a co-operative had a significant effect on his or her conditions of employment. So, for instance, unlike co-operative members and those on labour contracts, those on 'agreed' or specific, short-term contracts were not entitled to a medical certificate or holidays and were not covered by the standard office working regulations. Hired labour did not have the same rights as members and, since they could participate in general meetings but not vote, they were unable to influence decisions associated with, for example, the distribution of income.

People working in co-operatives were classified in terms of the way in which their earnings were determined. The basic division was between members and contract labour. The latter were paid a contract wage and perhaps a bonus, but they did not participate, as a right, in the co-operative's profits, which might be either distributed amongst the members or reinvested. A division also existed amongst the membership. Those who invested more in the enterprise were entitled to a larger reward – which amounted to their receiving a return on their capital. In certain specified cases, members' incomes would reflect the value of the property (assets) which they had contributed to the organisation. This dual reward system created a distinction between 'wages' and 'dividends'. The formation of a two-class membership based on those who drew an income and those receiving both an income and a dividend was politically problematic for a socialist government and unacceptable to large numbers of Soviet citizens. Nevertheless, there was evidence that some workers in this sector considered that the entry fee and share deposit were 'laughably small' and should be increased, since the dividends payable on them were quite inadequate to serve as an incentive and reward.[100] In 1988 the Charter regulating consumer co-operatives allowed shareholders to receive a dividend on their actual deposit. The amount paid out as a dividend was permitted to rise to 40 per cent of the total profit. Apart from dividends being small, all fully paid-up shareholders received the same payment irrespective of their personal labour input to the co-operative's activities. The crucial issue of profit distribution was widely acknowledged as being in need of amendment.

In January 1989 the Government issued a long decree on price formation.[101] Among other things it specified a range of measures designed to equalise prices in the co-operative and state sectors by encouraging equal competition. Priority in the allocation of supplies, credit facilities and advantageous tax and other privileges would be shown to those who delivered at prices no higher than those charged by the state. Local soviets and construction ministries were to investigate ways of supplying building co-operatives with materials and equipment at the same prices as those charged to state building organisations and to pay them for work carried out at the same rates as state contractors. This reflected a good deal of wishful thinking; nonetheless a start to changing the system had been made.

The Law also established a procedure akin to that introduced in England and Wales, whereby local authority services have to be 'put out to tender'. However, the transfer to co-operatives of works canteens and other eating places in enterprises, schools, building sites and other organisations currently run by central catering departments was prohibited unless it had the consent of those working in these enterprises. As far as restaurants were concerned, charges had to be the same as those in state restaurants of a similar quality; in any case, they were not to exceed those set for the highest-category restaurants. The general aim in this sphere of co-operative activity was to 'suppress speculative tendencies in certain co-operatives which has given rise to justified popular censure'. Like so many other stipulations in this particular sphere of activity, the intention was laudable, but the outcome could and did cause confusion and anomalies.

The spirit of the decree on prices was designed to counter critics of the co-operative movement, partly by introducing stricter accounting procedures. An income declaration, to be submitted quarterly, became the co-operative's principal financial document, defining its relationship to banking and financial institutions. It set the size of the co-operative's revenue and the personal incomes of both its members and employees in order to determine the level of taxation and their other obligatory payments. The whole issue of income declaration and penalties incurred for giving false information was dealt with subsequently.

Ultimately, those 'converted' to the movement defensively pointed out that the 'enviable advantages of co-operative membership' were dependent on profits being made, for 'without profit there can be no technical development, no expansion of production and no new markets'.[102] The language used by supporters and popularisers of co-operatives sounded didactic and condescending; for instance, they pointed out that, since losses did sometimes occur, part of the income earned in good years should be placed in an insurance fund. Alternatively, everything could be paid out in the form of wages, in which case employees were warned that they would themselves have to make provision for the 'rainy day'. This all presupposed the existence of a commercial infrastructure and ethos. Yet it was precisely the absence of an infrastructure of institutions, knowledge, norms and values which constituted one of the most formidable barriers to radical economic reform. Eventually, in order to overcome these barriers, radical reformers decided to take the fast lane to the market by liberalising prices and privatising state assets.

The exclusive right to apportion revenue to wages, investment, production and social expenditure resided with the general meeting. The size of a member's wage was made dependent on his labour contribution. No upper limit was placed on labour earnings, which were payable in both cash and kind. These and other 'privileges' annoyed functionaries in the state sector and they found irksome ways of retaliating. For example, producer and mining co-operatives in Poltava were told by the State Committee for Labour and Social Issues that: 'There is nothing to stop you forming a co-operative, but if you do so then you will forfeit all privileges available to workers in the mining industry, including pensions, because the Law on Co-operatives has nothing to say on the subject of these privileges'.[103] Bureaucratic insensitivity and callous pedantry were not, of course, the prerogative of Soviet institutions and remain distinguishing characteristics of the post-Soviet Russian Federation and other former republics of the USSR.

An important role was assigned to taxation, which was expected to encourage co-operatives to choose profitable areas of activity in terms of product assortments, technologies employed and services for which a demand existed. It also had to differentiate between the needs of the various types of co-operatives, offering tax credits to co-operatives introducing new, high-quality goods which increased production costs. These were to be fixed (as a rule) for a five-year period, sufficiently long to provide an incentive to increase output. In June 1989 a decree by the RSFSR Supreme Soviet set the tax on the revenue of trading co-operatives at 60 per cent, rising 'in some cases' to 85 per cent. For co-operative publishers the rate was 45 per cent and for construction co-operatives 25 per cent.

A major point of controversy focused on the taxation of the co-operative's income (profit) and the personal incomes of co-operative members and other people working in the organisation under contract. In 1988 income tax was still a constant 13 per cent tax levied on monthly earnings exceeding 100 roubles in the state sector (i.e. the maximum marginal tax rate for factory and office workers at their principal place of work). The Draft version of the Law had recommended that a progressive tax be established for the 'personal incomes of co-operative members and people working in it under a labour contract'.

Under its proposals, people working in co-operatives would, like all other employees in the economy, pay income tax at a flat rate of 13 per cent, but then, after a monthly income of 500 roubles, marginal tax became 30 per cent, rising to 50 per cent over 700 roubles, 70 per cent over 1,000 roubles and 90 per cent on each rouble over 1,500 roubles.[104] This rate was vigorously defended by the Minister of Finance in an interview, heatedly debated at the meeting of the Supreme Soviet to ratify the Law on Co-operatives, and then rejected. While the clause on higher rates was retained in the final Act, the actual rates to be set remained undetermined.[105] A decree by the Presidium of the USSR Supreme Court suspended an edict issued in the previous March by the Supreme Court introducing progressive tax rates and requested that the Government 'rethink its tax proposals'.[106] Rules introduced in June 1989 meant that the actual take-home pay of workers earning 600–800 roubles a month would be reduced by half. Since the national average monthly monetary income at that time was only 202 roubles there were good grounds for making it more progressive.

Yet, in true, classical economic reasoning, protagonists of the co-operative pointed out that the 'danger in creating a steeply progressive tax was that it might kill off the motivation to work'.[107] A clearer distinction between income and profit ('corporation') taxes was definitely required in order to discourage the distribution of a good year's earnings in the form of income (or dividend). However, the successful inculcation of a norm of 'deferred gratification' would always be dependent on the development of capitalist attitudes and co-operative members' anticipations of a stable political-economic future.

That the tax structure needed to be revised was widely accepted, even by the co-operative supporters. It was the somewhat arbitrary and devious manner in which the tax increases had been introduced into the RSFSR that caused concern.[108] As a way of registering their grievance, delegates to the first national congress of producer and consumer co-operatives recommended that co-operatives badly affected by tax regimes imposed by local soviets should move to other republics where the tax burden was less onerous, such as Latvia and Estonia, where the tax rate was to be 50 per cent lower than in the RSFSR.[109] Within the RSFSR, local governments such as the Komi SSR (population: 1.3 million) suspended the decree on income tax relating to co-operatives for purely pragmatic reasons: it did not want to force into liquidation co-operatives which made substantial contributions to the supply of goods and, through local taxes, to city budgets. While such resistance by local authorities might be commendable, it was nonetheless further evidence that legislative acts of the central government could be disobeyed with impunity.

For advocates of the co-operatives the true intention behind this impost was the destruction of 'co-operatives as a class'. An alternative and more (generous) interpretation was that either the legislators were guided by ill-informed economists or they chose not to heed sound economic arguments.

Local Soviets

Long experienced with their own bureaucracies, the framers of the legislation on co-operatives took care to try and prevent local authorities from acting obstructively, as they had done even in tsarist days. So, if a local soviet refused to register a prospective co-operative's statutes, the latter was allowed to appeal to a higher-level soviet or to the courts. The legislation also aimed at curtailing the age-old practice of state officials extorting bribes from those who feel weak in the face of authority. Nevertheless, the local authorities reserved the right to judge the professional competence of individuals wishing to set up a co-operative. Again, some commentators believed that the market rather than officials should be the arbiter of competence, even if the would-be co-operators were palpably unqualified to provide the service they were proposing. Protagonists of the new law adopted this rather stridently contentious stance because co-operatives were being hampered by local officials afraid of their greater efficiency and therefore of the potential threat they presented to the jobs of employees in the state sector.[110] The powers of officials were increased in October 1989 by amendments made to the Law on Co-operatives. Local soviets now had to set maximum limits on the prices which co-operatives could charge.

Little systematic investigation was ever undertaken on the behaviour of local soviets towards economic and social institutions located within their administrative jurisdictions during the early reform period of the late 1980s.

For example, in 1988, the large Ukrainian industrial city of Dnepropetrovsk adopted a hostile stance on co-operatives, issuing a circular directing local state enterprises not to sell any of their output to co-operatives.[111] We know nothing of the politics behind this decision: which department within the soviet issued it and who, in any case, was responsible for co-operative affairs and the local economy more generally.

From the earliest discussions on the draft legislation on co-operatives in 1988, it was never clear who should oversee their activities and how tightly they should be controlled. At the heart of Gorbachev's vision of perestroika lay the notion of economic and political decentralisation. The co-operative movement represented one particular manifestation of decentralisation in the economy and production, while increasing the *de facto* power of the local soviets represented decentralisation in the political realm. There were sound logical reasons for placing responsibility for overseeing the activities of co-operatives with the local soviets. It had frequently been argued that more power should be given to lower tiers of government since they had a far better understanding of local needs and demands.[112] It was therefore assumed that they should be allowed to exercise discretion on the manner and degree to which moral and material support should be given to co-operatives. For instance, they would be able to advise the latter on where to find inputs of raw materials and equipment for their operations, provide them with information on the markets which they wanted to supply, and also assist them in surmounting legal and bureaucratic formalities.

Unfortunately, reformers, co-operators and local soviet officials were unable to overcome a tragic and critical systemic contradiction, namely, how to produce commodities and capital equipment for a private market (or non-state sector) when there were insufficient supplies to meet the needs of the state sector itself. In the face of this situation, priority for supplies was accorded to state enterprises. This inevitably generated tensions and conflicts as co-operatives competed with state firms to obtain materials and led both sectors into illegal activities to meet their supply needs.

As already remarked, the absence of a wholesale market for capital goods constituted a critical flaw in the whole economic system, especially as far as co-operatives were concerned.[113] Under these circumstances, cases were reported of gatekeeping officials within the local soviet executive committees becoming co-opted as members of co-operatives.[114] In a survey of 80,000 co-operatives aimed at discovering who the extortionists were, almost one-third of the chairmen replied that officials working in local authority departments were the worst offenders; only 7 per cent of respondents cited criminal protection racketeers as the principal extortionists.[115] This finding was also significant from the point of view of the escalating crime rate, particularly the rate of violent crimes against persons and property, which even then was receiving a high profile in the media. Extortion, which may be regarded as an extended form of 'bribery', is a practice with deep roots in the culture, and is by no means confined to employees in local authorities. On some occasions a co-operative's creditworthiness was not necessarily the criterion for granting a loan; frequently bank credit was only made available after the payment of 'illegal monetary inducements'. One consequence of this practice was that banks were unable properly to fulfil their regulatory function in their relationship with co-operatives, a factor which contributed to a higher than anticipated level of bankruptcies and defaulting in this sector.[116]

Class and Property

A thorough class analysis of the Russian co-operative movement has never been undertaken, although prior to 1917 authors on co-operatives did sometimes draw attention to the social class dimension. Unfortunately, the majority of the writers were visibly partisan on the subject. The same can be said of those writing on co-operatives at various times since the October Revolution.

Public opinion surveys carried out in the 1980s indicated that broad sections of the population were hostile to co-operatives, frequently because of their association in the public mind with the private sector, which people had been socialised to understand as being synonymous with exploitation. Members of older age groups and those on low incomes and/or unskilled were at the beginning of 1990 less sympathetic to co-operatives than the younger generation and members of the intelligentsia. More specifically, co-operatives were least popular amongst pensioners and agricultural workers (9.2 and 14.2 per cent respectively) and most popular among specialists and managers (22 and 25 per cent).[117] Perhaps predictably, trade unions took a critical stance towards them. Paradoxically but understandably, the social groups making least use of co-operatives were amongst their sternest critics. This may be explained by the types of products and services provided by co-operatives, such as architects and restaurants, and the high prices these charged..

Some of these attitudes were of course the product of political socialisation. For instance, the longer individuals had been exposed to regular doses of ideological information on the iniquities of capitalism, the more hostile they could be expected to be towards organisations associated with capitalism. Similarly, the more clearly their interests as political 'activists' were attached to those sections of the Communist Party critical of the changes taking place, the more opposed they were to co-operatives.

Yet, it would be a mistake to consider that all salaried Party functionaries refused to accept as legitimate and just any property form other than state property. After all, local party secretaries were themselves 'achievers' and were admirably placed to be well informed about the inefficiencies in the management of the state sectors within their administrative jurisdictions. Many of these members of the *apparat* sat at the centre of a complex web of personal and institutional relationships which enabled them, should they so wish, to keep in touch with public opinion. As a result they had the pulse of local demands and feelings. Intelligent Party members and functionaries who had been watching the waning fortunes of the Party would no doubt have adapted their organisational talents to the emerging economic sector. Although the co-operatives were institutionally weak and vulnerable to harassment by boorish bureaucrats, they could muster a strong defence because they attracted the educated and articulate and a section of the existing élite, whose members were neither highly educated nor articulate but politically astute.

The co-operative appealed to certain types of individual: one survey of 586 co-operative chairmen revealed that 68.2 per cent regarded the opportunity 'to be creative' as their primary motivation for joining a co-operative. Another important motivating factor was that it offered individuals the opportunity 'to be in control' or master of the work situation.[118] Soviet society had closed off most avenues for individual initiative and creativity, leaving one major peephole or avenue of escape – scientific research. For this reason, perestroika was particularly welcomed by academics; many co-operatives were started by academics with a background in mathematics and the natural sciences.

In 1923 Lenin finally came to see the huge and growing bureaucracy as the key problem facing the new Soviet state, which led him to publish one of his last works, *Better Fewer, But Better*. Gorbachev *began* by specifying the bureaucracy as the prime obstacle to restructuring, before realising that the greatest impediment to change was the conservatism of the population itself.

Lenin with some justification also saw social class as a problem, but a surmountable one. Stalin with scarcely any justification perceived the ubiquitous class enemy as the principal social problem, for its aim was the restoration of capitalism. For Khrushchev the Soviet state was 'a state of all the people', for there were no longer any classes. This meant that conflicts arising as a consequence of perestroika could not be couched in terms of class conflict. Gorbachev was inhibited from adopting a Marxist analysis of class and ethnic conflict in the Soviet Union no doubt partly because of his knowledge of the country's past: the putative existence of a ubiquitous class enemy justified Stalin's policy of 'terror'. The last General Secretary of the CPSU was unwilling to stray down a path signposted 'capitalist class'.

Conclusion

By creating different property forms the Government was seeking to distinguish between what the state was obliged to do (minimally and maximally) and what corporate bodies, social and occupational groups and private citizens should expect to pay for. The notion of full cost accounting, the foundation stone of co-operatives, allowed for insolvency and bankruptcy. This required expansion of the social insurance system to provide for those employees (whether in state or co-operative enterprises) who lost their jobs. Indeed, the co-operative appeared to be a crucial component in the process of restructuring social welfare as well as the economy. Now that a large number of state enterprises were to face closure because they were insolvent or unprofitable (perhaps due to the lack of demand for their products), the ministries responsible for them could lease or sell the bankrupt state enterprise's assets to co-operatives.[119] To the extent that this could offer jobs to those made redundant, this strategy resembled the management and worker buy-outs employed by the British Labour Government in the case of the Meriden motorcycle firm in England. In some of these cases, because many of the co-operatives formed during the initial 'shake-out' were far from being fully independent but remained 'attached to' state enterprises, their establishment was a device used by the accomplished bureaucrat or manager to avoid certain state controls or to reap benefits not allowed to them as managers of state property.

Producer co-operatives were intended to demonstrate how enterprises could be efficient and technically innovative and allow their workforces opportunities to exercise initiative and responsibility. It was hoped that the principles and practices employed in co-operatives would have a ripple effect throughout the economy as the advantages of this form of property and its mode of organisation and work patterns and incentives became evident.

Ironically, allowing individuals to form co-operatives in order that they could exercise their entrepreneurial skills appealed to those who enjoyed the 'game' of gaining a 'competitive edge' and 'achieving'. It thus attracted those who carried the germ of the capitalist spirit.

In the event, it proved too easy to declare in the first three years of perestroika that, by combining personal, group, collective and state interests, co-operatives were implementing Lenin's vision of 'socialism as a system of civilised co-operators based on the joint ownership of the means of production'.[120] The view that co-operatives appeared as 'an essential component in the renewal of socialism and as an important condition for its further progress'[121] was not at that time supported by empirical evidence. Hence, the statement that it was 'justifiable to conclude that the more co-operation that exists, the more socialism'[122] was more a profession of faith than a statement of fact. Abalkin, one of the co-operative movement's staunchest proponents, conceded that their future development would not be a straightforward or easy process. For the reformers, the path ahead was strewn with snares laid by bureaucrats who had interests to preserve; on the other hand, the 'defenders of socialism' could see in the co-operative beast 'negative phenomena associated with group interests coming to prevail'. The perceptions of both parties were essentially correct. The 'defenders of socialism' could point to the fact that already a number of co-operatives were in reality small, private firms employing hired labour. In fact, radical reformers such as Shmelyov regarded the conversion of co-operatives into joint stock companies as being both necessary and inevitable.[123]

Furthermore, many of those operating in the black economy were unconvinced of the benefits which would accrue to them if they legalised themselves by registering as co-operatives. As Soviet citizens with long experience of the mechanisms of their society, they were reluctant to be drawn into the bureaucratic labyrinth. Officials might have asked searching questions about their previous activities and networks and then refused to register them as co-operatives. In other words, at the time, whereas individuals working in (or recently made redundant from) state enterprises could have regarded forming or joining a co-operative as a rational and rewarding choice, those operating successfully in the informal sector tended to judge otherwise.

There was also evidence that people functioning in the black economy and criminals engaged in bribery, extortion, drugs, protection and robbery were laundering their earnings through co-operatives. The still highly marginal position of co-operatives in society also left them open to demands from common criminals for protection money and from officials for bribes.[124]

In a number of respects, Soviet co-operatives provided a fascinating object of sociological analysis: the dynamic of their formation in the interplay between individual citizens and bureaucratic forces; the socio-economic background and education of prospective and actual members, and of their advocates and antagonists; the political and ideological orientations of members; attitudes towards achievement and acquisition on the part of members and non-members; the value attached to freedom from the petty tutelage of officials and the Party. This minority, on whom the reformers depended to boost and reorientate the economy, were, as a social category, like the Old Believers who performed a function akin to Protestants in Weber's analysis of the rise of capitalism.[125]

The Mayor of Moscow epitomised the ambivalence of sections of the country's leadership towards co-operatives:

> If we want the co-operative movement to develop and become an integral part of the economy and way of life, it must fight to win the sympathy and support of the broad mass of the working population. . . . We expect co-operatives to make a real and substantial contribution to solving social problems, not making them more complicated.[126]

Yet newspaper and magazine articles critical of co-operatives conveyed to the public an impression that the economic crisis – high prices, inflation, shortages of consumer goods – were attributable to co-operatives, even though the latter accounted for a mere 1.5 per cent of gross domestic production.[127] But if nothing else, and regardless of its future, the co-operative sector has occupied a definite place in the transformation of the Soviet social system.

From their inception the co-operatives had to endure unconcealed and widespread public hostility.[128] On the one hand, these feelings expressed a moral outrage: the emerging co-operatives were alien to socialism – as it had for so long been officially described. On the other hand, dislike was bred by a righteous envy felt by the majority of the population towards high earnings. The two facts were linked by the high prices that co-operatives frequently charged. Underlying those resentments towards co-operatives was a more profound fear of change and the insecurity associated with the uncertainties of change.

And yet uncertainties in the population bred insecurities in the co-operatives, just as they did during NEP. Thus, the prospect of an uncertain and insecure future led co-operatives to a form of rational behaviour that was not in the best interests of the state or society: instead of investing their profits, they consumed them in the form of wages or bonuses. This only reinforced the antagonisms of large sections of employees in the state sector who were annoyed at the higher earnings of those working in the co-operatives.[129]

The decision to create co-operatives, as one of several new property forms, had the unintended consequence of initiating a real class struggle in the Soviet Union. It was a class struggle because it involved a contest for control over political and economic resources. An administrative class, jealous to preserve its patrimony in land and capital, was challenged by a nascent bourgeoisie harbouring under a co-operative cloak. Finally, by creating different national bourgeoisies, they were instrumental in undermining the old unitary ruling class and thus in initiating the break-up of the Union.

Co-operatives became a focus of many of the major conflicts and contradictions in the Soviet (and post-Soviet) economy, extending to the society at large. As a non-state property form, they evoked strong sentiments amongst both the supporters of a 'deep' restructuring and those who wanted to restrict the process of restructuring to a minimum. In general, criticisms of co-operatives were scarcely concealed criticisms of perestroika, both of which were considered to be undermining socialism.

Co-operative ventures have emerged in Russia at critical points in the society's economic and political evolution. Their re-emergence in 1987 was not the result of popular action from below, but of 'the executive of the modern state' acting according to Marxism in its characteristic, but in this case only in a semi-conscious, way as a 'committee for managing the common affairs of the whole bourgeoisie'.[130] The alacrity with which many people responded to the changed economic and political climate demonstrated the presence among a section of the population of a desire to 'truck, barter and trade'. This aspiration among some was countered by an urge among others to enforce equality, to preserve the communism of the barrack room.

In 1998 it is still not certain whether the Pied Piper's march towards a market economy is being led by precariously perched regional and national élites, or by civil servants (primarily those in the Ministry of Finance).[131] It is certainly not being established by popular demand. Nor is it certain that the visible changes and the Panzer attack approach of their delivery are desirable and more than superficial. In 1881 Marx wrote to the Russian revolutionary, Vera Zasulich, that autocratic, tsarist Russia stood at the crossroads in terms of its future development. A century later, Mr Gorbachev realised that authoritarian, Soviet Russia over which he presided stood at another crossroads. While he dithered, pondered, protested and sought to negotiate, Yeltsin pushed him aside and chose the path to capitalism, which the society is now stumbling along.

Notes

1   *Materialy XXVII S"ezda KPSS*, Politizdat, Moscow, 1986, pp. 39, 59; *Izvestiya*, 28 June 1988.
2   M. Gorbachev, *Political Report of the CPSU Central Committee to the 27th Party Congress*, Novosti Press, Moscow, 1986, p. 51.
3   Ibid.
4   Postanovlenie TsK KPSS i Soveta Ministrov SSSR, 'O merakh po dal'neishemu razvitiyu potrebitel'skoi kooperatsii', SP SSSR, 1986, no. 8, art. 45; Postanovlenie Soveta Ministrov SSSR, 'O sozdanii kooperativov po proizvodstva tovarov narodnogo potrebleniya', SP SSSR, 1987, no. 10, arts 41 and 42; Postanovlenie Soveta Ministrov SSSR, 'O sozdanii kooperativov po bytovomu obsluzhivaniyu naseleniya', SP SSSR, 1987, no. 11, art. 43; Postanovlenie Soveta Ministrov SSSR, 'Voprosy kooperativov po zagotovke i pererabotke vtorichnogo syr'ya', SP SSSR, 1987, no. 26, art. 90; Postanovlenie Soveta Ministrov SSSR, 'O sozdanii kooperativov po razrabotke programmnykh sredstv vychislitel'noi tekhniki', SP SSSR, 1988, no. 14, art. 37; Postanovlenie Soveta Ministrov SSSR, 'O nekotorykh voprosakh kooperativnoi i individual'noi trudovoi deyatel'nosti', SP SSSR, 1988, no. 15, art. 41; Postanovlenie Soveta Ministrov SSSR, 'O prodazhe v 1988-90 godakh kooperativnom nekotorykh vidov transportnoi i sel'sko-khozyaistvennoi tekhniki', SP SSSR, 1988, no. 29, art. 80; Postanovlenie Soveta Ministrov SSSR, 'Ob organizatsii zagotovki i pererabotki vtorichnogo syr'ya na kooperativnom osnove', SP SSSR, 1988, no. 11, art. 44.
5   N. Baklanov, 'Masterskaya, salon-auktison', *Izvestiya*, 6 April 1987; B. Yakovlev, 'Kooperativy est' – kooperativa net', *Vechernaya Moskva*, 2 February 1987.
6   Zakon SSSR, 30 June 1987, 'O gosudarstvennom predpriyatii (ob"edinenii)'. Perhaps the most radical aspect of the law was in its provisions that the management should be elected by the workforce, who would elect a works council that in turn would ratify the enterprise plan. See A. Aslund, *Gorbachev's Struggle for Economic Reform: The Soviet Reform Process, 1985–88*, Pinter Publishers, London, 1989.
7   For details on the content of the body of legislation enacted in 1987, see *O korennoi perestroike upravleniya ekonomiki. Sbornik dokumentov*, Izd. polit. lit., Moscow, 1987.
8   Postanovlenie TsK KPSS i Soveta Ministrov SSSR, 17 July 1987, no. 824, 'O sovershenstvovanii deyatel'nosti respublikanskikh organov upravleniya'. Ultimately, this decree created the preconditions for the clash between Armenia and Azerbaijdzan over Nagorny Karabakh, then for the secessionist steps taken by the Baltic republics ard finally for the conflict between Mr Yeltsin as President of the RSFSR and Mr Gorbachev as President of the USSR.
9   *Pravda*, 21 November 1986.
10 *Izvestiya*, 12 February 1987, p. 2.
11 Zakon SSSR, 'O kooperatsii v SSSR', Izd. Izvestiya Sovetov narodnykh deputatov SSSR, 1988.
12 'Proektnyi zakon o kooperatsii', *Pravda*, 6 March 1988.
13 Even so, in 1998 they are still largely agglomerations of individuals who readily spun off into totally new orbits seeking new asteroidal groupings. The dismissal of the whole Russian Cabinet by Yeltsin in March 1998 and references to the power of the multi-millionaire businessman, Berezovskii, suggest that the formation of a party identifiable as representing capital may be imminent.
14 M. Gorbachev, *Political Report of the CPSU Central Committee to the 27th Party Congress*, Novosti Press, Moscow, 1986, p. 49.

15 'The Novosibirsk Report', published in *Survey: A Journal of East & West Studies*, vol. 28, no. 1; M. Yanowitch, *A Voice of Reform: Essays by Tat'yana Zaslavskaya*, M. E. Sharpe, London, 1989; T. I. Zaslavskaya, *The Second Socialist Revolution: An Alternative Soviet Strategy*, I. B. Tauris, London, 1990.

16 Gorbachev, op. cit., p. 50.

17 A. Aganbegyan, *The Challenge: Economics of Perestroika*, Hutchinson, London, 1988, p. 26.

18 Gorbachev, op. cit., p. 50.

19 Gorbachev, op. cit., p. 60.

20 The (revised Third) Party Programme (adopted at the XXVII Party Congress) spoke in a similar vein of the housing problem being solved by 'large-scale state-funded housing construction, more extensive development of *co-operative* and individual house building as well as reconstruction, renovation and better upkeep of the available housing and closer control over its distribution'.

21 Gorbachev, op. cit. (1986), pp. 69–70, 73.

22 *The Programme of the CPSU*, Politizdat, Moscow, 1986, p.43

23 A. S. Tsipko, 'Vozmozhnosti i reservy kooperatsii', *Sotsiologicheskie issledovaniya*, no. 2, 1986, p. 50.

24 Elsewhere in Central Europe the Marxist orthodoxy was ritually chanted. In Czechoslovakia, for example, while the co-operatives were allotted a role in the building of socialism, they were to remain subordinated to the task of 'constructing and developing socialist relations of production on an ever higher level'. See K. Pernica, 'The Social Functions of the Czechoslovak Co-operative Movement and the Role of the Central Co-operative Council', in *The Co-operative Movement in Socialist Czechoslovakia*, Prague, 1967, p. 11.

25 Tsipko, op. cit., p. 51.

26 Ibid., p. 55.

27 It is worth remembering that the Reformation was a revolution in people's minds which took place over a period of centuries. Although the timescale might well be shortened, it will be many decades before that transformation in thought occurs in Russia.

28 A. Zaichenko, 'Sale of the Century', *Moscow News*, no. 19, 5–11 October 1990, p. 10.

29 In a letter to Bebel in 1886 Engels pointed to the necessity of relying on large-scale co-operative production in the transition to a pure communist economy with the provision that the state, through its ownership of the means of production, would prevent the particular interests of co-operative associations prevailing over the interests of society as a whole (K. Marx and F. Engels, *Socheneniya*, 2nd ed., Moscow, 1955–81, vol. 36, p. 361). See also his *The Peasant Question in France and Germany* (1892), in which he propounded the co-existence of state and co-operative property.

30 K. Marx, *Inaugural Address to the Working Men's International Association* (28 September 1864), in K. Marx and F. Engels, *Selected Works*, (2 volumes) vol. 1, Moscow, 1962, p. 383.

31 K. Marx and F. Engels, *Socheneniya*, vol. 16, pp. 10, 169; vol. 25, part 1, p. 483 .

32 V. I. Lenin, *Draft Programme of the RKP (b)*, in *Collected Works*, vol. 29, p. 14.

33 V. I. Lenin, *Collected Works*, vol. 32, p. 347.

34 V. I. Lenin, *Collected Works*, vol. 33, pp. 468–9. In fact, most of his remarks on co-operatives outside the field of agriculture are concentrated on pages 468–71. As late as 1990 the protagonists of modern co-operatives persisted in demanding a talmudic attention to Lenin's teaching: 'The question of what Lenin meant in totality when he spoke of the co-operation of Russia's entire population *requires further in-depth study*'

(my emphasis). He was applauded for his striving 'to employ to the maximum possible extent the materialist dialectic, the principle of the unity of opposites in the process of elaborating the strategy of socialist construction' (see *The System of Civilised Co-operatives is the System of Socialism*, Novosti Press, Moscow, 1989, pp. 11–12).

35 The weight of the past on the course of the October revolution and its aftermath continues to weigh on the present. Autocracy and dictatorship have given way to a wilful but less harsh authoritarianism which relies on a 'serf-consciousness' within Russian culture, cultivated by tsarism and Stalinism. See, for instance, Stalin's note to Lenin in 1921 in which he advised that those appointed to the staff of GOELRO should act according to the principle of 'the order carried out'. R. McNeal, *Stalin: Man and Ruler*, Macmillan, London, 1988, p. 138. Also, R. W. Davies, *Soviet History in the Gorbachev Revolution*, Macmillan, London, 1989, p. 15; T. Szamuely, *The Russian Tradition*, Fontana Press, London, 1974/1988.

36 V. I. Lenin, *Polnoe sobranie sochenenii*, Moscow, 1960, vol. 45, p. 100.

37 The justification was that European (and other 'far abroad') food standards do not comply with those applied by Russian authorities. Not all Western products are 'better' than their Russian equivalent, a fact which Westerners and Russians alike must acknowledge.

38 In fairness to (Soviet) Russia, the same complaint could be made about many other recipients of foreign aid. The indelible principle at the heart of the present post-Welfare State mission statement is that poverty (domestic European poverty as well as that in the Third World and transitional countries) cannot be 'solved by money alone'. The unfortunate (albeit implicit) slogan of the Anglo-Saxon welfare to work policy is '*Arbeit macht frei*'.

39 V. I. Lenin, *Polnoe sobranie sochenenii*, vol. 44, p. 364.

40 Tsipko, op. cit., p. 52.

41 However, if the analogy is to be pursued, then it must not be forgotten why the Mycenaean Greeks fought the Trojan War.

42 O. L. Luzhbina, 'S kem idem k s"ezdu'?, *SPK*, no. 1, 1989, p. 2.

43 L. Abalkin, 'Vozrozhdenie kooperatsii', *SPK*, no. 2, 1989, p. 6.

44 Ibid.

45 A decree of April 1989 placed responsibility for deciding whether or not to lease capital to co-operatives on enterprise managements and government agencies. See *Ekonomicheskaya gazeta*, no. 16, 1989.

46 *BBC Summary of World Broadcasts: Soviet Union*, 24 November 1989, p. (i) and 29 November 1989, p. c/2.

47 *Pravda*, 10 March 1990.

48 The controllers of urban real estate (such as the Mayor of Moscow) and of agricultural land (the chairmen of state and collective farms) are unwilling to surrender a resource which gives them power and income.

49 *SPK*, no. 1, 1989, p. 17.

50 'Commerce or art?', *Moscow News*, no. 33, 1989, p. 1.

51 Postanovlenie Soveta Ministrov SSSR, 'O regulirovanie otdel'nykh vidov deyatel'nostei kooperativov v soostvestvii s Zakonom O kooperatsii v SSSR', *SP SSSR*, 1989, no. 4, art. 12.

52 A large number of radical reformers in Russia had a rather naive and distorted image of Western capitalism and parliamentary democracy. Then and subsequently they seemed neither to understand nor to contemplate that liberal societies could and did impose restrictions on 'freedom'.

53 For instance, the regulations did not prevent the establishment of a co-operative ('Amico')

specialising in offering 'bed and breakfast' accommodation for foreign tourists. (See *Moscow News*, no. 30, 1989, p. 7.) Such developments were in harmony with the privatisation of accommodation and the beginnings of a real estate market.

54   *Izvestiya*, 20 February 1989.

55   *Pravda*, 4 October 1989.

56   The objective of consumer co-operatives was to 'develop trade and public catering in towns and villages'. They were to supply the population with their own products as well as those obtained from the state, producer co-operatives and private citizens. 'Another task facing us is to buy, process and market agricultural products. . . . we are to offer various everyday goods and services to the population' (P. Fedirko, Chairman of the Board of the All-Union Society of Consumer Co-operatives (Tsentrosoyuz), *We're Working With the Prosperity of the Peasants in Mind*, Novosti Press, Moscow, 1989, p. 6.

57   *SPK*, no. 1, 1989, p. 7.

58   In the Soviet Union it was far more common to use the word 'obtain' (*dostat'*) than 'pay for' (*platit'*), signifying the greater significance of social networks than purchasing power for the acquisition of goods.

59   In 1986 the official rouble–pound exchange was still 1:1, as it had been for many years. The black market rate in the mid-1970s was about 7:1, rising to 25:1 in 1988. By 1991 the official rate was 318:1 and the rouble was re-denominated by 1,000 at the end of 1997 after the rate reached 9,617:1. I am grateful to the Moscow Narodny Bank, London, for providing me with the rates since 1991.

60   'Gorodskoe potrebitel'skoe obshchestvo: pervye shagi', *SPK*, no. 2, 1989, pp. 21–2.

61   P. Bunich, 'I soyuzniki i konkurenty', *Ogenok*, April 1988.

62   Ibid. Co-operatives also 'mean shops, schools, hospitals and house-building projects in the countryside which state-controlled building contractors regard as too unprofitable to undertake'. See A. Bekker, *Moscow News*, no. 31, 1989, p. 10.

63   *Moscow News*, no. 33, 1989, p. 7.

64   *Moscow News*, no. 30, 1989, p. 10.

65   A. Borodenkov, 'Co-operatives for Peace and Survival of Mankind', *Moscow News*, no. 31, 1989, p. 2.

66   *SP SSSR* 1988, no. 356, art. 99. This decree was preceded by an article in which the author applauded the value attached to charitable activities in pre-revolutionary Russia. See D. Granin, 'O miloserdii', *Literaturnaya gazeta*, 18 March 1987.

67   As opposed to full-time work. The female participation rate in the labour market in the USSR was almost total. Many women wanted to work part-time. The Government was already moving in this direction in response to the demands by women and the objective needs of society in the face of a declining birth rate (approaching the basement of the replacement level) and rising juvenile delinquency.

68   A. Bossart, 'Zhizn' zanaves naloga', *Ogenok*, July, 1988.

69   V. Saikin, 'Reputatsiya. Kakova ona segnodnya u Moskovskikh kooperatorov?' *Nedelya*, no. 50, 1988.

70   F. Pankratov, 'Kommercheskaya rabota', *SPK*, no. 4, 1989, pp. 18–21.

71   I. Prikhod'ko, 'Trud v kooperative: pravovoe regulirovanie', *SPK*, no. 2, 1989, pp. 36–9.

72   *Moscow News*, no. 39, 1989.

73   *Moscow News*, no. 30, 1989.

74   *Moscow News*, no. 28, 1989, p. 12.

75   'Commerce or art'? *Moscow News*, no. 33, 1989, p. 11.

76   Bunich, op. cit.

77   Ibid. 'People are saying that co-operatives bought up coffee so that it would soon be

impossible to obtain any at all. The same was said about cloth, fabrics, thread, buckles and clasps . . . about everything'.

78   Saikin, op. cit.
79   'Shagi perestroika', *SPK*, no. 2, 1989, p. 8; Goskomstat, *Narodnoe khozyaistvo za 70 let*, Moscow, Finansy, 1987, pp. 454–57.
80   'Shagi perestroika', op. cit..
81   *SPK*, no. 2, 1989, p. 11.
82   A. Danilov and S. Selivertsov, 'Vdokhnut' v kooperativy novuyu zhizn'', *SPK*, no. 1, 1989, p. 34.
83   R. Loshkin, 'Goszakazy i roznichoi tovarooborot', *SPK*, no. 1, 1989, p. 30.
84   Danilov and Selivertsov, op. cit., p. 34.
85   *Izvestiya*, 5 March 1990.
86   Saikin, op. cit.
87   A. Samoilov, 'Co-operatives, To Be or Not To Be?', *Moscow News*, no. 28, 1989, p. 2.
88   The speech, delivered in April 1929, was reprinted in J. Stalin, *Leninism*, Lawrence & Wishart, London, 1940, pp. 240–93.

   The mistake Bukharin and his friends make is that they identify the growing resistance of the capitalists with the growth of their relative importance. But there are absolutely no grounds for such an identification . . . because the fact that the capitalists are resisting by no means implies that they have become stronger than we are. The very opposite is the case. The dying classes are resisting . . . because Socialism is growing faster than they, and they are becoming weaker than us. And precisely because they are becoming weaker, they feel that their last days are approaching and are compelled to resist with all the means in their power. Such is the mechanics of the intensification of the class struggle and the resistance of the capitalists (p. 259).

89   S. Golovina and A. Shokhin, 'Tenevaya ekonomika: za realizm otsenok', *Kommunist*, 1, 1990, pp. 51–7.
90   In 1989 the 257,000 detected 'economic crimes' were estimated to have comprised just 1 per cent of all such crimes. Yu. Kozlov, 'Tenevaya ekonomika i prestupnost'', *Voprosy ekonomiki*, 3, 1990. Since that date crime of all kinds has escalated to the extent that, in some estimates, it accounts for 40 per cent of Russia's GDP.
91   I am very grateful to Professor Phil Hanson of the Centre for Russian Studies, University of Birmingham, for allowing me to draw upon his paper 'Von Mises' Revenge. Ownership Issues in Perestroika', presented at the Conference: Perestroika: A Socio-Economic Survey, Munich, July 1989.
92   'Proektnyi zakon O sobstvennosti', *Izvestiya*, 18 November 1989.
93   P. Savchenko and P. Mar'yanovskii, 'Koopertivnaya sobstvennost' pri sotsializme i vozhmozhnosti i perspektivy', *Planovoe khozyaistvo*, 2, 1988.
94   Ideas on ownership undoubtedly had a long gestation period before their appearance in Gorbachev's speeches. See, for instance, *Problemy sobstvennosti v strankakh real'nogo sotsializma*, Moscow, IEMSS, 1987; L. Abalkin, *Perestroika: Puti i problemy. Interv'yu s akedemikom*, Moscow, Ekonomika, 1988; M. Gorbachev, *Potentsial kooperatsii – delu perestroiki*, Moscow, izd. Politicheskaya Literatura, 1988
95   The Law on Individual Labour Activity of November 1986 allowed for the licensing of individuals to operate small-scale businesses using family labour only. Able-bodied people of working age were not permitted to work full-time in such ventures.
96   K. Khubiev, 'Kooperativy, arenda, sobstvennost'', *Ekonomicheskaya gazeta*, 2, 1989, p. 8; Yu. Sukhotin, 'Sobstvennost': perestroika otnoshenii', *Ekonomicheskaya gazeta*, no.

1, 1989, p. 17.

97 V. Loshak, 'Two Thousand and One Laws', *Moscow News*, no. 31, July, 1988, p. 12; also, *Moscow News*, no. 33, 1989, p. 7.

98 L. Kunel'skii, 'Kooperatsii – dinamizm razvitiya', *Ekonomicheskaya gazeta*, no. 34, August 1988, p. 12.

99 *SPK*, no. 1, 1989, p. 7.

100 Danilov and Selivertsov, op. cit., p. 35.

101 Postanolvenie Soveta Ministrov SSSR (5 June 1989), 'O merakh po ustraneniyu nedostatok v slozhivsheisya praktike tsenoobrazovaniya', *SP SSSR* 1989, no. 8, art. 25.

102 *Moscow News*, no. 28, 1989, p. 8.

103 A. Bossart, 'Zhizn' zanaves naloga', *Ogenok*, July 1988.

104 For a very useful background study of the evolution of Soviet taxation policy, see M. A. Newcity, *Taxation in the Soviet Union*, Praeger, London, 1986.

105 P. Bunich, 'I soyuzniki i konkurenty', *Ogenok*, April 1988.

106 Postanovlenie Verkhovnogo Soveta SSSR (29 June 1988), 'O poryadke nalogooblozheniya dokhodov chlenov kooperativov', *SP SSSR* 1988, no. 27, art. 72.

107 V. Gurevich, 'Co-operatives Demand the Right to Exist', *Moscow News*, no. 28, 1989, p. 9.

108 Samoilov, op. cit., p. 2.

109 A. Bekker, 'Komi Republic's Government Blocks Decision', *Moscow News*, no. 31, 30 July 1989, p. 10.

110 V. Tolstoi, 'Kooperativ ishchet soyuznikov', *Izvestiya*, 13 August 1988; V. Matukovskii, 'Zavist' i len'', *Izvestiya*, 8 August 1988.

111 *Moscow News*, 20 November 1988.

112 See G. Andrusz, *Housing and Urban Development in the USSR*, Macmillan, London, 1984, Chapter 3.

113 N. Shemelev, 'Libo sila, libo rubl'', *Znamya*, no. 1, 1989.

114 *Moscow News*, no. 5, 1989.

115 *Izvestiya*, 3 February 1990.

116 *Sovetskaya Rossiya*, 11 October 1989.

117 *Ekonomicheskaya zhizn'*, 16, 1990.

118 *Sovetskaya Rossiya*, 20 October 1989.

119 V. Romanchuk, 'Kooperativy vykupaet zavod', *Izvestiya*, 27 February 1989, p. 2.

120 L. I. Abalkin, 'Vozrozhdenie kooperatsii', *Sovetskoe potrebitel'skoe obshchestvo*, no. 2, 1989, p. 5.

121 Ibid.

122 Ibid.

123 G. Shmelyov, 'No need to Scare with Hiring', *Moscow News*, no. 26, 25 June 1989, p. 3.

124 V. Loshak, 'Co-operatives under Fire', *Moscow News*, no. 33, 1989, p. 7.

125 See, for example, A. Gerschenkron, *Continuity in History and Other Essays*, Harvard University Press, Cambridge, Mass., 1968; *Europe in the Russian Mirror*, CUP, Cambridge, 1970.

126 V. Saikin, 'Reputatsiya. Kakova ona segodnya u Moskovskikh kooperatorov?', *Nedelya*, no. 50, 1988.

127 *Sovetskaya kul'tura*, 6 August 1989.

128 In so far as co-operatives epitomised the direction demanded by reformers for the whole econonomy, the most trenchant populist criticism of perestroika, by Nina Andreyeva, applies equally to co-operatives. See *Sovetskaya Rossiya*, 13 March 1988; *Molodaya Gvardiya*, no. 7, 1989.

129 *Ekonomicheskaya gazeta*, 13, 1989.
130 K. Marx and F. Engels, 'Manifesto of the Communist Party', (1848) in *Selected Works in Two Volumes*, vol. 1, FLPH, Moscow, 1962.
131 O. Kryshtanovskaya, 'Ktopravit Rossiei?', *Argumenty i Fakty*, no. 30, July 1998. The article is based on an interview with the Speaker in the Khanty-Manyiiskii Autonomous Region [*okrug*] Duma in the Russian Federation.

PART III
HOUSING CO-OPERATIVES
IN EUROPE

Introduction to Part III

Housing co-operatives represent one of a number of forms of non-profit housing[1] which collectively comprise a distinctive form of social housing tenure.[2] They are distinguished by the fact that central to their philosophy and statutes is the guaranteed role for tenants or members in determining policies directly relevant to the co-operative. In general, the tenants' or residents' councils set up by non-profit housing associations act in an advisory, not decision-making capacity. Countries vary considerably in terms of their attitudes towards the issue of equity: strictly speaking, co-operatives are limited equity associations. This means that on leaving the co-operative members receive a limited return, if any, on the capital appreciation of the property in which they have been living.

In the view of one writer on the subject, 'the marks of the housing co-operative' are 'voluntary and spontaneous formation, group responsibility, equality of rights and duties, common ownership, permanent or temporary and common services'.[3] For another author, a 'housing co-operative enables people to collectively own and control one of their fundamental human rights – housing – on the basis of mutual aid rather than of individual gain or distant bureaucracy'.[4] It is a co-operative society which corporately owns a housing estate in which each member occupies, or is a prospective occupier of, a dwelling. No member owns a separate flat or house but each is an equal shareholder in the co-operative society which owns the whole development. Should the association find it has a surplus, it is left to the general meeting to decide how it should be allocated. In some cases it is distributed according to principles laid down in the ICA charter,[5] while in others it can be used to develop more co-operative dwellings or used for more general social purposes such as providing benefits for the elderly or pre-school facilities.

The policies adopted by housing co-operatives place them in three economic categories:[6] the first allows each member who leaves the co-operative to benefit from any increase in the market value of the land and buildings, which means that the member can take a capital gain on this equity or loan share. These are essentially co-operatives of owner-occupiers who might provide a range of services (for themselves) on a collective basis. The

145

second category regards payments made by members as mortgage repayments; on departure from the co-operative the member is allowed to take a sum related to the mortgage principal which has been paid during the tenancy. The third type is referred to as a *par value* co-operative, which means that a member who leaves sells back his or her membership loan share to the society: that is, withdraws no more than the original capital contribution. These are frequently referred to as tenants' co-operatives. There are also hybrid versions of these three types.

A third leading specialist on the subject speaks of 'attempting to define' a housing co-operative, 'because the only way to do so is through a detailed study of all the different types of organisation calling themselves co-operatives'. However, a minimum definition is that 'they are a voluntary association by means of which dwellers can collectively own their own housing and control the process of housing'.[7]

The principal distinction between housing co-operatives lies in whether they are 'collectively owned' or 'individually owned'. In the case of the former, following the construction of accommodation the co-operative maintains ownership, while the latter sees the transfer of the accommodation to its members. Even in the second instance, the co-operative may continue in existence in order to maintain and manage the property for its members. This might be a wholly newly constituted 'management co-operative'.

Just as industrial co-operatives differ from a variety of 'participatory' schemes, so the housing co-operative differs from (local authority) housing associations or tenant management schemes. The critical difference is that co-operatives own the enterprise or house.

By the beginning of the 1980s it was already noticeable that housing starts in Western Europe were falling and costs were rising, while in the construction industry both unemployment and costs were rising. The timing and incidence of these phenomena differed from country to country. Apart from the unemployment issue, they were also apparent in East and Central Europe. By the end of the decade all European countries were experiencing major problems in the housing sector, which in the CEECs intensified in the years following the political upheavals of 1989–90.

During the 1990s, the falling output of dwelling units and the decision to privatise the public housing stock in a number of European countries, spectacularly so in Russia and the UK, have short- and long-term implications for housing consumers. High unemployment in the economy at large affects people's ability to pay their rents or repay loans. At the same time a high proportion of low-income households receive some form of state housing benefit.

Where the state has not played a prominent role in housing provision or is seeking to reduce its role, and where house prices are above the means of large sections of the population, especially during a recession, then alternative forms of housing assistance have to be found. Two other conditions make an alternative even more pressing: firstly, where landlords are converting rental accommodation into condominiums, thereby reducing the stock of accommodation available for renting;[8] and, secondly, where household formation is increasing, particularly amongst young single persons, as part of changing demographic patterns, wealth distribution, career paths and life styles.[9]

The development of the modern theory of property rights in the 1970s is thought by some to constitute one of the most important advances in economic thinking since 1945. It can be helpful to interpret housing as falling into three categories of property right. First of all, there is the right to use an asset (*ius usus*), which has to be distinguished from, secondly, the right to a return on the asset (*ius usus fructus*), which has in turn to be distinguished from the third component, the right to dispose of the asset (*ius abutendi*). To a determinate degree these correspond to the public (state, municipal), co-operative and private types of housing tenure.

Housing, when studied in terms of tenure and thus in terms of its associated property rights, may act as a barometer of tectonic shifts in society. Household movements between housing tenures represent adaptations to the rights enjoyed by individuals in other tenures and to a changing environment in which social rights of citizenship are being reformulated. As a result of their 'propertyless' status, homeless people, refugees and squatters are frequently caught in a process of being excluded, which means that they are denied a variety of political and social rights. Variations in tenure, and thus in property rights, between countries, serve as important signifiers of a society's social and economic behaviour in many other contexts.

Co-operative housing is frequently seen as a form of self-help for those who do not have an immediate claim to state rented accommodation and cannot afford to pay the rents charged for private rented property or to enter the home-owner sector. By extension it has been a way of meeting the needs of homeless people who may or may not also be squatters. In the past the term 'squatter' has referred to people occupying land to which they have no formal legal title, in order to farm it and/or to build shelter for themselves.[10] In recent decades the term 'squatter' has in Europe applied to those gaining entry to and occupying housing or other buildings as a means of meeting their need for shelter. With few exceptions, squatting has been an urban phenomenon associated with the movement of people from the countryside into the larger cities and with the absence of cheap housing.[11] Housing co-operatives have sometimes emerged out of squatting.

Governments are looking for ways to meet housing needs that do not wholly rely on state-subsidised provision or depend exclusively on private financing to build or buy. Politicians in various countries in the European Union have favoured the re-expansion of the privately rented sector. It remains to be seen whether co-operative and other types of non-profit housing will become credible tenures for policy makers to cultivate.

Notes

1   In Germany, 'non-profit' means that the association has to: (a) charge a reasonable rent, taking into account a tenant's income and the general market rent level; (b) provide accommodation for the broad mass of the population, with special regard for low-income earners; and (c) not exceed a 4 per cent ceiling on profit distribution.

2   Two principal types of social housing are found in the member states of the EU: (a) that which is constructed and managed by public organisations or by non-profit organisations (which normally work in close collaboration with local councils); (b) that built and (in the case of rental accommodation) managed by private investors. It includes housing built for renting and for sale. See *Funding of the Social Housing*, published by the Belgian Presidency for the 5th Annual Meeting of the European Housing Ministers, Brussels, 1993, p. 6.

3   M. Digby, *Co-operative Housing*, Occasional Paper, No. 42, The Plunkett Foundation for Co-operative Studies, Oxford, 1978, p. 2.

4   J. Hands, *Housing Co-operatives*, Society for Co-operative Dwellings, London, 1975, p. 30.

5   'The economic results arising out of the operations of the society belong to the members of that society and should be distributed in such a manner as would avoid one member gaining at the expense of others. This may be done by: (a) provision for the development of the business of the co-operative; (b) provision of common services; or (c) distribution among the members in proportion to their transactions with the society.'

6   Hands, op. cit., pp. 30–36, where the author presents a clear, concise summary of the arguments for and against each of the three main categories of housing co-operative.

7   J. Birchall, *Building Communities the Co-operative Way*, Routledge and Kegan Paul, London, 1988, p. 20.

8   J. van Weesep, *Condominium: A New Housing Sector in the Netherlands*, Department of Geography, Rijksuniversiteit Utrecht, Utrecht, 1986.

9   It is now being suggested that the downsizing of the welfare state makes the rebirth of the multigenerational family household inevitable. Increases in life expectancy, rising costs of child support and residential care, growing working flexibility and mobility, increased home working and the growth of 'cyber schooling' could, it is believed, lead individuals to group together in larger households. See G. Leach, *2020 Vision*, Barclays Life, 1998.

10   In the immediate aftermath of the Second World War, the housing shortage led groups of people to squat on land in the south of England, where they erected dwellings for themselves. See D. Hardy and C. Ward, *Arcadia for All: The Legacy of a Makeshift*

Landscape, Mansell, London, 1984.

11 In 1983, 27.9 per cent of the total urban population in Turkey was classified as squatters. In Ankara and Istanbul squatters accounted for 65 per cent and 45 per cent of the respective populations. See F. Yavuz et al., *Sehircilik: Sorunlar-Uygulama ve Politika*, Ankara Universitesi, Ankara, 1978. Cited in A. Sule Ozuekren, *Workers Housing Co-operatives in Turkey: A Qualitative Evaluation of the Movement*, Sectoral Activities Programme (SA 2. 18/WP. 29), International Labour Office, Geneva, 1990, p. 3.

5 Soviet Russia: The Struggle against Statism

This chapter examines the role in the Soviet Union of a form of housing tenure which was neither 'private' nor 'state'. The fortunes of housing co-operatives improved when Soviet society was in a phase of political liberalisation. As capitalism hardened in Russia, the hegemonic market model of social and economic development zealously promoted by the USA pushed the co-operative tenure aside in favour of private ownership by individual home-owners or by private landlords. Those opposing this drift have tended to remain stalwart supporters of state-subsidised municipal accommodation.

Failed Beginnings Prior to 1917

In spite of the popularity of the co-operative form, on the eve of the revolution in 1917 housing co-operatives remained an untried alternative. According to a contemporary Russian commentator, consumer associations in Russia had still not attempted to build housing for their members, principally because construction co-operatives were 'still weakly developed'. The fact that the All-Russian Council of Workers' Co-operatives had placed the housing question on its agenda and that a resolution had been passed were looked upon as signs of progress.[1] Even where they were established, such as the Third Basin Society in St Petersburg, which erected a four-block complex, membership was 'beyond the means of most people, including the lower middle class'.[2] A delegate at the March 1917 Congress of the Russian Workers' Co-operatives pointed out that, since municipal authorities would be quite unable in the foreseeable future to provide new housing on a large scale and philanthropy and charity should be totally rejected, the working class could only solve the housing problem through the creation of house-building associations. War and revolution broke out before this solution could be tested.

Housing Tenures 1917–90

Soviet housing policy was established under the exigencies of revolution and civil war between 1917 and 1920, when two new forms of housing tenure were created – the municipalised and nationalised sectors. The former was owned and operated by the local soviets and the latter by economic agencies and public institutions, who retained the accommodation already attached to these bodies. (That is to say, when a factory or museum was nationalised so was the accommodation belonging to it.) The introduction of the New Economic Policy in 1920 brought changes in housing policy; the private sector was resuscitated and co-operatives were set up.

In 1991 the four tenure categories which had emerged by 1924 were still the pillars of house ownership: (i) local soviet (municipal housing); (ii) state ministries, enterprises, trade unions ('departmental sector'); (iii) house-building co-operatives; and (iv) individual home ownership.[3] Although the Housing Code is to a large extent obsolete, a new code has not yet been finalised. This means that the 1984 Code remains in effect if its provisions do not contradict the numerous legal acts which have been adopted since then. In light of the paradigm shift and privatisation of the state housing stock by selling it to sitting tenants, a recent reclassification of the housing stock virtually reversed the above order by nominating 'private housing owned by citizens or their association' as the first type of tenure – the abolition of 'soviets' means that this tenure is now referred to as the 'municipal stock', and 'co-operatives' no longer exist as a separate category, having been subsumed either within the private sector or the fourth category 'social, consisting of property belonging to social organisations'.[4]

For three decades after 1960 the state was responsible for erecting 76–85 per cent of all accommodation in towns. Even after the economy slid into decline after 1983, this figure was 81 per cent in 1988. Its contribution was lower if housing construction in the countryside was included: it rose from 51 per cent in 1960 to 59 per cent in 1965, peaked at 75 per cent in 1980 and declined to 71 per cent in 1988.[5] The structure of housing tenures in 1989 is shown in Table 5.1.

In the 1980s the local authorities[6] controlled less than half of the nation's public housing stock.[7] The rejuvenation of the local soviets, which was one of Gorbachev's priorities, could have seen an accelerated progress towards the completion of the very slow transfer of accommodation belonging to enterprises and organisations into their jurisdiction that had been government policy since 1957. The aim of the transfer was to reduce the state subsidy to housing by rationalising the management of the state-owned housing stock.

Table 5.1 Structure of housing ownership in 1989 (per cent)

Owner	Town and country	of which	
		in towns	in rural areas
Overall of which:	100.0	100.0	100.0
State-owned of which:	54.7	72.3	24.0
Municipal	*23.0*	*35.4*	*1.3*
Departmental	*31.7*	*36.9*	*22.7*
Social organisations (e. g. Union of Writers)	2.6	0.6	6.0
Co-operatives (ZhSK)	3.7	5.7	0.2
Owner-occupation	39.0	21.4	69.8

Source: Goskomstat, *Narodnoe khozyaistvo SSSR v 1989 g.*, Moscow, 1990, p. 165; Goskomstat, *Statisticheskii press-byulleten'*, Moscow, 1990, no. 20, p. 13. See also E. M. Blekh, *Povyshenie effektivnosti ekspluatatsii zhilykh zdanii*, Stroiizdat, Moscow, 1987, p. 19.

The transfer envisaged a shift of property between 'state' bodies and therefore remained part of state property. However, with the privatisation of the economy during the 1990s, departmental housing has increasingly become the property of financially independent enterprises. Not all of them now want to surrender control over 'their' real estate.[8] On the other hand, the EU includes in its technical assistance programme (TACIS) projects directly concerned with helping enterprises and organisations to divest themselves of accommodation and other 'objects of collective consumption' by transferring these resources to the local soviets free of charge or at a negotiated price.

Even where the transfer does take place, in the longer term local authorities might well divest themselves of responsibility for the management and ownership of at least part of their vast housing stock. As is discussed below, an enhanced role for co-operatives became a possibility and probably would have been preferable to the policy that is emerging. For reasons which are not entirely clear, neither the British Government nor the EU Commission has adopted a policy on housing in Russia (and other countries in the former Soviet Union and in East and Central Europe). As a result they have been persuaded to use the American condominium model instead of the culturally and ideologically more appropriate social and non-profit housing models found in Western Europe.

For a short period, between 1955 and 1961, the Soviet Government encouraged private housing construction. In 1956, prior to the re-establishment of co-operatives as a tenure form, the central government sent out an instruction to employers asking them to make building materials, transport and credit facilities available to those employees wishing to build their own homes. The Government's sirenic approach to the owner-occupier sector was accompanied by admonitions to those seeking to gain 'unearned incomes' from private renting at usurious rates. Evasion of the law was widespread, particularly in suburban areas of large cities. By 1962 a Government-inspired campaign was well under way in legal journals and the national press against the alleged abuses by private home owners. This was the prelude to new legislation on co-operatives.

The Rise and Decline of the Housing Co-operative, 1924–37

The introduction of NEP in 1921 was accompanied by a thaw in attitudes towards co-operatives. The planning and construction of the workers' settlement in Moscow, Sokol, designed by the leading architects of the time (including Shchusev, the Vershenin brothers and Kolli), was carried out under the auspices of a decree on housing co-operatives.[9] In Lenin's view, now that the working class controlled the means of production, the development of co-operatives had become a 'positive necessity'. On the assumption that the only thing needed to achieve socialism was to demonstrate to the masses the advantages of co-operation, Lenin threw his weight behind the advocates of the co-operative movement and in doing so gave an undoubted fillip to the decision to set up housing co-operatives. Nevertheless, widespread antipathy within the Party to the co-operatives generally had a dampening effect on their development. Doubts and hostility notwithstanding, on 16 May 1924 the XIII Party Congress passed a resolution which, in stressing the need to pay greater attention to the housing question and the necessity of drawing upon the 'independent activity of the population', proposed the creation of housing co-operatives. Subsequently, on 19 August 1924, two quite distinct forms of co-operative association were established: the house-leasing co-operative association (ZhAKT) and the house-building co-operative association (ZhSK). The former was charged with managing the socialised housing transferred to it and the latter with new house building.

The House-leasing Co-operative (ZhAKT)

The failure of departments of the local authorities (local soviets) to maintain their properties in a satisfactory condition led to the gradual transfer of the housing that they controlled to the ZhAKTs. By the late 1920s they were widely regarded as the most efficient way of running and managing municipalised accommodation. Besides having the right to lease and then rent out municipalised housing, they were allowed to convert this accommodation into co-operative property by deducting rent to redeem the cost of the building.[10] The individual associations were combined into urban, provincial and republican unions of housing co-operatives, at the apex of which stood the All-Union Council of Housing Co-operatives (*Tsentrozhilsoyuz*). By the end of 1926, two-thirds of the housing stock belonging to the local soviets, representing almost 40 per cent of the total state sector, had been leased to the ZhAKTs. A decade later, these associations were administering 42 per cent of the whole socialised sector (which included housing belonging to enterprises, ministries and other public bodies) and 84 per cent of the municipalised stock.[11]

Government support for the leasing co-operatives rested on the understanding that the co-operatives would maintain the existing housing stock and, by undertaking structural repair work, increase the amount of living space.[12] The co-operatives were also charged with organising kindergartens, crèches, communal dining rooms, laundries, clubs and recreation rooms. Additionally, their brief included taking steps to tackle the problem of illiteracy – although there is little evidence that in practice their activities were this wide-ranging. From a more theoretical and ideological standpoint, they were regarded as a way of involving the 'broad masses' in the field of administration and of 'drawing us out of the petit-bourgeois swamp of the individual economy and leading us to a collectivised way of life on a socialist basis'.[13]

The House-building Co-operative (ZhSK)

Unlike the ZhAKTs, which were a sort of management co-operative, the task of the ZhSKs was to contribute directly to the housing stock by erecting new dwellings. Reflecting the Government's pervasive preoccupation with social class, the ZhSks were divided into two categories: workers' co-operatives (RZhSKTs) and general citizens' co-operatives (OZhSKTs). Only employees in state, co-operative and other public organisations (or individuals equal to them in rights, such as invalids) could be members of the former, whereas any citizen could join the latter. This meant that, although the OZhSKTs were able to attract individuals with private capital, they could not claim the same privileges, such as access to state credit and building materials, as workers' co-operatives.[14] By the mid-1920s, the ZhSK was alleged to be very popular, despite the fact that labour costs were relatively high, building materials expensive and work always behind schedule, and that building organisations tended to treat workers' co-operatives in a very offhand way.[15] The Government was intent on making the co-operative the principal vehicle for dealing with the acute shortage of housing and, to this end, in 1927 ruled that the share contribution for workers' co-operatives should be reduced to 13 per cent of the estimated building cost with the balance repayable over 60 years, at an annual interest rate of 0.25–2 per cent a year. These measures were an attempt to counter charges that monthly payments were too high.

Then in 1928 the Government issued a decree which envisaged that the role of the co-operative should be further enhanced since it was 'necessary to attract substantial sums of private capital for the construction of large houses'.[16] Partly as a consequence of this policy, the amount of living space erected by ZhSKy during the period 1928–32 was almost three times greater than in the preceding five-year period (1923–27). However, this absolute increase cannot conceal the fact that the ZhSK's contribution relative to other sectors was halved between 1929 and 1937, from 14.6 per cent to 6.8 per cent. Paradoxically, it was during the second Five-Year Plan that the XVI RSFSR Congress of Soviets (15–23 January 1935) passed a resolution to the effect that 'urban soviets must cease their unhealthy practice of undermining the role of housing co-operatives'.[17]

This critical comment on the behaviour of local authorities is a classic and tantalising example of how, during the rising tide of centralising Stalinism, policy directives emanating from the central government (and Party) were ignored by local authorities. In their defence it should be said that local authorities (like all other agencies) were frequently given tasks and targets which they were unable to carry out for lack of resources.

Demise of Housing Co-operatives

In the 1980s the change in official policy towards this sector came to be explained in terms of the incapacity of housing co-operatives to cope with the scale of the new problems and tasks created by rapid urbanisation[18] and the attendant need to embark upon a massive building programme, which would require the increasing use of industrialised construction technology. Secondly, the larger budgetary revenues at the disposal of local soviets reinforced their authority, power and ability to assume greater responsibility for the management of housing.[19] This meant that the soviets could resume their housing management function. A third and damning indictment of the ZhSKs was that the houses which they built were effectively the private property of their individual members – even though up to 90 per cent of the cost of construction was financed by the state through direct loans and by industrial enterprises, which were diverting to the co-operatives resources designated for their own house-building projects. The momentous societal transformation that had occurred over the previous decade made it virtually inevitable that major changes in housing policy would be introduced. These came with the publication of a Law on 17 October 1937 entitled 'On the Preservation of the Housing Stock and Improving the Housing Economy in Towns'. Among other things, it abolished both types of co-operative.[20]

For the dozen years of their existence, co-operatives were looked upon as highly successful. They were also popular, at least among higher-status, better remunerated groups. Yet issues concerning the size of credit and the length of the repayment period, the unhelpful attitude, if not deeply rooted animosity, of the local soviets towards them, and their social composition have still not been sufficiently well researched. All these factors continued to be a cause of contention into the 1990s. Detailed studies remain to be conducted on the legal entitlements of co-operative members and to discover the extent to which, as has been frequently asserted, co-operative property had been converted into private property.

In the eyes of the Government, the co-operative form of housing management and construction had been 'dialectically' superseded by more strictly socialist forms of organising house building and management, namely the local soviets and state firms[21] and agencies. Undoubtedly, there were good 'objective' reasons for their abolition; however, ideological imperatives also played an important role in their demise. In 1936 Stalin declared that socialism had been achieved; and since Lenin had defended the co-operative as a form of organisation well suited to the period of transition to socialism, they were duly abolished in the following year. The interaction of substantive arguments, such as the fact that the centralisation of administrative control in the hands of local soviets would lead to greater economic and organisational efficiency, and that the co-existence of different property forms had been ideologically anathematised, requires further study.

In the final analysis, the co-operative tenure probably was incompatible with the rigid parameters set by the administrative-command economy, based as it was on the centralised allocation of building materials. The abolition of a market for building materials undermined the case for preserving this alternative (housing property) form. In other words, the key decisions taken in the realm of economics (on markets and prices), politics (preferred forms of property) and sociology (social class) determined the fate of housing co-operatives. The role of 'property' and 'class' in the 1920s and 1930s as objective realities and ideological (policy-legitimising) constructs determining housing policy began to be re-enacted in the 1980s, albeit under different historical circumstances, and in 1998 continue to exert an influence in the evolving housing policy.

The House Building Co-operative, 1953–86

Structure and Organisation

If standards of living were to improve, as socialism promised and as the destruction, privations and sacrifices caused by war made socially and morally imperative, then far more resources would have to be directed into house building. This meant, among other things, that in the aftermath of Stalin's death in 1953 it was inevitable that the goals and *modus operandi* of the system which had evolved under his leadership would have to be modified. Although by 1953 the output of consumer goods and services was beginning to increase, more drastic improvements were necessary. In July 1957 the Government issued a major housing decree proclaiming its intention to eliminate the housing shortage within ten to twelve years. In revising the house construction programme upwards, it prepared the ground for re-establishing the house-building co-operative (ZhSK) as a tenure form. The decree itself made no mention of the co-operative, but chastised local soviets and heads of enterprises for not organising builders into house-building collectives. The absence of any reference to co-operatives in the decree was rectified less than a year later. In practice, however, individual (private) builders continued to receive preferential treatment over the co-operative: the former were granted credit for a seven- to ten-year period, whereas co-operative members remained deprived of any state assistance, having to deposit the full cost of construction in the bank before they could start building. But, because of the financial unattractiveness of the co-operative form, the 1958 decree failed to attract an influx of would-be co-operative members.[22]

The Government was forced to re-think and no doubt overcome antipathies within its ranks towards co-operatives. Four years later legislation was passed making co-operatives eligible for state loans to cover up to 60 per cent of the estimated cost of construction, repayable over a ten- to fifteen-year period.[23] Just two years later a decree, 'On the Further Development of Co-operative Housing Construction', increased the credit facility from 60 to 70 per cent in rural areas, the Far North, Kazakhstan and 'other remote areas'. In other words, the state regarded the co-operative flat as a signifier of status and privilege, but, more importantly, as a reward for the above-average hardship experienced by households willing to migrate to and work in particularly harsh conditions. At the same time it extended the repayment period to twenty years. The loan bore an annual interest charge of 0.5 per cent rising to 3 per cent for overdue payments.[24]

Eighteen years later, in August 1982, the Government reduced the initial deposit to 30 per cent of the estimated construction costs for the country at large and to 20 per cent in Siberia and 'other similar regions'. The repayment period for these loans of 70–80 per cent was simultaneously extended to 25 years.[25] The actual size of the loan and the repayment period were decided in each individual case by Construction Bank (Stroibank) officials in conjunction with the co-operative's board of management and the local soviet's executive committee (*ispolkom*). By now the modern house-building co-operative was being defined as a voluntary association of citizens set up with the objective of combining their resources for the joint acquisition of accommodation and future use of communal services at their own expense.[26] (This wording, in speaking of 'voluntary association', indicates how near to dramatic change Soviet society now stood.)

Since the authorities had always envisaged that co-operative houses should be multi-storey blocks with five or more floors, with up to 300 apartments, the number of shareholders would under most circumstances exceed the required minimum membership, which ranged from twelve in rural areas to no fewer than sixty members in Moscow and Leningrad. Because it had to cover its capital expenditure, management and maintenance costs, the co-operative had a real interest in increasing the number of members, for this lowered the contribution required of each member towards the running and upkeep of the building.

A group of individuals wanting to form a co-operative would approach the housing department either of the local soviet or, more often, of the enterprise at which they worked, where they had to involve the local trade union branch in all negotiations. A general meeting of the applicants was then convened. Those present at the meeting would decide to set up a co-operative and nominate a group of three to five persons to deal with the necessary preliminary organisational matters such as examining potential locations and preparing the draft constitution. From the moment of registration, the ZhSK became a juridical person, which owned the property. Thus, houses built by the ZhSK belonged to the co-operative 'as a right of co-operative property'. This meant that it had the exclusive right of disposing of the property belonging to it. In other words, members of the co-operative did not acquire a 'right of personal ownership' to the co-operative but a right, corresponding to their share, to the property and use of specific parts of it. Although this meant that it was for the co-operative to find a replacement member, and merely to refund the departing member's capital outlay, the person leaving could exercise wide rights of nomination, which frequently enabled the departing co-operative member to reap a windfall gain.

With the systemisation and formalisation of the housing market, the state had not seen much to be gained in restricting the practice of paying 'key-money'. The payment of key-money was an instrument in the commodification and marketisation of housing. Tolerated rather than encouraged, like other black economy or illegal practices, key-money would eventually 'mature into' a formal market-economic mechanism. In fact, so widespread were these housing transactions that they constituted what was tantamount to a parallel market; the additional (key-money) charge represented the difference between the subsidised price for a flat and its market price, which nullified the real income gain which citizens received through the subsidy. Of course, it also meant a large unearned income gain for those disposing of an inherited property.

From the point of view of the co-operative management and membership the social attributes and financial standing of the prospective member were of paramount concern. Thus, financial solvency and personal recommendation were critical determinants in the selection of new entrants. If it were later discovered that a shareholder had joined the co-operative by deception, for instance, by presenting false documentation and information, or by purchasing a share from unearned income or from illegal use of resources belonging to state, co-operative or public bodies, the local authorities had prima-facie grounds for requesting that shareholder's eviction.

Ironically, this last legal provision may well have served to extend the network of individuals systematically or occasionally engaged in corruption and bribery. Officials in local government and other organisations directly involved in accommodation transactions were in a position to seek personal gain from individuals perpetrating even a minor crime in order to secure entry into a co-operative. Perhaps because they knew the ramifications of prosecuting so well, the authorities and the courts rarely resorted to eviction. The pervasiveness of corruption in its various manifestations, from nepotism to blackmail, also explains the importance attached, firstly, by Andropov to rooting out corruption, and then by reformers to establishing the 'rule of law'. It also explains why, especially after the initial flush of glasnost, the principle of 'social justice' was so appealing to the population and why it was the *primus inter pares* in the reformers' lexicon. The tragic irony is that the majority of the people have been so accustomed to acquiring goods and services 'informally' or 'illegally' that the implementation of rules to ensure justice would affect them all adversely: of course, some more adversely than others.

The Government established certain minimum conditions for applicants wishing to join a co-operative, and so not everybody was eligible for membership. Normally, applicants had to be registered with the militia as a permanent resident in the district where the co-operative was being formed. The principal criterion for offering a place in a ZhSK was that the applicant's living space fell below the average amount of living space per person found in that locality.[27] This norm varied from district to district and depended on the size of the local housing stock. In Novosibirsk and Ufa (both cities with populations of over one million), individuals with less than eight square metres of actual living space were eligible to be placed on the local soviet's waiting list, while for residents of Odessa the figure stood at a niggardly four square metres.[28]

Since large numbers of people found themselves in this situation and co-operative membership was regarded as a privilege, other factors were taken into account when the local authority examined the list of potential members submitted to it. Theoretically, those given preferential treatment reflected the general ethos of Soviet society, which was essentially meritocratic whilst protecting the weak. In other words, as already mentioned, it rewarded those whom it deemed to have 'sacrificed' by working (or serving) in harsh climatic conditions where, moreover, cultural and living standards were also low; secondly, it rewarded those whose past efforts had been recognised by some honorific reward. It also sought to provide for those who, through no fault of their own, had become disadvantaged: invalids and people whose houses were to be demolished as part of an urban renewal project or because they were beyond repair. This is a reasonably accurate description of the broad parameters of social policy, as defined and rationalised by those directly responsible for the allocation of accommodation. However, since Gorbachev's initiation of his policy of 'openness' (glasnost), there has been a flood of evidence testifying that the above depiction of housing policy is a misleading representation of reality: privilege, paternalism and corruption, rather than being peripheral or random anomalous events in the process of allocation, were much more pervasive in effecting access, not only to co-operatives but to all other forms of housing tenure.[29]

In 1989, the Belorussian trade union council passed a resolution deploring the operation of the waiting list system and the frequent infringements of social justice that were perpetrated in the distribution of accommodation.[30] It is now clear that the censure was fully justified, even though many such resolutions contain a strong element of hypocritical self-castigation. The acute shortage of housing and the modes of its production and distribution lay at the heart of the problem and no amount of condemnatory resolutions have removed the social injustices that occur. However, 'the market' which is now so ardently recommended by Western (predominantly United States) advisors is far from a panacea for Russian citizens.

Hence, only in a very formal sense could 'any group of individuals' decide to form a co-operative. Both the enterprise management (often in conjunction with the trade union branch of a factory or organisation and, formerly, the party group) and the housing department of the local soviet controlled access to the formation of a co-operative. They also determined who could join the waiting list to form a co-operative.

The Housing Situation during the Early Years of Perestroika

The country's leadership, echoing popular sentiment (and resentment), acknowledged that the housing situation was dire. Between 1959 and 1989 over 100 million square metres of housing space was constructed each year, equivalent to 2.0–2.2 million flats. Nevertheless, about 27 million urban inhabitants (15 per cent of the total) and 2 million (2 per cent) of rural inhabitants were registered as not having a home of their own.[31] They lived in hostels, barracks and rented rooms in the private sector. A further 3 million families consisting of four or more members lived in one-room flats. One family in five with five or more children were living in one- or two-roomed flats. Single-person households 'suffered particularly harsh living conditions', with 7 million living in hostels and privately rented rooms. The housing waiting list – which stood at 14.3 million families in 1990 – was only very slowly declining. In many towns those fortunate enough to be eligible to join a queue had to wait for ten years to be rehoused. The average amount of living space per person – and there were wide fluctuations around this average – was 15 square metres. If the target set in 1989 of building 2.3 billion square metres in the period 1986–2000 were to be achieved and the average raised to 18 square metres, the USSR would still be well down in the international league table (see Table 5.2).[32]

Table 5.2 Average flat size and per capita living space in selected countries (square metres)

	Average per capita living space	Average flat size
USSR	15	56
GDR and Czechoslovakia	15+	80
France	30+	100
FRG	40+	120
USA	50+	150
Belgium and Norway	75+	200

Source: S. V. Nikolaev, 'O zhilishchnom stroitel'stve na trinadtsatuyu pyatiletku i period do 2000 goda', *Zhilishchnoe stroitel'stvo*, no. 4, 1989, p. 7.

Furthermore, even meeting that target of 2.3 billion square metres, which would require substantial adjustments to the financing of house building, would not ensure that 'each family will be provided with its own house or flat'. It had long been acknowledged that the state could not continue to provide virtually 'free' accommodation; now this understanding was being openly articulated, with the recommendation that state-provided accommodation should be gradually reduced from 57 per cent in the twelfth Five-Year Plan (1986–90) to 17.5 per cent by the year 2000. Secondly, this reduction in centrally funded house building would have to be compensated by directing an increased proportion of enterprise profits towards new building. Thirdly, two-thirds of the state's budgetary saving on housing construction should be used to provide the infrastructure for house building undertaken by the co-operative and the owner-occupier sectors. These changes were part of a major shift in attitude within the Government to the way in which rents were determined and the ways in which the different tenures were subsidised.

Already by 1989 housing provided evidence of a move away from universalism to selectivity in social policy. It was said on the one hand that 'payment for the consumption of living space over the norm must be increased' and, on the other hand, that those on low incomes must be given a guaranteed right to free accommodation.[33] These policy shifts had considerable implications for housing co-operatives.[34]

Supply and Demand

There can be little doubt that this tenure never developed as rapidly as the Soviet leadership hoped or anticipated. The reasons for its enthusiasm for house-building co-operatives were always relatively clear. Essentially, they offered an economic benefit to the state and introduced an element of flexibility into the housing system by creating a tenure form advantageous to different social groups. Resolutions passed at the XXIII (1966), XXIV (1971), XXV (1976), and XXVI (1981) Party Congresses, which pointed to the need to increase the amount of building carried out on behalf of ZhSKs, may be regarded as definite statements of intent. But it proved difficult to translate intention into action. Co-operative house building declined steadily through the 1970s, reaching a nadir in 1980. It fell from a national peak of 10.8 per cent of all housing built in towns in 1970 to a low of 6.7 per cent in 1980. After that date it showed a steady recovery until 1989. In 1990 for the Russian Federation the figure was 5.0 per cent.[35] (See Table 5.3.)

In terms of the geographical distribution of housing co-operatives, two features in particular stand out. Firstly, there were tremendous variations between the fifteen constituent republics of the former Soviet Union and 121 provinces (*oblasts*) in terms of the contribution made by co-operatives to new house construction. In 1988, Lithuania held first place (17.5 per cent), followed by Belarus (12.0 per cent), Georgia (11.9 per cent), Latvia (10.2 per cent) and Estonia (9.9 per cent). The Russian Federation (5.7 per cent) was below the USSR average of 6.6 per cent. If the highest rates were concentrated in the Baltic States (although not exclusively), the lowest were to be found in Central Asia: Turkmenia, Kazakhstan, Tadzhikstan, Kirghizstan (2.1 per cent, 2.9 per cent, 3.6 per cent and 3.8 per cent respectively).[36]

Table 5.3 Co-operative housing construction in the USSR, 1971–88

Year	Total construction (million sq. metres)		Co-operative construction		
	Town and country	Towns only	million square metres	% of total building	% of total building in towns
1971–75	544.8	377.4	32.6	6.0	8.6
1975	109.9	76.3	5.8	5.3	7.6
1970–80	527.3	378.7	27.4	5.2	7.2
1980	105.0	76.3	5.1	4.9	6.7
1981–85	522.2	384.8	32.8	5.9	8.5
1985	113.0	77.1	7.8	6.9	10.1
1986	119.8	82.0	8.2	6.8	10.0
1987	131.4	90.3	8.9	6.8	9.9
1988	132.4	91.7	8.7	6.6	9.5

Source: Goskomstat, *Narodnoe khozyaistvo SSSR v 1989g.*, Finansy i Statistika, Moscow, 1990, p. 165; Goskomstat, *Statisticheskii press-byulleten'*, no. 20, Moscow, 1990, p. 13.

Secondly, it would appear that co-operatives were to a very considerable degree concentrated in the larger cities. For example, in 1970 Moscow and Leningrad accounted for 33.4 per cent of all co-operative house building in the RSFSR. In fact, in 1980 alone ZhSKs erected 830,000 square metres in Moscow and Leningrad, which may be compared with the 900,000 square metres built during the whole of the tenth Five-Year Plan (1976–80) in the countryside and was equivalent to 16.3% per cent of all ZhSK construction in that year.[37]

One reason for such concentration in capital cities (Moscow, Leningrad, Kiev, Yerevan, Alma-Ata) and provincial centres is that it enabled the ZhSKs to make use of standard designs, preferably of high-rise blocks constructed from prefabricated panels. Such buildings could only be erected in the vicinity of a major construction base. However, such technical factors were not the sole explanation. The attraction of the metropolitan centres to scientific, cultural and administrative organisations has been such that the state found it politic to make provision for its young, talented élites, who were able to appreciate and avail themselves of the right accorded to ZhSKs to introduce modifications to the design and furnishing of their apartment block and individual flats within it. Many architects regarded the housing co-operative as the only way of overcoming the stultifying uniformity of so many towns arising from the use of industrialised, prefabricated building techniques.[38] In the overwhelming majority of cases, allowing higher standards of decoration, better fixtures and equipment in a small number of architect-designed and individually negotiated housing co-operatives did not lead to the construction of extravagant, luxury apartments.

Although modifications were real and important to the residents, in the main they were quite minor. At the time the policy shift towards housing co-operatives was less concerned with placating the demands of various élite groups than with finding alternatives to the way in which housing was financed; above all, means had to be found to reduce the size of the state's budgetary allocation to accommodation.

The Cost and Financing of Housing Co-operatives

Although the initial deposit on a flat in a co-operative was a relatively high outlay relative to incomes, co-operatives were nonetheless still quite heavily subsidised. The state, apart from granting low interest credit, provided the infrastructure, which amounted to one-fifth of the cost of erecting residential buildings.[39] Fortunately, the price of building land was determined by Marxist economic theory, which meant that it could be no higher than the opportunity cost of the yield from lost agricultural land.[40]

In return the state benefited from the fact that the loan was repaid. Moreover, the state did not bear the burden of amortisation costs, including capital repairs, which were paid for out of a special fund contributed by the members. This amounted to an annual charge of 1.1 per cent of the estimated cost of construction. Finally, co-operatives were faced with annual service charges, which covered, *inter alia*, repairs to lifts and gas installations (not paid by tenants in state accommodation) and management fees. These too were charges for which tenants in state property were not responsible.[41]

Therefore, during the loan repayment period, the current outlay of co-operative members was 3–5 times as great as that paid by tenants in state accommodation. After the loan had been repaid, the cost of housing for co-operative members was 1.9–2.3 as great as for state tenants. One of the primary objectives of the new policy was to raise the rent tariff in order to reduce the state subsidy to cover huge running and maintenance costs and, ultimately, to equalise annual expenditures on running costs in the co-operative and state sectors.

According to one calculation, a strong case could be made for a housing reform which entailed changes to the system of charging rent in the state sector, lowered still further the deposit to be paid by co-operatives and encouraged their growth.[42] The comparatively large initial downpayment – relative to other prices, costs and the proportion of income spend on accommodation in non-socialist countries – together with a high monthly outlay on repayments of capital and interest was not in itself a deterrent to individuals wishing to join co-operatives, since the very high propensity to save in the Soviet Union meant that substantial deposits were held in personal saving bank accounts. Thus, the availability of funds for a deposit was not the determining factor of whether or not a person became a co-operative member.[43] However, as might be expected, savings were not evenly distributed: statistics published in 1989 revealed that 5 per cent of savers had holdings of over 20,000 roubles. The aggregated deposits of this small group represented 50 per cent of total savings. On the basis of this uneven distribution of 'wealth', one leading housing specialist concluded, in support of her case for maintaining a 'social guarantee' of accommodation, that 'all research demonstrates that most of the population lack savings sufficient to purchase housing'.[44] Our understanding of class structuration, which was taking place in the Soviet Union prior to perestroika, would be improved if it was known whether a correspondence existed between the size of a household's savings account and co-operative membership. It is likely that parents 'who saved for their children' were also willing to offer their married progeny financial assistance to join a co-operative, in order to reduce the enormous pressure on the family's inadequate living space.

Reducing the direct financial cost of housing to the budget was not the sole reason propelling the Government to reform the housing system. The transfer of control and responsibility for property was associated with a more pervasive problem, that of the universal disregard for publicly owned goods (state property), as reflected in the popular phrase 'public property is no one's property'. Co-operative members and owner-occupiers were not infrequently contrasted with tenants in state accommodation, who, 'having no stake in the property', 'behave like barbarians' towards their flats, 'quickly reducing them to an unsightly condition'.[45] One indicator of this negative attitude was the high level of rent arrears in the state sector. Although co-operative members were on occasion unable or unwilling to repay their loan, the scale of this problem paled into insignificance in comparison with the size of rent arrears. This phenomenon was a manifestation of the population's passivity and dependency caused by the linkage in Soviet Marxism between social progress under socialism and the 'permanent statisation of property'.

In four short years, 1986–90, this orthodoxy had not just been attacked and eroded; by September 1990 it had become a conservative heresy, doomed in its opposition to the new doctrine based on the virtues of privatising state property. A fatal flaw in the country's paternalistic culture and statisation of property lay in its inculcation of an 'irresponsible' attitude towards resources', including accommodation. The 'human factor' (Marx's *homo faber*[46]) had been neglected.

Each increment of privatisation was deemed a measure of social progress. A representative view of the 'new orthodoxy' is to be found in an article by one economist: 'Today's economic proposals all point in one direction – privatisation. Our economy simply cannot survive without private ownership. ... We cannot afford to wait decades or centuries for private ownership to evolve naturally as in other countries. We need a fully-fledged market economy now. ... Privatisation must involve giving away state property to the public or selling it for just symbolic sums'.[47] As has already been remarked, it is not a new phenomenon in Russian history for those politically in charge to demand, as they do today, the complete and immediate transformation of economy and society.

At the heart of the complaint raised by reformers and radicals was the over-involvement of the state in all economic and social affairs, and thus the need for it to cease acting as the principal provider of accommodation. Although housing privatisation was in the air, in 1990 co-operatives, implying as they did self-financing, self-governance and independence, were the main policy prescription for overcoming alienation and enabling people to exercise initiative and to feel in greater control of their lives. Both the individual and public interest would be maximised in the very premises of co-operation. Yet it was far from clear who would reap the greatest gain from co-operative enterprises and housing.

At the beginning of 1980, 1.1 million people were on the waiting list to join a ZhSK.[48] By 1985 over 1.3 million applications had been registered[49] and in 1989 it stood at 1.8 million.[50] The chairman of a Moscow co-operative estimated that the actual number of people interested in joining a ZhSk was 10–20 times greater than this.[51] The average annual rate of construction of co-operative flats – 102,000 in 1976–80, 116,000 in 1981–85, and 150,000 in 1988 – was not even sufficient to meet the demand of those for whom there was no alternative to the co-operative as a means of obtaining accommodation. This included, in particular, families working on contract in the far north, single-person households of 'average age' and young families living with their parents and thus formally provided with housing.[52]

Before the attempted coup against Gorbachev in August 1991, followed by his eclipse and the demise of the USSR, housing co-operatives seemed set to establish themselves as an important type of tenure. The shift in attitudes during the late 1980s towards the 'form of ownership appropriate under socialism' had a dramatic impact on housing policy. By 1990 it was no longer a matter of the form of ownership appropriate under socialism, but of that appropriate for the country.

Co-operative Housing: Zenith and Nadir

Notwithstanding injunctions by senior government officials and housing specialists on the imperative of expanding the co-operative sector, it was by no means certain that the hopes placed in co-operatives would come to fruition in the foreseeable future.[53] Although the central government undoubtedly regarded the development of co-operatives as a means of saving on its housing budget and more people had the wherewithal to finance housing construction, the underperformance of this sector suggested that local institutional barriers and local informal mechanisms were impeding policy implementation and the establishment of house-building co-operatives.[54]

Explanations for underperformance are largely to be found in the 'supply side'. For instance, co-operatives did not pay the cost of survey work, site clearance and preparation; neither did they bear the cost of providing social amenities and shops and other daily services, which amounted to 6 per cent of housing construction cost estimates. Therefore, since the legislation governing co-operatives did not specify where the resources for site clearance, development and landscaping were to be found, local authority building departments were less than keen to increase the number of co-operatives. Many local authorities were also recalcitrant in their approach to this tenure because they were socially and ideologically biased against it on the grounds that it encouraged queue jumping, especially by office workers and members of other social groups not well placed on the priority list for new state accommodation.

Annual surveys conducted by a central government department (Gosstroi) revealed that local councillors and full-time officials procrastinated in providing the design and cost estimate documentation which co-operatives required, and also failed to meet construction schedules;[55] for instance, against an average construction time in the state sector of 9–12 months, co-operative apartment blocks frequently took over five years to complete.[56] The chairman of the board of governors of one Leningrad co-operative complained that they were being treated as badly as 'private traders' (i.e. they were being harassed and generally mistreated); 'even though cost estimates had been prepared and the money was available to carry out urgent roof repairs, the plan to carry them out had not even been included in the five year plan'.[57]

Legislation enacted in March 1988, 'On Measures to Accelerate the Development of Housing Co-operatives',[58] attributed poor performance to 'a serious underestimation by virtually every major institution of the social and political significance of house building co-operatives'. Two main reasons were cited as being responsible for this situation: firstly, local authorities were adopting a 'formal bureaucratic approach towards them', which makes the 'allocation of a building site and the furnishing of designs and cost estimates a protracted process'; secondly, there was a general expectation that the state would provide funds for building.

The preamble of complaints then stated that the new provisions were designed to make housing co-operatives 'one of the main directions for expanding housing construction . . . so that by 1995 it will contribute no less than 2–3 times more than at present to the overall volume of housing construction'. In other words, the Government intended that this sector would account for 14–20 per cent of all new building.[59] By the end of the century, nationwide, the co-operative and owner-occupied sectors would be supplying 45–50 per cent of all new house building.[60]

The manner in which this expansion was to take place included a novel element. The law defined two types of co-operative. The first consisted of house-building co-operatives created for the purpose of constructing and running dwellings by and for the benefit of the membership. They were also allowed to acquire buildings in need of major capital repairs, renovate and then occupy them. The second type of housing co-operative was not concerned with building at all: it was set up in order to acquire newly erected or renovated housing from enterprises, organisations and the local authorities. In a number of respects it resembled the leasing co-operatives (ZhAKTs) of the 1920s and 1930s. Both types of co-operative had much to commend them, in particular their organisational flexibility, which gave them the potential to renovate and modernise the existing stock. It had long been recognised that, unless more attention was paid to this aspect of housing policy, it would be impossible to solve the housing problem.[61] After almost twenty years of government criticism that insufficient funds were being directed to major capital repair work, in 1988 the state was assigning 11.3 per cent of total investment in housing to this purpose,[62] which was quite insufficient to deal with a task that, in any case, official data grossly underestimated.

In order to encourage local authorities to adopt a more positive and less obstructive stance towards co-operatives, the decree allowed them to place a 15 per cent surcharge on co-operatives located 'in the most favourable neighbourhoods and places', and to treat it as a budgetary revenue. This policy innovation had a twofold significance: firstly, it was a fiscal device to strengthen the financial base of local soviets, which among other things increased their autonomy. Secondly, the payment represented a differential rent and as such was an important step towards making rental charges for accommodation reflect its location.

In order to stimulate the construction of housing and subsequently its sale to housing co-operatives, specialist banks were allowed to grant credits to enterprises and local soviets for this purpose. Loans could range up to a maximum of 50 per cent of the estimated cost of construction, with repayments due within a six-year period after receipt of the loan. At the same time, co-operative members could be advanced loans repayable over ten years at an annual interest rate of 2–3 per cent – the differential depending on whether the property was located in a rural or an urban area.[63] People who used the money borrowed for purposes other than house purchase were to be surcharged at 12 per cent on the total loan.

Enterprises were recommended to offer financial assistance to employees wishing to join either form of co-operative. The source of this aid was increasingly to be the enterprise's social development fund (SDF), generated from above-plan profits. With the state cutting its direct investment in housing from 70 per cent in 1986 to 15 per cent by the end of the century, the profits made by enterprises and organisations would have become a far more important source of capital for investment in housing.[64] Local authorities were also empowered to make loans or grants to employees working in education, health and other occupational spheres in the so-called 'non-productive sector' (all low-paid occupations) from their local budget and other unspecified financial sources.

Another innovation allowed local architects to make changes to the standard designs and draw up individual plans for their co-operative clients. This extended and formalised existing practices (both legal and illegal) whereby co-operatives could pay for and enjoy higher levels of service (for instance, appointing a concierge) and modify the standard interior design. If the co-operative membership had the necessary financial resources, they could now request the construction of additional buildings to meet individual household needs, including garages and leisure facilities. Besides the flexibility to vary exterior forms and structures and adopt higher space standards, co-operative members were permitted – again at their own expense – to commission building and interior design co-operatives to improve upon the normal level of interior finishing.

The 1990s witnessed astronomical increases in the price of housing, especially in Moscow. The Government cut back sharply its funding of new construction from the state budget. The behaviour of the emergent finance markets, real estate agents and the whole gamut of institutions associated with private housing markets were conspicuous contributors to the view of Russia, in particular the capital, as a new Klondike, only the 'frontier' where the wealth lay was not a new country but another system – capitalism. The reaction of tenants and house-seekers ranged from squatting, setting up for a few months in 1991 a 'cardboard city' adjacent to Red Square, and the formation of organisations for homeless people to the foundation of an International Tenants' Union. As part of a broader and amorphous housing movement they were an indicator of the growth of civil society.

The first post-war housing association, 'Our House' (Nash Dom), was formed in 1991 on the Sol'yanka in the centre of Moscow. It was established as a share-holding society by the residents in one large old house. The aim was to combine their various resources in order to renovate their homes. They received no assistance from the local authority. Because of the opposition which Nash Dom and another housing association (Domstroi) met from the Moscow city council, they were pushed into joining forces to form the All-Russian Foundation for Promoting the Elimination of Communal Flats, which brought together roughly 500 housing associations throughout Moscow and in another eleven cities. It then created a Specialist Housing Cheque-Investment Fund (Zhiltovarishch) and a commercial bank (Zhilkredit).

These developments were the direct consequence of the country's rapidly and radically changing social and housing policies, which generated considerable anxiety about the future, and of the enthusiastic embrace by so many people of their newly granted freedom to organise in order to solve their own housing problems. Housing associations looked forward to taking over the administration of their accommodation and becoming the real owners.

Various housing movements recognised that, while many people were willing to invest their savings in housing, a central supportive role remained for the state. The housing association (*zhilishchnye tovarishchstva*) constituted one of the basic forms of grass roots housing movements. In 1992 representatives from 95 housing associations petitioned the Mayor of Moscow for assistance. This resulted in a series of decrees removing some of the bureaucratic obstacles hindering the development of housing associations.[65]

Needless to say, impediments remained, one of the most important of which was the absence of appropriate financial mechanisms. This led to complex schemes – sometimes ingenious, sometimes hare-brained, sometimes unscrupulously fraudulent – for raising the necessary finance to build low-rise housing estates.

During a particularly busy phase in the growth of voluntary organisations (*neformalnye*) in 1991, housing co-operatives in Moscow formed themselves into a Union. Co-operatives were now regarded as closer in form to housing associations and condominiums.[66] (In Estonia, where only 20 per cent of the housing stock remains in public ownership, in 1996 'the most important housing questions concern the creation of condominiums'.)[67]

But disillusionment with glasnost and self-help activities soon set in. Changes in the law empowering people, including knowledge of legal rights, could not and cannot easily overcome habituation to dependence on the state for building, allocating and maintaining housing. Hostile local officials, combined with a weariness and apathy amongst tenants, helped enthusiasm for housing associations to evaporate. The euphoria of the peaceful revolution inaugurated by Gorbachev had been longer than that which had accompanied the revolutions of 1917, but the civil war had been shorter. In both cases the outcome of the fierce change that had occurred in society has been a form of state capitalism, only those behind Lenin had anticipated socialism as being the final goal, whereas the forces behind Yeltsin look forward to the gift of capitalism.

As a result of political developments and changes in the housing system (especially the privatisation of publicly owned accommodation), in 1994 a group broke away from the Moscow Union of housing co-operatives to form a Union of flat-owners of municipal, co-operative and departmental housing.[68] Co-operative members began to exercise their rights under the Law on Property[69] to dispose of their flats, either by selling or by bequeathing them.[70] In this way, the co-operative apartment block crossed an important threshold from co-operative to becoming private property, thus furthering the development of a housing market. According to one estimate, in 1996 co-operatives accounted for 3.8 per cent of the housing stock in Russia.[71]

Conclusion

In the 1980s, as in the 1920s, the housing co-operative was regarded as a necessary component in an overall strategy for meeting the nation's demand for accommodation. Furthermore, in both periods, the co-operative form of housing tenure was tending to cater for a proportion of the society's different élites, including members of the working-class aristocracy. It was a tenure that was equally attractive to the white-collar middle class,[72] which, lacking status and power, was poorly placed in the queue for state housing (provided by more productive firms with high profit margins and by local soviets). On a practical level, it brought cost advantages to the state; ideologically, involving collective activity, it represented a step away from the inherent individualism of the private sector. Nevertheless, there remained a strong and large constituency for cheap, state rented accommodation which was supported by housing specialists who reaffirmed that the goal of providing 'each family with its own home by the year 2000' should be achieved 'predominantly by state forms of construction and distribution'.[73] Rents in the public sector, which accounts for roughly 40 per cent of the housing stock, are still very low.[74]

Overall, the co-operative sector mirrored changes in policy towards privately owned housing. Both had been called upon to aid economic development during crises and periods of stagnation: NEP, post-war recovery, 1955–61 and again in the late 1980s. They formed part of the society's reward structure designed to raise labour productivity, grant housing access to social groups weakly placed in the Soviet socialist housing allocation system and draw upon private savings.

The democratic virtue of co-operatives – that, largely because they are small in scale, they are controlled by their membership – was of importance to only a minority of applicants to join them. As early as 1990 the revolutionary decrees on Housing Co-operatives issued in March 1988 and the Law on Co-operatives ratified the following May could already be seen as historical, politico-legal landmarks on Russia's calvary towards large-scale privatisation of housing and of its publicly owned assets. It is another sad irony that wide sections of the population should have been so hostile to co-operatives in most spheres of activity, including house building, not knowing, expecting or wanting the privatisation which lay just three years ahead.

Notes

1   V. Ostrovskii, *Zhilishchnyi vopros i kooperatsiya*, Izd. -vo Kniga, Petrograd, n. d., c. 1916, p. 5.
2   W. Brumfield, 'Building for Comfort and Profit. The new apartment house', in W. Brumfield and B. Ruble (eds), *Russian Housing in the Modern Age: Design and Social History*, Cambridge University Press, Cambridge, 1993, p. 77.
3   See G. Andrusz, *Housing and Urban Development in the USSR*, Macmillan/CREES,

London, 1984; G. Andrusz, 'Housing Policy in the Soviet Union', in J. Sillince (ed.), *Housing Policies in Eastern Europe and the Soviet Union*, Routledge, London, 1990.

4   M. G. Masevich, 'Pravovoe regulirovanie otnoshenii po povodu nedvizhimosti', *Pravo i ekonomika*, No. 13–14, 1996, p. 5.

5   Goskomstat, *Narodnoe khozyaistvo SSSR za 70 let*, Finansy i Statistika, Moscow, 1987, p. 508; Goskomstat, *Narodnoe khozyaistvo SSSR v 1988 g.*, Finansy i Statistika, Moscow, 1989, pp. 150, 152.

6   The term used in the Soviet Union (and frequently still in the post-Soviet republics) for 'local authority' was 'local soviet'. In 1997 the term more commonly used is 'municipality' or 'local government'.

7   The degree to which it was concentrated in their hands varied tremendously between republics and between cities; for instance, it exceeded 80% in Armenia but was 37.9% in Kazakhstan and still only 37.9% in the RSFSR. See P. I. Sedugin, *Pravo na zhilishche v SSSR*, Yuridicheskaya literatura, Moscow, 1983, pp. 11, 60, 69.

8   The situation now is the exact reverse of that in 1917–19 when accommodation belonging to private enterprises (factories) and public institutions (museums) was nationalised at the same time as the enterprise or institution.

9   Postanovlenie Sovnarkoma, 'O zhilishchnoi kooperatsii', no. 726, 8 August 1921. In 1979 this one- to two-storeyed garden suburb of 119 houses, now an island amidst Moscow's multi-storey housing estates, was designated a conservation area.

10   I. P. Prokopchenko, *Zhilishchnoe i zhilishchno-stroitel'noe zakonodatel'stvo*, Izd. 2-e, Stroiizdat, Moscow, 1986, p. 44.

11   B. B. Veselovskii, *Kurs ekonomiki i organizatsii gorodskogo khozyaistva*, Moscow, 1951, p. 141.

12   V. Belousov, *Kul'turnye zadachi zhilishchoi kooperatsii*, Moscow, 1926, p. 7.

13   Ts. Ryss, *Zhilishchnaya kooperatsiya SSSR*, Moscow, 1926, p. 44.

14   Sh. Chikvashvili, *Zhilishchno-stroitel'naya kooperatsiya v SSSR*, Moscow, 1965, p. 4.

15   International Labour Office, *Housing in Soviet Russia*, vol. 12, no. 2, Geneva, 1925, p. 259; Belousov, op. cit., p. 9.

16   *SZ RSFSR* 1928, no. 6, art. 60.

17   A. Ya. Vyshinskii, *S"ezdy Sovetov RSFSR*, Moscow, 1939, p. 463.

18   The urban population rose by 29.8 million between 1926 and 1939.

19   Prokopchenko, op. cit., p. 50. It is, however, questionable whether they were in fact in a position to do so.

20   *SZ SSSR* 1937, no. 69, art. 314.

21   During the Soviet period, the term 'enterprise' or 'undertaking' was always used to translate the word *predpriyatie*, in order to distinguish it from the capitalist 'firm'. Since the collapse of the socialist system the word 'firm' is commonly used and in the present text it is used synonymously with 'enterprise'.

22   *SP SSSR* 1958, no. 5, art. 47.

23   *SP SSSR* 1962, no. 12, art. 93.

24   *SP SSSR* 1964, no. 25, art. 147.

25   *SP SSSR* 1982, no. 23, art. 120.

26   V. Batishchev, 'Ekonomicheskaya suchnost' zhilishchnoi kooperatsii', *Zhilishchnoe i kommunal'noe khozyaistvo*, no. 5, 1982; G. Matveets, 'ZhSK: Skol'ko obyazannostei, stol'ko i prav', *Literaturnaya gazeta*, 21, 1982.

27   In the former Soviet Union, the Housing Code of each republic allowed the local authority to decide on the amount of living space below which individuals were entitled to be placed on a housing waiting list.

28 *Argumenty i fakty*, 1988, no. 32. p. 5.
29 G. D. Andrusz, 'A Note on the Financing of Housing in the Soviet Union', *Soviet Studies*, vol. 42, no. 3, July 1990; G. D. Andrusz, 'Housing Reform and Social Conflict', in D. Lane (ed.), *Russia in Flux: The Political and Social Consequences of Reform*, Edward Elgar, Aldershot, 1992.
30 *Zhilishchnoe i kommunal'noe khozyaistvo*, 1989, no. 5, p. 6.
31 S. V. Nikolaev (Director, TsNIIEP zhilishcha), 'O zhilishchnom stroitel'stve na trinadtsatuyu pyatiletku i period do 2000 goda', *Zhilishchnoe stroitel'stvo*, no. 4, 1989, p. 7.
32 Ibid.
33 N. V. Kalinina, 'K voprosu o sotsial'nom garantirovanii predstavleniya zhil'ya', v Sbornik: *Sistemnoe modelirovanie protsessov intensifikatsii obshchestvennogo proizvodstva*, Gor'kii, 1986; S. S. Shatalin, *Funktsionirovanie ekonomiki razvitogo sotsializma*, M. G. U., Moscow, 1982; A. Bavilov and E. Sasburov, 'Kvartirnyi vopros', *Narodnyi deputat*, no. 4, 1990; N. V. Kalinina, 'Guaranteeing Housing Reform in the USSR: A Few Suggestions for Reforming the System of Housing Provision', paper prepared for International Conference: Housing Debates – Urban Challenges, Paris, 3–6 July 1990.
34 The director of the leading Soviet housing research institute (TsNIIEP zhilishcha), based in Moscow, produced a number of forecasts indicating different variants on the role that co-operatives could play in meeting housing need.
35 Goskomstat, *Narodnoe khozyaistvo RSFSR v 1990 g.*, Finansy i Statistika, Moscow, 1990.
36 Goskomstat, *Narodnoe khozyaistvo SSSR v 1988 g.*, Finansy i Statistika, Moscow, 1989, pp. 150, 152, 158.
37 D. S. Meerson and D. G. Tonskii, *Zhilishchnoe stroitel'stvo v SSSR v XI pyatiletke*, Stroiizdat, Moscow, 1982.
38 In 1985 the State prize for architecture was awarded for the design of a co-operative property. See D. Rybakov, 'Zhiloi kooperativnyi dom v Pyarnu', *Arkhitektura SSSR*, no. 3, 1986.
39 R. A. Iskenderov, 'Edinovremennye i tekushchie zatraty v domakh ZhSK', *Zhilishchnoe stroitel'stvo*, no. 3, 1989, p. 14.
40 In 1988 the average cost of construction of one square metre of state housing was 272 roubles, which was a 27 per cent increase over 1980 and 7 per cent over 1985. (See Chapter 4, note 59, for details of the exchange rate.) See Goskomstat, *Narodnoe khozyaistvo SSSR v 1988 g.*, p. 162.
41 Iskenderov, op. cit. p. 15.
42 Ibid., p. 16.
43 According to the Government's official statistical handbook, 29.4 million families (41 per cent of all families) saved for the sake of their children. See Goskomstat, *Narodnoe khozyaistvo SSSR v 1988 g.*, pp. 96–7.
44 Kalinina, 'Guaranteeing Housing Reform', p. 4.
45 S. Smusenok, 'Vremya obeshchanii proshlo', *Sovety narodnykh deputatov*, no. 7, 1987, p. 47; A. Tsipko, 'Vozmozhnosti i rezervy kooperatsii', *Sotsiologicheskie issledovaniya*, no. 2, 1986, p. 55.
46 S. Avineri, *The Social & Political Thought of Karl Marx*, CUP, Cambridge, 1968, chapter 3.
47 See A. Zaichenko, 'Sale of the century', *Moscow News*, no. 19, 5–11 October 1990, p. 10.
48 L. Grafov, 'Strasti po ustavu', *Literaturnaya gazeta*, no. 5, 1980.
49 'Stroit' kooperativ', *Pravda*, 30 September 1985.

50 Kalinina, 'Guaranteeing Housing Reform', p. 3.
51 'Vokrug kooperativnoi kvartiry', *Izvestiya*, 23 March 1986.
52 O. Bessonova, 'Problemy zhilishchnoi kooperatsii', *Ekonomika i prikladnaya sotsiologiya*, no. 1, 1988.
53 Ibid., p. 41.
54 N. Alekseev, *Ekonomicheskii eksperiment. Sotsial'nye aspekty*, 'Mysl', Moscow, 1987, pp. 195–6.
55 D. Pudikov, *Finansirovanie i kreditovanie kooperativnogo i individual'nogo zhilishchnogo stroitel'stva*, 'Finansy', Moscow, 1980, p. 63.
56 M. Buzhevich, 'Stroitel'nyi kooperativ', *Pravda*, 30 September 1985. According to personal informants, construction delays have not been reduced since then.
57 V. Arkhangel'skii, 'Kooperativnyi dom', *Sotsialisticheskaya industriya*, 11 March 1986, p. 6.
58 *SP SSSR*, 1988, no. 16, art. 43.
59 *Zhilishchnoe i kommunal'noe khozyaistvo*, no. 5, 1989, p. 6; Goskomstat, *Narodnoe khozyaistvo SSSR za 70 let*, Moscow, 1987, pp. 515–16. In Belarus co-operatives were to contribute 26 per cent of new building in the period 1991–95, compared with 11.5 per cent in 1981–85.
60 V. M. Loktionov, 'Zhilishchnoe stroitel'stvo – ob'emy i struktura', *Zhilishchnoe stroitel'stvo*, no. 2, 1989, p. 2.
61 V. I. Babakin, *Pereustroistvo zhilishchnogo fonda*, Stroiizdat, Moscow, 1981.
62 Goskomstat, *Narodnoe khozyaistvo SSSR v 1988 g.*, Moscow, 1989, p. 167; V. I. Popov, 'Prakticheskie dela – velenie vremeni', *Zhilishchnoe i kommunal'noe khozyaistvo*, no. 5, 1989, pp. 2–5.
63 Invalids, war veterans and individuals of equivalent status did not have to pay any interest.
64 Tsentral'nyi nauchno-issledovatel'skii i proektnyi institut tipovogo i eksperimental'nogo proektirovaniya zhilishcha (TsNIIEP zhilishcha), *General'naya skhema obespecheniya k 2000 godu kazhdoi sovetskoi sem'i otdel'noi kvartiroi ili individual'nym domom*, (Goszakaz No. 2-18-0043-88 p. I. 2), Moscow, 1988.
65 No. 300 of 9 April 1993; no. 813 of 24 August 1993 and no. 600 of 9 August 1994. Cited in: Materialy k vystupleniyu na mezhdunarodnom ekspertnom seminare 'Zhilishchnoe dvizhenie i mestnye vlasti', 17–19 May 1995, Prezident-Hotel, Moscow.
66 E. S. Shomina, 'Zhilishchnye tovarishchestva v Moskve', paper presented at: Mezhdunarodnyi ekspertnyi seminar 'Zhilishchnoe dvizhenie i mestnye vlasti', 17–19 May 1995, Prezident-Hotel, Moscow.
67 The Institute for Urban Economics (Moscow) and The Urban Institute (USA), *International Conference on Rental Sector Reform in Eastern Europe and the Newly Independent States*, Moscow, 11–13 November 1996.
68 This represented just one of many tenants' and residents' groups which emerged at the time. There were self-management committees, organisations of 'people on housing waiting lists' and a trade union association prepared to take over the management and maintenance of housing, its allocation and construction. Together they comprised an amorphous housing movement.
69 *SZ SSSR*, 1990, 'O sobstvennosti', *Izvestiya*, 10 March 1990.
70 In November 1994, Luzhkov, the Mayor of Moscow, issued a decree 'On the Specificities of Registering the Right to Ownership of Accommodation in Housing Co-operatives and House Building Co-operatives'. The short decree was concerned with the right to bequeath and inherit a flat in a co-operative dwelling.
71 The Institute for Urban Economics (Moscow) and The Urban Institute (USA), op. cit.

72 Pudikov, op. cit., p. 64. In the case of Georgia and Armenia, white-collar workers and technicians accounted for 76 per cent and 74 per cent of the membership of house-building co-operatives.

73 E. M. Blekh, *Povyshenie effektivnosti ekspluatatsii zhilykh zdanii*, Stroiizdat, Moscow, 1987, p. 14.

74 The monthly cost of housing and outlays on utilities for a family of three in a 54-square-metre flat was calculated to be US$ 23.2. The cost in Estonia and Poland is already much higher; rental and utility charges for a flat of the same description would now be in the region of US$ 56. In Slovenia the figure is US$ 169. The estimated cost of the same flat of medium quality and location on the open market was US$ 90, or US$ 450 in Moscow. In Estonia and Poland the respective rents would be US$ 207 and US$ 500. See The Institute for Urban Economics (Moscow) and The Urban Institute (USA), op. cit.

6 Marxist GDR: Cyclical Fortunes

PRUE CHAMBERLAYNE*

The reputation of the GDR as the most centralised Eastern European economy concealed its historical variegation. In fact, the 'socialist offensives' of 1952–53, 1958–60 and 1971–75, which involved concerted nationalisation, were remarkably shortlived. In the more enduring liberal periods the private sector was given rein, sometimes pragmatically for its responsiveness to the demand for goods and services, sometimes more positively as part of 'socialist teamwork'.

In the 'New Course' of 1953–57 and the 'New Economic System' of 1960–70 explicit parallels were drawn with the New Economic Policy pursued by the Soviet Union in the 1920s and with Lenin's theorisation of state capitalism. Petty commodity, capitalist and socialist sectors were expected to continue to co-exist for a long time: co-operatives were to spur concentration among peasant and artisan petty-commodity producers, while Chinese-style, semi-state enterprises would represent the highest form of state capitalism.[1]

In Ulbricht's 'golden' era from 1963 to 1970, the GDR was a front runner in technology, occupying fourth place in the world micro-electronics league. The idealistic 'cultural theory' proclaimed that rapid economic change would bring the 'new man'. Moreover, enthusiasm for the reform movement in Czechoslovakia, though never official, was widespread. Policies prefigured many 'Gorbachev-style' measures: increased labour productivity, intensive mechanisation and modernisation and a balancing of micro-markets. By contrast, the next 'socialist offensive' under the Brezhnevite Honecker forced

---

* Prue Chamberlayne is Director of the Centre for Biography in Social Policy at the University of East London. She would like to thank the West German housing specialists who generously supplied archival material on the history of GDR housing co-operatives and colleagues, especially Dr Juliane Roloff and Prof. Wolfram Speigner, at the Institute of Sociology and Social Policy of the Academy of Sciences in East Berlin, who arranged interviews with key informants and offered library facilities in 1987 and 1988. Information on Treptow and Riesa was collected in the course of a study of tenant and neighbourhood organisations, during a three-week visit financed by the British Academy in 1987.

the GDR back into a gradualistic, Comecon mould. But then a quiet revolution in 1976 brought the renewed assurance that 'the task of private craftsmen and entrepreneurs lasts far into communism'. State support for the private sector continued in the 1980s, though in the service sector rather than in manufacturing.

Stalin's projection of a reunified, neutral Germany was one of the reasons for the survival of the private sector. But the strength of the small-scale entrepreneurial tradition which had flourished from the 1880s to the 1930s also played a part. This tradition was underpinned by the myriad organisations of the co-operative movement, which, although inspired by the Rochdale model, developed along more commercial lines in Germany than in Britain. Herzog distinguishes three main strands within the co-operative movement:

- banking, distributing and marketing co-operatives, initiated by Raiffeisen (1818–88) to service small peasants, which, with 4 million members in 1930, formed the largest co-operative in the world;
- the more middle-class tradesman, in the craft and credit tradition of Schulze-Delitzsch (1808–83);
- the more working-class consumer movement, including housing co-operatives and, in the 1920s, trade union co-operative factories.

In 1902 the last-mentioned of these detached itself from Schulze-Delitzsch's movement and divided into two branches, the Social Democratic and Christian. Under Hitler the proletarian consumer movement was liquidated and subsumed within the *Arbeiterfront*. The more nationalistic and petit bourgeois Raiffeisen and Schulze-Delitzsch organisations were incorporated into national socialist structures.[2]

The social and political heterogeneity of this historically short period may well have accounted for the GDR's ambivalence towards co-operatives. In agriculture, horticulture, handicrafts, building, trade and retail, catering and consumer outlets, co-operative forms remained prevalent and even dominant. Only the wholesale supplier and manufacturing sectors were eradicated. But the regime's attitude towards co-operatives was volatile. At times they were used pragmatically to promote the productivity and output of the small-scale private sector, with fluctuating degrees of independence, while linking into the planning system. At other times the co-operative form was portrayed more positively as a stepping stone to a 'higher', more fully socialised system. In practice it was so centralised and so incapable of adhering to co-operative principles of self-employment and self-management as to be virtually indistinguishable from the state sector.

Housing co-operatives were a case in point. They were so intertwined with the state sector that some West German commentators, particularly in the wake of the sudden nationalisation of private manufacturing in the early 1970s, predicted their 'cold socialisation', that is, their absorption into state property.[3] The policy change was justified by the argument that these co-operatives depended more on state credit than on more autonomous sources such as savings banks. Co-operatives also had to use industrialised building systems and were subject to the housing plans of local authorities, who vetted their membership and allocations and placed tight controls on the amount they spent on maintenance.

Yet a strong case can be made that the state sector, far from being a more advanced social model to which housing co-operatives should aspire, increasingly drew inspiration from co-operative traditions and experience. A variety of principles first developed in the co-operative sector were, in the 1980s, modified and grafted on to the GDR state housing system: for instance, the close involvement of enterprises and trade unions in mobilising labour and resources for housing; the playing on mutual self-interest for social policy purposes; the adoption of the voluntary principle in administration and maintenance; and user management through small-scale house collectives.

Before exploring the argument that the state housing sector took its lead from the co-operative sector, it is first necessary to examine the meaning attached to 'co-operative' principles in the GDR's housing system. Thus, the first part of this chapter outlines the development and organisational characteristics of housing co-operatives from the late 1940s onwards. The second part considers the broader co-operative movement in the GDR, particularly agricultural and handicraft co-operatives. This provides a backcloth against which to discuss the prospects of housing co-operatives as these appeared in the late 1980s, when housing choice and quality were beginning to emerge as centre stage issues. At that point it seemed as if housing co-operatives might once again be recast, drawing on the experience and ideologies of other more dynamic co-operatives.

Housing Co-operatives

Tenure Fluctuations

The 1976–90 drive to 'solve the housing question as a social problem' led to a massive rise in output in both the state and co-operative sectors (Figure 6.1).

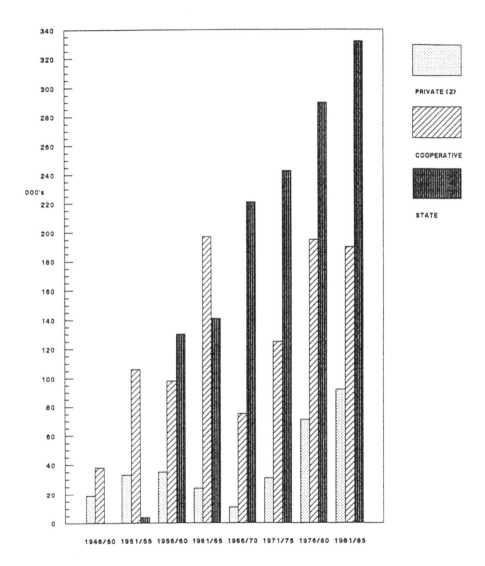

Figure 6.1 Number of newly-built(1) dwellings in the GDR in different property forms (in 5-year periods)
(1) Without repair, renovation, rehabilitation etc. (2) Until 1970, this category includes social organisations as well as part-state enterprises
Sources: Melzer 1983; for 1981–85 *Statistisches Jahrbuch*; Based on estimates and calculations of the DIW (Deutsches Institut für Wirtschaftsforschung)

Yet the survival of pre-war housing and the privately rented sector meant that the housing stock overall was, to a surprisingly large extent, private. This fact was obscured in the official figures, which concentrated on completions. It also seemed possible in the late 1980s that the rapid decline of the privately rented sector through the crash programme of state building might yet be counterbalanced by the growth in self-build, in more privatised forms of co-operatives and even in the 'right to buy'.

The average age of dwellings in 1973 was 59 years;[4] as late as 1983 less than 40 per cent of stock had been built in the post-war period. (See Table 6.1.)

Table 6.1 Age of stock in 1983 (per cent)

pre-1919	1919–45	1945–83
42.4	18.7	38.9

Source: M. Melzer, 'The GDR Housing Construction Program: Problems and Successes', *East Central Europe*, vol. 11, pts 1–2, p. 86.

Table 6.2 shows the declining importance of the private sector, about half of which in 1971 was rented property;[5] typically, these dilapidated tenement blocks (*Mietshäuser*) were built in all major cities during the 'founding' period (the *Gründerzeit*) of German industrialisation (1870–1918).[6] Frozen rents and absentee landlords living in the West[7] led to the neglect of this stock, which only began to be rehabilitated in the 1970s in an innovative state programme using industrialised methods. (See Figure 6.2.) A parallel modernisation programme tackled the appalling lack of basic amenities (see Table 6.3).

The owner-occupied sector, largely consisting of older properties, predominated in small towns and rural areas. In Berlin less than 10 per cent of housing was owner-occupied, although a large number of people owned weekend houses in the outlying forest and lakeside areas.[8] A generously subsidised self-build scheme (*Eigenheimbau*) had also been introduced. Originally intended for large families and young couples, this sector was increasingly used to reward and stabilise the skilled industrial workforce, but in doing so, it took the mantle of co-operative housing as provider of accommodation for this economically and politically important segment of the population. By the mid-1970s self-build annually accounted for a steady 10 per cent of newly built dwellings, and 15 per cent after 1979 (see Figures 6.1 and 6.2).

Table 6.2 Tenure forms in 1971 and 1983

	Total stock (million units)	Composition (per cent)		
		state	co-operative	private
1971	5.9	27.4	9.9	62.2
1983	6.7	33	15	50

Source: W. Homann, 'AWGs im Rahmen der Wohnungsbaupolitik der DDR', *FS-Analysen*, Berlin, 1981, p. 51; W. Homann, 'Veränderungen beim sozialistischenen Eigentum im Bereich der Wohnungswirtschaft der DDR', *FS-Analysen*, No. 3, Berlin, 1983, p. 8.

Table 6.3 Provision of housing amenities, 1971 and 1981 (per cent)

	Central heating	Bath/ shower	Indoor toilet	Running water	Hot water
1971	11	39	39	82	26
1981	36	68	60	94	64

Source: Statistisches Jahrbuch, Berlin, 1986.

The management and building of housing constituted separate functions within the state sector. As Table 6.2 shows, by 1983 one-third of the overall stock was managed by local authority departments (*KWV – Kommunale Wohnungsverwaltung*). But a substantial proportion of the new development built by state enterprises was allocated to co-operatives, so that in fact the state sector managed less property than it built.

A major housing survey conducted in 1971 revealed the full legacy of neglect (Table 6.3), and placed housing centre stage in the 'unity of economic and social policy as the chief battleground of domestic policy'. In order to meet the target of 2.8–3 million new or renovated units over the twenty-year period 1971–1990, by the mid-1980s 200,000 new and renovated dwellings were being built each year. Most construction used prefabricated systems technology carried out by state enterprises on ever larger estates, 69 per cent of which were located on the outskirts of large towns.[9] In Berlin, each of the two new residential districts, Marzahn and Grünau, had 35,000 dwellings.

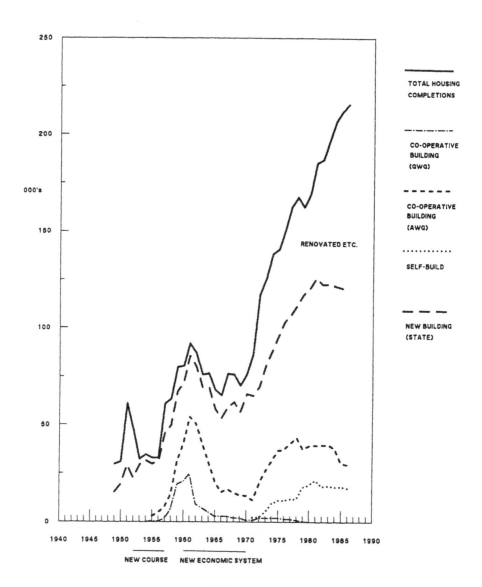

Figure 6.2 Housing completions (including renovations) in different tenure forms 1949–86
Source: Statistisches Jahrbuch (various years)

Despite widely expressed enthusiasm for inner city renovation and the notion of 'community', relatively little was done because of the limited speed at which new buildings could be erected. But questions had arisen about high infrastructural costs on peripheral estates and in satellite towns, internal design and room size. The issue of 'anonymity' became the subject of intense sociological inquiry in Marzahn[10] and much effort was devoted to the nurturing of small-scale neighbourhood organisations and tenants' associations on large estates.[11] Housing authorities recognised that the 'housing problem' would not be solved even if the 1990 target was achieved, since the population was beginning to demand higher quality standards.

These problems rebounded on the co-operative sector, which was dependent upon state sector building; it was allocated at least 30 per cent of new housing on estates, towards which it contributed 15 per cent of the building costs by using members' shares and labour contributions. As Table 6.2 shows, by 1983 it was managing 15 per cent of the housing stock, which included a substantial proportion of the pre-war stock. At its peak, in 1961, under the impetus of the housing boom of the second 'socialist offensive' (1958–60), co-operatives produced 58 per cent of all new dwellings, though this achievement was not maintained. Under the third socialist offensive, 1971–75, they were projected to take over 35 per cent of new construction, rising to 45 per cent in the period 1976–90. Although these targets were never reached, as Table 6.4 reveals, production for this sector remained high, accounting in 1985 and 1986 for 25 per cent of new building; the figures are lower if renovations are included in measures of state output.

The reasons for the failure to meet targets varied. In the 1960s and early 1970s local authorities tended to deprive housing co-operatives of building capacity in order to prioritise the achievement of their own targets.[12] Later still, the greater availability of state sector housing decreased the attractiveness of co-operative accommodation. Yet co-operative housing maintained its higher social status, even though members continued to be burdened with loan repayments (which exceeded the rent charged for state accommodation) and with labour contributions. Single people not catered for by the state sector found a real advantage in co-operatives, since young people wishing to leave home could choose between marriage (and being rewarded with a state apartment) or expending time, energy and money on a co-operative flat. Further discussions took place in 1988 on measures to increase the attractiveness of co-operatives, particularly by reducing the waiting period, with officials optimistically maintaining that the target of housing one-third of the population in co-operatives was imminent.

Mobility within and between housing sectors was encouraged in order to

Table 6.4 Projected and actual co-operative construction 1971–86

	Percentage of total new building		Actual number
	Projected	Actual	
1971–75	35	30	25,040
1976–80	45	36	39,496
1981–85	45	30	37,318
1986	45	25	29,551

Source: Statistisches Jahrbuch, 1987

facilitate labour mobility and optimise the use of living space. Although ratified by the local authority, most exchanges occurred informally through newspaper advertisements or workplace contacts, the latter actively promoted by workplace housing commissions.[13] Co-operatives had more control over occupancy than local authorities, whose only power lay in letting property, whereas co-operative members underusing space could be invited to move by their executive committee, and even compelled to do so by the co-operative's general assembly.[14] A household transferring to a smaller unit would be paid a modest fee, while the local authorities provided a range of services dealing with legal questions, decorating, sale and acquisition of furniture, and transport, on a means-tested basis.[15]

In summary, fluctuations in tenure patterns seemed likely to continue, with co-operatives in a particularly uncertain position. The projection that one-third of GDR citizens would live in co-operative housing by 1990 was unrealistic. For that goal to be achieved, there would have to be changes in terms of ease of access, cost, choice, space, quality and independence, relative to other sectors. In the late 1980s co-operatives scored rather low on these criteria, for reasons already indicated and further explored below. By contrast owner occupation had taken on a new lease of life and become more effective than co-operatives in mobilising the hidden resources of personal savings and individual effort. Moreover, the greater autonomy accorded to self-build schemes, despite strict cost limits, was allowing improved quality and variety in design. At the same time, innovative rehabilitation work was being undertaken using prefabrication. The primacy of rapid output in the 1980s precluded housing co-operatives from establishing an innovatory role, and the aim of gaining in efficiency caused them to lose a great deal of autonomy. Nevertheless, they retained an institutional framework which contained the potential for greater independence and innovative effort.

Types and History of Housing Co-operatives

The main type of housing co-operative, the Workers' House-building Co-operative (*Arbeiterwohnungsbaugenossenschaft – AWG*), was established in 1954 as part of the 'New Course', itself a response to the uprising of June 1953, and the subsequent 'Decree on the Further Improvement of Working and Living Conditions of Workers and of the Rights of Trade Unions' of December 1953.[16] The Mutual House-building Co-operative (*Gemeinnützige Wohnungsbaugenossenschaft – GWG*) was founded three years later on the basis of pre-war housing co-operatives. Agricultural and handicraft co-operatives also erected housing for their members, but these small sectors were not separately identified in the statistics.

Co-operatives during the inter-war period were mainly organised under two umbrella bodies, the Saxon and Middle German co-operatives. By 1957 there were still 393 such co-operatives in existence, varying greatly in size, with a total of 167,000 members. (See Table 6.5.) They were characterised as 'crippled capitalist relics', unable to fulfil their inherited financial commitments, deal with war damage, settle up with members who had left for the West or house those on their waiting lists – 40 per cent of their membership – or engage in new building. Their situation had been exacerbated by the 1:10 currency devaluation which took place in 1948, the increase in ground rent (now paid to the state) and the lowering of some rents.[17] The 1957 legislation, in the more pluralist manner of the 'New Course' period, aimed to restore their viability, to utilise their experience in housing construction and administration and to rekindle the confidence of their members and their collective energy in management, maintenance, rehabilitation and new building.

The 1957 legislation remodelled the pre-war co-operatives along the lines of the newly-formed AWGs on the basis of non-payment of dividends, non-liability and protection from bankruptcy. Their debts, including state loans, were written off, their liability to state charges and taxes was abolished, their finances were reorganised into three specified accounts and new closing and opening balances were established.[18] This allowed them to settle up with individuals who had left or wished to leave, up to a total value of 10 per cent of their holdings. Those who were not citizens or had not adopted permanent residence in the GDR, whose whereabouts were unknown or who refused to

Table 6.5 GWGs – Membership size before restructuring in 1957

Number of members	Number of GWGs
10–100	110
100–300	149
300–500	51
500–1000	48
1000–2000	22
2000–4000	10
4000–8000	2
over 8000	1
Total (average size 425)	393

Source: Manfred Hoffman, 'Gemeinnützigkeit in der DDR – Das Beispiel der gemeinnützigen sozialistischen Wohnungsbaugenossenschaften', *Archiv für öffentliche und freigemeinnützige Unternehmen*, Band 10, Heft 1/2, 1970, p. 62.

accept the new terms of the model rules, such as the commitment to work contributions, were excluded from membership.[19]

Aided by 75 per cent interest-free state loans, GWGs began to build new housing and their contribution accounted for 29 per cent of total completions during 1959–61, a level which then fell rapidly as they switched to maintaining and rehabilitating the older stock.[20] In so far as the Government was emphasising housing for industrial purposes, the fact that they were 'general', that is, neighbourhood-based rather than work-based, may have also placed them in disfavour. The 1957 legislation allowed amalgamations with AWGs, either as AWGs or as GWGs, in order to widen the distribution of larger units in older buildings and to draw GWG expertise into the AWGs. New model rules in 1968 made them almost identical with AWGs and from 1972 the two types were commonly bracketed together as 'socialist housing co-operatives'.[21]

Three main themes can be highlighted in the ensuing key enactments of

1957, 1958, 1963 and 1973: (i) a broadening of membership entitlement, (ii) a closer integration in local authority planning, with close attention being accorded to industrial requirements, and (iii) the expansion and easing of loan facilities.

Broadening membership entitlement The first AWGs were based at industrial workplaces and required that at least 60 per cent of members must be workers. Building levels were low until the adoption of the 1957 and 1958 statutes. These allowed other enterprises to affiliate to parent AWGs. They also restructured and lowered the cost of shares,[22] introduced bridging loans for shares and raised interest-free credit for co-operatives from 80 to 85 per cent of total building costs.[23] By 1959 agricultural and handicraft co-operatives also became eligible to build on a co-operative basis. As a result of these changes co-operative building soared in the years 1959–64, although not necessarily in the areas of direct housing shortage. Moreover, housing co-operatives were signing up members far in excess of their capacity, which led to long waiting periods. In 1963 legislation restricted waiting lists to those who could be housed within three years and made shares refundable after the expiry of that time limit.

In 1973 accessibility was improved for those unable to afford the initial deposit or additional monthly payments for loans by allowing up to 40 per cent of share values to be replaced by labour contributions. The value of work contributions[24] carried out for one co-operative could also be transferred to another. This meant that an AWG which had reached its membership limit could still organise work contributions and procure housing for its would-be members.

Integration into the planning framework A key development accompanying the new model rules of 1963 was the responsibility imposed on regional authorities to tie housing co-operatives to 'plans and economic possibilities and needs'.[25] Both the location of the building and allocations criteria came under increasing state control.

The later years of the New Economic System, 1963–70, saw a low level of housing output overall, and a sharp decline in co-operative house building. Local authorities were criticised for monopolising building materials and acting dismissively towards housing co-operatives. Legislation passed in 1973 sought to overcome these problems by obliging all tiers of local government to involve co-operatives in the various stages of the house-building process, from the preparation and planning to implementation. Enterprise directors were now entitled to attend co-operative meetings and nominate committee members. Their direct involvement exemplified the new emphasis on collaboration between enterprises and local authorities, which was identified as the unity of economic and social policy.

Loan extension State subsidies to co-operatives were massively increased in 1970, when local authorities took over the repayment of 80 per cent of co-operatives' loan costs, leaving them with only 1 per cent to pay.[26] In fact, this had the effect of removing all financial independence from co-operatives; in 1972 credit facilities were transferred from savings banks to the industry and trade bank (*Industrie- und Handelsbank*) and in 1974 to the state bank (*Staatsbank*).

Size and Structure

At first GWGs were relatively large, averaging 400 members in 1957, whereas AWGs were, until the early 1970s, much smaller. (See Tables 6.5 and 6.6.) In the late 1980s, in order to minimise administrative costs, state policy aimed to increase their average size to 1,000–4,000 and even 6,000 members. While total membership had grown to one million, the number of co-operatives remained much the same as in the late 1950s. Although still numbering 235, a quarter of all co-operatives, GWGs received no mention in GDR literature.[27]

Legislation passed in 1963 encouraged amalgamations between co-operatives. Later on government policy promoted exchanges of buildings between co-operatives on the grounds that a single co-operative in a particular neighbourhood could organise more activities and build a stronger sense of identity than would occur with widely dispersed buildings. However, while this weakened the bond between workplace and the housing co-operative, this policy only reinforced a process that was happening in other ways, through individual exchanges, and the transfer of the value of work contributions from one co-operative to another in order to overcome membership restrictions. This particular trend typified the recurrent Eastern European conflict between associations created in the workplace and those established at the neighbourhood level; and also between corporatist privileges accorded to key workplaces as against overall social need. In general, changes were tending in the direction of services, including accommodation, being locality-based. The chairperson of the executive committee, who tended to be a trade union or enterprise representative, could none the less be lobbied and was often a figure of some influence. Enterprises were enjoined to increase their support to local authorities and there were a number of enterprise budget headings

Table 6.6 AWGs (housing co-operatives) 1954–80

Year	Number	Members	Average number of members
1954	264	15,000	57
1957	739	78,850	107
1958	846	137,500	163
1959	850	160,000	188
1964	864	*370,000	428
1970	*800	394,000	493
1977	731	750,000	1026
1980	684	850,000	1243
1985	889	930,000	1046

* Estimated
Sources: Hans Lewitzky, 'Arbeiterwohnungsbaugenossenschaften im Siebenjahrplan', *Stadt und Gemeinde*, Heft 12, 1959, pp. 26ff.; *Neues Deutschland*, 31 August 1965, p. 3; *Neues Deutschland*, 7 February 1972; *Neues Deutschland*, 25 July 1977; *Tribüne*, 9 October 1980, p. 5.

relating to local authority activities upon which co-operatives could make claims. Moreover, the inherent conflicts between enterprise labour requirements for housing and local authority prioritising of social need gave rise to much bargaining. It was not so easy to 'unite economic and social policy'.

Yet, for many people, larger did not mean more efficient. It was argued that the chief advantage of co-operatives lay in their small size and personalised services. The largest housing co-operative in Berlin, based on the electricity industry in Lichtenberg, had 10,000 members and was described as 'an elephant', though that was still modest compared with Lichtenberg's local authority stock of 50,000 units and staff of 700. 'Vorwärts', another of the 30 AWGs in Berlin, was based on a men's clothing factory and 50 affiliated workplaces. In 1985 it managed almost 6,000 flats and several maintenance depots (*Stützpunkte*), and employed thirty craftsmen as well as white-collar staff.[28] Another, 'Tribüne', had 1,283 members and 17 staff in 1988 and was vehemently opposed to exceeding 3,000 dwellings. In the steel town of Riesa, with a population of 49,000, half the housing belonged to AWGs and was centrally administered, allegedly in as bureaucratic a manner as the local KWV. Smaller-scale administration was considered more responsive and more efficient, and the lack of rent arrears in the co-operative sector was cited in support of this view.[29]

Organisation and Management

The sovereign body in a housing co-operative in the GDR was the members' assembly, which elected the executive and auditing committees. The members' assembly wielded some general legal authority, such as ratifying or modifying decisions from other bodies, and exercised exclusive competence over a range of matters which no other body could decide, such as the adoption of the constitution, election of committees, recall of members and decisions on various plans.[30] The five-member executive committee (*Vorstand*) elected its own chairperson for two years and was responsible for day-to-day affairs. Housing co-operatives were in effect a section of the trade union (FDGB),[31] and from 1973 enterprise leaders or their representatives were eligible to attend AWG meetings and nominate committee members. Discussion had taken place on whether the chairperson's role should become a full-time, salaried position, especially given the growth in membership size. But it was considered important to retain both the voluntary and the elective nature of the post, and it was customary for the chairperson to receive 'assistance' from the enterprise. These particular attributes might lie behind the claim that co-operatives generated a greater sense of involvement among their members than did the state sector.

Housing co-operatives were enmeshed in a complex web of relationships at central, regional, local and neighbourhood levels, including the state, auditing bodies, enterprises, trade unions, local authorities and the political parties, which were organised through the National Front. The nature of these relationships was frequently the subject of sharp and acrimonious discussions. Journal and newspaper articles reported conflicts over the roles and responsibilities of enterprises, trade unions and local authorities in relation to housing co-operatives. These revealed the nexus of power and influence within which co-operatives were situated and also the way in which principles of democracy and control could be made part of the public discourse.

The growing complexity of these relationships led to a dilution of the 'self-management' function and an attenuation of direct access to the central state. Apart from falling under the auspices of the Finance Ministry, housing co-operatives had no national body to represent their interests; yet housing co-operatives were not altogether powerless, for they were well placed to profit from the above-mentioned tensions between enterprises and local authorities.

In 1960, legislation ordered the establishment of regional and county level co-ordinating committees (*Beiräte für die sozialistischen Wohnungsbaugenossenschaften*), with the latter also acting as a court of appeal – for example in cases involving the expulsion of a member from a co-operative.[32] In 1963, the regions were required to integrate housing co-operatives into their five-year plans, and in 1973 the involvement of co-operatives in local authority planning and implementation was made mandatory. These measures were attempts to remedy the allegedly negligent attitudes of local authorities towards housing co-operatives, whose real achievements were not being fully acknowledged. It was pointed out that the overall value of members' shares and labour contributions to building and repairs, of their voluntary services – which halved administrative costs relative to state housing – and of their social function in organising community activities for all age groups in collaboration with the National Front, just like a 'mass organisation' needed to be recognised.[33] The quarterly meetings of the regional and county-level committees, which were attended by the Mayor, offered opportunities for co-operatives to be consulted over regional developments and amalgamations, and for the problems of particular co-operatives to be discussed.

In 1959, a leading figure in the FDGB upbraided the trade unions for failing to ensure that enterprises met their obligations to housing co-operatives. These included, firstly, protecting members from chairmen who abused their status and authority; and, secondly, undertaking their educational task of developing socialist consciousness. The function of trade union housing commissions was to represent the interests of shift workers, the elderly and disabled and to remedy the situation where members felt like tenants rather than members and regarded the committee as a landlord.[34]

Other authors asserted co-operatives' right to be consulted over location, the range of flat sizes being built and the organisation of major repairs, irrespective of the difficulties that non-specialists might have in understanding large-scale industrialised building technologies. They were also to be involved in scheduling and organising work contributions, which were restricted to digging ditches, landscaping and interior decoration; and in the transfer to the co-operative of the value of work contributions conducted as outside-hours building work at the factory.

One West German critic, with some justification, characterised 'participation' in GDR housing co-operatives as nothing to do with an 'emancipatory realisation of interests', but rather the 'mobilisation of additional labour resources'. Moreover, the rationalisation of planning and implementation processes meant that genuine initiatives by citizens would be more hindrance than help.[35] Certainly the scope for ordinary members to influence decisions beyond such matters as the effective organisation of work contributions for maintenance and repairs and of social events was quite negligible. At the same time, however, this critical interpretation not only overlooked the scope for negotiation afforded to co-operatives in the arena of local authority relations with enterprises, but also underestimated participation rates at neighbourhood levels.[36]

Enterprises drew up annual local contracts (*Kommunalverträge*) to carry out renovation work, built sports facilities and provided school meals from the enterprise canteen. These services were bargaining counters in negotiations with local authorities over how much housing would be assigned to the enterprise. Enterprises also had an annual collective fund (*Betriebskollektivvertrag*), part of which could be used to contribute to co-operative members' shares. Resources for housing co-operatives might be negotiated under either of these heads and also under a section of its budget entitled 'Work and Living Conditions' (*Planteil Arbeits- und Lebensbedingungen*). There was undoubtedly scope for a dynamic chairperson to influence decisions.[37]

The complexity and ambiguity of the triangular relationship between enterprise, local authority and housing co-operative was highly visible in the system of housing allocations. Although housing co-operatives lost their autonomy over allocations in 1963, they were not incorporated into the annual local authority allocation plan, which was a published list of names worked out in conjunction with enterprises on the basis of need, urgency and labour requirements. Enterprises were assigned a share of available dwellings for their own distribution. But, as will be seen, their criteria of 'need' tended to conflict with those of the local authority.

Housing co-operative allocations involved several stages: admission to membership, allowing entry onto the waiting list, was followed by payment of a deposit and the making of labour contributions. Normally, a flat would be allocated within three years of membership. The crucial question of admission to membership and the waiting list was formally subject to exactly the same criteria as were applied to people joining other housing queues. Applicants' housing conditions were investigated by the trade union leadership committee (*Betriebsgewerkschaftsleitung – BGL*). Points were also awarded for a person's work record and extent of involvement in social organisations. The co-operative executive committee then submitted a housing allocation plan to the members' assembly. However, since that plan had to be approved by the local authority, the 'decision' by the general assembly was actually a 'proposal' to the local authority, which also decided how many new members might be allowed to join.[38]

Since the motivation for workplaces to support housing co-operatives was the opportunity it gave them to keep their young workforce and to stabilise their key workers, industrial employers needed to be able to allocate dwellings on grounds other than need and urgency, which were the principal criteria established by the local authorities. In this way, young people, and one suspects particularly young men, gained access to housing through housing co-operatives which they could not acquire under the terms of 'solving the housing problem by 1990', a target which excluded young single people.

Formal procedures notwithstanding, there seemed to be prima-facie grounds for believing that considerable negotiating 'space' existed between local authorities and enterprises – space in which housing co-operatives could intervene. The executive committee, and particularly the chairperson, who might be the nominee of the enterprise leadership, had roles to play here; by encouraging the enterprise to contribute more to local authority affairs, more accommodation could be expected to be allocated to co-operatives and to enterprises themselves.

Funding

As in other Soviet-type systems, the German Government provided the population with highly subsidised accommodation, which ensured that on average only 3–5 per cent of household income was spent on rent and heating. Co-operative housing payments, called 'service charges' (*Nutzungsgebühren*), were lower than this because the state paid a 5 per cent return on members' shares and work contributions, which was regarded as an investment that members had made in their housing. The charges for street cleaning, water, waste disposal, insurance, credit repayments, repairs and administration, were calculated on a fixed monthly rate per square metre of living space, taking into account the quality of the flat. The state was also nominally responsible for the cost of repairs beyond what the co-operative could finance or carry out itself,[39] such as the structural restoration of roofs and balconies. Early accounts of housing co-operatives in the GDR abounded with eulogies to their efficiency in achieving low costs in repairs and administration. For instance, in 1960 the AWGs were said to 'provide the most convincing example of how the initiative of the individual worker and the collective spirit of the co-operative can make fuller use of the allocation of state funds'.[40] At first, state subsidies took the form of a flat rate per dwelling and savings accrued to co-operative funds. By 1963 they became cost-related and adjusted to take into account flat size.

Nevertheless, arrangements still preserved their open-ended and costly character. So, the general drive to cut unit costs in housing led in 1983 to a rigorous tightening of budgeting and accounting regulations and procedures in housing co-operatives. Among other things this involved enforcing adherence to norms and directives on the use of energy, other material resources and management. The central auditing body was made directly answerable to the Minister of Finance and charged with taking a more active role in support of local authorities in their dealings with housing co-operatives.

Both savings ('dead capital') and labour were important resources to the state and were drawn upon to pay the deposit of 15 per cent of building costs required from members. While land was free, it was frequently disputed whether or not site clearing and infrastructural costs should be paid for by the co-operative. The cost of cash shares (equivalent of two months' salary and repayable over three years) and the expected labour contribution varied according to the size of the flat. The hourly value of the work performed (which usually included the papering and painting of a member's own flat) also varied, depending on the degree of skill involved.[41] Perhaps not surprisingly, members did not necessarily undertake the work themselves. Newspaper advertisements invited paid, informal help, while friends also often lent assistance; 200 hours of labour could easily be performed over two weekends by a group of ten friends. A two-room flat required 330 hours in all, but the work share could be increased to reduce the financial share. After a special drive in the early 1970s the 'work component' reached 40 per cent of members' total contributions.

Agricultural and handicraft housing co-operatives were financed differently: the state made a 7,000 Mark flat-rate loan, leaving the members to contribute the remaining 3,000 Marks. Many of these dwellings were individual houses rather than flats, and members were more involved in building and design. As with AWGs and GWGs, a plot of land of up to 500 square metres (for self-build) was provided free on an indefinite lease. Co-operatives had to show considerable ingenuity and initiative in their search for financial support and materials, frequently turning to the parent and affiliated enterprise. This regularly brought them into competition with local authorities, whose own building operations were always overstretched and under pressure and who had to rely on individual and collective self-help measures to carry out routine (and sometimes major) repair and restoration work. They too required materials, machinery, skilled labour and transportation, and they too turned to the enterprises. Housing co-operatives also found themselves competing with a number of other local authority departments and social and neighbourhood organisations in negotiating for resources such as recreational facilities and the maintenance of open space. The state wisely encouraged co-operatives and other organisations to improve their financial status by collecting secondary raw materials like glass, paper and scrap iron: shortages rather than environmental considerations led the state to nurture a more ecologically benevolent attitude towards resources.[42]

Collective user control over routine maintenance was also exercised by 'house collectives' of 10–12 households grouped around a staircase, or a couple of floors in the case of high-rise flats. In the state housing sector these collectives entered into annual repair plan contracts with the local authority, whereby they carried out repairs for themselves and were authorised to call in craftsmen for emergencies up to a certain value. The contract also included clauses stipulating the range of actions that the local authority was duty-bound to undertake. In the case of co-operatives, members were obliged to give twelve hours of labour towards maintenance annually and entered into annual repair plan contracts similar to those in the state sector.

From the point of view of the state, the advantage of co-operatives lay in their lower administration and maintenance costs, reduced arrears, better use of space and in their saving the state 15 per cent of the total building cost. From the point of housing co-operatives, many retained a special cohesion and engagement which derived from several sources: the initial commitment made by individual members in terms of their work contribution and financial investment; their limited (but nonetheless respected) responsibility for their own affairs; and, their smaller and more personalised scale of administration. Overall, however, these attractions were insufficient to bring about a major increase in new members, especially in light of the sacrifices that membership entailed and the greater availability of state housing.

By the late 1980s it would seem that housing co-operatives were primarily attractive to young workers. Skilled workers were more easily stabilised (that is, enticed to remain in the same enterprise) by offering them the opportunity to build their own individual, detached dwellings (*Eigenheimbau*) for which they also received a subsidy. Moreover, they shared a number of the benefits enjoyed by the co-operative sector: land was free, weekly repayments were no higher than an average rent and the building work was supported by enterprises.

Conclusions

Although in absolute terms housing co-operatives in the GDR maintained the size of their stock, by the time of the Republic's final demise co-operatives had already been experiencing a loss in dynamism over the last fifteen years. Projections made during the third socialist offensive (1970–75), when it was claimed that the Government would 'solve the housing problem by 1990', estimated that housing co-operatives would be responsible for 42–45 per cent of all new dwellings and would house every third citizen. However, by the mid-1980s completions by co-operatives had fallen to 25 per cent of the total. The enthusiasm which they had previously enjoyed had been transferred to the new renovation programmes and self-build schemes. There were no significant changes to co-operative model rules after 1973, and co-operatives scarcely aroused attention, let alone debate in social science journals. In the 1950s and 1960s their participative forms of management were praised and judged to become important models to be imitated in the state sector. But the reality of participation was seriously diluted by the imposition of stringent regulations and guidelines and, perhaps especially, architectural designs. However, co-operatives in other spheres were flourishing in an environment characterised by an intensified debate about 'rights' and 'interests'. It seemed quite possible that under these conditions housing co-operatives would face their own revival in the near future, drawing on ideological arguments and legal forms rehearsed in these other co-operative sectors. The fact that quality, design and choice had by 1990 been placed on the public agenda strengthened this likelihood.

General Co-operative Activity

The co-operative movement in the GDR was as diverse as that of pre-war Germany: retail co-operatives maintained continuity with their earliest origins; agricultural co-operatives were refashioned in the Soviet mould; manufacturing co-operatives were nationalised out of existence in 1972; and, handicraft co-operatives, after various fortunes, came to be heralded as the saviour of repairs and services.

In 1986 members of co-operatives represented only 9.1 per cent of the total workforce, or 14.7 per cent together with other non-member co-operative employees (see Table 6.7). Yet they dominated in several sectors of the economy: for instance, 92 per cent of cultivation; 83 per cent of livestock;[43] 41.4 per cent of repairs and servicing; 34 per cent of retailing. In addition 4.3

Table 6.7 Workers in co-operatives and in the total workforce in 1986

	In co-operatives (members and workers, but not including apprentices)		Total workers in sector	
	Number	%	Number	%
Industry	54,300	4.4	3,221,500	37.7
Handicraft (not building)	72,600	5.8	263,899	3.1
Building industry	110,100	8.8	574,100	6.7
Agriculture and forestry	730,400	58.1	926,500	10.8
Retail (*Handel*)	233,600	18.4	877,800	10.3
Communications			627,400	7.3
Other productive	3,300	0.3	251,400	2.9
Non-productive	54,400	4.3	1,805,200	21.1
Total	1,259,700	100	8,547,800	100

Source: Statistisches Jahrbuch, Berlin, 1986

million people out of a population of 17 million were members of 200 consumer co-operatives.[44] In 1965 Konsum, the national dividend consumer co-operative, ran 38,000 shops, 1,500 factories, 5,500 restaurants, 300 laundries, 1,100 repair workshops, 6,000 repair reception points, a made-to measure clothing service, a mail-order system processing 1 million orders annually, and recreational facilities.[45]

This consumer co-operative was established in 1845 in Chemnitz (which became Karl-Marx-Stadt during the GDR period), one year after the Rochdale co-operative was founded. Under its aegis trade unions in the 1920s set up factories as wholesale societies (*GEGs – Grosseinkaufsgesellschaften*), such as the soap, pasta and match factories in the southern town of Riesa. Konsum upheld all the traditional co-operative activities, including the provision of health care, training and education, and cultural and recreational facilities for its workers. It also maintained a complex system of elected bodies such as shop advisory committees (*Verkaufsstellenausschüsse*), members' committees (*Mitgliederaktivs*), co-operative councils *(Genossenschaftsräte)*, review commissions (*Revisionskommissionen*) and an annual delegate conference. Lastly, it played an active role in the International Co-operative Alliance.

All consumer co-operative property, which had been expropriated under Nazism, was restored to the consumer co-operatives in 1945. As a working-class movement consumer co-operatives enjoyed socialist credentials, and their expertise proved indispensable in the aftermath of war. Reorganised on a county basis in the 1940s, they were given advantageous terms in the 1948 currency reform (1:1 rather than 1:10).[46] Then a rival state retail network (*Handelsorganisation*), a 'socially higher form of property',[47] was established, and in 1953 the consumer co-operatives were directed to the rural areas to help convince the peasants of the advantages of collective association. Since the village and town consumer co-operatives were too small to succeed, they were enlarged and in 1963 renamed 'socialist' co-operatives.

While their large size and elaborate structures meant that they played a significant part in the society and economy, it is difficult to evaluate the socialist co-operatives' level of democracy and efficiency, since they were excluded from the political arena. Their nationalisation was never mooted, but in 1960 they suffered a great loss in autonomy from the nationalisation of their wholesale suppliers (*Eigengrosshandel*). In 1988 consumer co-operatives were nominated to play a leading role in co-ordinating local trading organisations and they began to be allowed to draw up their own contracts with suppliers, which was welcomed by their personnel as a significant step towards greater independence and improved productivity.

Although agricultural co-operatives as such were not a major feature of pre-war Germany, small farmers and peasants were serviced by a large number of credit, supply and marketing co-operatives. These had their origin with Raiffeisen, who used joint stock finance provided by wealthy associates to offer loans to farmers as a means of protecting them from merchants and money lenders. The loans also supported the provision of ancillary services, normally the use of hired-out machinery. The joint stock company which became Raiffeisen's German Bank was founded in 1876 and his national union of agricultural co-operatives was established in the following year. Raiffeisen's motives were philanthropic and moral rather than egalitarian. He aimed to promote mutual aid and religious devotion and insisted on small, neighbourhood-based co-operatives in order to ensure personal knowledge of the economic viability and creditworthiness of its members. Profits were paid into a reserve fund or to charities. The administration of these co-operatives was principally in the hands of middle-class people, if for no other reason than that it was performed on a voluntary, unpaid basis.

Raiffeisen was greatly influenced by the theoretician Huber (1800–69), who had visited England. Huber advocated increased bargaining power for small-scale craftsmen and farmers through mutual- and self-help organisations against the overwhelming power of capitalist corporations. But his major concern was the insecurity and spiritual impoverishment of the population as a consequence of the individualisation engendered by urban industrial society. Co-operatives were regarded as a means of providing the organic social association necessary to social, moral and spiritual elevation.

Huber's philosophy made no claims to be socialist. This was in contrast to the communist egalitarianism of Weitling (1808–71), for whom co-operatives would provide equal living standards, and to the 'scientific socialism' of Rodbertus (1805–75), who sought a form of state socialism in which land and capital would be held in common possession.[48] Nor did the tradition of Huber and Raiffeisen stress self-management, whereas Marx and Engels, who rejected the ideology of self-help as 'bourgeois', valued co-operatives in so far as they were 'independent creations', the 'first sprouts' of a new form of society managed by workers.[49]

The greatest influence on co-operative forms in Germany came from Schulze-Delitzsch, regarded by many as outside the co-operative movement. As early as 1849 he began to set up commercial associations of shopkeepers, small manufacturers and craftsmen, whose principal aims were to purchase joint supplies, co-ordinate sales and organise mutual credit. His General Union, established in 1864, became the German Association of Co-operatives (*Deutscher Genossenchaftsverband*) in 1920. Schulze-Delitzsch, while an espouser of the law of self-interest, sought to create freer competitive conditions for the weak. He believed in the sharing of profit and loss through dividends and collective liability and rejected all forms of philanthropy or state aid. He worked prodigiously to produce enduring legal and organisational forms, which, despite his individualistic philosophy, served socially useful ends.[50]

It is perhaps not surprising that with this ideologically complex and contradictory inheritance the GDR was ambivalent in its attitude towards co-operatives. Neither is it surprising that, at the same time, the rich legacy of expertise and experience found in these traditional institutions should have been repeatedly called upon. These two themes will be pursued in the course of a more detailed examination of agricultural and handicraft co-operatives, both of which were at the centre of the reappraisal of property forms and of the relation of the individual to society in the GDR of the late 1980s.

Agricultural Co-operatives

In 1945 land holdings in excess of 100 hectares or belonging to war criminals were confiscated and distributed to poor peasants, agricultural labourers and migrants. The move was designed to destroy the Prussian Junker class and win political sympathy for the regime. In the same year all traditional Raiffeisen co-operative forms were re-established in order to promote agricultural production as rapidly as possible. Within six months 6,325 co-operatives with 800,000 members had been set up. A new type of co-operative, a union of mutual peasant help (*Vereinigung der gegenseitigen Bauernhilfe*) was also established to co-ordinate peasants politically, give specialist advice and lend machinery. Greater state control over co-operative activities was effected through a central union of agricultural co-operatives set up in 1949 and through the affiliation of the rural co-operative banks (*Landesgenossenschaftsbanken*) to the state peasant bank (*Deutsche Bauernbank*).

As a step towards the collectivisation of land, the first, shortlived 'socialist offensive' of 1952 introduced three types of co-operative affiliation. While type I allowed the joint use, but individual retention, of property and equipment, type III required their full collectivisation. Type II represented an intermediate form. Peasants with small holdings benefited greatly from participation in larger-scale production, but the more self-sufficient peasantry with medium-sized and large holdings resisted. As in the brief retreat from collectivisation in Soviet Russia in 1929, when the East German Government introduced its New Course in 1953, 698 newly founded co-operatives dissolved themselves.[51] Campaigning intensified in the 'second socialist offensive' (1958–60), and the remaining collectivisations were forced through within a few weeks in 1960.

In the process, only one traditional form of service co-operative survived, the peasant trading co-operative (*Bäuerliche Handelsgenossenschaft*). Its activities had been restricted in 1951 to working with individual peasants. Two years later, some of its other functions, such as providing animal feed, manure and seeds, information on accounting, transport, animal breeding and drying systems, were resuscitated. All of these were essential for establishing the new co-operatives. Threatened with closure in 1960, it could still not be dispensed with. In the 1970s many of its functions were transferred to state institutions and thereafter it concentrated on household, farmyard and garden provisions, building materials and banking services.[52]

By the 1980s agricultural co-operatives were almost exclusively of the fully collectivised Type III variety, whose number had been greatly reduced by amalgamations (see Table 6.8). The average membership size was about 200, but some employed 5,000 members and workers.

Table 6. 8 Agricultural co-operatives 1960–86

	Number of co-operatives	Type I & II %	
1960	19,313	38.0	(1961)
1970	9,000	16.9	
1986	3,890	1.2	(1975)

Source: Statistisches Jahrbuch, Berlin, 1987

Specialisation and co-ordination became the major themes in the 'third socialist offensive' in the 1970s; the restructuring of industry into combines (*Kombinate*) paralleled the emphasis on planning and leadership from above. 'Industrial-style' agriculture with giant horticultural and animal production units, introduced by Ulbricht in 1968, had brought economies of scale. It also brought management problems. In order to overcome the latter, the early 1970s witnessed the introduction of co-ordinating bodies (*KOE – Kooperative Einrichtungen*) whose aim was to link production units and co-operative councils (*Kooperationsräte*) in order to improve communication links between co-operatives and county authorities.

In contrast, the new model rules of 1977 bore the hallmarks of 'the unity of economic and social policy', which stressed the co-operatives' responsibilities for their members' health, living and working conditions, the elderly and culture. The general assembly of 300–400 members and workers remained the sovereign body and met twice yearly, though meetings of delegates could be held in the intervening period. Delegates were elected for three years by their brigades and departments, which might also have their own councils. Rights and duties in relation to work, sickness pay, holidays and participation were to be documented in written agreements.[53]

In the 1980s, such organisational and democratic forms and practices received considerable attention from political philosophers and lawyers. The position of KOEs (co-ordinating bodies) was strengthened: they were to assist in the drawing up of very specific agreements and targets and in achieving economies through a more efficient use and sharing of labour and transport between co-operatives.[54] Stress was laid on the rights of members to call upon the co-operative for support in the cultivation of individual plots of land and to use small buildings for private animal husbandry. The danger to democracy from domination by superordinate bodies such as co-operative councils was also addressed. Co-operative councils were reminded that they were elected to represent ordinary co-operative members and workers, not just 'the leadership'. Others argued that, although co-operative councils derived their executive authority from the county council and their rights and duties prevailed over those of the individual co-operative, the legal independence and economic self-reliance of individual co-operatives remained; co-operation and self-reliance were symbiotic. The sophistry of the argument revealed the salience of the issue.[55]

In the late 1980s, journal articles began to reassert the durability and distinctiveness of co-operatives as a property form within socialism. The earlier perspective had referred to a 'merging process' (*Verschmelzung*) and the 'gradual transition to ever higher forms of co-operative production'.[56] Now, however, notions of a 'convergence' process (*Annäherungsprozess*) were criticised as artificial. Instead, it was argued, agricultural co-operatives needed to strengthen their legal independence, economic self-reliance and identity as a specific property form. Promoting the use of small parcels of land and small buildings by private individuals was suggested as a means for hastening this process. At the same time, it was necessary to clearly stipulate and delineate the ownership and responsibilities for facilities shared between different co-operatives or between co-operatives and state farms.[57]

Not only was Lenin coming to be quoted on the subject of 'personal interest' as an essential ingredient of revolution, but clearer definitions were being demanded for the authority to use, possess and dispose of property and for co-operatives to be given greater scope to influence state decisions. Warnings could be heard against excessive state direction. Extending the decision-making powers of co-operatives was a precondition for enhancing their feeling of responsibility; while the state should be responsible for the general, long-term strategy, operational decisions must belong to the co-operatives. The key issue in this revisionist view was to be found in inner co-operative democracy, which offered the only way for a community to develop which 'associates, produces and owns (*aneignet*)'.[58]

This debate arose in the context of an economic imperative to improve the involvement of individuals in their work and communities. The impulse for change emanating in the economic sector did not diminish the dynamic towards genuine forms of democracy attendant upon more active forms of participation. The passions expressed by writers during the latter part of the 1980s suggested a motivation beyond economic necessity.

Handicraft Co-operatives

Members and workers in handicraft co-operatives (*Produktionsgenossenschaften der Handwerker – PGH*) represented 1.86 per cent of the total workforce and 13.24 per cent of all co-operative workers.[59] The ranking of the five largest categories within the handicraft sector is shown in Table 6.9.

Table 6.9 Handicraft sections 1986

	Number of co-operatives	Number of members	All co-operative workers	% of all handicraft workers
Building handicraft	1,064	52,750	53,154	33
Services	400	39,326	41,069	25
Machine/ vehicle construction	341	19,836	20,055	12
Electronics	320	22,642	22,379	14
Carpentry	194	7,233	7,337	4.5
Other				11.5
Total	2,319	141,524	144,257	100.0

Source: Statistisches Jahrbuch, Berlin, 1987

Of all the different types of co-operative in the former GDR, the history of the handicraft co-operative is the most fascinating. The majority had their origin in the self-interest, profit-based sections of the co-operative movement which owed so much to Schulze-Delitzsch; on these grounds alone they posed dilemmas for the Government of the GDR. They were essential to the economy and to political stability, but were also prone to profiteering and creating instability. Since handicraft workers were self-employed they owed no automatic allegiance to socialism; indeed, their proclivity to emigrate in large numbers before the building of the Berlin Wall in 1961 was certainly a factor in their careful treatment in the GDR. Their role was further enhanced by the goods and services which they produced for a population tantalised by Western consumerism.

The history of handicraft co-operatives in the early period parallels that of the agricultural sector. After 1945 co-operatives were actively promoted in their pre-war form and championed for their 'true democratic spirit'. In 1952 an attempt was made at their socialist transformation through modification of their co-operative form. The regime hoped that the pressure of high taxation and problems over obtaining supplies and orders in the private sector, as compared with the benefits from state contracts, would induce self-employed handicraft workers to join these co-operatives 'voluntarily'. A choice of model rules was offered, as in the agricultural sector: one involved sharing privately owned tools and machinery, the other established common ownership. Leading figures in the Chamber of Trade (*Handelskammer*), the main co-ordinating body for supplies, were purged. The response to these measures alarmed the Government. First of all, there was a mass exodus of self-employed craftsmen to the West and an alarming drop in the production of consumer goods. Then, following dramatic concessions to the private sector which aroused resentment in the state factories, came the June 1953 uprising. In the hurriedly introduced 'New Course', 347 newly nationalised firms were denationalised and 4,450 new private enterprises set up.[60] In spite of these pacifying initiatives, by 1954 there were still only 50 handicraft co-operatives (PGH), with 1,449 members. Even when PGHs were exempted from tax in 1955, artisans remained reluctant to join them.

So favourable were the conditions for the private sector in the 1950s that the GDR became nicknamed the 'Artisan and Peasant State'. Co-operatives, which had been encouraged as 'socialist' in 1952, were once again deemed 'capitalist'. Indeed, in the more liberal conditions of the 1950s they did promote profitability, assisted by legislation which allowed the Purchasing and Distributive Co-operatives (*Einkaufs- und Liefergenossenschaften – ELG*) to be exempted from tax and to distribute 77 per cent of their profits to their members – in true Schulze-Delitzsch tradition.

The second socialist offensive, 1958–60, declared war on artisans and peasants, and simultaneously proclaimed that the GDR would by 1961 overtake the Federal Republic in the production of consumer goods.[61] PGHs were encouraged through tax concessions, access to supplies and investment finance. Recalcitrant artisans who would not join them were denounced. Nevertheless the private sector flourished again under the New Economic System of the 1960s. According to Asland the structures of 'state capitalism' (the continuance of some, especially small-scale, capitalist enterprise under the socialist state) were too complex to be easily dismantled. Not only was the traditional handicraft sector vital to economic revival in the wake of the second socialist offensive, but its nationalisation would have been prohibitively costly, as the collectivisation of agriculture had shown.

Nevertheless, industrial PGHs were suddenly nationalised in 1972 during the third socialist offensive as part of the new post-Ulbricht political settlement.[62] The nationalisations were an attempt to stop the erosion of labour from the state sector to the more lucrative and congenial non- or semi-state sectors, and to stem resentment at the lavish lifestyles and amassed fortunes enjoyed by their élites.[63] But services and repairs remained a persistent, embarrassing problem. The state service sector showed little improvement and, fearing their nationalisation, those in the remaining private handicraft sector were extremely reluctant to join PGHs. New model rules in 1973 certainly emphasised state control: PGHs 'carry out their tasks on the basis of plans conveyed to them by the superior state body'. Their goal was 'to provide better and more effective services through an improved use of capacity'. This view has to be contrasted with the 1955 model rules, which referred to 'protecting and developing the high quality traditions of German handicraft' and to 'protecting, tending and expanding co-operative property in order to develop a model of co-operative work'.[64]

The tenth Party Congress in 1976 marked a quiet but major turn towards handicraft in all its forms, and particularly in the guise of PGHs. The assertion of *Bündnis* politics as a principle rather than a tactic was particularly designed to reassure handicraft workers.[65] The watchwords became 'socialist teamwork' and 'socialist integration' rather than 'socialist transformation'. The term *'Gewerbepolitik'* (trading policy) was revived after long disuse. The simple form of lump-sum taxation was reintroduced; credit quadrupled for new private-sector initiatives and for rationalisation; 30,000 new handicraft and 7,500 trade and catering licences were issued during 1976–78; apprenticeships were greatly expanded; state enterprises were asked to assist with buildings and machinery. Many of the newly self-employed were organised in co-operatives. The policy as a whole was extolled for easing labour shortages, since in family businesses relatives helped out to minimise labour costs. Service and repair output duly increased by 38.7 per cent in the period 1975–80, compared with 3.3 per cent during 1972–75.[66] The remarkable resilience and capacity of this traditional sector to recover was demonstrated once again.

Major efforts were made from the late 1970s onwards to co-ordinate and rationalise the service sector in parallel with the agricultural co-operatives. By 1979 regional and county handicraft and trade workgroups (*Arbeitsgruppen für Handel und Gewerbe*) had been set up by the National Front, modelled on the renowned Stralsund project of 1977. This 'outstanding ideological work' mounted 'constructive discussions and exchanges of opinion' between state, co-operative and private sectors on how to rationalise resources. As a result, fifty concrete proposals were incorporated into the local plan.[67] After 1973 a number of co-ordinating bodies (KOE – as in agriculture) for particular service areas (*Versorgungsgruppen*) were also established. By 1981, 45 per cent of co-operatives and private producers belonged to such groups.[68]

As already noted, later theoretical work on handicraft co-operatives criticised orthodox (Soviet-Marxist) assumptions that class differences could be rapidly removed and that greater equality meant greater progress. The role played by co-operative and private handicraft workers in the reproduction process was now expected to last far into socialism: under the secure leadership of the working class and its party they were 'joint owners of social property overall' (*Miteigentümer des gesamtgesellschaftlichen Eigentums*), whose socially useful work entitled them to a share in social wealth. Furthermore, modern technology, contrary to earlier interpretations, was now regarded as enhancing the importance of services and repairs and of small-scale production. Falconere cited the revival of small businesses and services in the US and Britain as a positive development offering quality, innovation and adaptability. Thus handicraft workers developed 'interests, needs, relationships, attitudes' in accordance with the interests of the whole society.[69]

Oscillating between Raiffeisen, Schulze-Delitzsch and state socialist principles, handicraft co-operatives were in the main of more recent foundation and had a more varied history compared with their agricultural counterparts. Efforts to co-ordinate and rationalise them took place in the relatively tolerant conditions of the *Bündnispolitik*, a period in some ways akin to the New Course and New Economic System of the 1950s and 1960s, but which also laid great stress on participation (*Mitgestaltung*) captured in the slogan 'Work, plan, rule together!' (*Arbeite mit, plane mit, regiere mit!*).

Handicraft co-operatives were far smaller than agricultural co-operatives, less amenable to strict state control and more accessible to active participation. In the Berlin borough of Treptow, eight handicraft co-operatives, each with about eighty plumbers, electricians and other tradesmen, worked in conjunction with the local authority building department. Each had standard executive and auditing committees, but also committees for such matters as innovations,[70] health, recreation, pensioners – functions which involved the majority of the membership and which would be organised through trade union structures in state enterprises. Furthermore craftsmen often worked individually on household repairs and jobs 'on the side'. As has been indicated, the agricultural sector also increasingly facilitated individual undertakings.

In general, the craftsman tradition in the GDR was law-abiding and conservative in comparison with the speculation and corruption that characterised equivalent sectors in other Eastern European countries. Asland attributed this to the strength of upright, German co-operative traditions and to the relatively short post-war period of economic breakdown and rampant speculation. The GDR repeatedly drew back from nationalising the private retail and handicraft sectors, allowing them a continued existence with substantial state support, at least until 1972. In Asland's view, policies in that period may well have destroyed the law-abiding tradition, since the state itself encouraged a black market in repairs and services to compensate for its own inability to meet the demand for services. Tax-free earnings of 3,000 Marks were allowed 'on the side' and in 1972 the self-employed salary was 3.7 times the average. There are good grounds for agreeing with Asland's opinion that 'an underground economy had been deliberately created'.[71]

Conclusion

Ever since 1976 there had been a clear trend towards giving positive emphasis to the difference between co-operative and state property forms in both handicraft and agriculture. After that date, concern with motivation brought greater attention to subjective aspects of co-operation: individuals' needs, interests and rights. There was a fresh interest in the importance of self-reliance and inner co-operative democracy as ways of spurring individuals to become more engaged in the workplace and in society and to show greater responsibility. This new approach took a firmer hold in the 1980s, in sharp contrast with earlier 'convergence' theories of co-operatives as a transitional form towards full state socialisation.

Two reasons tend to be put forward to explain why debates around agriculture took a more central place in discussions compared with the handicraft, housing or consumer sectors. Since the 1950s change in the co-operative form had been pioneered in agriculture; their model rules set the pattern for other sectors, and they were the first productive area to be fully collectivised through the co-operative form (in 1960). Their credibility lay in their vanguard role and it seemed likely that new thinking initiated in the agricultural sphere would be extended to other co-operatives in due course. Secondly, agricultural co-operatives, confined in their actions by state directives for nearly thirty years, needed to democratise their structures, whereas handicraft co-operatives offered more scope for individual initiative by virtue of their smaller size and more personalised and specialised functions.

Intellectuals spoke confidently of the long-term future of co-operatives under socialism and the Gorbachev reforms seemed likely to blow wind in their favour, even though in official circles perestroika was deemed redundant and glasnost ruled out. Others felt Gorbachev's position was by no means secure from the old guard, in which case the GDR might yet see a clampdown. Asland argued that economic pragmatism maintained the private sector in the GDR, but one might add that political pragmatism periodically, as in 1972, countered it. The tension between offering high prices to stimulate goods and services and controlling profiteering had led to abrupt swings in policy as in the nationalisations of the late 1950s and 1960s. The great scope to amass wealth through co-operatives, individually and collectively, in the 1980s, might well have led to another turnabout.[72] The scenario no one considered was a West German takeover.

The early 1970s saw the highpoint of state collectivism in the GDR, in co-operatives too. Agricultural and housing co-operatives were almost indistinguishable from their respective state sectors, and handicraft co-operatives, reduced to a minimum, were used as instruments of state planning. Subsequently there was a gentle thaw towards the pole of individualism and market mechanisms. Individual undertakings were encouraged as satellite activities in agriculture; the self-employed in the handicraft and service sectors were generously facilitated; and consumer co-operatives were empowered to make direct contracts with suppliers. The highly subsidised self-build scheme in housing actually belonged to the owner-occupied sector, although it bore co-operative features.

Credit co-operatives scarcely existed[73] and housing co-operatives remained close to the collectivised, state pole. Redesigning industrially built housing blocks for quality and choice would require immense material and creative resources. Democratisation and marketisation were possible courses, drawing on ideological and legal premises already being rehearsed in other sectors. Entirely new model rules and fiscal policies would be required and it seemed a daunting task to break the pattern of rents at 3–4 per cent of household income while unspent savings were invested in buying weekend houses at inflated prices and extortionately priced secondhand cars. In comparison to such spending patterns the 15 per cent of housing costs raised by co-operative members' contributions was paltry.

An obvious way to direct hidden resources into the formal economy was to marketise investments, as was beginning in some Central European countries. Many feared this would bring excessive social differentiation and competitive individualism. The question was whether marketised investments could be increased without losing the collective traditions which had been developed. The co-operative form offered hope for this and the GDR stage seemed set for such discussion. With unification in 1990, however, the GDR stage appeared totally irrelevant. It will take another study and the passage of more time to see whether GDR perspectives and experience were quite as irrelevant as they suddenly seemed.

Notes

1   A. Asland, *Private Enterprise in Eastern Europe*, Macmillan, London, 1985, pp. 151–3, 174.
2   H. J. Herzog, *Genossenschaftliche Organisationsformen in der DDR*, Mohr, Tübingen, 1982.
3   W. Homann, *AWGs im Rahmen der Wohnungsbaupolitik der DDR*, FS-Analysen, Berlin, 1981.
4   I. Markovits, 'Pursuing One's Rights Under Socialism', *Stanford Law Review*, Vol. 38, No. 3, 1986, p. 725.
5   M. Melzer, 'Wohnungsbau und Wohnungsversorgung in beiden deutschen Staaten – ein Vergleich', *Deutsches Institut für Wirtschaftsforschung – Beiträge zur Strukturforschung*, No. 74, 1983, p. 190.
6   G. Staemmler, 'East Germany (the GDR)' in M. Wynn (ed.), *Housing in Europe*, Croom Helm, London, 1984, p. 230.
7   Some privately rented property in East Berlin was owned by residents, mostly old ladies, and administered by private agencies. The majority was owned by landlords resident in the West and administered by local authority housing departments. The legal relations varied. Rents were fixed and the properties dilapidated; compensation was paid if a building was redeveloped or taken over for major renovation.
8   Thirty to fifty per cent of Berlin households were said to own such highly sought-after, and appropriately priced, plots.
9   G. Staemmler, 'Wohnungsbauplanung und Wohnungspolitik in den Städten der DDR', *Bauwelt*, Vol. 73, No. 35, 1982; Staemmler, 'East Germany (the GDR)'.

10   A. Kahl, J. Wilsdorf and H. Wolf, *Kollektivbeziehungen und Lebensweise*, Dietz, Berlin, 1984.
11   P. Chamberlayne, 'Citizen Participation in Local Government in the GDR', *East Central Europe*, Vol. 14–15, 1987–8, pp. 81–116; P. Chamberlayne, 'Neighbour and Tenant Participation in the GDR', in B. Deacon and J Szalai (eds), *Social Policy in the New Eastern Europe*, Avebury, Aldershot, 1990.
12   M. Hoffmann, 'Genossenschaftlicher Wohnungsbau in der DDR' in *Jahrbuch für Nationalökonomie und Statistik*, Vol. 187, No. 6, 1973, p. 536.
13   Workplaces elected housing commissions through the trade union. They worked actively with the enterprise, the local authority and housing co-operatives on housing issues affecting the workforce.
14   Homann, op. cit., p. 36.
15   S. Bergmann and K. Zieger, 'Wohnungstausch und Verantwortung der Betriebe und Wohnungsbaugenossenschaften bei der Wohnungsversorgung', *Neue Justiz*, No. 10, 1986.
16   M. Hoffmann, 'Genossenschaftlicher Wohnungsbau in der DDR', *Jahrbuch für Nationalökonomie und Statistik*, Vol. 187, No. 6, 1973.
17   Herzog, op. cit., 1982.
18   K. Gittel, 'Die Umbildung der alten Wohnungsbaugenossenschaften', *Deutsche Finanzwirtschaft*, No. 12, 1958.
19   R. Müller, '400 gemeinnützige Wohnungbaugenossenschaften werden umgebildet', *Deutsche Finanzwirtschaft*, No 12, 1958; Gittel, op. cit.
20   Melzer, op. cit., p. 79.
21   Herzog, op. cit., 1982.
22   Shares were originally uniform at 2,500 Marks. After 1958 each share cost 300M, the number required depending on the flat size; for example:
     1 room with kitchen and shower recess – 3 shares 900 Marks
     1 room with kitchen and bathroom – 4 shares 1,200 Marks
     2 room flat – 7 shares 2,100 Marks
     Source: Homann, op. cit., p. 30.
23   Homann, op. cit.
24   In addition to shares, 'work contributions' were a prerequisite for gaining access to co-operative housing. Depending on the size and amenities of the flat and the hourly value of the work performed, an individual member was required to contribute 200–400 hours. Annual contributions of about 12 hours, as decided by the members' assembly, were also required for maintenance and repairs, but this time could be paid for in cash equivalent (Statut für Arbeiterwohnungsbaugenossenschaften, Berlin, 1973).
25   R. Beckmann, 'Das Neue Musterstatut der AWG', *Die Wirtschaft*, Vol. 18, No. 3, 1964.
26   Hoffmann, op. cit., p. 527.
27   Melzer, op. cit., p. 81; FDGB, *Wohnungskommission*, Schriftenreihe Die Kommissionen der Betriebsgewerkschaftsleitung, Berlin, Tribüne, 1968, p. 20.
28   R. Breunung, 'Die Werkschaften und die AWGs', *Weltwerkschaftsbewegung*, No. 2, 1985.
29   Although rents were low, arrears reached 16 million Marks in 1973, the last date for which published figures were available (Markovits, op. cit., p. 724). Rent allowances were payable to single parents and to large and pensioner households.
30   Herzog, op. cit., chap. 2.
31   The FDGB (*Freier Deutscher Gewerkschaftsbund*) was the main trade union, structured around different occupational groups.
32   Homann, op. cit., p. 35.

33 Political and many social activities were organised through mass organisations, which included the political parties, the women's, youth and pensioners' organisations and others to do with sport, culture, Soviet friendship etc. Mass organisations were co-ordinated in local government through the National Front.

34 B. Sommerer, 'Arbeiterwohnungsbau – ein Teil der ökonomischen Hauptaufgabe', *Die Arbeit*, No. 4, 1959.

35 Staemmler, *Wohnungsbauplanung und Wohnungspolitik.*

36 Chamberlayne, 'Citizen Participation in Local Government'.

37 FDGB, op. cit.

38 Bergmann and Zieger, op. cit., p. 421; Breunung, op. cit.

39 Melzer, op. cit., p. 163.

40 Homann, op. cit., p. 50.

41 Friedrich-Ebert-Stiftung, *Wohnungs- und Städtebau in der DDR – zur Wohnungsfrage*, Neue Gesellschaft, Bonn, 1981, p. 25.

42 Chamberlayne, 'Citizen Participation in Local Government' and 'Neighbour and Tenant Participation'.

43 R. Mecklenburg, 'Zu einigen staatstheoretischen Aspekten des Verhältnisses von Staat und genossenschaftlichem Eigentum in der Landwirtschaft der DDR', *Staat und Recht*, Vol. 36, No. 8, 1987.

44 Herzop, op. cit., p. 48.

45 Verband der Konsumgenossenschaften der DDR, *Konsumgenossenschaften der DDR*, Berlin [East], 1965.

46 The 1948 currency reform of 1:10 was necessitated by the growing disparity in the value of East and West German Marks. Certain sectors were granted preferential terms of 1:1 or 1:3. In the 1960s similar industrial price reforms were gradually introduced in three stages, the last one in 1967. Socialised firms contracting with the private sector were allowed to use the old prices, whereas the private sector had to use the new rates (Asland, op. cit., p. 172).

47 Herzog, op. cit., p. 26.

48 *Beiträge zur Theorie des Genossenschaftswesens*, Oesterreichischer Wirtschaftsverlag, Vienna, 1937.

49 Association of Consumer Co-operative Societies of the GDR, *Articles on Theory and Practice of Co-operation*, Berlin [East], 1976.

50 *Beiträge*, p. 84; P. Lambert, *Studies in the Social Philosophy of Co-operation*, Co-operative Union, Manchester, 1963.

51 Herzog, op. cit., p. 66.

52 Ibid., pp. 15/16.

53 R. Hähnert, 'Zu einigen eigentums- und kooperationsrechtlichen Aspekten in der sozialistischen Landwirtschaft', *Staat und Recht*, Vol. 36, No. 4, 1987; W. Schneider, 'Der Vertrag als Mittel zur Gestaltung von Beziehungen zur LPG und ihren Mitgliedern', *Staat und Recht*, Vol. 35, 1986, pp. 959–65.

54 R. Lehmann and D. Sachse, 'Kooperationsräte – bewährte demokratische Gremien', *Einheit*, No. 4, 1980.

55 K. Ahrends, 'Die Vertiefung der Kooperation zwischen LPG und VEG der Pflanzen- und Tierproduktion – Faktor des Produktions- und Effektivitätswachstums', *Wirtschaftswissenschaft*, Vol. 33, No. 11, 1985.

56 Association of Consumer Co-operative Societies, op. cit.

57 Hähnert, op. cit.

58 Mecklenburg, op. cit., p. 670.

59   *Statistisches Jahrbuch,* Berlin, 1987.
60   Asland, op. cit., p. 146.
61   The Soviet Union's hopes until 1961 of a united, neutral Germany also played a part in the careful treatment of the self-employed and small-scale producers.
62   Asland, op. cit.
63   Ibid., pp. 176–8.
64   M. Haendcke-Hoppe, 'Neue Statuten für die PGHs und die Handelskammer der Bezirke', *Deutschland Archiv,* Vol. 6, No. 8, 1973, p. 837.
65   *Bündnis,* or alliance politics, emphasised respect for different social groups represented through the mass organisations. The SED (Socialist Unity Party) retained its 'leading role', but the other four parties were represented at all levels of government: the CDU (Christian Democrats); LDPD (Liberal Democrats); NDPD (National Democrats); BP (Peasants).
66   Asland, op. cit., pp. 204, p. 198.
67   H. Lehmann, 'Der Beitrag des Handwerks zur Erfüllung der Hauptaufgaben, *Einheit,* No. 7, 1977; H. Schütze, 'Handwerk und Gewerbe – Zwischenbilanz einer Initiative', *Einheit,* No. 6, 1979.
68   M. Haendcke-Hoppe, 'Kurskorrekturen in der Handwerkspolitik der DDR', *Deutschland Archiv,* Vol. 14, No. 12, 1981.
69   I. Falconere, 'Zur Rolle der Handwerker und Gewerbetreibenden im gesellschaftlichen Reproduktionsprozess der DDR unter veränderten Reproduktionsbedingungen der 80er Jahre', *Wirtschaftswissenschaft,* Vol. 30, No. 9, 1982, p. 1350.
70   Technological innovation and rationalisation were encouraged by the introduction of the voluminous 'invention' laws which offered rewards for proposals which would aid production. The 'value' of an invention was determined by 'innovation committees'.
71   Asland, op. cit., p. 198.
72   Handicraft workers were said to charge three or four times the set rate and frequently to demand payment in Western currency. High official prices were paid for fruit, vegetables and livestock to improve fresh food supplies. Small producers sold everything they could and shopped for their own consumption at a fifth or so of the price they had sold at.
73   GHGs (*Genossenschaftskassen für Handwerk und Gewerbe*) were extant credit co-operatives. Each bank was owned by a co-operative, whose members were, for instance, private craftsmen, retail traders or proprietors of restaurants. Capital resources were formed from shares; any group which included handicraft co-operatives was also entitled to state credit (I. Jeffries and M. Melzer, *The East German Economy,* Croom Helm, London, 1987, p. 197).

Further Reading

P. J. Bryson, *The Consumer under Socialist Planning – the East German Case,* Praeger, New York, 1984.

M. Hoffmann, 'Die Wohnungsgenossenschaften in der DDR in der "sozialistischen Entwicklungsperspektive"', *Gemeinnütziges Wohnungswesen,* Vol. 27, no. 11, 1974.

H. W. Jenkis, *Wohnungswirtschaft und Wohnungspolitik in beiden deutschen Staaten,* Hammonia Verlag, Hamburg, 1976.

R. Klein, 'Grosse Leistungen im genossenschaftlichen Wohnungsbau', *Presse-Informationen,* No. 139, 1978.

7 Socialist Yugoslavia: Embryo of a Co-operative Republic

LARS NORD*

Some champions of the co-operative idea foster a dream that the whole of society should be organised on co-operative principles. In such a society, democratic association would form the key structural component of the political-administrative system with control over production as the logical consequence of consumer co-operatives. The ultimate goal of co-operation is the establishment of a co-operative republic.

Advocates of this idea have yet to see its materialisation. Despite their advances, Israeli kibbutz and Mondragon co-operatives in Spain are far from being the central organisational units in society at large and by no means constitute the foundation of either country. Socialist Yugoslavia, for the almost fifty years of its existence, came closer to the image of a co-operative society that visionaries foresaw: elements of co-operatism permeated the society. Its outstanding achievement in this regard was to apply to the system of government the same guiding principle as do co-operatives, that is, self-government. The assumption that people better promote a common cause when they unite and co-operate than when they act alone or when the state acts on their behalf was the core conviction underlying the country's political-administrative system from the 1950s until the dissolution of the federal state in 1991.

This chapter examines the extent to which socialist Yugoslavia could be said to have been a co-operative republic. This involves observing co-operatism in two ways: as a phenomenon in the nation's governance and as a movement within the society. The focal point of the analysis is co-operation within the housing sector.

Yugoslavia's experience in this field is not of purely historical and academic interest, for it has a relevance for its fragmented successor states, to whom responsibility for legislating on co-operatives was passed in 1971, twenty years before the demise of the federal state. As the examples of other

---

*   Lars Nord is Senior Lecturer in the Department of Government, University of Uppsala.

former socialist countries in East and Central Europe confirm, it can take time to change housing laws and housing practices.[1]

The Co-operative Republic

Studies on co-operation and the co-operative movement usually point to the absence of a common understanding of the concept. Its etymological derivation is the Latin word, *cooperatio*, meaning people working together for mutual benefit. But beyond this general definition lies an abundance of different approaches and schools concerning its meaning. In some instances, the psychological dimension is to the fore: an unspecified human willingness to join for a common cause is looked upon as the root of co-operation.[2] This willingness might in turn be traced back to human nature[3] or to human resources in general,[4] or divided into fundamental and universal components of human nature and experiences,[5] or to an expression of 'a community instinct'.[6] Another alternative is to explain co-operation and the co-operative movement by theories developed within the social sciences, employing concepts like action, expectation and social movements.[7] Yet another approach is to turn to political theories associated with the history and tradition of the co-operative movement, whose most prominent ideological forerunners were Robert Owen, Charles Fourier and Henri St Simon. It is on the latter that proponents of the idea of a co-operative republic mainly rely. However, perhaps the most eloquent spokesman for the co-operative republic was the French economist Charles Gide, whose vision was outlined in his two books, *La Coopération* and *Sociétés coopération de consommation*, on which the following section draws heavily.[8]

Gide's Vision

According to Gide, since the purpose of co-operation was to satisfy people's needs, it was superior to capitalism, which he considered would be superseded by a new economic order founded on co-operation. However, in contrast to the Marxist conceptualisation of the development of capitalism, which envisaged a constant evolution before it finally transformed into socialism (and then communism), Gide foresaw capitalism returning to a pre-capitalist stage, which would in essence be a family economy based on solidarity.[9]

In his view, the guiding principle for the new economic order was 'la loi naturelle de l'association',[10] which governed nations and societies. The new order implied control over the distribution of goods and that production should rest with co-operatives. While rejecting the market as a means of producing goods, he did not advocate state ownership. It was enough that consumers 'controlled' the means of production.[11]

Gide's scheme embraced both industry and agriculture. He was, however, aware that they could not be treated in the same way. As far as industry was concerned, the crucial point was not the supply of capital, but the sale of products. Co-operatives had to have many thousands of members or be associated for common purchases, so that there would be sufficient numbers to make manufacturing feasible.

Industrial production was dependent on the supply of raw materials. Consumer co-operatives also sold goods which were produced on farms. According to Gide, therefore, it was necessary that the production of raw materials and food should be in the hands of co-operatives, which would thus have to own land (and mines). Public services would also have to be co-operatively run. However, the supply of utilities (gas, water, electricity), transport and other public goods presented a problem. Since they could not be allowed to grow organically in proportion to the increase in new members, but had to be completed 'in one go', they had to be established by large, private or public companies. For Gide, municipal enterprises, when viewed closely, were co-operatives,[12] since their purpose was to satisfy consumers' needs effectively without making any profit; any gains would be returned to consumers (or tax-payers) or used for public works. They, therefore, constituted a kind of co-operative whose members were all inhabitants of a municipality.

One problem connected with membership of a municipality was its compulsory character. While membership of a co-operative society is voluntary, an individual is not formally allowed to remain outside a local community. He circumvented this problem by pointing out that a citizen could settle down in any municipality. In addition, needs that are satisfied by public enterprises are so general and fundamental that everyone shares them. For these reasons, the difference between a co-operative association and a municipality was, for Gide, only a matter of degree.

Gide's reasoning took it for granted that there was no conflict between members of consumer co-operatives and of producer co-operatives. But this was not always the case. Since co-operatives could also be established by workers irrespective of their needs as consumers, what would happen to profits produced by such co-operative enterprises; should surpluses belong to the worker or the consumer?

Two arguments were advanced justifying the allocation of profits to workers: firstly, associations of producers would be more competent than consumers in handling production; consumers should not, for instance, be required to make their own shoes. The consumer's role in the production process is as a sort of 'supervisor'; at the same time, involvement in the process would make consumers better educated in the economics and social relations of production. Secondly, only producer co-operatives, by making workers their own employees, who themselves reap the fruits of their work, can liberate the working class by abolishing wage-labour. Although people employed by consumer co-operatives remained traditional wage-earners and dependent on the employer in the same way as in a private company, the employer would not be a capitalist. Workers could and would be members of the consumer co-operative for which they worked and as a result would be working for themselves.

In his view there had to be pure consumer as well as pure producer co-operatives, existing independently alongside one another. This would be necessary because, for a very long time, many workers would, in their capacity as producers, stand outside consumer co-operatives. This would apply to people employed in a whole range of occupations and economic sectors. However, Gide recognised that a dilemma would arise if consumer co-operatives established enterprises to produce their own goods and producer co-operatives established consumer co-operatives in order to sell their products. A consequence of this development could be a merger which, should it occur, would be a 'higher form' in accordance with 'a natural law of development'.[13]

Yugoslavia: A History in Three Parts

A Kingdom and Empires

Major wars can be dangerous for empires. The social and economic upheavals that follow more often than not destroy old-established structures and power relations, as occurred in the aftermath of the First World War, which witnessed the collapse of the Habsburg Empire and the formation of a new state on the Balkan peninsula.[14]

The new state was established by Slav peoples who had come to the region in the fourth century. After centuries of German and Turkish domination, and in the wake of the national liberation movements of the nineteenth century and the First World War, an independent Kingdom of Serbs, Croats, and Slovenes was established. From the beginning, the country was characterised by multiple cleavages between the three peoples in terms of:

- religion: Orthodox on the part of the Serbs, Roman Catholic on the part of the Croats and the Slovenes, Muslim in Bosnia-Herzegovina;
- language: Serbo-Croat and Slovenian;
- alphabet: Cyrillic in Serbia, Latin in Croatia and Slovenia; and
- history: for 500–600 years, Serbs had been ruled from Constantinople, Croats from Budapest, and Slovenes from Vienna.

The new country embraced many other nations, including Hungarians, Macedonians, Albanians, Germans, Romanians, Turks and Italians, some of whom were members of another world religion – Islam. Social cohesion in such a heterogeneous community was preserved by the creation of a strong, centralised, unitary state with Belgrade as its capital and with Serbs dominating its government and administration. This unholy mixture contained, as future events were so sadly to demonstrate, an enormous fissiparous potential.

The agrarian economy was characterised by small plots cultivated by heavily indebted farmers. Industry, too, was based on small-scale units or was under the control of foreign capital. Illiteracy was widespread, which contributed towards an unstable polity. A monarchical dictatorship was installed in 1929 and the name of the state changed to the Kingdom of Yugoslavia.

At the onset of the Second World War Yugoslavia declared itself neutral, but the country's strategic position ensured that it did not retain this neutrality for long. Invasion by the Axis powers was followed by the capitulation of the army and the outbreak of civil war along several fronts: indigenous fascist groups collaborated with the enemy and fought against the bourgeoisie and communist guerillas, who were also fighting between themselves; Croats and Serbs were in a state of feud, as were Serbs and Muslims. In the end the communist partisans commanded by Josip Broz Tito emerged victorious from the multilateral combat. Highly disciplined, strongly motivated ideologically, and with a clear and unequivocal policy on the national question and a range of social and economic issues, the Communist Party came through as the true ruler of the country when the new European order came into being in the post-war period.

A People's Democracy

Socialist Yugoslavia became a federation of six republics – Serbia, Croatia, Bosnia-Herzegovina, Slovenia, Macedonia and Montenegro. (Serbia also contained two autonomous provinces of Voivodina and Kosovo.) Officially, it included five peoples – the Serbs, Croats, Slovenes, Macedonians and Montenegrins – and a number of other national minorities, all of whom had the right to use their own language and to preserve their culture. This, it was hoped, would make political and ethnic subjugation, so characteristic of the inter-war period, a thing of the past.

The new regime was confronted with the enormous task of post-war recovery. The country had suffered severely in both human and material terms; the war had seen the loss of between 1.1 and 1.2 million people (7–11 per cent of the population.) Industrial production in the textile, food processing and metals sectors was less than half of the country's pre-war capacity. The whole of the railroad network was seriously damaged; only 23 per cent of locomotives and 10 per cent of wagons were in operation. In agriculture the number of cattle, horses, sheep, and pigs had fallen by 50–60 per cent and about 80 per cent of ploughs and harvesting machinery had been destroyed. Merchant shipping and other important sectors of the country's economy had also suffered severe losses.[15]

Housing was no exception to this general pattern of destruction. One-quarter of the population, or about 3.3 million people, had been made homeless. Every fifth house had been demolished or badly damaged, with the figure in Belgrade and other large cities rising to two-fifths of the pre-war housing stock.

The Yugoslav communists looked to the Soviet Union and its system of centralised state socialism for a model on which to base their policy of reconstruction. In order to transform the country from a bourgeois order into a People's Republic, they put into practice socialist premises of nationalisation, collectivisation, industrialisation and electrification. Private property was nationalised, a Five-Year Plan was launched and, following the established Soviet pattern, consumer needs and agriculture were neglected.

A Socialist Democracy

The type of regime which was officially referred to in the 1980s as 'the centralised administrative period' lasted for little more than five years, for in 1948 Yugoslavia's communist party and its leadership were expelled from the Soviet-inspired Communist Information Bureau (Cominform), and thereby from the world brotherhood of communist parties and countries. Challenged to find an alternative to Stalinist state-centralism, the Yugoslav communists developed their own brand of socialism, one based on decentralisation and self-government in politics and the economy, which none the less continued to function under the dominion of the Party.

The state was transformed from an owner of the means of production into 'an association of free producers' – a formulation that should satisfy champions of a co-operative republic provided that consumers were not excluded. Its best-known institution was the workers' council, which in 1976, as part of the continuing search for ways of further decentralising the economic system, was made the main decision-making body within the 'basic organisation of associated labour' (BOAL), which was considered to be the fundamental economic unit.[16] The BOALs could be seen as a step towards the formation of producer co-operatives. They were run by the workers and constituted divisions which could join together to form an enterprise. The enterprise was an autonomous legal entity allowed to enter into contractual relations for the purchase of capital goods, raw materials and workers.

The principal determining features of this unique Yugoslav model of socialist democracy were the transfer of, firstly, administrative-political power to the communes and, secondly, economic management to the enterprises, with the workers' council as the main decision-making body. In order to ensure a more balanced economic development, the new approach witnessed a shift in investment away from heavy industries into other sectors, including consumption. These changes in the domestic economy were matched by a foreign policy of neutrality; in the 1990s Yugoslavia's non-aligned stance (ironically) contributed, quite literally, to its undoing.

In the 1960s the processes of democratisation and decentralisation were taken a step further when, in order to encourage greater competition within a 'free socialist market', enterprises were given almost complete operational independence. The 1974 Constitution continued the process of federalisation by granting the republics and autonomous provinces still more authority to manage their own affairs, while at the federal level the position of head of state became annually rotated within a Presidency, composed of representatives of each of the republics. Even the Communist Party underwent a process of decentralisation and in doing so abandoned many of Lenin's cherished conceptions of the Communist Party as a monolithic and disciplined organisation, based on the principle of 'democratic centralism'.

However, theory and practice do not always coincide. One study of Yugoslavia's labour-management system, published in 1984, stated that should an economist wish, as an experiment, to study the effects of such an economic model, it would probably be advisable not to choose Yugoslavia as the object of the investigation because of its many disparate elements, the roots of which have already been briefly mentioned. Apart from cultural and religious differences, the country was characterised by considerable disparities in levels of economic development between republics, the most advanced of which were Slovenia and Croatia in the north and west. Their well-being may be contrasted with the situation in Bosnia-Herzegovina, Macedonia, Kosovo and Serbia proper.[17] Thus, while some republics and regions in Yugoslavia were at a level of social and economic development approximating that found amongst (the poorer) countries of Western Europe, there were other republics and regions which, measured by the same criteria, were closer to that of less-developed countries.

Conclusion

Therefore, any discussion of co-operatives in Yugoslavia has to be seen in the context of a young nation state, which had been established after the First World War on the ruins of disintegrating empires, and which, from the beginning, had been encumbered by a legacy of serious political, social and economic cleavages and a small-scale, agrarian economy. In the wake of the Second World War and subsequent domestic turmoil and social revolution, a new regime had been installed, initially relying on Stalinist state socialism as a model for the country, and later on its own original form of self-managed socialism. Yugoslavia's turbulent history up to the end of the first half of the twentieth century framed the setting for the development of housing co-operatives.

Co-operative Principles

In Gide's vision of a co-operative republic, the principles guiding organisation and management of co-operatives were taken for granted. To him the Rochdale pioneers were the fathers of co-operation. They had managed to formulate the principal ideas and practical rules that were adopted by co-operatives all over the world for years to come.[18] These guidelines were also approved as the basis for the work of The International Co-operative Alliance (ICA) when it was founded in 1895. These same principles provide the basis of the analysis used in this chapter, although the wording is that of the Rochdale principles as agreed in 1966. In short they consist of the following points:[19]

- Open and voluntary membership;
- Democratic decision making;
- A limited rate of interest, if any, on shared capital;
- A fair distribution of surplus and savings;
- Education in co-operative principles and practices; and
- Co-operation between co-operatives.[19]

The unabridged version of the principles contains additional information on the interpretation of these points. Thus, the first one, open and voluntary membership, consists of two requirements, although both have in common a repudiation of discrimination on any social, political, racial or religious grounds. The clause on open membership, sometimes referred to as the 'open door', implies that anyone who can make use of the service of a certain co-operative and accept the responsibility of membership should be accepted as a member of that co-operative. 'Voluntariness' means that members should join of their own free will.

Democracy is an equivocal concept. The ICA had four criteria of democracy in mind when agreeing the tenet on democratic decision making. The first concerned the appointment of the administrative staff: it stipulated that they should be chosen by the members. The second related to the responsibility of this staff: namely, that they should be answerable to the members for their work. The third took up the issue of the right to vote and specified that the rule of one member, one vote should be applied. And the fourth criterion dealt with participation: every member had an equal right to take part in decisions concerning the co-operative's affairs.

Whether it is in line with the co-operative idea to take interest might be a matter of controversy. The basic attitude among ICA members seems however to be, at least according to the requirement of a limited rate of interest, that unearned incomes are a bad thing. The best alternative is no interest at all. If there must be any, it should be as low as possible. As regards the question of a fair distribution of surplus and savings, the ICA's view of fairness was that economic results should be shared by members in such a manner that nobody should gain at the expense of others. The subject of education includes principles as well as techniques. It is a question of learning democratic decision making and economics and pertains to staff as well as to members and the general public. Finally, the ICA presumed that co-operation between co-operatives would take place at local, national and international levels.

The rules for democratic decision making, which Gide took for granted, were very much applied by BOALs. Power and management lay in the hands of a workers' council which was elected by the workers. The council in its turn elected a director and board of management, who were responsible for the employment and dismissal of personnel. It also decided on such matters as annual financial reports and economic plans. A further democratic guarantee was that major decisions concerning the enterprise in its entirety had to be voted on by all of the BOALs. In the application of other ICA principles to ensure that surplus and savings were fairly distributed, the workers' councils were given the power to decide on the use of funds and the distribution of earnings between investment and personal income. Adherence to the principle of education was observed by encouraging participation in decision making. For instance, alternating halves of the workers' councils were elected each year for two-year terms of office, and no one could serve more than two consecutive terms. In addition, Workers' Universities gave courses in self-management.

However, two ICA principles were not adhered to. In part this concerned the issue of membership. The principle of voluntarism was followed. A person was free to choose the enterprise in which he or she would work. The same respect was not accorded to 'openness'. True, the Yugoslav Constitution recognised social, political and religious rights such as freedom of thought, speech, press information and religion. However, freedom of the press and information was circumscribed by the important addition that it could not be used 'to destroy the basis of the socialistic, democratic order'.[20] Contrary to the ICA principle, such a formulation gave room for discrimination on political grounds.

The clause on a limited rate of interest was not applied, simply because share capital did not exist in Yugoslav enterprises. The basic concept of property was 'social property' which was owned by 'society' and not by private capital or by co-operatives.

Views on how to deal with violations of the ICA principles differ. Thus Erwin Hasselman does not consider political and religious neutrality a precondition, provided it concerns a 'free' organisation which can change its policy whenever its members want to.[21] On the other hand, this was not the case with the Yugoslav self-managed enterprises. They were constitutionally forbidden to deviate from socialist precepts. However, the Soviet co-operative movement had been a member of ICA since 1921, as was the Yugoslav co-operative. Therefore, in practice at least, the Alliance did not make loyalty to the principle on discrimination an unconditional requirement of membership.

'While voluntary association and democracy are cardinal tenets that have to be met for an organisation to be recognised as a co-operative, this does not apply to *share-holding*: Co-operatives may or may not have shareholders.'[22]

Thus, overall, ICA principles were adhered to in Yugoslavia's self-managed enterprises. This picture changed when the position of BOALs in the political-economic structure of society was taken into account. The problem arose because according to the constitution they were holders of all social-sector assets; this may be compared, for example, with the Mondragon co-operators, who on the whole do not have access to national social security arrangements.[23]

BOALs were given a key political role in government, especially in the 1974 Constitution, where they found expression in the composition of the local assembly. This consisted of three chambers elected by local communities, the so-called socio-political organisations (e. g. the communist party and the trade union) and 'organisations of associated labour' (i.e. enterprises, institutions and other workplaces).[24] In other words, by sending delegates to the main decision-making body in the municipality, the enterprises were given decisive influence on matters which in capitalist Western democracies are considered to come under the jurisdiction of the local authority (city council, municipality).

The 1974 Constitution contained another interesting institutional innovation: the so-called 'self-managing community of interests' (*Samoupravne interesne zajednice, SIZ*) which was charged with managing public amenities and objects of collective consumption such as public utilities, education and welfare, including housing. The basic motivation for creating this institution was to establish a framework within which those providing resources would be able to combine with those using them to decide how services would be allocated.[25]

Each municipality contained 15–20 SIZ. They could also be found at all other levels of society: some covered small residential estates, others covered the municipality or were inter-communal, republican or federal, depending on the scope and significance of the service concerned. Usually the suppliers and consumers met once a year in order for each group to set the budget and the level of contributions for the coming year. A professional staff implemented its decisions.

In the sphere of housing, a SIZ dealt with issues concerning the construction, management and the maintenance of buildings. It was formed, on the one hand, by enterprises and institutions providing housing, and, on the other hand, by all the consumers within this sector, whether tenants, owner-occupiers of apartments and single family dwellings, owners of office space, or members of co-operatives.

The crucial role of financing the public sector accorded to the self-managed enterprises by the SIZ system meant that they lacked the degree of independence required by Gide's conception of a producer co-operative. The position and importance given to the self-managed enterprises in Yugoslavia's political-administrative system is reflected in the conception of co-operatives.

The Yugoslav Conception of Co-operatives

In his study of the history of co-operatives, Erwin Hasselman maintained that no sizeable co-operative movement can avoid political involvement unless it wants to endanger its own interests. However, it would be wrong to equate co-operative and political interests. Therefore, a co-operative should not support a single political party, although it might now and then endorse the standpoint of a political party on a single issue when defending the co-operative's interests. Overall the movement should adhere to the principle of neutrality.[26]

On the other hand, traditional Marxist theory regards such a stance as sheer bourgeois idealism for, in principle, co-operation cannot be treated as an independent socio-economic factor working and acting autonomously in relation to the state and its policies, since it is an instrument employed by the state to promote the interests of the ruling class.[27] In this interpretation, which conflicts with the view held by Lenin at the end of his life, a socialist state made no difference to the position of co-operatives in the society. In Yugoslavia, where the state was regarded as an agent of the working class, the character of the co-operative movement as a means of implementing the goals and objectives of state and society had not changed.

This instrumental view of co-operatives, which prevailed under the socialist regime, was considered to be useful in tackling the old problems of agriculture inherited from pre-war Yugoslavia, hence the predominance of co-operatives within this sector. In a study published immediately after the war, the leading Yugoslav politician and official theorist, Edvard Kardelj, referred to the organisational tradition of agricultural co-operatives and their appeal to farmers as the main argument for employing them as a vehicle for transforming agriculture. It was a question of using them to achieve a victory for socialism in the countryside. At the first Congress of the National Union of Co-operatives, in 1946, the man responsible for Yugoslavia's first Five-Year Plan, Boris Kidrič, spoke out against the old co-operative ideology which, in his opinion, was incompatible with the objectives of what he called 'the people's co-operation', which in the first place should further the implementation of the Plan.[28] In his words, co-operation should serve as 'a gigantic school of socialism for the masses'.[29]

The introduction of self-management and the establishment of workers' councils in 1950 changed nothing in that respect. The co-operatives continued to be looked upon as a means of propagating socialism. But the transformation of the state, from an owner of the means of production to 'an association of free producers' who did not have to rely on the state apparatus to run the economy and the country, also changed the role of the farmer in the co-operatives. From being a farmer and member of a co-operative he was now a worker and member of a co-operative.[30] The farmer as producer was thereby separated from the farmer as owner; and the interests of a farmer in his capacity as a producer became the same as those of any producer. A co-operative member was not considered to have an interest meriting the particular interest of a political-administrative system based on the participation of different interests in the decision-making process. For, in Kardelj's opinion, such interests must be 'authentic', a qualification which apparently excluded those who claimed membership of a co-operative.[31] The co-operative had in this way been turned into 'an association of direct producers' and thereby ceased to exist as such, i.e. as 'a co-operative in the classical sense'.[32]

In practice this meant that a co-operative, whether in agriculture or any other sphere, was looked upon in the same way as any other enterprise or institution and had to be run according to self-management principles. The implication of this was that a co-operative might be very democratic according to the tenets of socialist democracy, but not according to the Rochdale principles as later developed by the ICA and adopted in 1966.[33] Above all, the rule of 'one member one vote' was set aside. Even though everyone working in a co-operative had the same formal voting power as in the workers' council, the main decision-making assembly in an enterprise, no distinction was made between members and non-members: an employee in such an enterprise had as much say as any member of the co-operative.

However, agricultural co-operators had a privilege not enjoyed by workers, in that they were entitled to a larger share of the enterprise's income reflecting their individual contribution, through labour or other resources, to the generation of that income.[34] This rule underscored the fact that Yugoslav co-operatives did not conform to the 'classical' notion: the practice of giving benefits to members according to the number of shares which they held in the co-operative contravened Gide's view of the co-operative. The issue that 'capital should yield profit but not interest'[35] was taken into account when the law was modified in order to allow a 'limited rate of interest'. It was also a question central to the polemic on co-operatives which occurred in the Soviet Union in the late 1980s.

In conclusion, the co-operative in Yugoslavia was not regarded as a value in itself, but as a means for the establishment of a socialist political order.

The Development of the Yugoslav Co-operative

Co-operatives between the Wars

One of the first offshoots of the Schulze-Delitzsch co-operative outside the founder's native country, Germany, appeared in Slovenia in 1856. It was a credit co-operative and, in characteristic form, was established by craftsmen.[36] It was this type of co-operative which came to dominate co-operatives in pre-Socialist Yugoslavia.[37] The first co-operative in Croatia was of the type associated with another German, F. W. Raiffeisen and was founded on the island of Korcula in 1864.[38]

Because of its close connection with agriculture, the Croatian co-operative represented a good example of pre-socialist Yugoslavia's co-operative movement. At the beginning of the twentieth century 93 per cent of all co-operatives and 83.5 per cent of all members worked in agriculture.[39] On the eve of the Second World War, in Yugoslavia as a whole there were almost 11,000 co-operatives, organised into about forty federations with a total of more than 1,400,000 members.[40] With 2,500 associations in 1938, consumer co-operatives formed the second largest type of co-operative.[41]

Co-operatives first appeared in Serbia in 1870 as a response to rising prices consequent upon a general rise in the level of demand following a population increase. Their emergence was closely connected with the name of Svetozar Marković, the 'first Balkan socialist of European stature',[42] according to whom, in the tradition of the Russian Populist, Chernyshevskii, co-operatives could break 'the stranglehold of capital on labor'. This overtly socialist political-ideological stance exposed the movement to very hostile opposition from the Government, which contributed to the movement's short life.[43]

In the opinion of some authors, 'health co-operatives' were Serbia's 'chief contribution' to the field.[44] Established in the early 1920s, they provided villages with resident doctors and pharmacies and were also engaged in general public health work and educational activities.[45] Estimates vary on their actual number: one official source states that there were 134 officially registered health co-operatives but only 93 active associations, with little more than 65,000 members; while another study, without source references, cites 114 member societies of the Union of Health Co-operation, with a quarter of a million individual members.[46] Since they received a state subsidy, the Government was able to intervene in order to foster its own political aims: tax-exemptions and other forms of economic aid were used as a means of securing the votes of certain classes of peasant.[47] This was not an atypical feature of the co-operative movement. For example, the Slovenia People's (Catholic) Party fostered co-operation among peasants as a way of improving cultural and economic standards among the peasantry, while by the second half of the 1930s the Croatian Peasant Party had established a successful co-operative arm. The involvement of co-operatives in politics, on the whole, disadvantaged the movement.

It is tempting to explain the predominance of agricultural co-operatives by reference to the *zadruga* (similar to the Russian *mir*), which was a traditional social and cultural institutional form found among the southern Slavs. This was a communal, multiple family consisting of, at most, up to a hundred members but normally less than ten, related by blood or adoption, sharing property and often living and working jointly on collective land and regulating their formal internal relations communally.[48] The *zadruga* as an institution dissolved when rural life evolved into more advanced social and economic form; however, it contained many co-operative traits, such as collective property and democratic decision making. It differed significantly in that its activities concerned the whole life of a peasant in a way that a co-operative never does. As an institution, the *zadruga* predisposed the peasantry towards understanding the meaning of co-operatives and to participate in them.[49]

The argument holds appeal until it is remembered that in pre-socialist Yugoslavia agricultural co-operation, like co-operation generally, was most successful in Slovenia – a part of the country where the *zadruga* institution did not exist. Moreover, in 1927 in Slovenia, credit co-operative federations charged their member co-operatives between 8 and 9 per cent interest on loans, while Serbian and Croatian federations charged between 12 and 20 per cent. It was also only in Slovenia that agricultural credit co-operatives were more than a subsidiary source of credit for agriculture. Of further significance is the fact that a collective endeavour such as the co-operative working of land aroused very little interest in pre-socialist Yugoslavia.[50] In fact, Slovenia's dominant economic ranking in Federal Yugoslavia might suggest that, for co-operation to develop and flourish, such factors as a higher cultural level and a less far-reaching subdivision of agricultural property are of greater importance than the existence of strongly collectivist, cultural traditions.[51] With the exception of Slovenia, the co-operatives became centres of corruption and mismanagement. People who understood little or nothing about business used them for personal gain.

Co-operative History under Socialism

The co-operative alternative reached its highest levels of membership and diversity in the immediate post-war years, during the so-called 'administrative period', when the Government sought to emulate the Soviet system. It was then that co-operation reached its peak in terms of membership and diversity, flourishing particularly in agriculture, as in the so-called 'Farmer Working Co-operatives'. In 1950 they numbered almost 7,000 with over two million members, who together cultivated two and a half million hectares of land. Twenty years later there were only seven left, with 1,000 members and only 10,000 hectares of cultivated land.[52]

Another kind of agricultural co-operative was the 'Specialised Farmers Producing-Processing Co-operative: in 1945 they had over 120,000 members; by 1970, they had all but completely disappeared. One of the reasons for their demise was, as in the case of Farmer Working Co-operatives, that not all of their members could take part in their activities, because of the way in which the production, buying and selling of agricultural products was organised. By far the most common form of co-operative was the Farmer General Co-operative, whose number declined from almost 5,000 at the end of the 1950s to 500–600 in the 1980s.

The General Co-operatives passed through at least four developmental stages. During the first ten years after the war they had a very universal character, managing the purchase of industrial goods, the sale of agricultural products, the extension of credit, the production of handicrafts and the running of hotels and restaurants; they also established libraries and theatre groups.

The second phase began with the introduction of self-government. A new law in 1954 adapted the General Farmers Co-operatives to the new conditions. This meant in effect that the principle of workers' self-government was applied to the running and organisation of the co-operatives. In this way, as elsewhere in the economy, co-operative councils and boards were established, to which people representing those working in co-operative organisations were elected in proportion to the size of their co-operative.

With the third phase, beginning in 1958, agricultural co-operatives were transformed into self-managed enterprises within agriculture. During this period co-operation between co-operatives and individual farmers was encouraged in order to raise productivity and increase economic integration. The transformation of the co-operatives continued during the fourth phase which started with the economic reform of 1965, when market competition was introduced.

One co-operative of quite short duration was founded by workers and civil servants as a continuation of the pre-socialist consumers' co-operatives, in which the dividend paid corresponded to the amount that a member spent in the co-operative. It had difficulty in competing with the growing state-controlled retail trade. The same fate befell Handicraft Production Co-operatives, when they were co-opted as instruments in the post-war planned economy after losing ground in the marketplace to state-supported handicrafts; in most cases they were transformed into enterprises of a more general type. Nevertheless, within the craft sector co-operatives did survive by, among other things, combining with non-co-operative enterprises and by specialising within their own sphere.

Another type of co-operative, although on a much smaller scale, was the Credit Co-operative. While in the pre-war period these were confined almost exclusively within agriculture, they now came to play a most important role in urban areas among craftsmen and civil servants, railway personnel and university teachers.

Finally, a type of co-operative which, unlike the others, began to grow in the 1950s was the 'School Co-operative', which taught pupils the theory and practice of co-operation. For example, using land donated by agricultural co-operatives, they would lay out gardens and grow crops, applying the latest findings in agricultural science, run small chicken farms and beehives and collect medicinal herbs and forest products. In 1978 there were 1,776 such co-operatives with more than a quarter of a million members. Since, according to information cited above, the total number of co-operatives did not amount to that number for any year in the 1980s, it would appear that school co-operatives were not recorded in official statistics on co-operatives. As Table 7.1 indicates, by no means all the co-operatives mentioned here were to be found in the official statistics. It also shows that agricultural co-operatives predominated, followed by handicraft co-operatives.

Enterprises described as 'co-operatives' frequently did not correspond to the normal understanding of the term. The primary activity of some farming co-operatives was anything but agriculturally oriented, but was concerned with manufacturing, mining, tourism and construction. Most 'handicraft' co-operatives were involved in the building trade, with consumer and credit co-operatives playing a very minor role.

As Table 7.2 shows, co-operatives were not evenly distributed throughout the country. In terms of ranking, first place was occupied by Croatia, followed by Serbia, Macedonia, Slovenia, Bosnia-Herzegovina and Montenegro.

In sum, the number of co-operatives declined considerably over the forty years of socialism, falling from 11,000 to about 1,500 by the time of the

Table 7.1 Number of various types of co-operative 1981–85

Type of co-operative	Number of co-operatives				
	1981	1982	1983	1984	1985
Agricultural	531	555	585	628	665
Producer	1	77	79	93	91
Handicraft	389	425	463	520	574
Other	110	126	243	279	323

Source: Calculated from figures in *Statistički godišnjak Jugoslavije, 1986*, Savremena administracija, Belgrade, 1986, p. 104.

country's dissolution in the 1990s. Housing co-operatives, which were not included in the above review, are dealt with in the context of the Government's post-war housing policy.

Housing

Housing production and tenure

As has already been mentioned, housing was not spared from the destruction which affected other sectors of the economy during the Second World War. Then, because it was classified as 'consumption' in Stalin's Soviet model, it was not accorded priority status in the immediate post-war years. Only in the mid-1950s did policy change, but even then housing conditions improved only marginally.[53] Nevertheless, at the end of the 1980s three-quarters of the housing stock had been erected since 1945.

Because, officially, state property had replaced private property, it would have been reasonable to assume that the state would be the major housing provider. This, however, was not the case; in the early 1980s the state owned only 22 per cent of the housing stock, while 78 per cent remained privately owned.[54] The ratio remained the same at the time of the state's demise at the beginning of the 1990s.[55] The fact that only one-fifth of all housing was not in private hands almost forty years after the country's social revolution was a consequence of the Government's decision not to change the relationship

Table 7. 2 Number and type of co-operatives by republic in 1985

	Type of co-operative				Total
	Agricultural	Producer	Handi-craft	Other	
Yugoslavia	665	91	574	323	1,653
Bosnia-Herzegovina	35	19	62	8	124
Montenegro	14	2	19	4	42
Croatia	212	2	172	125	511
Macedonia	160	2	155	6	323
Slovenia	41	22	46	95	204
Serbia as a whole	193	44	120	85	442
Kosovo	*49*	*6*	*8*	*0*	*63*
Voivodina	*6*	*1*	*22*	*82*	*111*
Serbia proper	*138*	*37*	*90*	*3*	*268*

Source: Calculated from figures in *Statistički godišnjak Jugoslavije, 1986,* Savremena administracija, Belgrade, 1986, p. 439.

between the two sectors. Even after investment in housing began to rise in the 1960s, the state's share in overall investment in house building scarcely rose above 40 per cent. Following its peak in 1976, the amount erected by the state again began to decline. Overall, the number of dwellings built in 1988 was 60 per cent of that in 1981, although by this date the number of dwellings equalled the number of households.[56]

Since official statistics did not draw a distinction between co-operative and private-sector construction, the true size of the former was difficult to gauge. However, based on the fact that between 1966 and 1988 this sector built on average 5,000 to 6,000 units each year, a reasonable estimate of co-operative house building would be that it accounted for 4 per cent of total output.[57]

In the late 1980s, Yugoslav housing space standards were below the average for Comecon countries[58] (an average of 42.8 square metres of dwelling floor space compared with 49.0 square metres) and well below the average for other European countries (98.2 square metres).[59] However, although its citizens inhabited a much smaller living space, especially when compared with the average household in Western Europe, they fared better in terms of the number of detached dwelling units. But, as is amply illustrated below, since the statistics contain important omissions, unduly far-reaching conclusions should not be drawn from them.

One of the most interesting features of Yugoslavia's housing tenure was that, in so far as a housing co-operative has as its defining feature collective ownership by those living in it,[60] a truly co-operative form of tenure scarcely existed in Yugoslavia; a dwelling in Yugoslavia was owned either by an individual or by the state. In other words, the only alternative to being an owner-occupier was to rent accommodation. Nevertheless, while a co-operative tenure was all but absent, co-operatives were active in the construction process, where their role reflected their position and significance in society generally.

Co-operation within Construction

The limited impact of co-operatives is evident in the lack of statistics available on them. For instance, in the case of housing co-operatives the researcher has to rely for information on figures held by the federal organisation of housing co-operatives, which compiled data on its members. There were, however, co-operatives which were not affiliated to the federal body. With this caveat in mind, in 1986, in the country at large, there were only 320 co-operatives, with just over 350,000 members; by the end of 1988, nationwide there were 470 co-operatives with more than 500,000 members, most of whom were concentrated in large cities.[61] The number of co-operatives varied from republic to republic, from town to town and over time. Slovenia, for example, had a building co-operative in almost every municipality,[62] whilst in 1980, according to the federal organisation, Skopje was the only place in Macedonia with a co-operative.[63] There is reason to believe that their development peaked at the end of the 1950s and early 1960s when credit was available on very favourable terms.[64] There are no reliable figures available on the size of membership of each individual co-operative and the average number of members varied considerably over the years.[65]

The legislative framework and political climate heavily influenced the formation and development of co-operatives. When it was possible to obtain easy credit on favourable terms, amortisation and mortgage conditions were attractive and land was freely available, individuals found the prospect of co-operative membership appealing.[66] Thus, when Croatia adopted an unfavourable credit policy and there was a land shortage, a study of housing co-operatives found that the production of this type of tenure in multi-storey buildings declined. Because of tax exemptions, their place was taken by co-operatives established to procure building materials. In descending order of popularity, there were also 'building management co-operatives' for building single-family houses, co-operatives for building flats in multi-storey blocks and co-operatives for building offices, the acquisition of loans for their members, the construction of holiday homes and maintenance.[67]

Finally, 'housing co-operatives' were defined in terms of whether the source of membership was a person's place of work or the place of residence[68] – the same dualism was found in the Soviet Union. The former were referred to as closed co-operatives, and the latter as open. Not only have the latter existed for a longer period of time, but they were responsible for building more dwelling units and had a much higher number of members per co-operative unit. One further reason for the benign neglect of co-operatives within the housing sector was that, in contrast to agricultural co-operatives, they lacked an ideological foundation of their own within the country's socialist credo.

A common theme in the housing literature was that there had been no political or socio-economic imperatives for the development of co-operatives within this sector. In theory, if not in practice, housing policy was to promote the construction of more state dwellings.[69] The presumption was that citizens should rent their accommodation through the enterprise or institution for whom they worked. For people who were excluded from access to this system of allocation, 'solidarity' housing would be provided by the communes (local authorities or municipalities).[70] Such housing would be selectively distributed according to need. During the 1970s and 1980s less than one-fifth of all rental housing was being allocated according to social need criteria. In 1986 the figure had fallen to 12 per cent.[71]

Legislation governing housing distribution referred to need, number of family members, length of service and contribution to work as criteria for allocation.[72] In practice, BOALs had complete freedom in deciding the rules for gaining access to accommodation. As a consequence, allocation was partly determined by a person's position in an enterprise and partly by the latter's profitability.[73] The outcome of this distribution system is shown in Table 7.3.

Table 7.3 Requests by employees for accommodation and actual distribution, by occupation group (1986)

Occupational group	Unfulfilled requests	Fulfilled requests	
		Number	%
University-trained specialist	55,980	5,051	9
Vocational-school-trained specialist (advanced)	37,985	2,807	7
Vocational-school-trained specialist (intermediate)	134,864	7,117	5
Vocational-school-trained specialist (elementary)	30,591	1,430	5
Highly qualified worker	54,209	3,464	6
Skilled worker	158,229	7,952	5
Semi-skilled worker	55,847	2,425	4
Unskilled worker	60,714	2,807	5

Source: Raspodela stanova i kredita za stanove 1986. Statistički bilten 1675, Belgrade; Zavezni zavod za statistiku, 1988, p 11.

Table 7.3 provides some evidence of preferential treatment of applicants; twice as many university-trained specialists had their requests met as most other categories of employee. At least according to these figures, the criticism that power under the Yugoslav model of self-management was supposed to rest with blue-collar workers, but was in reality in the hands of managers and technicians within the enterprise,[74] is not borne out. The figures do not support the contention that, whereas peasants and unskilled workers built their own houses, the middle class queued for state apartments. Neither does it uphold the view that the social sector offered no solution to the housing problems for most citizens, who had to seek other means to meet their accommodation needs.[75] However, the system was probably more discriminatory than these statistics would seem to demonstrate. A more important source of inequality was the preference shown to higher social status groups in granting credit by enterprises to employees to invest in a co-operative housing construction project.[76] This was reflected in the social composition of co-operatives, over 90 per cent of whose members were under the age of 50 and the majority in the 31–40 age group. The huge costs connected with buying or building housing has meant that, despite the state's socialist orientation, social class had been a factor in affecting the ability of a household to gain access to co-operative accommodation. The Croatian study already mentioned found that 43 per cent of co-operative members had been to college and only about one-quarter had only had secondary education or attended a vocational school for manual workers. The same tendency is evident from an analysis of the occupational background of co-operative members, the majority of whom were specialists with college education and only one-fifth were workers. That higher education and white-collar jobs means better pay is shown by the fact that more than 60 per cent of the members had an above-average monthly salary.[77] Certainly in Croatia and to varying degrees elsewhere the typical member of a co-operative would be a well-paid family member in the prime of life.

Organisation and Management

Self-management was Yugoslavia's guiding organisational principle. The idea permeated every association, large or small and regardless of whether it was a political body, a trade union, or a small society in a village. Co-operatives within the housing sector were no exception to this rule.

Thus, every co-operative had an assembly as its main decision-making body, in which each member had a right to vote. This assembly in its turn elected representatives to assemblies at each administrative level – municipal, republican and state. Thus, at the federal level an assembly represented the Union of Housing Co-operatives of Yugoslavia. Each assembly had an executive, a president and a general secretary, who constituted its board of management. A variety of committees fulfilling different functions were attached to individual co-operatives.

Like all democratic bodies, co-operatives required extensive member involvement. Since the information available on these issues is drawn from the aforementioned study in Croatia, it cannot be properly representative of all the republics; nevertheless, the data demonstrate the state of affairs pertaining in the most developed parts of the country.

The study measured 'involvement' in different ways. A questionnaire was given to members of the co-operatives' management asking them for their opinion on the factors motivating individual members to take part in the work of the co-operative. In about 60 per cent of the co-operatives members were said to have average motivation, while the remaining 40 per cent were divided equally between those who were 'highly' and 'poorly' motivated. Furthermore, about three-quarters of the members elected to one or other of the co-operatives' committees regularly attended meetings.[78]

The leaders were also asked to assess how much influence the members were able to exert on the planning of their accommodation. In two-fifths of all co-operatives the influence was considered to be 'very considerable'; it was 'great' in a further 30 per cent, and 'small' in only about 10 per cent. As regards the level of influence on the quality of the work carried out, it was thought to be 'very considerable' or 'great' in about 30 per cent of the co-operatives, average in about 20 per cent, and low in about 6 per cent.[79] These fairly impressive figures might be distorted by the fact that they include members of co-operatives building 'private villas'; such people are frequently well placed to influence both planning and quality.

Such information on the interest evinced by members in co-operative activities should be interpreted in the context of the people who came together in order to establish a co-operative in the first place. While, theoretically, any group of people could set up a co-operative, in practice those taking the initiative and handling the affairs were enterprises, construction companies and local communities.[80] By 1988 the situation had changed and about 55 per cent of all co-operatives were established by individuals or employees. Trade unions took second place in the instigating stakes, followed by construction companies, public organisations active within housing, and municipal trade unions.[81]

Co-operatives and Local Government

The special position of housing co-operatives in Yugoslavia was most evident in their formal relations with the state and the municipality. Like all other forms of housing in the country, they fitted into a political-administrative system which was compatible with the principle of self-government. Ironically, perhaps, co-operative independence was a victim of the adherence to the principle of self-government. The form which state interference took depended on the type of co-operative. For example, in the case of co-operatives established to build apartments in multi-storey buildings, the state involved itself both during and after construction, for as long as the co-operative existed, and even after its dissolution, when the members had become owner-occupiers. This system and the rationale for it were related to the way in which public services were provided in Yugoslavia.

As previously mentioned, the 1974 Constitution introduced the SIZ (self-managing community of interests). Other social units apart from the SIZ were involved in the operations of co-operatives. There was, for instance, the tenant assembly, which managed all the apartments in a particular building through an executive body called the tenant council. The assembly consisted of all persons in the building, both those renting and owners, and took responsibility for matters relevant to the building, such as maintenance, parking arrangements, codes of behaviour and the redistribution of a portion of the revenue from rent. The tenants' assembly was also represented in the SIZ assembly.

Clearly, housing co-operatives share common interests with both SIZs and tenant assemblies. Since the SIZ decided on investments regarding construction and modernisation, and on urban planning, the maintenance of facilities and general management, co-operatives behaved as pressure groups, checking that their builders adhered to the plans and construction schedules.[82]

Since the whole tenure system in Yugoslavia came under the common SIZ umbrella, all residents in multi-storey buildings had to pay this body a regular sum of money to cover the costs of its various undertakings. Up to fifty variables were taken into account by a special commission within the municipality when assessing the amount of rent to be paid, including size, furnishings, location, exposure to sun and environment.[83]

Perhaps because the general housing standard, as measured by the criteria laid down, remained low, the majority of rents were extremely low. Even though in 1986 the average level in Slovenia was almost three times as high as in Bosnia-Herzegovina, by international standards they comprised a fraction of the cost of providing and maintaining the housing stock – in fact, in 1980 amounting to less than 1 per cent of the construction costs.[84] According to an official publication from the early 1980s, accommodation charges were 'obviously insufficient', with a specialist referring to them as 'absurdly low'.[85] Although, between 1980 and 1986, the consumer price index and the cost of living both witnessed a ninefold increase and mean income also increased almost ninefold, rents only rose fivefold.[86] In 1984 rents were estimated to cover barely one-fifth of the amount needed simply to maintain the housing stock.[87] As a result no more than 2.8 per cent of all household expenses in 1983 went on housing compared to, for example, 5.5 per cent on tobacco and beverages.[88] This low-rent policy certainly contributed to the poor standard of the Yugoslav housing stock. Of course, the Government could have committed larger sums from the state budget to cover the costs of maintenance.

The low rent level in the state sector exacerbated the social inequalities, already described, since a major market already existed for subletting renting, where rents were set according to market principles of supply and demand. Rents for subtenants in this market segment were in 1988 five to ten times higher than the monthly payments for equivalent state accommodation;[89] this discrepancy between a state rent and the charge made to subtenants increased in the years up to the demise of the Yugoslav Federal Republic.

Tenants paid their rents directly to the SIZ, from which a certain percentage was then returned to the block of flats where the tenant lived for the tenant assembly to use as it deemed fit. But it was the individual tenant who had to contact the SIZ to discuss (and complain about), for example, the rent level; the tenant assembly did not become involved in this matter, presumably because few people wanted to challenge the low rents being charged and those who were paying high rents were doing so illegally.[90]

Thus, from what is known about the socio-political system and the mechanisms for setting rents, membership of a co-operative *per se* did not increase a person's ability to influence housing decisions, including the level of rents charged. Since a household was a member of a co-operative only during the building's construction phase, it was only then that its expressed interests were taken into account. Delegates representing co-operatives could act like pressure groups within a housing SIZ, but were in no way different from delegates from other groups represented in its assembly. In many instances the voice of the co-operative was simply drowned in a choir composed of delegates representing a larger group of the population, whose members were trying to find solutions to their housing problems within the state and private sector.

Consolation for members of a building co-operative only came when the co-operatively produced building was completed and the members became owner-occupiers. Overall, housing co-operatives were few in number, their role within construction contracted, their function distorted and their membership socially unrepresentative. At the beginning of the 1990s they were not offering a solution to the country's pressing housing problems.

Legal Framework

As already noted, housing co-operatives did not occupy a special place in the country's socialist credo and no legislation dedicated to them was enacted for many years after the Second World War. It was only in 1959 that a law was enacted exclusively concerned with this type of tenure. This treated them as economic organisations like enterprises, with corresponding rights and duties.

The manner in which they were regarded is apparent from the description of their purpose, which was that, by drawing upon people's savings and by using funds set aside by enterprises for common consumption, they should be supplemental to public funds allocated to housing. The next law to affect this tenure, in 1968, continued the same basic approach: housing co-operatives were considered to be no different from any other enterprise. The main change was that registered businesses and organisations could no longer be members.[91]

As part of wider political-administrative changes, a more far-reaching law was enacted in 1971. This transferred legislative responsibility from the federal level to the republics and lower administrative tiers. Henceforth, co-operatives were governed by the specific rules and conditions of each republic, which meant that they did not all have the same legal status, were not all organised in the same way and did not deal with the same issues. In Bosnia-Herzegovina and Croatia, for example, they came to be treated as self-managed organisations, while in Slovenia and Serbia they were given their own unique status. Nevertheless, while the requirements for establishing a co-operative changed, with the number of people needed now varying between ten and thirty, depending upon the part of the country in which the co-operative was located, a common nationwide condition for being allowed to join a co-operative was unmet housing need. At the same time, their substantive tasks also became more uniform: they were now supposed to invest money in housing construction for their members, to organise savings for the purchase and construction of an apartment and to take care of maintenance. However, the manner in which these tasks had to be organised and performed allowed for variations between the republics.

The idea that housing was a social right and therefore should not form a large proportion of a household's living costs – a central *desideratum* in all socialist countries – militated against a co-operative solution to the housing problem. The 1959 legislation on housing co-operatives ameliorated this situation. Apartments built with money from public funds could now be bought by co-operatives on favourable credit terms: an individual member had to deposit 25 per cent of the accommodation's value, the remainder having to be repaid over a 40-year period at 1 per cent interest. Co-operatives were further privileged by not having to pay for building permits. However, because all private house-builders as well as members of co-operatives used this credit policy to improve their living conditions, the funds established for this purpose soon ran into difficulties. The outcome of the situation was the pursuit of a more market-oriented housing policy together with the revival of state construction; this two-pronged approach made the co-operative alternative less attractive. Greater emphasis was placed on the workplace as the channel for meeting housing needs. It was at this stage, in the early 1960s, that co-operatives became agents for buying apartments, trading in housing and, in some cases, engaging in speculative transactions.[92]

Households which in the 1980s were still acquiring accommodation with the help of a co-operative found that they no longer offered a cheap solution. An official Yugoslav booklet from 1980 informed would-be borrowers that credit was provided to cover only 40–50 per cent of the accommodation's value, with the repayment period reduced to 15–20 years and at the comparatively higher interest rate of 2–4 per cent.[93] By the end of the decade, credit terms had become still more onerous, not least because of rampant inflation, so that by 1986 it was not unusual for the annual repayment of the housing loan on an average apartment to exceed the average personal income.[94] Moreover, the rate at which money could be borrowed, the length of the repayment period and the size of the downpayment varied considerably across the country, depending on the location and the lender, whether it was public funder, bank or enterprise, all of which lent according to rules that were not uniformly applied.[95]

The implications of these credit conditions become clearer when related to the ratio of accommodation cost to personal income. Again, statistics on the private/co-operative sector are lacking; however, to a certain extent, figures from the state sector can be employed as an indicator. In 1982 the cost of a two-room, 50-square-metre apartment with standard furnishings was twelve times greater than average earnings.[96]

Conclusion

The first of the ICA principles, the 'membership clause', which affected all republics, was not without its problems.[97] One of the stipulations of Yugoslav legislation was incompatible with the ICA's 'open door' precept. The former specified that only individuals living in housing need could become members of a housing co-operative; thus, families living in accommodation which was officially defined as satisfactory were not allowed to join a co-operative. In other words, the legislation proscribed the fairly common practice in Poland whereby middle-class parents invested in a co-operative flat on behalf of their children so that the latter would, in the future, be able to live separately from them.

As far as housing co-operatives are concerned, the 'open door' precept has another dimension. Housing co-operatives could be established and registered by members at their place of work or where they lived. In the case of the former, they were in essence 'closed', since membership was restricted to individuals working at that particular factory, institution or office. On the other hand, in that they were non-discriminatory, since any employee was entitled to become a member, regardless of status, ethnicity or belief system, they did not infringe the ICA principle on openness. Territorially based co-operatves, that is, those formed at the local authority level, were completely open.

As regards the ICA tenet on 'democratic decision making', the guiding societal principle in Yugoslavia was the notion of 'self-management'. This permeated every association, whether large or small, manufacturing enterprise, trade union, or small village association. Housing co-operatives were no exception to this rule. Thus, every co-operative had a decision-making assembly which elected delegates to assemblies at the municipal, republican and federal levels. An assembly representing the Yugoslav Union of Housing Co-operatives met at the federal level. Every member of an assembly had a right to take part in the proceedings at each level and to vote. Furthermore, every assembly had a president, an executive and a general secretary to whom they were responsible. This system of governance may be said to have complied with the condition of democratic decision making. The expansion of the practice of self-management meant that the 'impulse to participation in the democratic decision-making process' could be met at the workplace.

Given the Yugoslav view on property, the ICA principle concerning 'limited interest on shares' did not apply. Similarly, the clause on 'a fair distribution of surplus and savings' was unproblematic as far as the ICA was concerned: its understanding of 'fair' was that any economic benefits should be shared by members in such a fashion that nobody should gain at the expense of anyone else. There is no evidence to suggest that Yugoslav co-operatives did not adhere to this principle.

It is less clear that Yugoslav co-operatives comply with the ICA requirement that co-operatives engage in educational work. According to the ICA the commitment to education applies to staff as well as members and the general public. Given that separate studies of housing co-operatives in Croatia and Slovenia found that 'professional competence' was a major problem,[98] it may be assumed that education in management and economics was inadequate. Books, articles and leaflets on co-operatives in Yugoslavia are characterised by an absence of reference to education. This may be explained by the fact that individuals were motivated to join a co-operative in order to satisfy their housing needs; as soon as they had achieved their objective, they quickly stopped attending meetings and lost interest in having any involvement beyond the minimum required.

On the final principle, that of 'co-operation between co-operatives' at the local, national and international level, all that can be said was that links did exist and there were no legal or structural impediments to the forging of connections between associations. The Yugoslav co-operative movement was also a member of the ICA.

Overall, Yugoslav housing co-operatives adhered to the ICA principles in some instances, only partly in others and not at all in others still. Co-operatives played a fairly insignificant role in the Yugoslav housing system; they did not exist as a separate tenure and were of little importance as builders. Their history mirrored the general trend of co-operatives in Yugoslavia in the post-war period; they received limited state support since they were regarded as ideologically incompatible with the prevailing view of socialism. Free, independent organisations, which co-operatives by definition should be, were inconsistent with the 'special form of the dictatorship of the proletariat', as specified in the 1974 Constitution. The very few studies of co-operatives which have been conducted in Yugoslavia provide no evidence that the general public were at all supportive of them.

The interesting question is whether our knowledge of the co-operative phenomenon is enhanced by identifying co-operative elements in the country's self-management system. With important exceptions, such as the fact that enterprises were totally integrated into the state's economic policy and therefore could not operate as free independent organisations, in the main the system functioned in accordance with ICA principles. It is also true that the number of co-operatives registered a continuous decline from the inception of the socialist period until the demise of the Yugoslav state.

Co-operatives in the housing sector existed only in the production of housing, and even then they accounted for only four in every hundred units built. Co-operative tenure based on collective ownership did not exist at all, since the category 'collective' could only be applied to social ownership. The division of tenures was therefore a simple one of social or private.

Despite the absence of co-operatives *per se*, Yugoslavia incorporated many co-operative elements into the country's socio-political system. To that extent the society may be said to have demonstrated the possibilities of a particular hybrid 'third (co-operative) way'.

Notes

1   Ample testimonies are for example to be found in J. P. Telgarsky and R. J. Struyk, *Toward a Market-Oriented Housing Sector in Eastern Europe: Developments in Bulgaria, Czechoslovakia, Hungary, Poland, Romania, and Yugoslavia*, The Urban Institute Press, Washington, DC, 1990; and in B. Turner, J. Hegedius and I. Tosics (eds), *The Reform of Housing in Eastern Europe and the Soviet Union*, Routledge, London, 1992.

2   Bob Briscoe, Susan Grey, Paul Hunt, Mary Linehan, Hugh McBride, Vincent Tucker and Michael Ward, *The Co-operative Idea*, Centre for Co-operative Studies, Cork, 1982.

3   Johnston Birchall, *Building Communities The Co-operative Way*, Routledge & Kegan Paul, London, 1987.

4   Alf Carlsson, *Cooperatives and the State: Partners in Development? A Human Resource Perspective*, Institute of International Education, Stockholm University, Stockholm, 1992.

5   W. P. Watkins, *Co-operative Principles. Today and Tomorrow*, Holyoake Books, Manchester, 1986.

6   Paul Lambert, *Studies in the Social Philosophy of Co-operation*, Co-operative Union, Manchester; Co-operative League of the USA, Chicago, Ill., Société Générale Coopérative, Brussels, 1963.

7   Ove Jobring, *Kooperativ rörelse. Om utveckling in teori och praktik*, The Co-operative Institute, Stockholm, 1988.

8   Charles Gide, *La Coopération. Conférences de propagande*, Paris, 1900; Charles Gide, *Sociétés coopération de consommation*, (Paris, 1904) was unfortunately available to me only in a Swedish translation of the third edition: *Konsumtionsföreningarna*, Kooperative Förbundets Förlag, Stockholm, 1918.

9   This and the following paragraphs on Gide are based on *La Coopération*, pp. 46–108, 145–65 passim, and on *Konsumtionsföreningarna*, pp. 31 and 279–310 passim.

10   Gide, *La coopération*, p. 57.

11   Gide, *Konsumtionsföreningarna*, p. 279.

12   Ibid., p. 290.

13   Ibid., pp. 309–10.

14   S. Clissold (ed.), *A Short History of Yugoslavia, from Early Times to 1966*, CUP, Cambridge, 1968; R. L. Wolff, *The Balkans in our Time*, Harvard University Press, Cambridge, Mass., 1956; G. Andrusz, 'Structural Change and Boundary Instability' in G. Andrusz, M. Harloe and I. Azelenyi, *Cities after Socialism: Urban and Region Change and Conflict in Post-Socialist Societies*, Blackwell, Oxford, 1996.

15   B. Kidrič, *Privredni problemi FNRJ*, Kultura, Beograd, 1950, p.103; E. Kardelj, *Borba za priznanje i nezavisnost nove Jugoslavije 1944–1955. Secanja*, NIRO Radnicka stampa, Beograd and Drzavna zalozba, Ljubljana, 1980, pp. 175–6.

16   Information on BOAL is taken from *Priručnik za polaganje stručnih ispita radnika u državnim organima, organizacijama udruženog rada i drugim samoupravnim organizacijama i zajecdnicama*, Savremena administracija, Belgrade, 1979, and *Zakon o Udruženom Radu*, Službeni list, Belgrade, 1976.

17   Voivodina, in the north of Serbia close to the Hungarian border, improved Serbia's overall rating.

18   Gide, *Konsumtionsföreningarna*, pp. 42–5.

19   *Report of the ICA Commission on Co-operative Principles*, International Co-operative Alliance, London, 1967, pp. 11–32.

20   *Priručnik za polaganje stručnih ispita radnika u državnim organima, organizacijama udruženog rada i drugim samoupravnim organizacijama i zajecdnicama*, p. 103.

21   E. Hasselman, *Rochdalegrundsatserna. De kooperative idéernas historia*, Rabén & Sjögren, Stockholm, 1971, pp. 45–6.

22   Watkins, op. cit., p. 54.

23   H. Thomas and C. Logan, *Mondragon: An Economic Analysis*, George Allen & Unwin, London, 1982.

24   *Priručnik za polaganje stručnih ispita radnika u državnim organima, organizacijama udruženog rada i drugim samoupravnim organizacijama i zajecdnicama*, p. 69.

25   *Priručnik za polaganje stručnih ispita radnika u državnim organima, organizacijama udruženog rada i drugim samoupravnim organizacijama i zajecdnicama*, pp. 32–5.

26   Hasselman, op. cit., pp. 86–91.

27   P. Milenkovič, *Odnos države i zadrugarstva u FNR Jugoslavije*, Universitet u Beogradu, Belgrade, 1961, pp. 24–5.

28   Kidrič, op. cit., pp. 89–90.

29   Ibid., p. 32.

30   A very similar distinction was made in the Soviet Union between a member of a collective farm (*kolkhoz*), who was classified as a 'peasant' and of a state farm (*sovkhoz*), who was defined as a 'worker'.

31   E. Kardelj, *Pravci razvoja političkog sistema socijalističkog samoupravljanja*, Komunist, Belgrade, 1977, pp. 63–76.

32   Milenkovič, op. cit., pp. 55–60.

33   *Report of the ICA Commission on Co-operative Principles.*

34   *Priručnik za polaganje stručnih ispita radnika u državnim organima, organizacijama udruženog rada i drugim samoupravnim organizacijama i zajecdnicama*, p. 35.

35   Gide, *Konsumtionsföreningarna*, pp. 144–7.

36   *Enciklopedija Jugoslavije*, Leksikografski zavod, Zagreb, 1971, p. 576.

37   R. L. Wolff, *The Balkans in our Time*, Harvard University Press, Cambridge, Mass., 1956, p. 172.

38   *Enciklopedija Jugoslavije*, p. 576.

39   Ibid.

40   *Yugoslavie, Annuaire statistique 1938–1939*, pp. 340–1, quoted in J. Tomasevich, *Peasants, Politics, and Economic Change in Yugoslavia*, Stanford University Press, Stanford, 1955, p. 614.

41   Ibid.

42   W. D. McClellan, *Svetozar Markovič and the Origins of Balkan Socialism*, Princeton University Press, Princeton NJ, 1964, p. 3.

43   The first co-operative movement in Serbia is treated in McClellan, op. cit., pp. 134–43.

44   Wolff, op. cit., p. 174.

45   Ibid, p. 174; Tomasevich, op. cit., p. 594.

46   *Yugoslavie*, op. cit., p. 420, quoted in Tomasevich, op. cit., p. 594; Wolff, op. cit., p. 174.

47   Wolff, op. cit., pp. 174–5.

48   Tomasevich, op. cit., pp. 178–84.

49   Wolff, op. cit., p. 172.

50   Ibid.

51   Tomasevich, op. cit., p. 133.

52   These and other data in this section are taken from *Enciklopedija Jugoslavije*, op. cit., pp. 576–80.

53   G. Masesich, 'Major Trends in the Postwar Economy of Yugoslavia', in W. S. Vuchinich (ed.), *Contemporary Yugoslavia. Twenty Years of Socialist Experiment*, University of California Press, Berkeley and Los Angeles, 1969, p. 209.

54   K. Petovar, 'Nonproductive Capital in Housing – The Counterproductive Effects of Limiting Private Property', paper for the Conference on Housing between States and Markets, Dubrovnik, 16–19 September 1988, p. 4.
55   M. Simoneti, 'Stambena reforma kao deo privredne reforme', *Komuna*, no. 2, 1990, p. 10.
56   P. Djukan, 'Prijedlog modela otkupa drustvenih stanova' in *Opština i grad u novim društvenim uslovima – prilozi*. Stalna konferencija gradova i opština Jugoslavije – XXVIII Skupština, Budva 1990 (mimeo), pp. 1f.
57   B. Mikoš, 'Novi elementi stanovanske politike u Evropi', *Komuna*, no. 9, 1977.
58   Comecon (CMEA) was the acronym for the Council of Mutual Economic Assistance. The organisation had been set up in 1949 in Moscow to facilitate trade between the USSR and East European Countries.
59   Economic Commission for Europe, *Annual Bulletin of Housing and Building Statistics for Europe*, vol. XXX, 1986, New York: United Nations, 1987, table 4.
60   J. Birchall, *Building Communities the Co-operative Way*, Routledge and Kegan Paul, London, 1987, p. 20.
61   G. Bežovan, 'Nalazi istraživanja' in G. Bežovan and S. Dakić, *Alternativna stambena politika*, Radničke novine, Zagreb, 1990, p. 123, note 39 and p. 122, note 37, quoting B. S. Repič, *Pogoji za razvoj zadružinstva u okviru družbeno usmerjene stanovansjske gradnje*, Urbanistički Institut SR Slovenije, Ljubljana; L. Levajac, 'Stambeno zadrugarstvo u novim uslovima', *Komuna*, no. 7/8, 1987, p. 42.
62   Bežovan, 'Nalazi istraživanja', p. 111, quoting Repič, op. cit.
63   *Stambeno zadrugarstvo u Jugoslavije*, Savez Stambenih zadruga Jugoslavje, Belgrade, 1980, p. 30.
64   G. Bežovan and S. Dakić, 'Individualna inicijativa i neprofitne organizacije az stambeno zbrinjavanje', in Bežovan and Dakić, op. cit., pp. 110–11.
65   It would be interesting to investigate why, in Croatia, between 1983 and 1987, co-operative membership rose from 157 to 260 and then went into decline.
66   T. R. Burns, O. Caldarovic, J. Kregar, D. Sekulic and A. Woodward, *Citizen Participation in Housing Management and Local Community Development: The Case of Yugoslavia*, Department of Sociology, Uppsala, 1981, p. 11.
67   Bežovan, 'Nalazi istraživanja', pp. 122–32.
68   *Stambeno zadrugarstvo u Jugoslavije*, op. cit., p. 33.
69   See, for example, G. Bežovan, 'Stambeno zadrugarstvo – kratak osvrt na razvoj i probleme' in G. Bežovan et al., 'Stambena politika i stambeno zadrugarstvo', Zavod za samoupravljanje, Zagreb, 1989, mimeo, p. 107.
70   This was the same as the distinction between the 'departmental' (*vedomstvennyi*) and 'municipal' (local soviet) found in the USSR.
71   Calculated from figures in *Raspodela stanova i kredita za stanove 1986, Statistički bilten 1675, 1988:10*, Savremena administracija, Belgrade, 1988.
72   J. Ostojić and M. Dedijer, *Komentar zakona o stambenim odnosima*, Savremena administracija, Belgrade, 1980, p. VI.
73   Burns et al., op. cit., pp. 4–5.
74   T. Baumgartner, T. Burns and D. Sekulic, 'Self-management, Market, and Political Institutions in Conflict: Yugoslav Development Patterns and Dialectics', in T. Burns, L-E. Karlsson and V. Rus (eds), *Work and Power*, Sage, London, 1979, pp. 96–102; H. Lydall, *Yugoslav Socialism*, Clarendon Press, Oxford, 1984, pp. 121–2.
75   D. Seferagić, 'Housing Perspectives in Yugoslavia', paper for the Conference on Housing between States and Markets, Dubrovnik, 16–19 September 1988, p. 4.
76   S. Mandić, 'Housing Provision in Yugoslavia: Changing Role of the State, Market , and

Informal Sectors', in W. van Vliet and J. van Weesep (eds), *Government and Housing. Developments in Seven Countries*, Sage, London, p. 265.

77 Bežovan, 'Nalazi istraživanja', pp. 184–5, 192.

78 Ibid., pp. 136, 207.

79 Ibid., pp. 137–8.

80 Burns et al., op. cit., p. 11.

81 Bežovan, 'Nalazi istraživanja', pp. 119–20.

82 Burns et al., op. cit., p. 11.

83 Ibid., p. 5; *Housing in Yugoslavia*, Standing Conference of Towns and Communes of Yugoslavia, Belgrade, 1980, pp. 31–4.

84 'Primena realnih ekonomskih kategorija u stambeno-komunalnoj oblasti i potreba izmna dogovora ostambenoj politici', *Komuna*, no. 4, 1987, p. 4; Lydall, op. cit., p. 231.

85 *Housing in Yugoslavia*, p. 32.

86 'Primena realnih ekonomskih kategorija u stambeno-komunalnoj oblasti i potreba izmna dogovora ostambenoj politici', p. 4.

87 Mandić, op. cit., p. 11.

88 *Statistički godišnjak Jugoslavije, 1986*, Savremena administracija, Belgrade, 1986, p. 181.

89 K. Petovar, 'Nonproductive Capital in Housing – The Counterproductive Effects of Limiting Private Property', paper for the Conference on Housing between States and Markets, Dubrovnik, 16–19 September 1988, p. 5.

90 Burns et al., op. cit., p. 6.

91 The information on legislation in this and the following paragraphs is based on *Stambeno zadrugarstvo u Jugoslaviji*, Savez Stambenih zadruga Jugoslavje, Beograd, 1980, pp. 43–5.

92 G. Bežovan and S. Dakić, 'Individualna inicijativa i neprofitne organizacije az stambeno zbrinjavanje', in G. Bežovan and S. Dakić, *Alternativna stambena politika*, Radničke novine, Zagreb, 1990, pp. 110–11.

93 *Housing in Yugoslavia*, pp. 19–20.

94 'Primena realnih ekonomskih kategorija u stambeno-komunalnoj oblasti i potreba izmna dogovora ostambenoj politici', p. 4.

95 Ibid., p. 7.

96 *Borba*, 16 July 1982, quoted in Lydall, op. cit., p. 230.

97 The information on membership rules is taken from *Stambeno zadrugarstvo u Jugoslaviji*, pp. 43–5.

98 G. Bežovan, 'Nalazi istraživanja', p. 142, and quoting B. S. Repič, *Pogoji za razvoj zadružnstva u okviru društveno usmerjene stanovansjske gradnje*, Urbanistički Institut SR Slovenije, Ljubljana.

8 Social Democratic Sweden: A Story of Success

BO BENGTSSON*

Introduction

Co-operatives play important roles in three major sectors of the Swedish economy: retailing, agriculture and housing. The historical and organisational links between these three co-operative branches are, however, fairly weak, despite the fact that both the consumer co-operative movement in retailing and housing co-operatives have their roots in the labour movement.

The autonomy of the three sectors means that co-operative housing is better understood in relation to developments in housing than as part of the co-operative movement in general. As a consequence, in this chapter greater attention is paid to housing co-operatives. After a brief introductory overview of the sector, the political and economic development of housing co-operatives in Sweden is examined in its organisational, institutional and ideological aspects. This leads into the second theme, namely the putative trade-off between different co-operative goals, which is discussed with reference to available empirical material on Swedish housing co-operatives. The empirical evidence referred to is collected from a number of Swedish sources.[1] The two themes are brought together and reformulated in terms of the notion of co-operatives as a third or middle way.

Independent though they may be, different co-operative sectors have much the same problems. In the concluding section of this chapter Swedish co-operative housing will be discussed against the background of five such 'eternal' co-operative problems: two concerning relations between individual, local and central levels of organisation, and the remaining three concerning the economic, democratic and social goals of the co-operative movement.

---

*   Bo Bengtsson is Senior Lecturer in political science, especially housing policy, at the Institute for Housing Research and the Department of Government of Uppsala University. He would like to thank Lennart J. Lundqvist, Lars Nord, and Stephan Schmidt for valuable comments on an earlier version of this chapter.

Elster's Co-operative Paradox

'If co-operative ownership is so desirable, why are there so few co-operatives?' is the provocative title of an article by Jon Elster.[2] Although his discussion concerns workers' co-operatives and their chances of survival and success in a capitalist marketplace, the same question could well be asked about housing co-operatives. Co-operative housing seems to have many friends and few opponents. Still, in most countries co-operatives play quite an insignificant role in the housing market.

Elster does not find one single and obvious solution to his co-operative paradox. Instead he provides us with an abundance of possible answers to explain why there are so few workers' co-operatives. His analysis suggests that co-operative failure may be ascribed to two essentially different types of problems: those that are fundamental and those that are transitional. The conventional explanations for their lack of success are that co-operatives are not economically viable, or that workers prefer working in capitalist firms. These might be called 'eternal' or fundamental co-operative problems. Workers may not want to participate in decision making, or they may lack the requisite technical competence. At the same time, participation may be costly, or co-operatives may be incapable of motivating people to work hard or of laying off redundant workers.[3]

Elster does not find any of these reasons convincing. Instead he concentrates on the problems that isolated co-operatives may face in an otherwise capitalist economy. These might be termed 'transitional co-operative problems', arising from, for example, adverse selection of co-operators, discrimination against co-operatives in the marketplace, or negative externalities in the relationship between the individual co-operative and the capitalist economy. Where such conditions exist, the failure of co-operatives is due to obstacles that arise precisely because there are so few co-operatives.[4]

The challenge to housing co-operatives is not simply to survive in a capitalist market system, but rather to compete with other tenures both on the market and in the policy arena. Nevertheless, the distinction between fundamental and transitional co-operative problems still seems useful. It does not take much imagination to translate the problems listed by Elster to housing. Fundamental problems could be that tenants do not want to participate in the management of their estate, that they lack the competence to do so efficiently, or that co-operative housing does not provide tenants and management with the right incentives. Transitional problems may be that only eccentrics or idealists are prepared to join co-operatives in a housing sector dominated by private landlords and the state. Furthermore, society may not be ready for co-operative solutions, and the legal and institutional framework may be unfavourable.

In housing as well as in other co-operative sectors, the main point is this: if the problems are fundamental, the co-operative case may be hopeless. If the problems are created by an adverse environment, they might be solved once a certain threshold has been crossed.

The Swedish Co-operative Movement

The Swedish co-operative movement covers a wide range of economic activities and in 1984 the sector as a whole employed some 5 per cent of the total labour force.[5] Other than housing, there are two main spheres where co-operatives are of special importance – in retailing and in agriculture and food production.

A co-operative may be regarded solely as a democratic way to handle the common affairs of a certain group of people. Most advocates of co-operatives, however, seem to have a more missionary attitude. To them the co-operative ideal is a way to improve society as a whole. The internal arguments in favour of a democratic organisation are reframed into external arguments in favour of a co-operative society.

The external arguments focus on autonomy and non-exploitation – values that make workers' co-operatives seem appealing to large numbers of people as a decentralised form of socialism. Again the argument has to be stated somewhat differently in housing. The concept of exploitation in a welfare sector is ambiguous to say the least, and a number of different external roles may be advocated for co-operatives in the housing sector. The common denominator seems to be that 'ordinary' people, including those with limited resources, should be able to solve their housing problems in an autonomous way through the co-operative sector. This will be designated the social aspect of co-operative housing.

Co-operative solutions have sometimes been portrayed as a third or middle way between the two traditional ways of organising production and distribution, between capitalism and socialism, plan and market, collectivism and individualism. In a pragmatic version, the notion of a third way means a compromise between state and market. In a more utopian version neither money nor power is seen as the driving force of the co-operative economy, but social norms promoting mutual self-help in a communitarian spirit.[6]

Consumer Co-operatives

The largest co-operative sector in Sweden consists of the co-operative retail societies; about half of all Swedish households are members of co-operative societies affiliated to the leading national organisation KF (the Co-operative Union and Wholesale Society). In 1984, 17 per cent of the total retail trade was managed by co-operatives, while their share of department-store trade reached 56 per cent.[7]

Other consumer co-operative branches of importance include co-operatives selling petrol, insurance and funeral services. The petrol co-operatives, which are part of the national organisation, OK (the Co-operative Society of Oil Consumers), have seen their market share increase steadily to 18 per cent of total oil and petrol sales in 1986 and a membership of 1.2 million people. In the 1980s OK was integrated into the KF organisation.[8]

The insurance company Folksam, which in 1984 managed in the region of one quarter of the household insurance market, is formally owned by its insurance-holders, though representatives to the general meeting are appointed by KF and other national co-operatives or by the national trade unions. The co-operative funeral society, Fonus, is not based on individual membership and handles about 30 per cent of all funerals in the country.[9]

The KF movement plays a dominating role in the consumer co-operative sector, and has often assisted other parts of the co-operative movement, with the exception of housing co-operatives, by providing capital and knowhow during their start-up phase.

Since 1945, and in particular during the 1960s and 1970s, consumer co-operatives have experienced a period of organisational concentration. Partly as a reaction to this centralisation process, new types of consumer co-operatives have appeared, independent of the established societies. These 'new co-operatives', which include, for instance, parents' co-operatives to provide child care, purchasing co-operatives and car pools, are an expression of the ideals associated with the 'alternative' movement. They are 'green' in political complexion, ecologically concerned, extremely self-help-oriented and small in size and are estimated to number about 1,000 in total.[10]

Producer Co-operatives

The producer co-operatives which may be said to be of any importance exist mainly in the agricultural sector. Although farming itself is dominated by private enterprise and family farms, co-operatives play a large role in the supply of goods to farms, in the provision of finance, marketing assistance and in the processing of agricultural produce.

The Federation of Swedish Farmers (LRF) is the main organisation within the overall agricultural co-operative movement. Since the LRF also represents the farmers in negotiations with the government over food prices and over their co-operative and other interests, farmers are well integrated in the organisation. Though politically independent, the agricultural co-operatives have strong links with the Centre (formerly the Agrarian) Party.

In 1984 agricultural co-operatives had about one million members, with farmers often being members of several co-operatives, operating in different fields, at the same time. The largest co-operatives are to be found in dairying (virtually 100 per cent) and slaughtering (80 per cent). Other important sectors include crop and meat marketing, forestry and banking. Producer co-operatives are also predominant in fishery, small-scale horticulture, taxis and heavy goods transport.[11]

In the last decades of the nineteenth century a considerable number of workers' co-operatives were set up, but they seldom survived for long. As elsewhere in Europe, both the consumer co-operative movement and the trade unions have historically adopted a largely negative stance towards them.[12]

In recent years, firms which have gone bankrupt as a result of the general economic crisis have been the subjects of takeovers by their employees or management. In some instances this has led to the creation of a 'new round' of workers' co-operatives. In 1987 there were about 100 employee-owned firms in the manufacturing sector with a total of about 3,000 employees, and a further 20,000 people were employed in jointly owned companies in the service sector.[13] If relations between housing co-operatives and other consumer co-operatives are limited, those between housing co-operatives and producer co-operatives are virtually non-existent.

A History of the Consumer Co-operative in Sweden

The modern co-operative movement in Sweden can be traced back to pre-industrial collective traditions. The first modern Swedish co-operative organisation was a wholesale co-operative founded in 1850. The growth of free trade in the 1860s witnessed a rapid growth in the number of co-operatives. Their lifespan, however, was normally very short. The situation began to change in the 1890s, when the socialist labour movement changed its previously negative attitude towards co-operatives, and the KF was established as a national organisation. Political activists came to see co-operatives as operating outside the established political and economic system with the long-term objective of replacing, or at least reforming, the capitalist economic system. Co-operatives were regarded as an ethically higher form of enterprise with a mission to educate consumers and provide them with 'clean and unadulterated products'.

The rise of the consumer co-operative movement often met with strong resistance. In the period after the First World War, KF had to overcome delivery blockades and other obstacles introduced by private monopolies and cartels. In order to combat these various impediments and reduce prices, KF founded its own factories for the production of, for example, margarine, flour, shoes, light bulbs, rubber products and leather goods. In doing so, however, it abandoned its earlier vision of a co-operative economy; co-operatives were now increasingly regarded more as a complement and corrective to private enterprise rather than as an expanding alternative. Henceforth, the co-operative movement was to look after not only the interests of its own members but also those of all consumers through, for instance, campaigning for improvements in government policy to protect consumers.

After the Second World War extensive structural changes began to take place within the consumer co-operative movement: efficiency gains were sought through concentration in larger units, automation and the shift towards self-service. Between 1952 and 1972 the number of co-operative shop units decreased from 8,200 to 2,600. At the same time the role accorded to co-operatives as a balancing competitive factor on the market was further accentuated.

In the 1970s the debate on the 'co-operative alternative' again intensified, and the co-operative movement sharpened its consumer-political profile, by introducing new lines of basic goods in, for instance, food, clothing and furniture. Even so, during the 1980s many co-operative societies experienced falling economic returns and diminishing market shares, which occasioned large-scale organisational changes. As a result of their actions they improved their competitive position *vis-à-vis* the private sector.

Organisation, Members and Activists

The co-operative societies, which form the organisational basis of the consumer co-operative movement, are all members of KF. In the early years co-operative societies were quite small, and, as with Tenant-Owner Co-operatives (see below), their boards were elected at general meetings, which were open to all members. Over time, however, their growth in size made it necessary to introduce an intermediary, district level into the organisation, as a result of which the influence of members gradually became more indirect.

The concentration process after 1945 worked the same way, with the number of societies declining from 680 to 170 between 1952 and 1977 and the number of elected representatives decreasing by 70 per cent.[14] By 1988 there were only 135 societies.[15]

The organisation of KF and the co-operative societies has often been criticised for being centralised and undemocratic. For some time the boards of the co-operative societies consisted of full-time directors, who were only formally nominated by the members. In 1967, however, the organisation was changed, and the managing director is now the only employee guaranteed a place on the board of the society.[16]

Membership of the co-operative societies grew steadily until in the 1980s co-operative societies had over two million members, which means that every second Swedish household belongs to a co-operative. However, it should be stressed that membership of a co-operative society does not have to be renewed, and that there is no annual membership fee. Lifelong membership may therefore well be the result of one single decision. This might account for the fact that co-operative societies have the most passive members of all Swedish voluntary associations. In a comprehensive study of member activity in Swedish associations only 7 per cent of members of co-operative societies describe themselves as 'active', and only 2 per cent had ever held an elected post. The corresponding figures for other co-operatives (including housing co-operatives) were 29 per cent and 15 per cent respectively.[17] According to a survey carried out in 1980, there were some 8,000 elected representatives in the KF organisation, equivalent to only 0.4 per cent of all members. Sixty per cent of the representatives were men, 73 per cent were forty-five years or older and 88 per cent inclined towards the Social Democrats.[18]

Until recently, members used to receive an annual dividend based on their purchases made in co-operative shops, but since the mid-1970s most societies have been forced for financial reasons to abolish dividends.[19]

Housing Co-operatives in Sweden: Key Agents

A primary question to be posed is: why are so many people attracted to co-operative housing? Here we may distinguish between internal and external arguments. The internal arguments focus on democracy. Co-operatives are looked upon as democratic organisations. By joining together on equal terms, it is held, members of a co-operative can take care of their common affairs in a spirit of participatory democracy, thereby obtaining a sense of shared responsibility, perhaps even personal self-fulfilment. This will be called the democratic aspect of co-operative housing.

Sweden as a Deviant Case

The social and democratic values of co-operative housing are often highly praised in the housing debate. So, why do housing co-operatives play such a minor, often negligible, role in most countries, at least in terms of their share of the market? Are the co-operative problems in housing fundamental or transitional? On the other hand, why does co-operative housing represent such a considerable share of the market in Norway and Sweden? By analysing the deviant case of Swedish co-operative housing, it might be possible to suggest ways of solving the co-operative paradox. Can the viability of co-operative housing in Sweden be explained by the actions, persuasiveness and energy of co-operative leaders or by the structural and institutional characteristics of the Swedish system of housing provision? Or do we have to attribute it to some particular Swedish 'culture of co-operation'?

About one-sixth of all Swedish dwellings are co-operatively owned. In multi-family housing, where owner-occupation is prohibited by law, the co-operative share is about 30 per cent, almost the same as that of the other two large multi-family sectors, namely, public and private rentals. In single-family housing the market is dominated by owner occupation, and the co-operative share has long been a modest 2–3 per cent. However, in the late 1980s, 30 per cent of all new single-family dwellings were erected by co-operatives, which may suggest a co-operative breakthrough into this segment of the market.[20] It is important to bear in mind that the characteristic Swedish co-operative tenure, *bostadsrätt*, is usually translated as 'tenant-ownership', indicating that the individual user's right of control lies somewhere between tenancy and ownership.

Most co-operative estates are owned by a tenant-owner co-operative (TOC) in which the individual tenant-owners are members. In organisational terms it is possible to distinguish between two main types of TOC. One type is organised within one of the two national organisations HSB (the Tenants' Savings and Building Societies) and Riksbyggen (the Co-operative Building Organisation of the Swedish Trade Unions). The other type of TOC is more heterogenous, consisting of co-operatives founded, for instance, by building companies, groups of households or local authorities. Since the TOCs of HSB and Riksbyggen are attached in a mandatory way to their respective mother organisations, they are referred to as 'attached' TOCs, in contrast to 'independent' TOCs.

HSB, the largest of the two national organisations, is based on the consumer co-operative principle of individual membership. It has three co-operative levels: TOCs, HSB societies and the HSB National Federation. Both the TOCs and their individual members are members of the regional HSB society, together with people on the waiting list for an HSB dwelling. The TOCs are primarily responsible for the management of existing houses and estates, and the HSB societies for the construction of new houses and the recruitment of new members. The HSB societies, being professional organisations, also offer the TOCs certain economic, technical and managerial services. The HSB National Federation, with the HSB societies as members, is responsible for the overall policy of the organisation and for assisting societies and TOCs in technical, financial, legal and administrative matters. Of great economic importance is the HSB Savings Bank, administered by the national federation.

The dominant owners of Riksbyggen are not individual tenant-owners, but the trade unions operating in the building sector. Some, but not all, TOCs attached to Riksbyggen also hold shares in the national mother organisation. The TOCs are organised in much the same way as those of HSB. Functions corresponding to those of the co-operative HSB societies are performed by district offices falling directly under the head office in Stockholm. The responsibilities of the head office are very similar to those of the HSB National Federation. However, Riksbyggen does not have its own bank but enters into special agreements with local savings banks with whom prospective tenant-owners hold accounts and take out loans.

SBC (the Swedish Central Organisation of Tenant-Owner Co-operatives) is a national organisation with independent TOCs as members. It is a service and interest organisation, and its links with member TOCs are far weaker than those between HSB and Riksbyggen and their attached TOCs. Only about one-third of all independent TOCs are members of SBC. In 1985 there were some 620,000 tenant-ownership dwellings in Sweden, and in 1992 about 650,000. In 1988 there were 300,000 HSB and 135,000 Riksbyggen dwellings, and a further 215,000 independent co-operatives.

By the end of 1987 there were about 3,500 active TOCs within HSB and about 1,500 within Riksbyggen. The average TOC managed about 90 dwellings, ranging from three to more than a thousand. The number of independent TOCs has been estimated to lie between 5,000 and 6,500, indicating an average size of between 30 and 40 dwellings.[21]

In 1985 more than 98 per cent of co-operative dwellings were classified as modern.[22] In Sweden, dwellings in multi-family houses, where most co-operatives are found, are relatively small. In 1985 the average size of a co-operative dwelling was between two and three rooms and kitchen, about the same as for private and public rentals.[23]

Tenant-ownership tenure completely dominates co-operative housing in

Sweden; housing co-operatives other than TOCs were in principle prohibited by the 1930 Tenant-Owner Act. Existing rental co-operatives were not dissolved, but they were no longer allowed to build or acquire new houses. The Act stipulated that tenant-ownership should be regarded as the normal tenure of housing co-operatives. By strengthening legal control over co-operatives, as well as the position of individual members, the Act contributed substantially towards the general credibility of co-operative housing, both in social and economic terms. It is estimated that in the 1980s there were between 1,000 and 2,000 rental co-operatives with a total of some 20,000 dwellings, most of them located on quite old estates.[24] The main exception is SKB (the Co-operative Housing Association of Stockholm), which is still building new rental housing on a co-operative basis. Rapidly rising prices for tenant-owned dwellings in the 1980s gave rise to renewed political interest in co-operative rentals, and the formation of new co-operatives of this type has again been allowed on a trial basis.

Economic and Political Success

By conventional standards, and certainly by Elster's, Swedish co-operative housing must be regarded as successful. In most countries housing co-operatives play a marginal role, rarely representing more than one or two per cent of the total stock, whereas in Sweden the co-operative sector is firmly established as an important component of the system of housing provision.

If we take seriously the possibility of transitional obstacles to co-operatives, we should look to history for an explanation for this deviant case. The question has to be posed: what factors made it possible for co-operative housing in Sweden to cross the threshold between failure and success, between marginality and integration? In the following brief historical account the focus is on the HSB organisation, which through the years has been the main force behind the development of the sector. Two periods seem to be of special importance. One is the 'consolidation period' of HSB from its foundation in 1923 up to the Second World War. The other is the 'expansion period' from the end of the Second World War to the mid-1960s.[25]

The consolidation period In retrospect, the breakthrough for co-operative housing in Sweden came when, in 1923, the Tenants' Association of Stockholm organised the first HSB society. Various attempts to form housing co-operatives had been made over the previous fifty years, but with limited success; in several cases co-operatives had been used by unscrupulous entrepreneurs who speculated with the tenants' savings. The non-speculative rental co-operative, SKB, was founded in 1916, but with the development of HSB it came to play a secondary role.

The decision to establish the first HSB society was triggered by political events. Earlier, in 1923, rent controls, which in common with many European countries had been introduced during the First World War, had been abolished, and the new organisation was regarded as a means of providing shelter at reasonable cost in a market that was anticipated to be highly speculative. The very next year, the Stockholm HSB Society founded the HSB National Federation, mainly as a means to start new HSB societies outside the capital. The period up to the Second World War witnessed a steady and systematic build-up of the HSB organisation. The foundations were laid, both ideologically and organisationally, for their future expansion after the war.

The vanguard role played by the HSB movement had an ideological dimension. During the inter-war period, HSB was virtually alone in representing the idea of non-profit housing in a privately dominated market. An often cited example of the social ideology was the initiative which it took to provide all dwellings with bathrooms, at the time considered by many a luxury unnecessary for workers. Other socio-technical innovations were refuse chutes, communal launderettes, children's playgroups, crèches and kindergartens. Its vanguard ideas were complemented and implemented by an elaborate organisation which from the mid-1930s took control of virtually all building and management functions. By 1940 the productive capacity of the HSB concern was in fact larger than was actually needed to meet the demands within the organisation.

Yet, in spite of the considerable ideological and organisational development, co-operatives still represented a minor part of the housing system; only some 20,000 HSB dwellings were constructed in the whole period 1923–39. Stockholm, however, was an important exception, since HSB had established a good collaborative relationship with the local authorities in the capital. Thus, here, in the 1930s HSB co-operatives accounted for as much as 10 per cent of housing construction.

The period of expansion The fruits of the gradual but consistent and sustained growth were reaped after the war. In political terms, the achievement was the adoption by the newly elected Social Democratic Government of a new comprehensive housing policy, which emphasised co-operative and, above all, public rental housing. As a result, in the period 1945–70, the co-operative share of the housing stock increased from 4 to 14 per cent, while public rentals rose from 6 to 22 per cent. The culmination of this remarkable expansion was the 'Million Programme' of 1965–74; of the one million dwellings built during that period 160,000 were co-operatively owned. Of organisational importance was the internal process of concentration that occurred in the 1960s, accomplished through a series of mergers between HSB societies. Today, the 60 HSB societies are typically professional organisations with a sizeable staff, covering a vast geographical area.

There are obvious links between the ideological and organisational consolidation before the war and the expansion after the war. The new housing policy was based on a programme formulated by the Government Commission on Social Housing that had been appointed as early as 1933. The importance of HSB was acknowledged by including Sven Wallander, the director of the HSB National Federation, as a member of the Commission. Nevertheless, the Commission's proposals gave co-operative housing a more modest role than the municipal housing companies. The latter were assigned the primary responsibility for preventing speculation and securing efficient production and management.

Wallander actually supported the priority given to municipal housing; he foresaw a growing market for HSB services from a fast expanding public sector. At the time, while most municipalities lacked the capacity to handle housing projects, HSB had built up a strong, almost oversized, professional organisation for such purposes. Therefore it was logical that both HSB and Riksbyggen (which was founded in 1940) should set up a large number of municipal housing companies in the years after the war. Today, more than 130,000 municipal rentals are still managed by co-operative organisations though they are formally under municipal control. Somewhat paradoxically, the emphasis on municipal housing companies in the new policy actually strengthened co-operative organisations.

In the 1970s demand for co-operative dwellings declined, as it did for multi-family housing in general, but in the 1980s co-operatives gained new ground. The 'attached' co-operatives of HSB and Riksbyggen increased their market shares, especially in single-family housing. And independent co-operatives, which had played a more limited role in the Million Programme with its emphasis on large-scale industrialised projects, now also expanded their market share. Nevertheless, in the late 1980s, the annual production of co-operative housing was still below that achieved within the framework of the Million Programme, even though fast-growing waiting lists and rising transaction prices provided ample evidence of booming demand. For example, the number of HSB members waiting for accommodation increased from 110,000 to 260,000 between 1980 and 1988, which seemed to indicate a new period of co-operative expansion.

The economic recession of the 1980s, changes in the political complexion of the Government and fundamental shifts in the global economic paradigm have not left the so-called Swedish welfare state model untouched. Although it is difficult to predict the long-term effect which these changes will have on the position that co-operatives have established in the Swedish housing system, they are unlikely to be under any immediate serious threat.

Political Support and Institutional Entrenchment

As already indicated, the success of housing co-operatives may to some extent be explained by the political support which they have received. Though officially neutral within the policy arena, both HSB and Riksbyggen have in practice been permanent members of the Social Democratic Party's informal 'Social Housing Coalition', alongside the National Federation of Tenants' Associations, the National Organisation of Municipal Housing Companies (SABO) and the labour unions operating in the building and housing sectors.

SBC, the organisation of the independent co-operatives, is also officially non-political, though its views on housing issues generally coincide with those of the non-socialist parties. On the whole, the non-socialist parties have not been hostile towards co-operative housing. Thus, the Liberal housing minister of the non-socialist governments in power between 1976 and 1982 initiated steps towards facilitating the conversion of rental houses into co-operatives, while the non-socialist government which took office in 1991 declared its intention to accelerate such conversions in the public rental stock.

The long period of political support has paved the way for institutional entrenchment. In the 1930s, the municipality of Stockholm assigned a major role to the local HSB society to provide the capital city with housing. After the Second World War, housing co-operatives were given an important role in the new national housing policy, and co-operatives gained ground in most cities and towns. Indicative of this enhanced status were the new institutional arrangements governing housing finance. In the early years, HSB and SKB could often obtain loans from the municipality of Stockholm, on condition that a proportion of the dwellings were allocated by the municipal authorities. Integral to the new, post-war housing policy was the government's greater involvement in housing finance. Today, tenant-ownership projects, together with owner occupation and public and private rentals, are included in the formula of 'tenure neutrality' which serves as the official guideline for housing finance and taxation in Sweden.[26]

One innovation which was important to market expansion in the 1980s originated completely outside the political sphere: from the mid-1980s, banks and other financial institutions came to accept a tenant-ownership certificate of a TOC dwelling as a collateral for long-term loans in much the same way as a deed for real estate. This change in financial practice undoubtedly contributed a great deal to the soaring prices of co-operative flats.[27]

The Steps to Success

In summary, during the inter-war period, HSB accrued considerable organisational strength and ideological credibility. The bridgehead in Stockholm was of great importance, as was the Tenant-Owner Act of 1930. Following the Second World War, housing co-operatives became firmly integrated into the new housing policy. From then on, institutional conditions, above all the system of housing finance and the complementary role played by the municipal housing companies, supported the growth in the co-operatives' share of the housing market.

In contrast, the co-operative housing boom which occurred in the late 1980s was not the result of political or institutional change; the co-operative organisations were now strong enough to compete successfully on equal terms with both rental housing and owner occupation. Co-operative housing was already safely embedded in the institutional framework of housing, as confirmed by the new practices of the banks.

Thus, ideological credibility and organisational stability nourished political and institutional support, which, in its turn, bred market success. Through the actions of both co-operative leaders and sympathetic political actors, institutional arrangements were designed that made long-term market progress possible.

Co-operative housing in the tenant-ownership form has undoubtedly crossed the threshold of co-operative success (whether this was achieved in 1930, 1946 or in the 1960s remains an open matter). The same cannot be said about its 'poor relation', the rental co-operatives. The legal and financial institutions governing the housing system have been working against them for decades. Moreover, their political support has been at best occasional, and their role on the housing market has remained marginal.

Social Ambivalence

The economic and political success of co-operative housing in Sweden raises the question of whether this has been achieved at the expense of the social and democratic aspects of co-operatives. In addition, to what extent has their organisational and institutional development had a negative impact on the values that made co-operatives look desirable in the first place? To paraphrase

Elster: when co-operatives are no longer an insignificant minority phenomenon, perhaps co-operative ownership has lost its desirability. The following section discusses the social and democratic aspects of co-operative housing.

Although 'social housing' is not a well-defined concept, it may be suggested that the social aspect of co-operative housing is related to the 'external' aim, namely to provide accommodation for people in general, and for those with limited resources in particular. Such an interpretation conforms to the use of the expression 'social housing' in the political debate. Sometimes the goals of social housing refer specifically to meeting the needs of working-class households, sometimes more generally to assisting households from other ('middle-class') households. Another goal, often referred to as 'social', is to prevent speculation in the housing field. The social orientation of an organisation can be evaluated in terms of its ideology, its practices and the outcome of its activities.

Ideologically, co-operatives may well be advocated from a liberal, a market-socialist or a communitarian world-view.[28] In Sweden, however, both the consumer co-operative and the housing co-operative movement have been strongly associated with the Social Democratic party. The expression 'social housing' was the ideological label attached to the comprehensive housing policy adopted by the Social Democrats after the Second World War: both HSB and Riksbyggen are members of the 'Social Housing Coalition', and they often describe their activities in terms of social housing.

The social aspect was undoubtedly a major motive behind the foundation of HSB in 1923, for it sought to provide shelter at reasonable cost within the framework of a speculative market system. The founders were Social Democrats and other people with leftist sympathies. HSB soon took on a vanguard role in social housing, and a leftist ideology can be traced behind the numerous initiatives taken by HSB during the inter-war period.

After the war, the social hegemony of the co-operative movement was challenged by the rapidly growing municipal housing sector, whose advantage lay in the fact that public rented accommodation, unlike co-operative housing, did not require a personal economic investment. However, since HSB and Riksbyggen succeeded in associating themselves ideologically with the new housing policy and organisationally with the municipal housing companies, they could still be regarded as an integral part of social housing.

With market prices for co-operative dwellings rising, the social role has gradually become attenuated, with the result that, today, HSB and Riksbyggen appear to be searching for a more directly ideological profile similar to that which they enjoyed in their early years. The majority of the leaders and activists within the co-operative movement unquestionably remain Social Democrats; it is their diminishing ideological credibility which has caused them a considerable amount of soul-searching and led them into new pastures where they have proposed a 'co-operative alternative' to the privatisation of municipal functions, such as day nurseries, home help and recreation facilities. Not surprisingly, the co-operative alternative is presented as the 'third way', a solution to the economic and ideological problems of local authorities in the current market-oriented climate. Thus, ironically, there are now signs that the formerly vanguardist co-operative movement is turning into a rearguard covering the retreat of the municipalities in the face of a torrent of legislation privatising and 'contracting out' services.

The actual policy of HSB during its first two decades contained several socially oriented ingredients. For instance, the construction of tenant-ownership houses for ordinary households at a time when the legal rights of tenants were still weak was in itself a social contribution. However, the new national housing policy after the war meant that the role of HSB as the nucleus of social housing was gradually taken over by the municipal housing companies. The most visible indicators of that development were the new transfer principles adopted by co-operative organisations.

There are three more or less 'social' reasons why a co-operative organisation may have an interest in controlling the transfers of its dwellings. Firstly, it may wish to have a decisive say in who is to be the buyer, in order to distribute dwellings internally to members on the waiting list. Secondly, it may wish to distribute vacant dwellings to households considered to be in urgent social need. Thirdly, it may wish to set the transfer price in order to prevent speculation with co-operative dwellings.

For more than forty years, HSB maintained a system of control over transfers and price. Transfers went via the HSB society, and prices were based on initial payments and amortisation. In the 1950s, with growing demand and inflation, these principles met with criticism from an increasing number of members. HSB leaders managed to resist changes until 1969, when market transfers were finally allowed. By then Riksbyggen had already taken the same decision. A moral vestige of price control survived until 1973: individual sellers and buyers were informed of the HSB recommendation on transfer prices *based on initial payments* and then they were allowed to agree on market terms.

Rapidly rising house prices in the 1980s more or less forced low-income households out of the co-operative market, especially in central parts of Stockholm and other large cities. This had the effect of once again placing the issue of transfer control on the co-operative agenda. Although HSB and

Riksbyggen discussed and carried out trials of different checking mechanisms, nevertheless, essentially, the principle of market prices prevailed. Recently, paralleling market expansion, HSB and Riksbyggen have initiated projects in fields such as housing for older people, housing for young households, service centres and tourist and recreation facilities. Such external initiatives may well signal a continuing redefinition of the role of co-operatives in society, but to label them 'social housing' would certainly be to stretch the definition of an already blurred concept.

One question in particular is frequently raised: to what extent can Swedish co-operative housing be described as 'social' in terms of outcome? It is true that the Tenants' Association in Stockholm initially established HSB in order to help solve the housing problems of the working class. Yet, as far as membership is concerned, HSB has never really been a working-class organisation. Even in the 1920s and 1930s, less than half of its members were workers and craftsmen. In the beginning of the 1970s, HSB officials characterised its membership as accurately reflecting the social structure of Swedish society and its political behaviour. A survey from 1970 indicated that the mean income of HSB members was by then already somewhat higher than the national average.[29] A similar picture is painted by 1985 census data on household incomes in different tenures. The proportion of immigrant households (12 per cent) in co-operative dwellings also corresponds to the national average.[30]

The socio-economic impact of the co-operative housing boom of the late 1980s had, in 1992, not yet been registered in official statistics. Yet, in all probability, the general trend will have only increased the middle-class character of the co-operative household structure. The typical co-operative household is better off in economic terms than the Swedish average, a fact reflected in the high market prices at which co-operative dwellings are often sold.

While the social dimension of co-operative housing is still an active ingredient in the official ideology of leaders and activists inside these organisations, it remains an open question whether co-operative policies or the outcome of the operation of the housing market could be described as social. Moreover, it is a moot point whether the recent advances of co-operatives into spheres of activity traditionally regarded as the purview of local authorities (municipalities) should be labelled 'social'. For some commentators, such as Lundqvist et al.,[31] developments in the 1980s make it no longer appropriate to regard Sweden's co-operative housing as the social tenure it was originally conceived to be. They regard tenant-ownership as a commodified tenure, similar to owner occupation. On the other hand, bearing in mind that the concept of social housing is lacking in precision, this conclusion might be premature. Nevertheless, there can be little doubt about the general trend which demonstrates that the social dimension of co-operative housing has been gradually eroded throughout the post-war period.

Democracy: Small-scale Elitism

One of the key defining principles of co-operatives adopted by the International Co-operative Alliance is that of democratic control. Today, normative discussions on democracy usually focus on the contrasting ideal types of participatory and representative democracy, associated with Mill and Schumpeter respectively. Co-operative democratic ideals are typically formulated in participatory terms; thus, small-scale organisations are said to offer the most suitable conditions for participation.

The formal organisation of a Swedish TOC combines the principles of direct and representative democracy. All members have the right to participate in the decision making that takes place at the general meeting, where members of the board are also elected. Between meetings the board is responsible for the affairs of the TOC, and is free to make most decisions concerning management without consulting the members. For example, the Tenant-Owner Act explicitly prescribes that changes in the rent level should be decided by the board.

Empirical data on the exercise of co-operative democracy within the TOCs are scarce and often of limited validity.[32] Between 1958 and 1983 participation of the membership in the TOCs of HSB has been studied on four occasions. During this period, the average participation rate at general meetings has varied between 20 and 30 per cent. A similar study conducted on Riksbyggen TOCs in 1979 showed an attendance one or two per cent lower than that in HSB.

Participation varies considerably with the size of the TOCs. The smaller the TOC, the larger the attendance. There is also a tendency towards higher participation during the first few years after the foundation of a new TOC. Interestingly, in contrast, participation in activities other than meetings, such as educational courses, excursions and festivities, are more often found in the larger TOCs. The reasons for this are readily understandable. Even though a fairly large number of people attend meetings, the majority remain rather passive; in only one-quarter of the TOCs of HSB did any member exercise the democratic right to submit a motion to the general meeting. However, the Riksbyggen study found that discussions were held at 68 per cent of the annual meetings. Finally in this catalogue of statistics, in 1984 some 30,000

(10 per cent of all) HSB members were on the board of their TOC or held other elected posts in the organisation; the corresponding figure for Riksbyggen was about 6 per cent.

These facts prompt the question: to what extent do TOC members themselves value the democratic aspect of the co-operative? The evidence from one study of Riksbyggen members is ambiguous: only 10 per cent of the respondents gave 'possibility of influence on housing conditions' as a main reason for having chosen a co-operative dwelling, while larger numbers cited 'quiet surroundings without social problems' and 'no possibility of getting a rental' as their reason for participating.[33]

In general, such findings should not be interpreted too cynically or negatively, for in the Swedish context a participation rate of 20–30 per cent at general meetings is actually quite high. Tenants' meetings in the rental sector, as well as general meetings of non-housing associations, typically have a much lower attendance. Since a considerable proportion of the membership also hold elected posts and take part in educational courses on housing and co-operatives, the TOCs would seem to function well as schools in democracy and in public-spiritedness, which are forms of social behaviour often advocated and applauded by participatory democrats.

On the other hand, the majority of the members do not take part in the democratic decision making and those who do attend meetings are often silent. The dominance of middle-aged men on the boards also casts some doubt on the representativeness of the elected members. The principle of electing only half the board each year and the common practice of allowing special election committees to nominate candidates may result in an extremely high degree of stability and conservatism in the representatives.[34] Furthermore, there is seldom more than one candidate for each post – although this fact may not be as serious and damaging to democracy as it might appear. While from a participatory viewpoint the high percentage of non-participants and the lopsided representation are unwelcome features, in fact many of the decisions taken by the board of a TOC are quite uncontroversial.

One reason for the seemingly low level of democratic activity within the TOCs may be their limited scope for decision making. Both the mother organisation and the individual tenant-owners hold formal and informal powers of veto, which put important constraints on the collective action of the TOCs. These are, of course, the normal problems faced by all democratic organisations. The opportunities for democratic decision making within a nation-state are constrained by the influence exercised by other nations or by powerful domestic pressure groups and by the rights held by individual citizens. Nevertheless, these limitations seem to be particularly powerful in co-operative housing, especially in the relations between the attached TOCs and their mother organisations.

In principle a TOC has full responsibility for its own affairs. Formally and in practice, however, the mother organisation has considerable influence on the attached TOCs. First of all, the mother organisation controls the planning, building and initial management of a new TOC. Not until the long-term financing of the project is settled do tenant-owners take over formal responsibility, and even then the mother organisation retains considerable formal and informal control. All deviations from the prescribed model statutes must be approved by the mother organisation, and it also appoints one member to the board of the TOC. Of crucial importance are the packages of 'co-ordinated housing management' offered by the mother organisations. In practice the TOCs are often left with the choice of either buying these well-defined packages or taking care of all the management themselves.

A study of housing democracy in Denmark, Norway, Sweden and Finland compared the respective influences of 'formal' and 'actual' agents on certain types of decisions. Among the organisations studied were the TOCs of HSB and Riksbyggen. Swedish TOCs were found to have a relatively strong formal influence on decisions concerning their own estates. In reality, however, the scope for decision making was often severely limited by economic, technical and legal factors and by the prior decisions made by the mother organisation. Even when the board of the TOC took the formal decisions, the professional organisation's greater resources of time, experience and expert knowledge meant that the latter often had a determining impact on the final outcome, exemplified by the fact that detailed proposals for TOC budgets were regularly prepared by the mother organisation.[35] Overall, however, although the level of membership participation certainly falls short of communitarian ideals, women and younger households are under-represented, and the range of decisions in which the majority of the members are involved is restricted, TOCs perform considerably better in this regard than do other organisations.

Not the Middle Way but Both Ways

Thus, we are left with doubts about both the social and, to a somewhat lesser extent, the democratic aspects of co-operative housing in Sweden. While the rhetoric of co-operative leaders still emphasises the ideology of social housing for the less well-off sections of the population, the actual policy and the market outcome seem to favour the interests of the middle classes. While democratic participation was found to be comparatively high, it was biased towards certain social groups and of low intensity.

There is much to indicate that social and democratic ambiguity is the price paid for economic prosperity. Ideological credibility and political support were certainly important in establishing viable co-operative organisations and in creating a favourable institutional environment. But once the organisation was consolidated, the main forces behind the economic success have undoubtedly been financial solidity, an efficient professional organisation and strong individual market incentives.

The conflicts between social, democratic and economic goals are to some extent reflected in the relative influence of the different organisational levels of co-operative housing. The actions of the primary co-operative, the TOC, are constrained by the powers of both the individual tenant-owners and the professional organisation. The scope of co-operative and democratic decision making is squeezed between claims by individual members for personal gains on one hand, and claims by professional managers for technical efficiency on the other. With the professionalisation of the local organisations, the main responsibility for maintaining co-operative housing's social dimension has been taken over by the national organisations. However, their influence on lower levels is limited, at least in the sphere of social issues. The main power base of the HSB National Federation is the savings bank; and banks have seldom been useful instruments for enhancing social responsibility.

The independent TOCs differ from the attached ones in certain important respects. The absence of a strong mother organisation should extend the formal scope of decision making, but other factors come into play to affect the level of participation. The forces supporting the social aspect of co-operative housing should be even weaker than in the attached co-operatives. However, since independent TOCs, and certainly their organisation SBC, do not claim to represent social housing, it is dubious whether the external arguments for co-operative housing are really of any relevance to them.

In both political and market economic terms, co-operatives have important competitive advantages over the other main tenures: private rentals, public rentals and owner occupation. Politically, co-operatives together with municipal housing companies have enjoyed the support associated with social housing. In reality, however, the burden of providing shelter for people of small means or with social problems has been carried almost completely by the municipal housing companies. As far as the economic side is concerned, co-operatives, like owner occupation, offer households an opportunity to invest their personal savings in property and to make a profit when moving. Since owner occupation in multi-family housing is prohibited by law, in this section of the market co-operatives meet with no real competition. Therefore, in times of housing shortage, buying a tenant-ownership secondhand is the only legal way for the slightly more prosperous to avoid queuing for inner-city dwellings. This too has the effect of eroding their social function.

As mentioned in the introduction, co-operatives are often discussed as a third or middle way between two traditional solutions, variously referred to as: the state and market, public and private, or collectivist and individualist. On closer examination this notion is far from unambiguous. In one version co-operatives are seen as a compromise. Thus, Kemeny[36] regards the co-operative tenure as a compromise between owning and renting, while Clapham and Kintrea[37] claim that the co-operative tenure can vary along a continuum from individualist to collectivist, resembling, at one pole, social rented housing and, at the other, owner occupation. Pestoff,[38] who does not confine his discussion to housing, also considers that co-operatives constitute a third way, an alternative to the 'mutual exclusivity of a simplistic markets vs. politics perspective'. However, he concludes that it is neither likely nor desirable that co-operatives will ever succeed in creating a synthesis between the two forces, going beyond market and politics.

But a third way does not have to be a middle way. Silver[39] criticises what she calls the 'Social Democratic' model of housing co-operatives as a compromise between extremes. Instead she argues that co-operative housing should be understood in communitarian terms, involving parochial, particularist and face-to-face relations. Thus, co-operatives should be analysed not in a state vs. market perspective, but by means of sociological terms such as human agency and the sphere of civil society rising.

How can Swedish co-operative housing be understood against the background of these notions of co-operatives as a third way? The first point that has to be made is that it is difficult to interpret the development of large-scale professional organisations, supported by legal and financial institutions, in Silver's communitarian perspective. Secondly, while it cannot be claimed that Swedish co-operative housing has reached a synthesis beyond market and politics, it has achieved a particular optimal balance between state and market.

The history of Swedish co-operative housing suggests that it has actually reached its present position not by finding a third, compromise way, but by walking firmly along both the traditional paths, sometimes being more social than public housing and, on other occasions, being more commercial than owner occupation. Co-operative organisations have skilfully managed to proceed simultaneously, or rather alternately, along the roads of state welfarism and market egoism. The price for this ambivalence has been paid in terms of the social and democratic aspects of co-operative housing.

From his notion of co-operatives as a compromise between owning and renting, Kemeny has suggested what might be called 'the supplementary theory of housing cooperation'. He argues that the co-operative tenure reflects the emphasis on dwelling type and lifestyle associated with the dominant tenure of a society. According to Kemeny, this thesis is supported by the differences between the large-scale Swedish housing co-operatives, mainly in multi-family houses, and the Australian small-scale co-operatives consisting of single-family houses.[40]

Yet the history of co-operative housing in Sweden does not fully support Kemeny's thesis. Before the war, when the housing market was totally dominated by private rentals, HSB based its development on its complementary role as part of the vanguard in the provision of social housing. After the war, when the new housing policy was initiated, HSB and Riksbyggen were able for a time to take advantage of their early start. When the municipal housing companies were ready to take over as the dominant social housing organisations, co-operative housing did not, however, confine itself to a supplementary role. Instead, it developed a niche based on the co-operative's monopoly in the market for non-regulated multi-family housing, that is, as a complement and not a supplement to other tenures.

Hence, the Swedish experience suggests that Kemeny's supplementary theory needs to be complemented (if not supplemented) by a 'complementary theory of housing co-operation'. Such a theory would imply that co-operative housing thrives where competition from other tenures is low, and complements them by invading vacant market segments. Of course, both the supplementary and the complementary theories are really derived from the same empirical fact: the indefinite and often flexible character of the co-operative tenure.

Conclusion: The Swedish Experience and the Paradox of Co-operative Housing

Can the political and economic success story of Swedish housing co-operatives help us to solve the paradox of co-operative housing? Does the Swedish experience give any clues about the necessary and sufficient conditions for establishing and maintaining a central role for co-operative housing? Can we even identify the historical threshold between marginality and integration?

Among the conditions that have favoured co-operative housing in Sweden, stress has been placed on the importance of the institutional environment, especially that affecting legislation governing tenures, housing finance and the market environment. Political support gave co-operative housing its breakthrough after the war, while the principal onus for providing social housing was placed on the shoulders of municipal housing companies. The absence of owner occupation in multi-family housing helped to fuel the market boom of the 1980s. The legal status of the tenure of tenant-ownership served as the institutional link between the state, the market and the housing co-operatives.

But the institutional framework and conditions did not come out of nowhere. The consistent build-up of social credibility, professional efficiency and solid finances by the co-operative organisations themselves substantially contributed towards the favourable environment. This development is probably best described as mutually reinforcing processes of internal organisational consolidation and external institutional integration.

This means, unfortunately, that little can be said about necessary and sufficient conditions, for there have simply been too many interacting conditions to make it possible to point at one or two as crucial. Indeed, the complex relations between actors and institutions indicate that, rather than seeking to find simple answers in terms of necessary and sufficient conditions, attention should be directed towards looking for favourable and unfavourable political and institutional mechanisms. By the same token, it might be advisable to avoid, or at the very least be wary of, settling for explanations couched in terms of a particular 'culture of co-operation'.

There is one respect in which the study of the deviant Swedish case has contributed to the solution of the paradox of co-operative housing. Co-operative problems have been transitional, not fundamental. After fifty years of co-operative failure, a species fit for survival and reproduction finally evolved. It required a further fifty years of consistent organisational and institutional design to find solutions to these transitional problems. Yet it has to be repeated that the complex interaction between several internal and external conditions means that it is impossible to point to one single critical threshold between failure and success. Perhaps a better metaphor would be a ladder of co-operative success, with a number of crucial steps of different character.

The paradox of co-operative housing will be better understood following comparative historical research on the interaction between co-operative organisations and their environment. Such comparative research should closely scrutinise both successful and unsuccessful attempts to build up co-operative organisations and to create supporting institutions. It should emphasise the relations between the behaviour of co-operative and political actors and their institutional settings, including the housing market. And it should not avoid or omit the issue of trade-offs between different goals and aspects of co-operative housing. After all, it has to be remembered that co-operative housing is an indefinite concept and a flexible phenomenon.

Notes

1   For a more comprehensive account of different aspects of co-operative housing in Sweden, with complete references, the reader is referred to B. Bengtsson, *Prosperous Ambivalence – Housing Co-operatives in Sweden*, National Swedish Institute for Building Research, Gävle, 1992.

2   J. Elster, 'From here to there; or, if co-operative ownership is so desirable, why are there so few co-operatives?', *Social Philosophy and Policy*, no. 6, 1989, pp. 93–111.

3   Ibid., p. 94.

4   Ibid., pp. 96–9, 109.

5   Society for Co-operative Studies, *An Overview of the Swedish Co-operative Movement 1976–1984*, Society for Co-operative Studies, Stockholm, 1986, p. 22.

6   Cf. H. Silver, 'State, market and community: low-income housing co-operatives in theoretical perspective', *Netherlands Journal of Housing and the Built Environment*, no. 6, pp. 185–203.

7   Society for Co-operative Studies, op. cit., p. 25.

8   S. -A. Böök and T. Johansson, *The Co-operative Movement in Sweden*, Swedish Society for Co-operative Studies, Stockholm, 1988, pp. 100–6.

9   Society for Co-operative Studies, op. cit., pp. 7, 25.

10   Böök and Johansson, op. cit., pp. 170–77.

11   Society for Co-operative Studies, op. cit., pp. 13–21.

12   Böök and Johansson, op. cit., pp. 42–4.

13   Ibid., p. 177.

14   SOU, *Kooperationen i Sverige*, Ministry of Industry, Stockholm, 1979.

15   KF, *Annual Report*, KF Group, Stockholm, 1988.

16   SOU, op. cit., p. 174.

17   O. Petersson, A. Westholm and G. Blomberg, *Medborgarnas makt* (The power of citizens), Carlssons, Stockholm, 1989, pp. 110–12.

18   M. Ahnlund, *Konsumentkooperationen och medlemmarna*, Arbetsrapport 5, Cooperative Institute, Stockholm, 1982.

19   Böök and Johansson, op. cit., p. 91.

20   Swedish Official Statistics, *Housing Construction 1990*, Statistics Sweden, Stockholm, SM Bo 20 SM 9101, 1991, p. 15; Swedish Official Statistics, *Yearbook of Housing ad Building Statistics 1991*, Statistics Sweden, Stockholm, 1991, p. 18.

21   K. A. S. Svensson, *Boende och kooperationen* (Housing and co-operation), Co-operative Institute, Stockholm, 1989.

22   Swedish Official Statistics, *Population and Housing Census 1985, Part 3, Dwellings*, Statistics Sweden, Stockholm, 1988, p. 227.

23   Swedish Official Statistics, *Yearbook of Housing and Building Statistics 1991*, Statistics Sweden, Stockholm, 1991.

24   Svensson, op. cit., pp. 9–10.

25   For a thorough study of the history of HSB, the reader is referred to L. Gustafson, *HSB under femtio-år – en organisationsstudie* (Fifty years of HSB – an organisational study), HSB National Federation, Stockholm, 1974.

26   See L. J. Lundqvist, *Housing Policy and Tenures in Sweden*, Avebury, Aldershot, 1987.

27   L. J. Lundqvist, I. Elander and B. Danerbark, 'Housing policy in Sweden – still a success story?', *International Journal of Urban and Regional Research*, 14, pp. 445–67.

28   Cf. J. Birchall, *Building Communities the Co-operative Way*, Routledge & Kegan Paul, London, 1988, pp. 26–58.

29   Gustafson, op. cit., pp. 24–5, 56–60.

30   See Bengtsson, op. cit., for details and references on the members and household structure of housing co-operatives.

31   Lundqvist et al., op. cit., p. 462.

32   See Bengtsson, op. cit., for details and references.

33   H. Mabon, *Basfakta om bostadsrätthavare* (Basic facts about tenant-owners), Riksbyggen, Stockholm, 1981.

34   Cf. M. Liedholm, *Boinflytande og medbestämmande*, (Tenants' influence and participation), Lund University, Department of Sociology, Lund, 1988, pp. 21.

35   T. Cronberg, 'Tenants' involvement in the management of social housing in the Nordic countries', *Scandinavian Housing & Planning Research*, no. 3, 1985, pp. 65–87.

36   J. Kemeny, *The Myth of Home Ownership*, Routledge & Kegan Paul, London, 1981, p. 53.

37   D. Clapham and K. Kintrea,, 'Importing housing policy: housing co-operatives in Britain and Scandinavia', *Housing Studies*, no. 2, 1987, p. 164.

38   V. Pestoff, *Between Markets and Politics*, Westview Press, Boulder, Colorado, 1991, pp. vii, 190–5.

39   Silver, op. cit.

40   Kemeny, op. cit., pp. 53–5.

Conclusion

In many European countries the First World War was a watershed for housing policy. Governments introduced rent controls during hostilities and in the years afterwards became even more interventionist by directly or indirectly subsidising housing construction and its modernisation (slum clearance). The Second World War (the 'people's war'), which was another major watershed in European history, gave a further impetus to government activity in the housing field. Housing policy was made an integral part of the Welfare State. It was treated as a need which it was the duty of the state to strive to meet. The production of housing was not be determined by market forces and neither should access to accommodation be dictated by ability to pay. In this way, housing was to varying degrees de-commodified[1] and its role in the Welfare State's commitment to a course of social inclusion was clearly stated.

On the territory of today's 'Euroland', the role of the state and its budgetary (and rhetorical) commitment to housing reached its apotheosis in the 1970s.[2] Shelter has been the first basic necessity (after food) to be recommodified and the first of the publicly owned assets to be privatised.

Decommodification applied especially to the former Soviet Union and CEECs, where rents tended to account for about 3–5 per cent of a household budget and did not cover running costs, let alone the capital cost of construction. Accommodation provided by co-operatives in Sweden and by local councils in the UK (where in cities with over 500,000 people one person in two was housed by the local authority), the Netherlands and the Marxist states was governed by the principle of the 'right to use'(*ius usus*).

In the countries of the European Union there has been a trend away from large-scale intervention by central and other tiers of governments in the provision of social housing. Subsidies and other forms of aid are now no longer directed towards the construction process, but are more closely targeted on individuals. Nevertheless, the price of renting or buying social housing is everywhere cheaper than the price paid on the free market.[3]

The revival of co-operative housing in the early 1960s in East and Central Europe was a step towards recommodification; the charge for a flat in a co-operative approximated more closely to the costs of construction and maintenance. The aim was to 'harness individuals' savings'. Those attracted to the co-operative tenure tended to be members of the middle class, primarily, young élites whose parents could provide a deposit, and white-collar workers low down on the housing waiting list.

Co-operatives have made a very limited contribution to solving the housing problem in England. In part this reflected the general attitude of the Labour Party and the trade unions to the role which they assigned to the state in meeting a range of basic needs, including housing. Municipal socialism was one manifestation of the success of social democracy and of the Parliamentary path to socialism: it was the duty of the central government, through its agent the local council, to provide housing. In the 1960s the Labour Party began to reorientate itself away from state as public landlord to the non-profit housing association and co-operative.[4] A similar legislative shift at that time in Russia was part of a 'socialist' solution to the problem of the enormous size of budgetary spending on housing provision. However, in neither country did a more favourable political climate bring about a major upsurge in co-operative construction, although by the 1980s in Russia the figure exceeded 10 per cent in some of the country's largest cities.

The housing situation in West Germany began to become more polarised during the mid-1980s, with low- and middle-income households finding it increasingly difficult to find affordable houses.[5] For those excluded from the luxury housing sector, co-operatives appeared to be an attractive alternative, although the scandals associated with the largest social-housing project, owned by the trade union, Neue Heimat, had a dampening effect on interest.[6] Nevertheless, the low rents charged in co-operatives, the possibility in some cases of paying with one's own labour (*Muskel-Hypote*), instead of with money, and the ability to participate in decision making continued to make the co-operative an attractive tenure form.[7] In some industrial areas, such as the Ruhr, there were some initiatives to convert company-provided accommodation into tenant co-operatives.[8]

In 1991 the National Association of Housing Enterprises (*Gesamtverband der Wohnungswirtschaft*) in east Germany published data which showed that 16 per cent of the total housing stock built in this part of Germany was managed by co-operatives.[9] Because of the low and regulated rents and the rising level of unemployment among tenants, the co-operatives (and other social housing projects) are now facing severe financial problems which reduce their ability to modernise existing properties and construct new ones.

The development of a specifically co-operative alternative in Germany has been hindered by the political decision taken in 1985 to abolish the charitable status of housing co-operatives.[10] The effect of this act was to compel co-operatives to adopt a more market-oriented approach and to encourage management reform. This is another illustration of a government choosing to make the climate uncongenial for co-operatives to germinate and flourish: they find it difficult to acquire affordable land and to borrow at cheap rates and find themselves disadvantaged by the tax system compared with owner-occupiers.

The role and significance of housing co-operatives in the former socialist countries has varied between the individual states and over time. They were particularly important in Czechoslovakia, where they were involved in the construction, management and maintenance of co-operative property. Following the post-war revival of the co-operative movement in 1959 it grew rapidly and by 1965 co-operative dwellings were contributing 49 per cent of all new housing. In 1988, in the Czech and Slovak republics, they accounted for 18 per cent and 20 per cent of the respective housing stocks.[11] Although their market shares declined slightly between 1980 and 1994, housing co-operatives remained major developers; output fell from 38 to 31 per cent in the Czech Republic and from 38 to 33 per cent in Slovakia.[12] They also fulfilled a number of other functions assigned to co-operatives, such as providing a range of social, cultural and recreational facilities for their members. The state contributed 55 per cent to the costs of construction, with members depositing18 per cent and the remainder coming from long-term credits. In 1988 in Poland co-operatives accounted for 36.7 per cent of the total urban housing stock.[13] Their contribution rose from 28 per cent in 1980 to 42 per cent in 1994.[14] Elsewhere in Eastern Europe they were virtually or wholly non-existent.[15]

In the Netherlands the number of co-operatives remains quite insignificant. Although housing associations build almost one-third of all new housing, the role of the government as funder is so important that it insists on setting policy. Because of this the housing associations, while carrying out the day-to-day running of the properties, lack independence. This means that they lack a key feature which enables an association to label itself a co-operative.

Sweden is one of the few countries where the housing co-operative has played a prominent role. This confirms Esping-Andersen's categorisation of the country as a 'social democratic regime-type', that is to say, one of a cluster of countries where the principles of universalism in the provision of welfare state benefits were extended to the new middle classes.[16] Swedish housing policy is widely regarded as having been the key to the success of the Swedish welfare state model. Non-housing benefits are also derived from the presence of a large and diverse stock of low-rent housing to which access is easy and security of tenure is assured.[17] Sweden's comparatively strong co-operative housing tradition is in a mutually reinforcing relationship with the co-operative movement more generally.

Because of the diversity of types of co-operative housing, while in some cases they adhere to the principle of the 'right to use', in many instances they signal a step away from the right of use to a property towards the right to derive a reward from housing, apart from its use, and towards the recommodification of accommodation. The final stage in the process towards recommodification is reached when users of the property have the right to dispose of it. These attributes of the third stage are characteristic features of postmodern society[18] and of the post-welfare state. A person's accommodation no longer simply provides shelter; it is an asset generated from personal savings, which can furnish a pension or a bond to cover health care or a collateral against other expenditure.

The initial impetus driving the foundation of the welfare state, as Esping-Andersen notes, was not confined to material social policy issues. It was also 'a mechanism for social integration, the eradication of class differences and nation building'.[19] This was most evident in the Swedish system and also, in theory at least, in the Soviet-type economies. However, the co-existence of different housing tenures is palpably inegalitarian and likely to cause social tension rather than social integration and feelings of solidarity. Privatising council housing and changing the statutes governing co-operative housing transforms accommodation from a use value into an exchange value and ensures that each household possesses a measure of wealth. Since individuals and households may not realise the benefits of owner occupation, or simply choose not to become owners, governments have provided additional stimuli to encourage rent-paying tenants to become mortgage-paying owners: huge discounts on the value of the property and increased rents in the public sector, together with rent deregulation in the private sector.[20] These policies do not remove inequalities, since the property owned by some has a greater exchange value than that held by others.

The satisfaction of one basic human need is coming to be regarded as a means of financing other needs at a later date. Thus, responsibility for taking action to cover for life's risks is being returned to the individual. This reverses a century-long trend culminating in the post-1945 consensus which transferred that duty to the society's representative and guardian, the state. At the same time, governments have undermined the mutual aid institutions which individuals created in civil society to protect themselves. In a sense, governments have reneged on their compact with their citizenry; first of all, in the post-1945 compact they took over many of the functions of mutual (self-help) institutions; secondly, those which were left were marginalised or atrophied. Those mutuals that survived were tempted to privatise themselves.

Ironically, the membership of those which resisted the temptation are growing, while building societies that became banks have been losing members. Overall, however, financing and ownership of housing are increasingly individualised, privatised activities

Yet the static nature of home ownership is at variance with the dynamic of a postmodern society which demands greater occupational flexibility and geographical mobility. Furthermore, home ownership is, arguably, less consumerist than rental housing: changing jobs and moving to new environments generates changes in lifestyle and offers new opportunities to choose new interior designs. The conclusion reached at a symposium organised by the Rowntree Trust on the future of private landlords was that: there was an urgent need for more homes to rent; since the cost of moving in the rented sector is cheap, private landlordism helped new households, jobseekers and divorcing families.[21] The most appropriate (and needed) housing tenure for late capitalism is the one that most arouses the appetite to consume. The choice between renting and owning constitutes another contradiction of the consumerist, postmodern society. At present, though, in spite of attempts in different European countries to revive the private rented sector, only in Germany and Denmark has private landlordism held its ground.[22]

The general trend throughout the continent has been for the state to build less accommodation and for the existing stock to be sold to sitting tenants. In the extreme case of the Russia Federation, in December 1992 the Supreme Soviet granted all tenants living in state accommodation the right to have their rented tenancies transferred to them as private property, completely free of charge, irrespective of their size, location or standard of amenity. Although a reversal of this trend is not to be anticipated, rented accommodation might better be provided by housing co-operatives and other forms of non-profit housing associations rather than private landlords or local councils.

Late capitalism and its postmodernist forms demand flexible boundaries and competencies between countries and regions, central and local government departments, private, voluntary (non-profit) and public institutions. For instance, whereas for owner-occupier residential estates the proper institutional authority for maintaining the environment is the municipal authority, which is also charged to keep its own tenants' housing and surrounding area in order, the co-operative takes on this responsibility for its tenants and members. The co-operative, non-profit method of providing housing extends the territory for which it is responsible beyond the four walls of each member's separate flat and beyond the walls of the block itself. In this way responsibility devolved from the state to the municipality becomes devolved still further. The co-operative tenant has an interest in the co-operative's financial probity and in its maintaining a high level of professional and prudent management.

Currently, this process of devolution, known as 'contracting out', means in effect the privatisation of services; they are 'devolved' to the private sector. In some cases they could be performed by co-operatives. The functions performed may not be confined to managing green spaces but may offer a range of services to the local residents which will vary depending on their place in the life cycle. This role is more likely to be performed not by co-operatives (which consist of individual members), but by a secondary or mother co-operative which is a federation of primary co-operatives and set up with the purpose of meeting the latter's need for professional management services and maintenance. It can serve as an information and educational resource centre and also assist in the development of new co-operative projects. The secondary co-operative in some cases, as in the German Neue Heimat, went much further in the range of services which it delivered or made available. In effect, co-operatives (housing associations) already provide a range of affordable, good-quality rented housing to meet widely differing requirements, including retirement housing schemes supervised by wardens who co-ordinate health and social care services and encourage or arrange social activities for residents. If high levels of public amenity are to be sustained in a low-tax economy, then mutuality and voluntary activity will have to expand.

The break-up of large estates into smaller units has begun. These may be local housing companies, with a minority local authority interest, housing associations or co-operatives. Different combinations are possible. The important fact is that downsizing is occurring in the housing sector as well as in the corporate sector. Ancillary services, such as the design of new housing estates, can also be on a smaller scale. Community architecture is a term that has been used since 1975 to describe the activities of a number of architects who try to make their services available to low-income and self-help groups. Like the notion of co-operatives, community architecture is more of a movement of ideas and social forces, rather than a tight definable set of practices. Experimentation with tenant management and participation and the substitution of slum clearance by rehabilitation created the conditions for future occupants to commission architects and become involved in the design of their future homes and environment.[23]

A propitious environment is the critical factor for co-operatives to succeed in a society. The public and their political representatives must believe in them and the legal and financial institutional frameworks must offer them at least an even playing field. This was evidently not the case in the USSR. City councils were mainly obstructive. According to the law, the latter had to allocate plots of land to co-operatives immediately, cover all the costs of site preparation, including the demolition of dwellings no longer fit for habitation, and lay the infrastructure. In reality, the construction sites assigned to them were in remote areas requiring expensive infrastructural preparation which they had to finance themselves. There were enormous delays in furnishing them with building designs and cost estimates, and contractors failed to supply the building materials required. They were also asked to cover the cost of building shops and other auxiliary buildings.[24]

While, overall, co-operative housing does appear to be a vestigial form, its very diversity preserves its vitality: in some contexts co-operative dwellings meet the needs of young and upwardly mobile people; in others they embody the spirit of self-help for low-income groups; they may be short-life or rehabilitation developments, which then become rooted communities. In poorer neighbourhoods they are identifiable by the absence of graffiti and other signs of vandalism; there are fewer vacancies and fewer tenants in rent arrears. As a result, administration, repair and maintenance costs are lower.[25] The national survey of housing co-operatives in England and Wales found a very high level of satisfaction amongst tenants of co-operatives, which convinced them that 'continued public investment in co-operative housing is fully justified'.[26]

The recommodification of housing, associated with the shift away from socially-rented accommodation, has been one of the most radical shifts in social policy in the last two decades of the twentieth century. All of these changes are occurring in a context of the restructuring of financial systems, including those directly concerned with housing. Until fairly recently housing policies were based on specific types of housing finance. Financial deregulation has allowed institutions which specialised in providing funds for housing (for instance, building societies) to assume the gamut of functions offered by banks. These changes are taking place simultaneously with two other processes: firstly, banks have begun to enter into the social housing sector and extend their activities in the private sector. At the same time governments are seeking to play a smaller role in the housing system and set limits to the level of aid which they provide. This is part of the broader strategy, stipulated in the Maastricht Treaty, to reduce public deficits and inflation, which requires containing and cutting public expenditure. Under these circumstances alternative sources of finance have to be found and mobilised. Mutual societies and other solidaristic (non-profit, non-market-determined) forms of financing have not exhausted their possibilities.

Housing, like employment, is a key factor in the process of social exclusion, which is now a major concern for the European Commission and Parliament.[27] Neither the Treaty of Rome (1957), nor the Single European Act (1987), nor the Union (Maastricht) Treaty of 1991, contains any statement to the effect that the citizens of Europe have a right to housing. The reason for this is that none of the Treaties stipulates that the Union has an overall competence in housing policy. The view taken by meetings of Ministers of Housing of the member states is that, because of the specific nature of each country's housing market, housing policy should remain a matter for individual governments.[28] It might well, however, establish guiding principles for co-operative and other forms of non-profit housing.

Notes

1   'De-commodification occurs when a service is rendered as a matter of right, and when a person can maintain a livelihood without reliance on the market', G. Esping-Andersen, *The Three Worlds of Welfare Capitalism*, Polity Press, Cambridge, 1990, p. 22.

2   The state's first major positive intervention in housing policy in the UK, for example, was in 1919, when it introduced a government subsidy for housing construction by local councils. Housing maintained a high ranking at all Parliamentary Elections until 1979. Education and health took its place as the *primus inter pares* on the political sparring agenda in all subsequent elections.

3   *Funding of the Social Housing*, published by the Belgian Presidency for the 5th Annual Meeting of the European Housing Ministers, Brussels, 1993.

4   The first ever national survey of housing co-operatives in the UK found that co-operatives were providing for a wide variety of types of household which would have difficulty in finding accommodation or are known to have difficulty in coping with poor conditions. See S. Underwood, S. Ross and C. Legg, *Who Lives in Housing Co-ops*, Solon Co-operative Housing Services and the National Federation of Housing Associations, London, 1986.

    A summary of the survey of 235 housing co-operatives (55 per cent of all co-operatives in England and Wales, of which 54 per cent replied) accommodating an estimated 9,800 tenants (of whom 16 per cent replied) recorded: one in five co-operative households were single adults; one in seven were elderly households; 10 per cent were single-parent households; nearly 20 per cent previously had no home of their own; one-third previously rented in the private sector; 50 per cent were on very low incomes; 25 per cent were unemployed.

5   I would like to thank Dr Ingrid Breckner of the Wohn-Forum München for her comments on the situation in the then Federal Republic of Germany.

6   K. Novy, *Genossenschaftsbewegung. Zur Geschichte und Zukunft der Wohnreform*, Transit, Berlin, 1983; M. Fuhrich, Ch. Neususs, R. Petzinger et al., *Gewerkschaften und Wohnungspolitik*, VSA-Verlag, Hamburg, 1983.

7   M. Arndt, H. Rogall and K. Schafer, *Wohnungsbaugenossenschaften im Wandel*, Institut fur Bauplanung im Produktions- und Dienstleistungsbereich, Berlin, 1989.

8   K. Selle, *Bestandspolitik: Zehn Beiträge zur Stadterneuerung und Wohnungspolitik,*

Verlag fur Wissenschaftliche Publikationen, Darmstadt, 1986.

9   Friedrich-Ebert-Stiftung, *Zwischen Markt and Sozialer Frage – Wohnen in den Neuen Ländern*, Forschungsinstitut der Friedrich-Ebert-Stiftung, Bonn, 1991.

10 See *Die Wohnungswirtschaft*, no. 2, 1992. (This was a special issue on housing co-operatives.) Another report on old and new co-operative movements in Germany was based on a conference on co-operatives generally, but including discussion of housing co-operatives. See W. D. Just and R. Reitz, *Alte and neue Genossenschaftsbewegung*, Evangelische Akademie, Haus der Begegnung, Mülheim/Ruhr, 1988.

11 P. Michalovic, 'Czechoslovakia', in D. Clapham, J. Hegedus, K. Kintrea, I. Tosics, with H. Kay (eds), *Housing Privatisation in Eastern Europe*, Greenwood Press, London, 1996, p.139.

12 J. Hegedus, S. Mayo and I. Tosics, *Transition of the Housing Sector in the East-Central European Countries*, Metropolitan Research Institute, Budapest, 1996, p. 24.

13 E. Kozlowski, 'Poland', in Clapham et al., op. cit., p.121.

14 Hegedus, Mayo and Tosics, op. cit., p.24.

15 In Bulgaria co-operatives owned a mere 0.2 per cent of the stock. However, Bulgaria was an anomaly within the socialist bloc; even before the collapse of the old regime, 84 per cent of the stock was individually owned.

16 G. Esping-Andersen, op. cit., 1990.

17 J. Kemeny, 'Swedish Rent-setting Policy and the Welfare State: Labour-led Corporatism in a Strategic Policy Area', *International Journal of Urban and Regional Research*, vol. 16, no. 4, December 1992.

18 As much of the literature on the subject testifies, the term 'postmodern' is difficult to define. See, for instance: T. Docherty (ed.), *Postmodernism: A Reader*, Harvester Wheatsheaf, Hemel Hempstead, 1993.

19 G. Esping-Andersen (ed.), *Welfare States in Transition: National Adaptations in Global Economies*, Sage Publications in association with the United Nations Research Institute for Social Development, London, 1996, p. 27.

20 In the UK this began in earnest with the 1972 Housing ('Fair Rents') Finance Act. In 1990 the Housing Minister of East Germany, prior to reunification, announced that rents would rise in stages over the next few years to cover the full costs of housing, including maintenance. (See J. Doling, 'Tearing Down the Wall: Building a New Housing Policy', *Housing Review*, vol. 39, no. 4, July-August 1990, p. 93.). In 1997 Russia inaugurated its own legislation to raise rents so that early in the next century they will reach 20 per cent of household income.

21 R. Best et al., *The Future of Private Renting: Consensus and Action*, Joseph Rowntree Foundation, York, 1992.

22 In 1990 private rental housing accounted for 49 per cent of the total stock in Germany and 18.4 per cent in Denmark. In 1992 it also accounted for 45 per cent of all new construction in Germany and 22 per cent in Denmark. The respective figures for the UK, France and the Netherlands were: 9 (6.2), 15 (10), 19 (8.3). See U. Pfeiffer and A. Dubel, *Private Rental Housing in the European Union*, report prepared for the Annual Meeting of the European Housing Ministers, Luxembourg, 1994, p. 10.

23 T. Woolley, 'Community Architecture – An assessment of the case for user participation in design', Paper presented at the *Housing Co-operatives Research Seminar*, Regent's College, London, November 1986.

24 B. Svetlichnyi, 'Sovetskim lyudyam – blagoustroennye zhilishcha', *Kommunist*, no. 6, April 1965.

25 A. Tinker, P. Dodd, P. McCafferty and S. Dougall, 'Co-operative Housing: Interim

Results of a DoE National Study', *Housing Review*, (36), no. 1, 1987; D. Clapham and K. Kintrea, 'Importing Housing Policy: Housing Co-operatives in Britain and Scandinavia', *Housing Studies*, (2), no. 3, 1987; Department of the Environment, *Tenants in the Lead*, HMSO, London, 1989.

26 Underwood, Ross and Legg, op. cit., p. 30.

27 There are 'at the minimum at least two and a half million known homeless persons in the European Communities', which is equivalent to about 7.5 per cent of the total population. However, this figure is based on a narrow definition of homelessness: those persons known to be without shelter or in receipt of public or voluntary/social accommodation in 1991 or 1992 (when the survey was carried out). See M. Daly, *Abandoned: Profile of Europe's homeless people. The second report of the European Observatory on Homelessness*, FEANTSA, Brussels, 1993, p. 3.

A further 65 million, according to another observer, are ill-housed, most of them from the most underprivileged and the poorest sections of Europe's population. See C. Ottolini, 'Social Europe: how and why', *The Role of Housing in the Building of a Social Europe*, Proceedings of the Conference held by Habitat International Coalition with the collaboration of the networks of the European Charter for the Right to Housing and Combating Exclusion and the co-operation of the Commission of the European Communities, Brussels, 1993, p. 115.

28 This is reflected in the size of the social housing stock in different countries: Belgium has only 25.7 units of social housing per 1,000 inhabitants, compared with 66.6 in France, 99.2 in the former West Germany, 104.5 in the UK and 136.5 in the Netherlands. (See R. Dury, 'Ensuring Housing Rights – for a Community Strategy', in *The Role of Housing in the Building of a Social Europe*, p. 120.)

Postscript

The co-operative is best understood as a social movement and itself part of a larger movement. In view of its long history it cannot be understood as a static form or idea, nor can co-operatives be divorced from the political and socio-economic environment in which they germinate. The pragmatism of English co-operators and the emergence of credit-oriented co-operatives in Germany in the nineteenth century and their implantation amongst nationalists in East and Central European countries before the First World War were conditioned by the circumstances of the time. The ideological nature of co-operatives in Russia prior to 1917, then when they re-emerged in 1924 and again in 1986, is obviously distinguishable from the co-operatives which evolved after the Second World War in Yugoslavia, Sweden and Denmark.

A deeply rooted premiss of the socialist model was that considerable economies were to be reaped from concentrating production in large-scale units. The theoretical foundation for this belief lay in a process which Marx foresaw would lead to a 'constantly diminishing number of the magnates of capital', eventuating in a situation where 'the entire social capital would be united, either in the hands of one single capitalist, or in those of one single corporation'.[1]

But it was not only Lenin who faithfully followed in this tradition.[2] The notion that economies of scale proceeded from mass production formed an integral part of Western conventional economic thinking. Following the Second World War and gathering pace in the 1960s and into the 1970s, 'Fordism', based on assembly-line technology and mass production for a mass society,[3] prevailed as the economic-technocratic paradigm. This model led to mergers between companies to form ever larger, more competitive units. According to Schumpeter it was necessary to accept that the large-scale establishment 'has come to be the most powerful engine of [economic] progress'.[4] This view was echoed by J. K. Galbraith, for whom it was a total fiction that technical change was the product of the matchless ingenuity of the small man forced by competition to better his neighbour.[5] Optimal plant size would be achieved through concentration so that, as a result of poor management, backward technologies and lack of capital, small firms would gradually wither away.

285

The antagonistic world systems of the Cold War also thought that the concentration of assets would eliminate unnecessary and wasteful duplication. It would also permit better command over inputs and outputs and thereby, through planning, allow them to exert greater control over the economic system. The two worlds of capitalism and socialism diverged in important ways but, in respect of organisation, they converged in their conviction that the growth in unit size was inevitable.[6] However, for a variety of reasons, the tendency in Soviet-type economies led to a level of concentration which was dysfunctional for both the economy and society.

In 1956, 13.6 per cent of employees in the manufacturing sector in Czechoslovakia worked in enterprises with less than 500 people. By 1988, the figure was 1.4 per cent. Over the same period the proportion of workers in firms employing over 2,500 people rose from 31.4 per cent to 55.8 per cent.[7] Throughout the EU, small firms account for 72 per cent of total non-farm employment and only about 12,300 businesses may be categorised as 'large', that is employing more than 500 people.[8] Thus, one of the features of the centralised planning system had been an extremely skewed size distribution of firms, in which small firms virtually ceased to exist.

Then, between 1975 and 1985 all the OECD countries underwent major industrial restructuring. The accompanying high levels of unemployment represented the jettisoning of the core tenet of the post-war political consensus in Western liberal democracies, namely that one of the primary tasks of government was to intervene in the economy in order to maintain full employment. The high levels of unemployment during the 1920s and 1930s had been a major contributory factor in the rise of fascism and in the attraction of Soviet communism for progressive, left-leaning European intellectuals. After the war the ideas of Marx and Keynes marched in time: unemployment was an evil and it was the task of governments to manage their national economies to ensure the maintenance of full employment. International organisations such as the IMF, World Bank and GATT were created in the 1940s to supervise governments in their fulfilment of this macro-economic objective.

Three decades later, it was evident that another radical paradigm shift had begun.[9] The unthinkable – unemployment (and at extremely high levels) – had become thinkable and acceptable. Corporatism – that institutionalised relationship between the state, trade unions and employers' organisations – had unceremoniously begun to be rejected by the, as it were, senior partner, central government, representing the universal interest (as opposed to the partial and sectional interests of trade unions and employers). The sanctification of market forces (the economy) and the famous denial of society was accompanied by the enhanced role now given to charity, so that the responsibility for providing welfare began to be transferred from state philanthropy to private philanthropy.[10]

Simultaneously, governments rediscovered the vitality of small enterprises, which were demonstrating remarkable resilience in this period of stressful economic turbulence, as the main providers of jobs. Greater general prosperity in Western societies had effected a change in consumer demand patterns; people were turning away from mass-produced goods to customised products and services. The flexible specialisation of small enterprises was admirably suited to the new consumerism and niche marketing.[11]

It was during this period that Gorbachev launched his policy of perestroika. In June 1990 the United Nations Industrial Development Organisation (UNIDO), in conjunction with various USSR government departments, convened in Moscow an 'Interregional Symposium on the Role of the Industrial Co-operative Movement in Economic and Industrial Development'. The background to the *aide-mémoire* that was circulated began by stating as a fact that 'In the USSR, the most widespread form of "ownership" of small businesses is the co-operative or collective form of ownership'. The purpose of the symposium was 'to provide a forum for the discussion of issues concerning the role of co-operatives'. It was 'anticipated that modalities and policy guidelines will emerge on adopting micro-economic methodologies for engendering decision-making based on market forces, rationalisation and competition'. The Symposium would identify ways in which international economic co-operation could enhance the role of co-operatives in the industrial development process.[12]

One of the practical purposes of co-operatives, especially in agriculture, is that they enable individual households to pool resources, particularly during the initial capital accumulation phase. Moreover, since they lack marketing, promotional and negotiating skills, the co-operative organisational form is *a fortiori* attractive in the former socialist countries (particularly to small-scale farmers). At the very least it may serve as a stepping stone towards capitalism in societies which have less experience of free markets and private ownership. This poses the question of the reasons for individuals and households deciding to remain in or withdrawing from co-operatives.[13] Subjective propensities play an important part in the choice made. However, outside ('objective') factors are of greater significance; capitalism has an inherent dislike of 'pooling' arrangements, for it reduces demand for capital equipment, accountants and financial advisors, lawyers and marketing specialists.[14] In the event, no stepping stone was required; capitalism preferred to erect a pontoon bridge from state to private ownership.

The merits of the Soviet system should not be wholly forgotten or rejected. But, while it did nourish human talents and offered certitudes and security for its citizens by guaranteeing work and wages and cheap housing and universal care, at the same time the structures which it constructed stifled individual initiative. At one level, individuals and families, assured of their life's necessities but almost totally forbidden from engaging in additional paid work, had an indifferent attitude towards work. At another level, heads of factories and organisations not only delayed for years the introduction of technical innovations, but left expensive, imported machinery to rust. It was Gorbachev, the Martin Luther of Russia, who, in calling for attention to be paid to 'the human factor', challenged the system from within and instigated the country's own Reformation.

Gorbachev recognised that some people aspired to a higher standard of living; but, in order for them to fulfil their ambitions, legal and bureaucratic obstacles would have to be removed. The non-state, co-operative property form was selected as the instrument through which individuals could enrich themselves; harnessing this energy would also help to maintain the Government's legitimacy with the population by allowing unmet consumer demand for goods and services to be satisfied.[15] At their conference in February 1990, the United Co-operatives of the Soviet Union passed a resolution to create a political party, 'The Party of Free Labour'.[16] This poignant name was indicative of the context within which the co-operative was evolving and of the various, sometimes divergent, interests of its membership, a very high proportion of whom had a higher education. There were differences on the legal form that co-operatives should assume, especially over the matter of whether members could draw profit from their capital investment as well as an income share based on their labour contribution, and whether a co-operative could employ non-members.

By the peak of the revolution in the Soviet Union and Eastern Europe in 1989–91, Western countries had been experimenting with legislation and institutional arrangements to help foster the small and medium-sized enterprise (SME) sector. Early on in the post-Soviet period, small and medium-sized enterprises came to be viewed as the vehicle for economic regeneration in the region.[17] But only a fraction of the myriad of companies that had been registered were in fact operating. Efforts had to be made to assist the rebirth of this sector; soon after the popular but nonetheless media-led euphoria had subsided, a disillusionment with market-based systems had manifested itself amongst large sections of the population, and this could lead to social unrest and political instability. Western civil servants recognised that their governments had a valuable idea to export to the former socialist countries; in their own countries they had themselves overseen a process of industrial and organisational restructuring similar to that which the Soviet-type economies were now embarking upon, as they dismantled their huge, centralised production units and transformed their monopoly-based systems into competitive, market economies.

Professional economists considered that the fundamental problem faced by the countries of Eastern Europe was that the majority of firms were based on a capital stock and technology that manufactured goods for which demand was limited; the transfer of state assets into private ownership would not, therefore, transform their value.[18] For economists, a robust entrepreneurial sector was of greater importance, and absolutely essential if new economic assets were to be generated. But, for that to happen, first of all, measures would have to be taken to remove legal and administrative obstacles to entrepreneurial activity, and, secondly, an institutional infrastructure conducive to the creation of a viable entrepreneurial sector would have to be established.

Politicians from both East and West, however, had a broader agenda than economists: privatisation and private property rights were of primary importance. They decided that it would be a good thing to create in the 'liberated East' institutions and procedures modelled on those found in the West. To this end they championed the transfer of assets into private ownership. Privatisation was the litmus test demonstrating that a country had recanted and returned to civilised behaviour, which included 'protection of private property, the free flow of trade, capital, investment and repatriation of profits'.[19]

The Secretary-General of the Conference on Security and Co-operation in Europe (the CSCE, predecessor of the OSCE) referred in his address in 1994 to a Seminar on SMEs in Bishkek to the 'standards enshrined in the Helsinki Final Act' (1975), which committed all participating states to 'human rights, democracy and the rule of law, economic liberty, social justice and environmental responsibility as well as the objective of developing market economies'.[20] These goals were related to SMEs by virtue of the association between 'the economic dimension' and a 'comprehensive concept of security'.[21] The representative of the European Commission at the Seminar referred to one of Mr Gorbachev's political neologisms, the 'human factor'. This linked into his exegesis of the CSCE's principles concerning human rights and freedoms, which 'constitute the very foundation of the market economy system, such as property rights and the liberty to contract'.[22]

In response to the demise of Soviet Marxism and the system which it supported in East and Central Europe, a new (intellectual) search has begun in the West for another alternative to capitalism; so far one outcome of the quest has been the notion of 'coupon socialism'.[23] The model claims to combine the market with a commitment to equality by devising a system in which all citizens would receive an equal number of coupons with which to buy ownership rights in companies. The coupons would be a separate form of currency, but one which could not be exchanged for ordinary money or transferred to other people. The model, which has its protagonists and opponents,[24] has been used in most East European countries and republics of the former Soviet Union as the principal means of privatising state-owned assets.

This political-economic development again mirrored a dual process occurring in West European societies: privatisation of publicly owned assets and management buy-outs, which throughout Europe reached feverish levels in 1988–89, as part of the economic restructuring process. In 1991 they still accounted for 55 per cent of all venture capital investments in the UK and 35 per cent in Europe.[25] They have become a principal form of privatisation in some of the republics of the former Soviet Union and countries in East and Central Europe. The problem for these countries is that many of the assets are grossly undervalued prior to privatisation.[26] The average size of such buy-outs between 1980 and 1992 (excluding the exceptional years, 1987–89) was £3.04 million. Since these are not such large sums, it is surprising that there are not more employee buy-outs. The explanation given for not involving all or most other employees is that it is difficult to involve large numbers of employees without prematurely disclosing the terms of the buy-out agreement. This not entirely satisfactory reason is, however, justified by the closed, aggressive and competitive economic system within which transactions concerning the future of companies and their employees are decided.

Nevertheless, employee share ownership plans (Esops) are a recognised device for involving the workforce in a buy-out. They enable employees to acquire a large shareholding stake in their company – whether public or private – without necessarily laying out personal capital.[27] The advantage of an Esop is that it not only raises cash for the buy-out, but also secures the commitment and participation of the workforce during an especially critical point in the company's existence.

Yet attitudes within financial institutions towards Esops (and by extension to co-operatives) reflect a blend of scepticism, cynicism, arrogance and paternalism. A mild expression of this outlook is found in the statement by a management and buy-out consultancy that: 'Managers are beginning to see the benefits of employees having a sense of ownership of the company'. On the other hand, trade unions remain sceptical, regarding these organisational and ownership innovations which increase the employees' stake in a company as a further instance of capitalist artifice. The negativity of their stance has been countered by the National Federation of Worker Co-operatives. Conscious of the need to project a more positive image of itself and of the importance of the Maastricht Treaty, it has recognised that ICOM should consider the merits of promoting forms of worker participation other than common ownership. However, the following statement by the chief executive of one Esop is a measure of the lack of workplace democracy and the distance that managements still have to travel: 'People feel that they are working for themselves, they can have an impact on the company and see a return on their investment by being *co-operative*'.[28] These developments are the diminishing seismic waves caused by industrial restructuring and the continuing restructuring of the financial services sector.

Industrial restructuring, management and employee buy-outs, and fragmentation[29] are embodied in an organisational form that has been revitalised in late capitalism, the small and medium-sized enterprise. The term 'SME' may be chosen because it appears to be value-neutral; it simply describes a phenomenon giving little mention to normative issues such as ownership and work relationships. The term 'co-operative' is, in contrast, value-loaded. In 1992 the Committee on the Development of Trade at the Economic Commission for Europe (ECE) produced a lengthy paper on SMEs. It dealt with the re-emergence of SMEs in developed market economies, their general characteristics, obstacles to their development, different government support programmes, examples of successful East–West joint ventures and SME development in Eastern Europe.[30] The document only once used the word 'co-operatives' and then as if *en passant*: 'a few more programmes which directly assist the financial health of SMEs . . . including . . . policies which assist in the creation of consortia and co-operatives to guarantee loans to small companies in Italy'.[31]

Thus it was that, with the formal dissolution of the Soviet Union on 26 December 1991, following Gorbachev's resignation on Christmas Day, the co-operative idea was put back into the politician's magician's box to be pulled out again as an acronym, the SME, which soon became better known than its full name. This entity has become the prime agent of a resurgent capitalism.

The raising of the curtain which Churchill pulled down in 1947 in Fulton finds the actors semi-frozen in their traditional and ideological attire. But they are being drawn together by the momentum of the same capitalistic process, one which sees the substitution of capital for labour[32] and higher productivity through greater competitiveness.

The Social Chapter in the Maastricht Treaty, the notion of the stakeholding society, and employee shareholding schemes have shifted the debate on property and participation on to a new jousting field. The political rhetoric of the major political parties in Europe cannot be too fanciful. It has to bear some relationship to reality, one with which, frequently, even politicians who consider themselves to be conversant are only just catching up. In the case of Brussels and the policies of national governments of the member states, flexible production and the need for flexible labour markets create novel opportunities for co-operative forms of labour organisation. At the time of this book's genesis, academics were speaking of a decisive moment in history having been reached, allowing totally new and much more democratic forms of organisation to be established, incorporating the informal sector into co-operative and other worker-controlled enterprises.[33] Conditions of flexible accumulation are seen as making worker and community control appear a feasible alternative to capitalism.[34] Reality may not have progressed so far as this; however, the direction of change is relatively clear.[35]

According to Samuel Brittan, citing the British Social Attitudes Survey (which he deems 'the most authoritative long-term snapshot of public opinion in the UK'), 'the British public remains hopelessly collectivist in its attitudes'.[36] His conclusion was grounded in the following. Firstly, despite the Conservative Government's rhetoric on the need to reduce public expenditure, it had done little more than stabilise the public expenditure ratio. Secondly, the Survey had found that a large majority of the population want to see public expenditure increase. Allowing for the fact that there might be some hypocrisy and self-deception, 'it is difficult to dismiss the fact that 60 per cent of the surveyed population favoured a policy of tax and spend against 5 per cent who supported a tax reduction', so that more could be spent on education, health and unemployment benefit. Most people believe that job sharing and a compulsory reduction in working hours should be used to reduce the level of unemployment. Finally, popular opinion in the UK would put greater controls on pay and working conditions than that envisaged by the Social Chapter in the Maastricht Treaty.

As already noted above, for co-operatives to succeed in a society, they must have the support of the public, the media and politicians.[37] The perennial dilemmas facing co-operatives, such as the distribution of surpluses, the creation of reserves, establishing a balance between internal and external financing, and raising long-term finance without jeopardising the exercise of control by their members, are no longer exclusively their problems. But, while SMEs are also familiar with these difficulties, co-operatives are further disadvantaged by a social climate which is generally unsympathetic to them

For instance, the dominant ideology in the USA, as in pre-Gorbachevian

USSR, is profoundly inimical to co-operatives. Having observed the success of co-operation and networking amongst small firms in Italy and Denmark, legislators from Oregon concluded that the 'every-man-for-himself ethic in the private sector has inhibited emergence of co-operative strategies'.[38] In the North American vision of the world, the norm is free enterprise and competition, and the pre-programmed goal of all actors and agencies is to maintain that norm and to return to it whenever there is a deviation from it. Even the notion of networking – which the American legislators understood as 'co-operative strategies' – appears as a suspect collectivist implant. It is unlikely that they fully understood the meaning and significance of co-operatives in Italy and Denmark.

The public (Oregon) purse was used in order to facilitate the return to normality and a world in which individuals, firms, cities, regions and countries compete: a world in which, moreover, competition is a good thing and the driving motor of invention; one in which competition manifests itself in the interplay between supply and demand in the marketplace which determines prices and profits.

On the other hand, social economics rejects the market as the final arbiter on decisions affecting society and its constituent communities and social and economic networks. The Catholic Economic Association, which was set up during the Second World War and later changed its name to the Association for Social Economics, has contributed, as have neo-Marxists, to a solidaristic school of thought.[39] The 'holistic, enriched economic discourse'[40] towards which these organisations have been described as tending has as an objective the search for novel conceptualisations of wealth creation in order to formulate alternative perspectives on economic progress, the measurement of progress and the apportioning of value to family and community activity and social cohesion. Voluntary associations do not produce private wealth, but create common wealth. The methodological tools available for this task now include evaluation and the social audit, which build upon welfare economics and cost-benefit analysis. Advances in qualitative methods of conducting research reflect the increased attention being devoted to trying to assess quality and value when, as in the case of voluntary organisations (the non-profit sector), activities are not driven by a profit motive.

Social economics is seeking alternative ways of understanding wealth and value creation in society. Even if there is no need to reject sociometric and econometric methods, traditional methods of measuring economic performance are being viewed with ever greater scepticism.[41] Globalisation is increasing the margin of error in national statistics and the rapidity of technological change makes it difficult to compare products over time.[42] This problem is compounded by the fact that conventional statistics were collected for tracing the production of physical goods, whereas today a growing proportion of output consists of 'ideas', for instance computer software. Attempts to refine our arithmetisation of the world in order to understand its processes better are contributing less than we expect (or pay for) to the *summum bonum* of society.

It would be impossible to chart the moment when the current shift from 'quantity' to 'quality' began. Brezhnev sanctioned the shift at the 1976 Communist Party Congress when he declared that the Soviet Union had moved from a quantitative stage of its development to a qualitative stage. In practical terms this was humbug, for on various indices living standards in the country remained low. But in Marxist-Hegelian philosophical terms it was more meaningful; a qualitative shift was taking place in the world led by technological change. The American sociologist, Daniel Bell, writing in 1973, had also identified that a qualitative change was taking place and that the United States was now a 'post-industrial society'.[43]

The word 'quality' was scarcely raised in the UK public services sector in the 1980s.[44] But, as in the Soviet Union, European central and local governments began to move away from focusing on quantitative outputs and head counts towards paying greater attention to the quality of products and services. An important underlying cause of the shift was the increasing pressure on central and local government budgets; since the quantity of goods and services could not be increased – because of budgetary restrictions or because there was already a surfeit in some cases – then the focus had to be on quality. This would be achieved through greater economy, efficiency and effectiveness (and, in some cases, greater equity). Explanations for the change in emphasis, couched in terms of the need to listen more attentively to 'consumers' and to raise the satisfaction level of 'service deliverers' (employees), are of secondary importance.

Economic activities are frequently divided into two categories: production and reproduction. As the proportion of activities falling into the second category has expanded, it was to be expected that the type of rationality which is imposed on the former would attempt to spread triffid-like to encompass the latter. Education, health care and social services – the so-called 'caring professions' have come to be subject to the same canons of quantitative assessment. This domain of social life is one of the last redoubts for defending values which combine elements found in both pre-industrial and modern cultures. In tone these values reflect the central premises of the co-operative movement: improving the quality of life, promoting non-exploitative relations, sharing responsibilities and rewards rather than expanding personal empires, improving working conditions, organising work to meet the needs of other members in a flexible fashion, and enjoying equal rights in decision making.

The desire by the governments in Europe and North America to reduce public expenditure – and using the voluntary sector as a means of doing so – inadvertently encourages the growth of co-operatives. Sweden provides a good example of this development.

Beginning in the late 1980s the Swedish state began to withdraw from directly providing care for the elderly and for pre-school children. In most cases this function was taken over by co-operatives, the majority of which were started by the parents as parent co-operatives. The remainder were set up by former staff (workers' co-operatives) and a few by religious groups. Research conducted into them raised interesting questions about different types of rationality.[45]

In view of the difficulties of measuring and evaluating efficiency within the public and voluntary sectors, rather than trying to set quantitative goals so that efficiency can be measured, the performance of these non-market domains might better be evaluated by examining the character, design and quality of the services and the long-term effect which they have on those delivering, receiving or otherwise associated with the service. As in the case of the co-operative Day Care Centres, the language of economics often seems inadequate for designing objectives. Good relations within the organisation, described in metaphoric terms of a 'family', were far more important than had been anticipated. The metaphor of the family implies a set of values which rest on reciprocity and understanding and an 'expressive rationality' that reflects an individual's need to make the world meaningful.[46]

Even those who express cynicism about the mutual movement[47] nonetheless believe that 'there is little doubt that mutuality is worth preserving', on the rather vague grounds that 'Something has to act as a bulwark against the banks and it is obviously a good thing to have some form of alternative to the joint stock company'. This view from within conventional (and conservative) financial circles is that co-operatives (mutuals), like the Church of England, are an embodiment of tradition, and therefore somehow *ipso facto* virtuous, and an alternative, and that they provide society with an insurance policy against a systemic malaise.[48]

Over a century ago, in 1888, George Holyoake quoted remarks made to him by the then Prince of Wales about 'The History of Co-operation in England' of which he was the author:

> The Prince has read with the greatest interest the details of the working of

the [co-operative] society with which you have supplied him, and he is anxious to express the extreme gratification which he experiences in finding that so large a body of the working men of this country are united in a determination to benefit themselves, both morally and physically, by endeavouring to carry out a scheme which his Royal Highness conceives is admirably adapted to raise the standard of their knowledge and intelligence, and to increase their welfare and happiness.[49]

Holyoake continued his introductory remarks by emphasising the encouragement given in the previous century by eminent personages ('prelates, peers and gentlemen') to co-operators,[50] who 'help themselves by Commercial and Industrial Associations, neither making war on Capitalists, nor supplicating aid from the State'.

One hundred years after the then Prince of Wales had paid his tribute to the principle of self-help found in co-operatives and friendly societies, another heir to the throne, through initiatives such as The Prince's Trust, has praised the actions of those who have tried to overcome the adverse circumstances in which they find themselves – being unskilled and/or unemployed – through voluntary schemes, such as using private and public investment to set up housing co-operatives and thereby help to revive run-down areas.

Dowager philanthropy has combined with the corporate sector and government and thousands of volunteers to stimulate self-help groups and other small formal organisations and informal groups that impart to civil society a vitality while remaining largely outside the market and thus untouched by market forces. Charitable and community work supported by the corporate sector is no longer confined to a handful of companies renowned for their philanthropy. The corporate sector has in recent years become more conscious of the need to demonstrate greater awareness of ethical issues involved in their business activities. This has led them to accept one of the guiding principles of the co-operative movement, namely an acknowledgement that they have social responsibilities to the community in which they are located which go beyond the pursuit of their functional economic objectives.

'Business in the Community', another initiative like the Prince's Trust, was established in 1982 in the wake of the inner city riots in England. In the self-help tradition BITC focuses on building relationships between business and local groups and providing specialist assistance to them through the secondment of employees from the corporate sector rather than through donating money. It also targets education and training, for this raises the quality of the workforce from which the benefactor draws its employees and makes the community more prosperous.[51] The benefactor is thus a beneficiary and a rediscoverer of the advantages of nineteenth-century so-called 'five per cent' philanthropy. Development Trusts,[52] also established in the late 1980s in the UK as independent, not-for-profit organisations, bring together the financial and other resources from the public, private and voluntary sectors to assist in the physical, social and spiritual renewal of an area.[53]

As a movement, co-operatives are linked to abstract social categorisations and realities such as the voluntary sector, charities, self-help, the informal (or shadow) economy and the social economy. The Community Enterprise Movement is an example of a self-help group which would in spirit fall within the embrace of the co-operative sector.[54] Consisting of trading companies, set up, owned and controlled by a local community (and thus definable as Community Co-operatives), it reinvests any profits locally to create more jobs or to provide additional services or to sponsor social welfare schemes. Community Co-operatives are created in areas of high unemployment, poor service provision and fragile economies, and their strength is alleged to lie in their ability to harness the commitment and talents of local residents, who take responsibility for their own community.

These developments of the 1980s and 1990s are a continuation and refinement of the community action and community development groups which proliferated in the 1960s. Over the past three decades there has been a multitude of accounts of community care groups and informal good-neighbour schemes formed to supplement statutory welfare services. Their existence complemented the ascendancy of a belief in the need to intensify (improve) democracy by encouraging and enabling the public to participate more fully in social and political affairs. They also complemented two other contemporary contradictory processes. On the one hand, during the 1960s and 1970s there was a widespread discussion of alternative communities, lifestyles and modes of economic organisation. On the other hand, these decades witnessed the growth in central and local government of planning and social welfare bureaucracies and, concomitantly, of jobs for the middle class.

This expansion in both the numbers and types of voluntary organisation was accompanied by increasing support for them from local and central government.[55] Although income from government has been growing over the past twenty years, especially through the 'contracting out of services', donations by individuals remain the principal source of funding for the voluntary sector.[56] The importance of the sector justified the setting up a government committee to investigate it. The result was the publication in 1978 of the Wolfenden Report.[57] In 1993 the sector was the subject of another thorough review.[58] Estimates of the number of active voluntary organisations in the UK range from 170,000 to 1.3 million. On a narrower definition, there are around 220,000. The largest sector covers social care, accounting for 37 per cent of all activity in the sector, followed by accommodation (19 per cent).[59] The total income of the voluntary sector rose from £12.3 billion in 1990 to £15.0 billion in 1995.[60] Registered charities in the UK now employ 620,000 paid workers, while the number volunteering has been estimated at 23 million people, although a survey by the Charity Commission found that four million adults had given time to charities in the previous month.[61] The accuracy of the estimates of the numbers involved, which vary depending on definitions of voluntary and charity, is less important than the fact that volunteering exists on such a large scale.

Attention has to be drawn to one important feature of the co-operative movement, namely that the prime movers within it have invariably been drawn from the middle class, which in the nineteenth century would have included tradesmen and artisans, the 'aristocracy of labour'. The same applies to the Victorian notion of self-help, with its theme of individual enterprise, initiative and self-advancement through education and self-discipline.[62]

Organisations which bear the banner inscribed with the 'self help ethic' are not, in the main, agencies of salvation for the poor and excluded. They have been promoted by and for those who possess a mind-set which is conducive to the dual idea of self-help and mutuality. Beveridge regarded mutual aid as springing from 'a sense of one's own need for security against misfortune and, realising that, since one's fellows have the same need, by undertaking to help one another all may help themselves'.[63] Mutuality can be seen as consisting of three components: being in need, helping oneself and helping others. The nineteenth-century Friendly Society and Building Society in Britain or the Raiffeisen society in Central and Eastern Europe appealed to the better-off members of the working class (as Marx and Engels and Proudhon observed and as Lenin doctrinally accepted) and to the middle class. According to the managing director of the Co-operative Bank, speaking in 1997, the Bank's growth in earnings could be attributed in part to the Bank having gone back to its roots: that is to say, it had attracted more members of the middle class, 'who were after all the pioneers of the co-operative movement'.[64]

Today, in the majority of cases the initiating agents in self-help groups are drawn from government and the private sector (public and private philanthropy); the target groups are the unemployed, women, young people, ethnic minorities and disabled people. Individuals falling into these marginalised or socially excluded categories are rarely themselves the instigators of self-help projects. Households inhabiting a dependency culture[65] cannot be rescued by charity and philanthropy; the vehicle for betterment is through a revived mutual aid movement, found in Friendly Societies, community development and co-operatives.[66]

Neither credit unions[67] nor 'local exchange and trading systems' (LETS), which are vehicles for allowing individuals from different income groups to work together to their mutual interest, emerge from those who are outside the labour market and experiencing a variety of deprivations: self-help is taken to them.[68] In any event, LETS are small in terms both of membership[69] and economic activity[70] and, despite considerable publicity, with about 35,000 members[71] they hardly constitute mass movements. However, like other 'alternatives', for example, medicine, organic food, health food shops and Friends of the Earth, they represent a social movement which is uneasy about many aspects of modern society. Moreover, these local systems of production, multilateral exchange and consumption, based on a local currency that is independent of, but related to, the national currency, are community- rather than commercially-oriented trading networks, and represent an aspect of the co-operative phenomenon.[72]

Local currencies can shape and define value in the course of negotiating a transaction between a buyer and seller; valuing work in terms of time can enable the specific conditions under which it is undertaken to be taken into account. The closed nature of the system raises problems, notably the fact that there has to be interchange with the wider economy, since most households need to pay rent or mortgages. But even the acquisition of highly technical goods such as computers and videos does not demand the incorporation of all households into the formal economic system; there are sufficient 'redundant' items in circulation for them to be used within LETS.

The LETS phenomenon has a tint of 'green', of conservation and recycling of bottles and other detritus, and the resale and re-use of 'nearly new' clothes and other products. A reflective regard for the quality of life and a philosophical interest in the moral economy are distinguishing traits of a LETS membership. As in the co-operative movement, LETS and the moral economy are reactions to impersonality and a desire to found relations on trust.[73]

The basic principles of co-operation find reflection in the idea of 'communitarianism'.[74] Its underlying premiss is that individuals in contemporary Western society have too much freedom and resent responsibility, commitment and obligation. The communitarians place personal responsibility to the community at the core of their theory. They reject economic explanations for crime, deviance and bad behaviour generally, preferring to attribute the rise in crime to the collapse of the family. Communitarianism builds upon a critique, emerging at the beginning of the

1980s, of 'the central features of the modern economic order and more especially its individualism, its acquisitiveness and its elevation of the values of the market to a central social place'.[75] According to this view we have come to inhabit a world in which trust is absent, the only loyalty known is to oneself, and the primary goals motivating action are self-enhancement and self-realisation.

The most knowledgeable defenders of liberal values, though sympathetic to communitarianism's concern to prevent further disruption of local communities, consider that the 'relatively old idea of workplace democracy *would require the creation of radically new economic institutions*'[76] (my italics). This is, of course, quite true, and one reason why the critique of communitarianism, co-operatives and collectivism generally by liberals is so trenchant.

The counter-assault on liberalism is directed against its invasion of all spheres of social life, with its demand that education, medicine, public broadcasting and national and local governance should be open to the forces and vagaries of the competitive marketplace. The re-ascendancy of the contract culture, echoing Bentham's nineteenth-century espousal of utilitarianism, can withstand the factional attack from what appears to be a romantic, conservative communitarianism. The latter has much in common with the nineteenth-century reaction, epitomised in France by Louis de Bonald (1754–1840) and Joseph de Maistre (1754–1821), to the Enlightenment, the 'Philosophes' and both the French (political) revolution and British (industrial) revolution.[77] Co-operators would broadly agree with many of the charges brought by communitarians against this culture of Narcissus.[78]

In 1995, the International Co-operative Alliance marked the centenary of its existence. Since its foundation there have been political and economic revolutions; societies across the world have passed through successive ideological phases and experienced radical restructuring. For 140 years Marx and Mill[79] were locked in struggle. In the late 1980s the political system associated with Marx went into accelerated decline. The eventual routing of the political heirs to Marx, symbolised in the demolition of the Berlin Wall, passed on to the International Co-operative Alliance the baton of opposition to the heirs of John Stuart Mill.

Although during this period of time it has survived enormous challenges and surmounted the tensions which existed between the co-operative movements in Germany and the Soviet Union during the inter-war period, and then succeeded in keeping the embers of co-operation alive in Soviet-dominated Eastern Europe after 1945, the ICA receives as little attention as do co-operatives in their individual national contexts.

The co-operative, as originally conceived in the articles of the Rochdale pioneers and then restated by the ICA, is an ideal type, which is opposite to Weber's ideal-typical 'bureaucracy'. Just as the condition of modernism could be measured by the extent to which organisations deviated from the ideal-type bureaucracy, the archetypal organisational form of modernism, so the condition of late capitalism (postmodernity) can be measured in terms of deviations from the ideal-typical co-operative. The co-operative movement, which in many ways conceptually embraces the voluntary sector, is appropriate to changing social relations between people and their changing expectations about the workplace, authority and hierarchy.

The experiment with co-operatives in Russia from 1987 to 1991 was almost as shortlived as the experiment with workers' control in the heady days of the Revolution in 1917 and the period of War Communism. The earlier attempt at a radical form of democracy was terminated with the suppression of the Kronstadt uprising, which had demanded an end to the communists' monopoly of power and more freedom for workers and peasants, and the introduction of the New Economic Policy in 1921. The timid word co-operative is ultimately a mask for 'workplace democracy'[80] and therefore still regarded as a challenge to the established order. Throughout Europe, most visibly in the UK and Russia, and with exceptions such as Sweden, Italy and Spain, the word 'co-operative' has been defined as a *vocabulum non gratum*.

Boris Yeltsin's triumph over Gorbachev and then over his own parliamentary opposition was also a victory for 'economic liberalism' and for that faction within the co-operative movement which had joined it in order to realise entrepreneurial aspirations. It was also a victory for global capitalism and a setback for the co-operative movement.

Notes

1   K. Marx, *Capital*, translated by E. Untermann, vol. 1, Kerr, Chicago, 1912, p. 836.
2   On the other hand, Lenin had also deduced that small-scale production could be found in all capitalist societies and was responsible for the constant reproduction of a broad stratum of small proprietors (the petite bourgeoisie). See V. Lenin, *The Development of Capitalism in Russia*, St Petersburg, 1899.
3   The notion of 'mass society' described the way in which contemporary society was viewed in the 1950s and 1960s. One justifiably much-cited book on the subject is: W. Kornhauser, *The Politics of Mass Society*, The Free Press, New York, 1959.
4   J. Schumpeter, *Capitalism, Socialism and Democracy*, (1st edition 1943) 5th edition, 1952, Unwin University Books, London, p. 106.
5   J. K. Galbraith, *American Capitalism: The Concept of Countervailing Power*, Hamish

Hamilton, London, 1956.

6   J. K. Galbraith, *The New Industrial State*, Hamish Hamilton, London, 1967.

7   The statistics are cited by D. Audretsch, 'The Role of Small Business in Restructuring Eastern Europe', paper presented at the Fifth Workshop for Research in Entrepreneurship, Växjö, Sweden, 28 November 1991, p. 6.

8   'A Big Role for Small Firms', *Financial Times*, 11 December 1990, p. 12. In 1986, the figures for the respective shares of manufacturing employment accounted for by firms with fewer than 500 employees were 38.9 per cent in the UK and 57.9 per cent in the Federal Republic of Germany (Audretsch, op. cit., p. 7).

9   The defining moments were the Arab–Israeli war and oil price rise in 1973 and then the ideological alliance between Margaret Thatcher and Ronald Reagan after their election successes in 1979 and 1980.

10   William Beveridge said of philanthropy that 'it springs from . . . the feeling which makes men who are materially comfortable, mentally uncomfortable so long as their neighbours are materially uncomfortable: to have a social conscience is to be unwilling to make a separate peace with the giant social evils of Want, Disease, Squalor, Ignorance, Idleness, escaping into personal prosperity oneself, while leaving one's fellows in their clutches.' W. Beveridge, *Voluntary Action: A Report on Methods of Social Advance*, George Allen and Unwin, London, 1948. I am grateful to Barry Knight for providing me with this quotation from Beveridge.

11   W. Sengenberger, *The Re-emergence of Small Enterprises*, International Institute for Labour Studies, Geneva, 1990.

12   Leading Soviet government officials and senior academics gave papers on: 'The Co-operative Movement in the USSR and the Strategy of Perestroika' (L. Abalkin); 'Co-operatives and the State: Problems and Prospects' (Y. Tikhonov); 'Socialism and Co-operation' (V. Nikilorov). UNIDO consultants spoke on 'Soviet Co-operatives: A Force for Major Economic Development'; and 'Co-operative Banks in the Soviet Union'.

13   These questions were investigated in a case study of two co-operatives in Hungary, 1991–93. The research examined the social characteristics of individuals making these opposed choices, including their social status, education, social networks and cultural background. See Katalin Kovacs, 'The Slow Transition Process of Hungarian Agriculture. The Case of Two Organisations', Budapest Department of the Centre for Regional Studies, Hungarian Academy of Sciences, 1994.

14   Ironically, these professions, although adopting formal company status and frequently describing themselves as 'Associates', function as co-operatives.

15   Gorbachev also directly advocated greater income differentials as part of a new incentive structure. This was to be accompanied by a much more progressive income tax: at the time income tax stood at a maximum of 13 per cent.

16   *Kommersant*, no. 5. 1990, p. 5.

17   SMEs are generally defined as firms employing less than 500 people.

18   Audretsch, op. cit., pp. 17–19.

19   The statement was made at a meeting of the CSCE in Bonn in 1990 and cited by W. Hoynck, 'Address by the Secretary General', at the seminar 'Promoting the Creation of Small and Medium-Sized Enterprises', Bishkek, Kyrgyzstan, 23–25 February 1994.

20   Ibid.

21   Ibid.

22   Statement of a Representative of the European Commission in the Plenary Session, 'Human Factors in the Economic Transition Process', CSCE Economic Forum, 'Promoting the Creation of Small and Medium-sized Enterprises', 1994.

23   J. Roemer, *A Future for Socialism*, Verso, London, 1994.

24   For instance, see the essays in: E. Olin Wright, *Equal Shares. Making Market Socialism Work*, Verso, London, 1996.

25   C. Bachelor, 'Proving their worth', *Financial Times Survey on Management Buy-outs*, 3 December 1992, p. I. Management buy-out is defined as: The purchase of a business by its existing management with the help of financial backers. The managers put up a relatively small amount of the total finance but usually gain a disproportionately large share of the equity. Ibid., p. II.

26   This was the case of the management buy-out of the (British) National Freight Corporation, where several of the managers became millionaires soon after privatisation. In 1992 the total value of deals was £4.2 billion. The management buy-out is now regarded as a way in which to restructure companies.

27   The scheme works in the following way. A company sets up an employee benefit trust (EBT) to acquire some of its shares. The trust buys shares from an existing shareholder using proceeds from a loan guaranteed by the company. Repayments are tax-efficient since payments from the company to the EBT are treated as payments to employees, while the trust uses the funds to repay the principal of the loan as well as meet the interest charges. Shares are then distributed through an Inland Revenue-approved profit sharing trust.

28   H. Thomas, 'Building up the team spirit', in *Financial Times Survey on Management Buyouts*, op. cit., p. VIII.

29   Large firms can choose to downscale through three fragmentation strategies. They can decentralise, in which case large plants are broken up into smaller units or new subsidiaries are created, with no change in ownership. Secondly, they can devolve; this occurs when large firms cease to own units directly, but through franchising and licensing retain a revenue connection. Finally, they might disintegrate. In this instance the large unit fragments into separate units of ownership, although the large firm retains ultimate control through its market influence or contractual power.

30   UN Economic Commission for Europe, *Small and Medium-Sized Enterprises in the ECE Region*, GE. 92-32210/3294c, November 1992.

31   Ibid., p. 11.

32   In one empirical study of eight cases in the UK, the commonality was that 'there had been substantial technical change over the last few years with considerable substitution of capital for labour'. R. Penn and B. Wigzell, 'The Attitudes and Responses of Trades Unions to Technical Change: A Case Study of Maintenance Workers in the North West of England', *Journal of Interdisciplinary Economics*, vol. 2, no. 1, 1987. This process has not abated over the last decade.

33   M. Piore and C. Sabel, *The Second Industrial Divide*, Basic Books, New York, 1984.

34   D. Harvey, 'Flexible Accumulation through Urbanisation: Reflections on "Post-Modernism" in the American City', paper presented at the Sixth Urban Change and Conflict Conference, University of Kent, Canterbury, 20–23 September 1987.

35   One example of this development is the FI Group, a provider of IT services. Between 1962, when it was founded, it has grown from 100 women working at home to 750 salaried staff and an equal number of freelancers in 1998. It is collectively owned: half the shares are held by employees. Democracy and equality, decentralisation and delegation and flexible working hours are distinguishing features in the company's culture.

36   S. Brittan, 'Better than you deserve', *Financial Times*, 3 May 1997.

37   'To conclude, SMEs play an important role in virtually all sectors of developed market economies. These firms do much to maintain dynamism through their flexibility and

innovation. However, it is not the size of a firm which makes it viable. What does create conditions favouring the success of a small- and medium-sized firm is the institutional framework in which it is placed'. UN Economic Commission for Europe, op. cit., p. 16.

38   'European economic development ideas take root in Oregon', *TransAtlantic Perspective*, The German Marshall Fund of the United States, no. 24, Autumn 1991, pp. 8–9.

39   The Association publishes its own journal, as do other organisations concerned with social economics, such as the (American) Association of Evolutionary Economists, the European Association of Evolutionary Political Economy and the (American) Society for the Advancement of Socio-Economics. To these organisations has to be added the (British) School for Moral Entrepreneurs, which was launched in 1997 by Michael Young as an agency to revitalise Britain's moral economy.

40   M. Lutz, 'Living Economics in Perspective', in P. Ekins and M. Max-Neef (eds), *Real Life Economics. Understanding Wealth Creation*, Routledge, London, 1992, p.119.

41   'The unmeasurable lightness of being', *The Economist*, 23 November 1996, p. 121. A report to the USA Senate Finance Committee on the consumer-price index (CPI) was (at the time of writing) expected to conclude that the CPI had overstated annual inflation in recent years by 1–2 percentage points – which implies that the real growth in GDP had also been understated. This would also mean that, because welfare benefits and government pensions would have been over-indexed, the budget deficit would be higher. (I am grateful to Chris Abbess in the Department of Mathematics and Statistics at Middlesex University for drawing my attention to this article.)

42   The World Bank has estimated that the cost of a transatlantic telephone call, which currently costs 1.5 per cent of what it did in 1938, will have fallen by another two-thirds to 3 cents a minute by the year 2010. The same source notes that the cost of a single transistor, which in the mid-1960s was about $US 70, is now less than one millionth of a cent. See Ingrid Scheithauer, 'Technology on the Edge of the Information Society', paper presented at the Salzburg Seminar in American Studies, 4 April 1998.

43   D. Bell, *The Coming of Post-Industrial Society. A Venture in Social Forecasting*, Heinemann, London, 1973.

44   L. Gasker, 'Can Quality be Measured?', *Going Local*, The Decentralisation Research and Information Centre, School for Advance Urban Studies, University of Bristol, No. 15, April 1990.

45   L. Westerberg, *Social service i kooperative regi – hot eller möjlighet for kvinnligt foretagande* (Social Services in Co-operatives – Threat or Opportunity for Enterprises run by Women), School of Business, Stockholm University, Research Report 1996:1. (The information cited here is from L. Westerberg, 'Social Services in Co-operatives – Women in Leadership', paper submitted to The International Society for Third Sector Research, Mexico City, 18–21 July 1996.)

46   The study concluded that: 'When women talk about the co-operative as a family, it is in terms of the ethics of responsibility in that they care for each other and act as friends instead of employers and employees and their concern for their work does not end at a specific hour of the day'. See Westerberg, 'Social Services in Co-operatives'.

47   'Like the established Church [of England], the mutual movement paddled along . . . largely protected from the harsh realities of commercial life. . . . And like the church is being dragged kicking and screaming into the late twentieth century' ('Comment', *Independent*, 11 September 1997, p. 17).

48   Following an unsuccessful attempt by a stock exchange speculator to take over the mutually owned Co-operative Wholesale Society (CWS) in 1997, the mutual movement, consisting of building societies, mutual insurers, friendly societies and co-operatives in

Britain, began to lobby the Government to offer them greater protection against market marauders. The failed take-over attempt, the conversion of so many mutuals to public companies, the resilience shown by other large mutuals in retaining their status against the pressure of this tide, might herald the creation of a formal alliance amongst mutuals to promote the benefits of mutuality over public companies.

49 G. J. Holyoake, *Self-Help a Hundred Years Ago*, Swan Sonnenschein & Co., London, 1888, p. iv.

50 Holyoake cited the Mongewell Shop, devised by the Bishop of Durham in 1795, which 'may be regarded as the mustard seed whence has sprung that vast network of Distributive Stores which now overspread Great Britain, constituting a self-helping movement which has grown into prominence during Her Majesty's reign, the like of which has arisen in no other nation on the earth' (ibid., p. v).

His book documented examples of such activity at the end of the eighteenth century, beginning with the establishment in 1793 of a Friendly Society at Castle Eden in Durham. By 1796 it had 200 members and a board of trustees consisting of the lord of the manor, the clergy and justices of the peace of the parish. The benefits provided by the society were recorded as: payments to men 'in sickness, lameness or infirmity'; the cost of a surgeon and apothecary to attend them; an annuity in old age; and a death benefit. Ibid., pp. 37–43.

51 R. Trapp, 'A decade of building communal bridges', *Independent*, 4 July 1992.

52 Department of the Environment, *Creating Development Trusts: Good Practice in Urban Regeneration*, HMSO, London, 1988.

53 They also engage in property developments. For example, the Coin Street project adjacent to Waterloo Station on the South Bank of London emerged out of a confrontation between local residents and planners who had intended redeveloping the small area as part of an urban renewal project. The outcome was the formation of a co-operative.

54 Community Business Scotland, *Self-Help Communities*, West Lothian, Scotland, no date (circa 1988); N. Hurley, *Community Enterprise in Scotland: A Report to the Scottish Office*, CENTRIS, Newcastle-on-Tyne, 1990.

55 P. Wilmers, 'Planning, Self-Help and Mutual Aid', *The Planner*, vol. 67, no. 3, May 1981, p. 59. In 1993–94, central government funding of the sector amounted to £3.56 billion (1.3 per cent of total government expenditure). However, 80 per cent of that sum was payments to housing associations. See *Meeting the Challenge of Change: Voluntary Action into the 21st Century*, The Report of the Commission on the Future of the Voluntary Sector, NCVO, London, 1996, p. 29.

56 Ibid.

57 Report of the Wolfenden Committee, *The Future of Voluntary Organisations*, Croom Helm, London, 1978.

58 B. Knight, *Voluntary Action: The CENTRIS Report*, Home Office, London, 1993.

59 *Meeting the Challenge of Change*, op. cit., p. 27.

60 Funding is, however, concentrated in a relatively small number of charities: less than 19 per cent of charities account for over 90 per cent of the gross income. Cited in: *Meeting the Challenge of Change*, p. 29.

61 Ibid., p. 31. The figure cited in the Wolfenden Report for 1975 was about 5 million.

62 The thread of self-help, with which the voluntary sector is associated, has its roots in two different traditions, one of which is: S. Smiles, *Self-Help*, John Murray, London, 1859. For a good discussion of Herbert Spencer, the social thinker who coined the phrase 'survival of the fittest' and was a zealous exponent of social Darwinism, see D. Wiltshire, *The Social and Political Thought of Herbert Spencer*, OUP, Oxford, 1978.

The tradition which derives from Smiles and Spencer is diametrically opposed by Kropotkin, who argued that the dominant factor in evolution was voluntary co-operation, not competition. (See P. Kropotkin, *Mutual Aid. A Factor of Evolution*, Heinemann, London, 1902.) He did not deny that in nature a struggle for existence does take place, but he thought that in the evolution of higher animals mutual aid was more important. (See G. Woodcock, *Anarchy or Chaos*, Freedom Press, London, 1944, pp. 46–52.)

63　W. Beveridge, *Voluntary Action: A Report on Methods of Social Advance*, George Allen and Unwin, London, 1948. Again I am grateful to Barry Knight for the quotation.

64　In response to criticism that the Bank's recent success was a result of its having moved away from its original customer base, he declared that 'It would be foolish to think that [the co-operative pioneers] were men of the soil or hewers of rock'. C. Godsmark, 'Co-op Bank executive calls for review at CWS', *Independent*, 11 September 1997.

65　Most of the attributes of the dependency culture were described and analysed by Oscar Lewis. See his classic essay: 'The Culture of Poverty', *Scientific American*, October 1966, vol. 215, no.4.

66　E. Brass and S. Poklewski Koziell, *Gathering Force: DIY Culture – Radical Action for Those Tired of Waiting*, The Big Issue, London 1997.

67　In the UK credit unions grew in number from 117 in 1987 to 547 in 1996, with the membership doubling from 88,000 in 1992 to 161,500 in 1995. In Ireland one-quarter of the population belongs to a credit union. See B. Rogaly, 'Giving credit where it's due', *Guardian*, 29 January 1997.

68　On the potential of LETS to assist informal economic development, see Colin Williams, 'Informal sector solutions to unemployment and social exclusion: an evaluation of local exchange trading systems', in H. S. Lloyd and I. Cundell (eds), *Tackling Unemployment and Social Exclusion: Problems for Regions, Solutions for People*, Regional Studies Association, London, 1994.

69　J. Croall, *LETS Act Locally: The Growth of Local Exchange Trading Systems*, Calouste Gulbenkian Foundation, London, 1997.

70　In 1993 in the UK the largest LETS group had 333 members, while the average number of members was 70. From P. Lang, *Lets Work*, Grover Books, Bristol, 1994 (cited by R. Lee, 'Moral money? Making local economic geographies: LETS in Kent, south-east England', AAG Conference, March 1995).

71　S. Royal, 'A fair share of optimism', *Guardian*, 19 November 1997.

72　Lee, op. cit.

73　On the subject of 'trust' see F. Fukuyama, *Trust: The Social Virtues and the Creation of Prosperity*, Free Press, New York, 1995.

74　A. Etzioni, *The Spirit of Community: Rights, Responsibilities and the Communitarian Agenda*, Fontana, London, 1995 (first published in 1993); A. Etzioni, *The New Golden Rule: Community and Morality in a Democratic Society*, Profile Books, London, 1997; D. Bell, *Communitarianism and its Critics*, OUP, Oxford, 1993.

75　A. MacIntyre, *After Virtue*, Duckworth & Co. , London, 1981, p. 255.

76　A. Gutman, 'Communitarian Critics of Liberalism', *Philosophy and Public Affairs*, vol. 14, no. 3, Summer 1985, reprinted in S. Avineri and A. de-Shalit (eds), *Communitarianism and Individualism*, OUP, Oxford, 1992.

77　See, for polemical introductions to their thought: I. Zeitlin, *Ideology and the Development of Sociological Theory*, Prentice-Hall, Englewood Cliffs, NJ, 1968; R. Nisbet, *The Sociological Tradition*, Heinemann, London, 1967.

78　C. Lasch, *The Culture of Narcissus. American Life in an Age of Diminishing Expectations*, Abacus Books, London, 1980.

79 Both authors published landmark works in 1848: K. Marx and F. Engels, *Manifesto of the Communist Party*, London, 1848; J. S. Mill, *The Principles of Political Economy and Some of Their Applications to Social Philosophy*, London, 1848.

80 The idea of 'workers' control' is politically defunct and the milder, but closely related notion of 'industrial democracy' has been nullified by the demise of manufacturing and the advent of 'post-industrial society'.

For Product Safety Concerns and Information please contact our EU
representative GPSR@taylorandfrancis.com Taylor & Francis Verlag GmbH,
Kaufingerstraße 24, 80331 München, Germany

Printed and bound by CPI Group (UK) Ltd, Croydon, CR0 4YY
08/05/2025
01864394-0003